Milton

ENGLISH MASTERPIECES · AN ANTHOLOGY OF
IMAGINATIVE LITERATURE FROM CHAUCER TO
T. S. ELIOT · UNDER THE GENERAL EDITOR-
SHIP OF MAYNARD MACK, YALE UNIVERSITY

Milton

edited by

MAYNARD MACK

Professor of English, and Fellow of Davenport College
Yale University

PRENTICE-HALL, INC.

Englewood Cliffs, N. J.

SECOND PRINTING . . . . . FEBRUARY, 1951
THIRD PRINTING . . . . JANUARY, 1953
FOURTH PRINTING . . . . SEPTEMBER, 1953
FIFTH PRINTING . . . . . . JANUARY, 1955
SIXTH PRINTING . . . . JUNE, 1956

TO THE READER

These volumes present a carefully proportioned collection of writings in English, from Chaucer to the present, which are primarily valuable as literary works of art. Writings in the less imaginative modes have been almost entirely excluded, and complete works have been preferred to excerpts. Where cutting or selection was necessary, an effort has been made to preserve what is crucial for an understanding of the artistic value of the whole piece. Since novels cannot be condensed or excerpted satisfactorily, they have been omitted. Separate reprints of prose fiction may be used to supplement the last three volumes of this set. The introductions try to focus the reader's attention on what is imaginatively interesting and valuable in the various selections. If they succeed, they will at the same time provide the justification for this anthology and distinguish it from the many other anthologies that are available.

28243

For

F. B. M.

noli equi dentes inspicere donati

Contents

Introduction

MILTON'S LIFE

John Milton was born in 1608 into the Puritan family of a well-to-do lawyer and private banker, living in London not far from the Mermaid Tavern. He showed from an early age the intellectual gifts that were to make him one of the most learned Englishmen of his time, and was accordingly destined (he tells us) to "pursuits of literature" and ultimately the church. Such was his appetite for knowledge throughout his life that from twelve years old, or about the time he entered St. Paul's school, he rarely left his studies before midnight. To this practice may be attributed the eventual loss of his sight.

In 1625, aged seventeen, Milton enrolled at Christ's College, Cambridge, and took there successively the B.A. and M.A. degrees. His university experience was not an altogether happy one. His own deep love of learning, and his idealism about the ministerial profession for which he (and every student who in those days went on to an academic education) was preparing, combined to make him critical of the ignorance, indolence, and sensuality that he saw illustrated in some of his classmates. About these matters he was honest (and also tactless) enough to speak out. The curriculum, moreover, of Milton's time—"a feast of sow thistles and brambles," he called it in retrospect—was uncongenial to a student of his broad training and interests. Since the universities were the seminaries of the clergy, it was heavily theological, consisting, in Milton's words, of turning over "those huge and almost monstrous volumes" of the medieval theologians, mastering their "warty controversies," and disputing superannuated subtleties with "a certain overboiling and truly laughable foam of words." On these deficiencies too, Milton spoke out. It was possibly some such sentiments expressed to his first tutor that caused him to be whipped and for a time expelled.

Leaving Cambridge in 1632, Milton spent a half-dozen years of further study at his father's country house near Horton, and then traveled for fifteen months in Italy, at this date still the artistic center of Europe. From there he returned, toward the autumn of 1639, to set up in London with a few pupils as a private tutor. He had now abandoned his intended career in the ministry, probably for a variety of reasons, but not least on account of the widening rift in the religious life of England. The opposition of the Puritans to Anglicanism, which had earlier (1620) sent the Pilgrims to America, and which grew in acrimony all through the reign of Charles I (1625-49), was about to break out in the Civil Wars (1642-51). The Puritans' aim, as the name implies, was to "purify" the Anglican church. By this they meant ridding it of the remnants of Roman Catholic ritual and doctrine, and particularly of government by bishops, in favor of simpler practices and purer methods of church government which they believed were laid down in Scripture. As their attacks on the established institutions increased, those who adhered to the Anglican side of the dispute retaliated with restrictions that eventually made it impossible for anyone to take orders without swearing to uphold the episcopate. This, Milton—an ardent Puritan as well as a determined individualist—could never have brought himself to do: it would have been, as he proudly wrote later, to "subscribe slave."

Another factor that must have affected his decision was his growing recognition that his best powers lay in poetry. He had already written at Cambridge and Horton, among many other pieces of less importance, his fine poem *On the Morning of Christ's Nativity* (1629), *L'Allegro* and *Il Penseroso* (1631?), *Comus* (1634, published 1637), and *Lycidas* (1637). Looking back in 1642 at this whole period from his university days onward, Milton acknowledged that an "inward prompting" had been growing steadily upon him to the effect that "by labor and intense study" he might leave something to aftertimes, such that they should not willingly let it die. What he had in mind was a poem of heroic scope in which he could exercise as a poet (with the same spirit of dedication to the service of God and nation) the influence that might have been his in the church. For the performances of poets, he wrote, are of power along with the pulpit "to imbreed and cherish in a great nation the seeds of virtue and public civility" and "to celebrate . . . the throne and equipage of God's almightiness, and what he works, and what he suffers to be wrought with high providence in his church."

Though Milton expresses here, in 1642, the spirit if not yet the plan of his great poem *Paradise Lost,* the composition of that work was obliged to wait. The Puritan-Anglican conflict came to a head at this time, and, taking in Milton's mind the shape of a gigantic struggle for freedom from all forms of tyranny, engaged his energies as a writer for nearly twenty years. In 1641-42, with pamphlets in behalf of liberty from the Anglican "oppressors" of the church. In 1643-45, after the Puritan parliament had come to power, with further pamphlets in behalf of liberalized divorce laws, freedom of the press (*Areopagitica*), and reforms in education. In 1649-54, with various defenses of the action of the parliamentary party in executing Charles I; and in 1649-60, under first the kingless Commonwealth and then the Protectorate of Cromwell, as Latin Secretary in what we should now call the Department of State. The theme of all Milton's prose in these two decades is liberty, and its movement is from a tone of high optimism to deep disillusionment as he came to realize how few men were capable of the self-disciplines that the full liberty of his ideal commonwealth required.

With the restoration of Charles II in 1660, Milton as a defender of regicide was in serious danger. He escaped, for reasons that are still uncertain, with only some loss of property, and thereafter lived retired. In the total blindness which had been his lot since 1651, he had already begun, before the Restoration, the dictation of *Paradise Lost* to his amanuenses and his daughters, and this poem he now carried on to completion and publication (1667), along with *Paradise Regained* and *Samson Agonistes* (1671). The best picture of the poet in these declining years, and one that gives much of what is known about his personal habits and appearance, is the following passage from an anonymous contemporary biography not published till 1902:

He was of a moderate stature, and well proportioned, of a ruddy complexion, light brown hair, and handsome features; save that his eyes were none of the quickest. But his blindness . . . added no further blemish to them. His deportment was sweet and affable; and his gait erect and manly, bespeaking courage and undauntedness . . . , on which account he wore a sword while he had his sight, and was skilled in using it. He had an excellent ear, and could bear a part both in vocal and instrumental music.

He rendered his studies and various works more easy and pleasant by allotting them their several portions of the day. Of these the time friendly to the Muses fell to his poetry; and he, waking early, . . . had commonly a good stock of verses ready against his amanuensis came; which if it happened to be later than ordinary, he would complain, saying *he wanted to be milked*. The evenings he likewise spent in reading some choice poets, by way of refreshment after the day's toil, and to store his

memory against morning. . . . And David's Psalms were in esteem with
him above all poetry. The youths that he instructed from time to time
served him often as amanuenses, and some elderly persons were glad for
the benefit of his learned conversation, to perform that office. His first
wife [Mary Powell, with whom his relationship was not at first an entirely
happy one] died [in 1652] a while after his blindness seized him, leaving
him three daughters, that lived to be women. He married two more
[Katherine Woodcock, d. 1658, and Elizabeth Minshull], whereof one
survived him. He died in a fit of gout, but with so little pain or emotion,
that the tide of his expiring was not perceived by those in the room.

MILTON'S EARLY WRITINGS

Background

Milton's poems concern themselves centrally with reconciling two
conceptions of man. In one traditional way of looking at him, man is
an eternal and spiritual being whose career on earth is but a pilgrimage to his final home in God. When we view man in this way,
we see him as part of a supernatural scheme or order—what the
seventeenth century called the order of grace. Within this order, man
is an actor in a vast spiritual drama, where his heredity is the corruption he inherits from the Fall of Adam, his environment the world
of spiritual existences, his community the church, his struggle is toward salvation, and his weapon is faith. On the other hand, according to an equally ancient way of regarding him, man is predominantly
a creature of this world—the order of nature, which he is equipped
with intellect to explore and senses to enjoy. In this drama, the
heredity that counts is simply genealogical, the environment is the
physical universe, the community is the state, the struggle is for
the goods that terrestrial life offers, and reason is the weapon.

These two conceptions are by no means mutually exclusive; in the
thinking of the seventeenth century they were about equally balanced.
The claims of the latter view had been recently quickened by all the
currents of intellect and feeling that we associate with the Renaissance:
the expansion of man's curiosity, geographical, astronomical, philosophical, and the emphasis on his independence, dignity, and rationality that was partly the fruit of the recovery of Greek and Latin cul-
ture. But in the same way, the Reformation and the Roman Catholic
Counter-Reformation had reinvigorated the sense of man's spiritual
destiny, and the favorite theme of that wing of the Reformation
which was English Puritanism became the old metaphor of pilgrimage—man's wayfaring and warfaring through the wilds of this world
to his home in the next.

Most of the controversies of the seventeenth century stem in one way or other from these divergent conceptions of man, and most writers of the period seek to supply some sort of *modus vivendi* between them. The thoroughgoing naturalist like Thomas Hobbes managed it by paying only lip service to the order of grace. Extreme Puritans, on the other hand, minimized nature: the world and man's reason were hopelessly darkened by the Fall, and the senses were the avenues of Satan (it is unfortunately this aspect of Puritanism that is chiefly remembered today). Then there was the type of compromise which accepted both orders equally, but in isolation from each other. Such was the tendency of a fideism like Sir Thomas Browne's, which passed back and forth with ease between the "divided and distinguished worlds" of reason and faith; or of an empiricism like Bacon's, which, though it may have desired the segregation of the two realms in order to be freer for the conquest of nature, did not dispute the claims of grace: "It is therefore most wise soberly to render unto faith the things that are faith's."

Much the hardest reconciliation to make was that which *united* the two orders; which took account of the values implied in the Renaissance as well as the Reformation; which looked on man's natural life as the soil in which the life of grace was rooted, and on the life of grace as something not hostile to nature but fulfilling it. "These three, faith, reason, and sense, being all God's works in man, cannot be contrary in their use, one to another; neither can any thing be true in one which is false in another . . . ; reason [perfects] sense; and faith, both sense and reason." This was the view of the liberals, both Anglican and Puritan, and it was the view of Milton. As he himself had put it, while still at Cambridge, "nothing can be accounted justly among the causes of our happiness, unless it some way takes into consideration both that eternal and this temporal life."

On the Morning of Christ's Nativity

The fusion of "that eternal" with "this temporal" is a problem that Milton brooded over as early as his poem *On the Morning of Christ's Nativity*. This poem is an enactment of the fusion, in which nature is not repudiated but transformed by grace. In its first movement (stas. 1-8, following the four introductory stanzas), it presents the natural order, hushed, glimmering, and expectant, in the presence of the new-born Christ, who is grace. Nature, guilty through the Fall and here personified at first as a sinning woman, is afraid; but there is to be not war but peace between these realms, for it is the virtue of grace to be forgiving (sta. 3) and the virtue of nature to repent (sta. 2). Moreover, the natural order instinctively senses and responds to the higher intuitions supplied by grace. Its kings sit still, divining the coming of the King of Kings; its stars stand fixed, no longer obedient to Lucifer (the name is significant: Milton was to use it later of Satan), but awaiting the command of One higher. Even the sun hesitates in his course, acknowledging "a greater Sun," and the shepherds, though they do not yet know it, are about to be greeted with news of the Great Shepherd.

The poem now turns in its second movement (stas. 9-17) to the order of grace. The half light and the hush of the first section give place to images of intense light and especially of music—the harmony of the angels and the spheres. As in Milton's poetry generally, this harmony is used as a symbol of the concord, felicity, and perfect union to be found in a world in which nature has been completed by grace and restored to it. Such harmony (Milton wrote in his lines "At a Solemn Music") sounded on earth before the Fall, but then sin

> Jarred against nature's chime, and with harsh din
> Broke the fair music that all creatures made
> To their great Lord, whose love their motion swayed
> In perfect Diapason, whilst they stood
> In first obedience, and their state of good.

Now, at Christ's birth, it is fit that it should sound again—a reminder of the re-Creation of nature and man (sta. 12) and the restoration of the golden age in the New Jerusalem (stas. 14-15), to be achieved after the Last Judgment (sta. 13) through Christ's atonement on the cross (sta. 16).

With this, the poem turns back in its third section (stas. 18-26) to the order of nature. The rout of the false gods is Milton's elaboration of an old saying that the pagan oracles ceased at the coming of Christ. In the poem, his description of the rout serves two purposes. It images the purgation that the order of nature must undergo as a condition of its restoration to grace. The false gods, we may say, in addition to being the pagan deities of history, symbolize the elements in nature that are alien to grace, especially the tendency of man to deify his own natural powers and those of his environment. Milton's attitude toward this purgation is by no means simple-minded; the poem rejoices at the flight of a brutal deity like Moloch, but there is an air of wistfulness in its farewell to some of the more innocent manifestations of nature worship:

> With flower-inwoven tresses torn
> The Nymphs in twilight shade of tangled thickets mourn.

There is always something lost in the advance from a lower level of values to a higher one, and Milton does not blink the fact that it is a loss which hurts.

The rout serves also to depict the triumphant might of the new dispensation. Militant Protestantism, or at any rate Puritanism, has never been entirely comfortable before a Christ suffering or a Christ who is really a helpless infant. When Milton attempted a poem on the Passion, he found himself unable to finish it. Similarly here, though the developing theme of the poem amply justifies the image, it is very characteristic of Milton to have conceived a nativity poem which *would* justify the image of Christ as an infant Hercules (sta. 25), symbol of power. But again this power is not hostile to nature as such. Rather, its operation is such that it can be likened to the natural progress of the dawn—the Sun of the opening section brought back now in a metaphor of the Son (sta. 26)—driving away the shadows of the night.

The last stanza is a kind of coda, replacing the third movement's atmosphere of darkness, discord, conflict, and might with a reminder of the harmonious brightness found at the center of the poem in the predicted reunion of grace and nature. Hence the number of allusions in this stanza which carry the mind back to earlier symbols—this "tedious song" to the music of the spheres and angels (stas. 9-14); this "youngest teemèd star" to the constellations of the first Creation (stas. 6, 12); these bright-harnessed angels to those who sang and shone (sta. 11)—culminating in the Christ-child himself, emblem of grace incarnate in nature, nature fulfilled in grace.

Comus

Comus shows Milton working out a similar poise of values in less specifically Christian terms. The poem was written at the request of Milton's friend, the musician Henry Lawes, as libretto for an entertainment to be performed in Ludlow Castle on the occasion of the Earl of Bridgewater's induction into the Lord Presidency of Wales. (This is the reason for the compliment paid that country in the role of Sabrina, nymph of the river Severn, which originates in Wales.) The parts of the two brothers and the Lady were acted by the Earl's three children, and the part of the Attendant Spirit by Lawes himself, to whose musical settings Milton turns a handsome tribute in the poem (494-6).

As a masque, an established form of aristocratic entertainment in the seventeenth century, *Comus* was bound by the conventions of its genre to present—with music, pageantry, and dance—an allegorical rather than a dramatic action. Milton takes fuller advantage of this priority of allegory than is pleasing to a modern reader, when he allows the elder brother to discuss his sister's safety as if it were last night's hand at bridge; yet *Comus* is more dramatic than most masques, and in the earnest moral purpose of its allegory stands very nearly alone.

The central metaphor, it will be noticed, is the metaphor of pilgrimage. The forest through which the three children make their way home—"the blind mazes of this tangled wood" (181)—is clearly in some sense an emblem of the perplexity and obscurity of mortal life, which constitutes God's trial of the soul (79, 329, 970-73). The chief danger that threatens in this wood is Comus. In an obvious interpretation, he stands for evil in its tempting disguises, as his train of brutish monsters stand for evil in its unmasked effects. But Comus is more complex than this. He stands also for evil considered in its philosophical aspect as a perversion of the good: the misuse of the order of nature which makes the human being sink downward in the scale of being to the status of brute. For this reason, Milton allows him to express truths which in his mouth become distortions of truth. Thus he uses the symbol of the harmonious dance of created things (see the lines from "At a Solemn Music," quoted earlier), but misapplies the symbol to justify the obscene rites of Cotytto (111-44). Again, in some of the most beautiful lines in the poem, he appeals to the duty of using and not repudiating the gifts of nature (666-755); but the ends to which he would put this doctrine of use, as the Lady reminds him (762 ff.), amount to a doctrine of abuse.

Set over against Comus in the poem is the Attendant Spirit. Both present themselves to the mortal eye as shepherds (276, 493), preside over dances (144 ff., 957 ff.), celebrate the sensuous riches of nature (706 ff., 976 ff.), and use the tetrameter metre that Milton allots to no one else (93 ff., 867-1023). As the powers of Comus seduce men to sink to the level of brutes, the Attendant Spirit would persuade them to rise to the level of angels—"Higher than the sphery chime." But his role is guardianship only. Though he descends from the realm of grace to secure the travelers in their journey through the wood (and thus images, perhaps, the operations of divine providence in the natural order), he exercises no supernatural powers. In the test that the wood presents, the victory of the Lady has to be won, by herself, and within; the Attendant Spirit, representing apparently a right use of nature in contrast to Comus's perversion, offers against the latter's arts simply a control derived from nature—"Haemony," or, as the Lady later puts it in her debate with Comus, the "holy dictate of spare Temperance." Though it is difficult to interpret the Spirit's final song, what it seems to say is that through temperate use of the natural order man may participate sinlessly in the life processes of nature (999-1003), and fuse them with grace (1004-11) in a union whose ultimate offspring will be eternal youth and joy. Remembering the meaning of the musical symbol in the poem on Christ's nativity, one recognizes the appropriateness of the Spirit's being depicted as Thyrsis, a musician and poet. Milton may be glancing in this, as he may also in his exaltation of music in the earlier poem, at the power of the poet (a power that he himself was in the act of exploring) to bring together the beauty of the senses and a high spiritual purpose: nature and grace.

But though the general outlines of Milton's theme in *Comus* are clear, the poem remains obscure at a crucial point. It fails to elucidate how a doctrine of temperance such as the Lady proposes in her retort to Comus relates to a doctrine of virginity, or abstention, which she proposes in the same speech. Moreover, the Lady declares to Comus that the "high mystery" of virginity has a positive spiritual value, as in Christian philosophy it has; but the poem nowhere succeeds in "realizing" this value for us in poetic terms—that is to say, in terms which enable it to compete imaginatively with Comus's great lines on fruition. The Elder Brother, who comes closest to realizing virginity in poetic terms, seems no clearer than his sister whether the value that is to be balanced against "imbrutement" is temperate use or renunciation. He seems to be celebrating renunciation (427, 448, 453); but if so, why is lust the only alternative? Why is not temperate use another?

Many interpretations have been brought forward to soften these perplexities, but the very variety and ingenuity of the explanations suggests that what we confront at this point in *Comus* is a fundamental irresolution in both its moral and artistic design.

Lycidas

We have seen that, in one sense, both *Comus* and *On the Morning of Christ's Nativity* hint at the power of the true Christian poet to mediate between nature and grace. And it would not be hard to interpret the rout of the false gods in the latter work as an image of Milton's resolution to purify his poetry henceforward of the paganism of the "smooth elegiac poets" like Ovid, who had hitherto been among his favorite models; or to interpret the slight blur that we have noticed in *Comus,* as the reflection of his own hesitation between incompatible ideals of renunciation and purified use.

However this may be, Milton's next important poem, *Lycidas,* sets the problem of the true Christian poet squarely in the foreground.

Lycidas was written to be included in a volume of other elegies on the death of Edward King, who was drowned in a shipwreck while en route to Ireland, in August 1637. King had been a fellow student of Milton's at Christ's College (likewise preparing for the ministry), and according to the elegists in the memorial volume, though they may have exaggerated his promise, a man of great learning, piety, and poetic skill. His death, as the poem shows, jostled Milton into a general taking stock. Having by now all but given up the notion of entering the church, having determined to serve God and his country as a priestly poet instead, Milton found himself at the age of twenty-nine with little to show in the way of concrete achievement. He had most of the poems that we now call his minor poems in manuscript, but there were as yet only plans for the great work that would justify his long preparation. Supposing that he himself—he was about to set out for Italy—should be cut off like King? Why was it that men of spiritual promise died, while men who had sold out (as Milton saw it) to material ease were allowed to continue unchecked their betrayal of the spirit? These are among the questions—valid in every age—that Milton agitates in *Lycidas,* counterpointing them against a tribute to his dead acquaintance.

   Feeling, in works of art, is necessarily formal. It has to be detached from its individual circumstances (the sob, the shudder, the groan) and distanced into the larger patterns of thought and sentiment that all men share. Milton effects this necessary depersonalization in *Lycidas,* partly by making King the symbol of all gifted individuals "dead ere their prime," and partly by the pastoral convention. The very fact that this convention has had a long history—that Virgil and Theocritus and Spenser and many other poets have used it for laments; and that it possesses established characteristics like the fiction of shepherds, grieving of nature, questioning of nymphs and gods, procession of mourners, strewing of flowers, apotheosis of the dead—is a part of the meaning it contributes to Milton's poem. The convention pays King the compliment of associating him with the poets for whom Theocritus and Virgil mourned. It assimilates his loss to a long tradition of loss, so that the mystery of the individual occasion is taken up into, and softened by, the general mystery of human fate. And it has, further, the advantage of eliminating irrelevant particulars in favor of what is essential and significant. Thus the countryside round Cambridge in reality has no hill; and Milton and King certainly did not pursue their mutual interests in poetry by driving flocks to pasture. Yet both the fictional hill, with its suggestion of the Muses' haunts, and the fictional life afield described in the succeeding lines, point to a threefold connection between the inspiration of poetry, the sensuous appreciation of the natural world, and the intuition of mysterious forces (fauns and satyrs) linking poetry and man and nature—which is *truer* than would be any of the actual facts of King's and Milton's stay at Cambridge.

Most important of all, with respect to structure, the pastoral convention affords a framework of established formal elements upon which, as upon the formal elements in a musical composition, can be based the modulations and resolutions which convey the individual artist's theme. Thus in Milton's poem, the conventional grief of nature and the questioning of the nymphs rise into the poet's more passionate questioning of God's providence: why scorn delights and live laborious days, as Milton was doing at Horton, if death comes arbitrarily to frustrate effort? Similarly, the pastoral procession of mourners (which can contain St. Peter because of the Christian comparison of Christ and his clergy to shepherds) expands into Milton's famous denunciation of a corrupt church which a living Lycidas would have helped to purify. And the formal element of the strewing of the dead man's bier likewise crescendoes, first, into the acknowledgment that there is no way of glozing over the dominion of death in the *natural* order (this meaning reinforced by the loss of Lycidas's body to the casual indignities of the sea), and then, into the intuitive perception that by way of natural death comes spiritual life, "through the dear might of Him that walked the waves."

Throughout the poem, it will be noticed, water is used with a double or even triple significance. There is the sea, impervious, blameless, but destructive—to which Lycidas and all men fall victims. There are the fountain of the Muses and the pastoral rivers, symbolic perhaps of poetry, and especially of its power to invest the brute facts of experience with moral meaning, as demonstrated in *Lycidas* itself. And last, just hinted in the final paragraph before the close, there is the water of grace, won through Christ, who by his mastery of "the sea" has given a new significance to water. In these last lines, where nature has been redeemed by grace—the old pastoral landscape taken up into a new kind with "other groves and other streams"—Lycidas becomes the Genius of the Shore (compare the Attendant Spirit in *Comus*), and is powerful, through the water of grace, over the water of the natural order.

Areopagitica

Of all Milton's writings in prose, the one most celebrated today is his defense of the liberty of printing, *Areopagitica*. This was his appeal to a Puritan-controlled parliament to reconsider and abolish the ordinance by which, on its own coming to power, it had reinstated the licensing controls that had been found so repugnant when administered by Anglicans. The pamphlet marks an important shift in Milton's thinking from conservative toward radical Puritanism, and it was largely this shift that produced the great passages on liberty by which later times have set store.

The Puritan platform, as noticed earlier, held that the Scriptures contained a divinely appointed plan of church government and that this plan did not include an episcopate. To replace the Anglican episcopal hierarchy with the Scriptural plan was the heart of the "reformation" which Puritanism sought. But when it came to determining just what the Scriptural plan was—and it came to that immediately the Puritans were in power—the range of disagreement proved to be immense. On the level of practice, the dispute was whether the Scriptural design for the church called for a strong centralized ministerial control of doctrine and discipline—the position of right-wing Presbyterianism; or, as the congregationalist Puritans and others still further to the left insisted, a looser organization leaving room for some variety of practice and belief. What the dispute amounted to philosophically, however, was simply a new version of the conflict between our two divergent conceptions of man. Presbyterianism, insisting on uniformity, tended to support its case by stressing the depravity of human reason, which required for guidance the authoritative scheme implicit in the Scriptures—and this scheme, naturally, was found to be Presbyterianism. On the other hand, Puritans less sure about the character of the Scriptural scheme, or those who were sure that at any rate it was not Presbyterianism, tended to allow more latitude to the powers of reason. Man's apprehension of Scriptural truth, they found themselves arguing, was partial and cumulative; different sects might grasp it by different facets, and each be right. The best program, therefore, was one which would allow liberty of reasoning and (within the limits of agreement on Protestant fundamentals) differences of discipline.

This is the position at which Milton has arrived in *Areopagitica.* Two years earlier, writing against episcopacy, he had accepted the belief of the Presbyterians that there was a clear plan of government laid down in Scripture, and had pointed, with them, to the inadequacies of reason: "Open your eyes to the light of grace, a better guide than nature." Now, in *Areopagitica,* he takes up the position of the Puritan radicals—men like Roger Williams (founder of Rhode Island) and John Robinson (pastor to the Pilgrim Fathers)—and pleads for the dignity of reason, the toleration of variety, the cooperative and cumulative nature of the search for truth: "Neither can every piece of the building be of one form; nay rather the perfection consists in this, that out of many moderate varieties and brotherly dissimilitudes that are not vastly disproportional, arises the goodly and graceful symmetry that commends the whole pile and structure."

Upon this principle of variety in unity Milton constructs his case against censorship. The gist of his argument is this: 1. Censorship has always been the tool of those who would hinder the Reformation and has never been approved by the great nations or great men of the past. 2. Censorship prevents the development of character and wisdom, for since good and evil are mixed in this life, he who can discriminate between them and prefer the good is "the true warfaring Christian." 3. Censorship can never be effective. It cannot close up the many other inlets of evil besides books, it cannot keep the fool from being a fool, it cannot ensure goodness (for enforced sinlessness is not goodness), it cannot eradicate differences of opinion, and it is impossible to administer. 4. Censorship stagnates the mind's traffic with truth, discouraging learning, relaxing our grasp on the truth we have and preventing the discovery of new.

It is not by these arguments that Milton's treatise stands out from the host of contemporary writings embodying similar ideas. What distinguishes *Areopagitica* is its eloquence and its appeal to the heroic mood. It has, on the one hand, the literary imagination which transforms the local and particular circumstances of an attack on a now forgotten ordinance into symbols of universal significance—"he who destroys a good book, kills reason itself, kills the image of God, as it were, in the eye"; "And who shall silence all the airs and madrigals that whisper softness in chambers? The windows also and the balconies must be thought on; [these] are shrewd books, with dangerous frontispieces set to sale; who shall prohibit them?" And it has, on the other hand, a confidence in the potentialities of human character (especially the English character) which make it one of the great objective correlatives of man in his more exalted frames of mind: "Methinks I see in my mind a noble and puissant nation rousing herself like a strong man after sleep, and shaking her invincible locks." "And though all the winds of doctrine were let loose to play upon the earth, so Truth be in the field, we do injuriously by licensing and prohibiting to misdoubt her strength. Let her and Falsehood grapple; who ever knew Truth put to the worse, in a free and open encounter?"

The heroic confidence of these sentences was to be profoundly qualified in the fifteen following years, which cost Milton his sight and also his hope of a community of saints on earth; but the heroic view of man they imply points directly ahead to the two great poems of his maturity, *Paradise Lost* and *Samson Agonistes*.

PARADISE LOST

The Theme

Epic poetry deals with the life of man in its heroic aspect. Its action is usually an incident in the career of some real or legendary individual, treated in such a way as to bring out its representative character and its exemplary heroic value. Homer, for instance, telling the story of Odysseus's homecoming, gives the action grandeur and universality by associating it with supernatural agencies, a great war, and the mysterious vastness of the sea. By stressing Odysseus's relations with Olympian gods and goddesses, by underscoring repeatedly his reminiscences of Troy and the reminiscences of the other great Achaian heroes who fought there, and especially by fostering in our minds a sense of what seem to be very great geographical distances stretching from the Trojan shores to the underworld itself, Homer's poem encourages us to see in Odysseus something more than an individual—to see, in fact, an emblem of man's own existence, as he wanders homesick but undefeated through a world he never made, looking for stability and peace.

Virgil does much the same thing in his epic of Aeneas, but he expands the grandeur of his hero by making him a symbol of self-dedication, and his universality by making him a representative of the Roman character. Aeneas, unlike Odysseus, has a mission to perform in a divine plan of history: he has been chosen by the gods to found Rome, the greatest force for order and stability that the ancient world knew. Therefore, though his actual wanderings still take place, like Odysseus's, among little precarious islands of patterned life that rise up above the anarchy of the sea, there is always present in Virgil's poem the consciousness that some day these scattered cells of civilization are to be united in the vast political organism of Rome; and, accordingly, that on the self-discipline of Aeneas depends not merely his welfare and his men's, but the future of mankind.

Writing against the background of spacious poems like these, and resolved to give the heroic mood a specifically Christian orientation, Milton chose for his own subject the Fall of Man. This time the hero was to be, not an individual or a nation, but mankind itself; and the stage, not the known geographical world, but the universe. Milton's epic was also to enlarge the theme. Its question was to be no longer, as in the *Odyssey,* how men may secure their little outposts of order and self-discipline against the disorders imaged in the suitors and the sea; or, as in the *Aeneid,* how they may accomplish a larger order, political and social, that will guard them from the anarchy latent in their own egoistic drives. The question for the Christian poet was how the seeds of anarchy had come into man and his world in the first place. Into a universe created by a benevolent and omnipotent God, how had a principle of disorder penetrated—and having penetrated, how could it be withstood?

This is of course the problem of evil, which is handled in *Paradise Lost* in traditional Christian terms. In these terms, with which the modern reader is sometimes insufficiently familiar, the origin of evil is sin. Sin is possible because God has created some orders of beings— men and angels—free to choose or not to choose His service. When they do so choose, they choose what is also their own highest good; when they do not, they choose something less, and anything less is evil. For evil in Christian thought lacks positive existence; it is simply a privation, a falling below the highest good. This is what Milton's Satan and the other rebel angels have done. They have elected to turn away from God's will, their highest good, to seek their own will, a lesser good. They have tired of serving and now aspire to rule. They have forgotten that they are only creatures and have tried to become like God. Inevitably, they wind up in hell because what they have done is precisely (in a spiritual sense) the Christian definition of hell: the preference of one's own will to God's. Inevitably, too, their own will does not prevail. The only change is that now they serve God's purposes involuntarily instead of freely.

One thing, however, they can do, and that is to seduce some other creature who enjoys the liberty of choosing between God's will and his own to choose the latter and join them in their ruin. Hence they set to work on man. Even here the triumph is short-lived, for though they can make man fall, God frustrates them by himself becoming a man who does not fall but rises. The sin of Adam, with the inheritance of evil that it brings to his posterity, is made good by the greater man, Christ, who, though he is tempted like Adam, resists, and though he dies like Adam, is resurrected. Thus in the completed Christian version of the Old Testament story, man may yet be saved, through Christ's atonement, in spite of Adam's Fall; good is made to spring from evil; and the original temptation in the garden expands to include the whole of human history till the Day of Judgment.

This is the "great argument" that Milton outlines in abstract in the first fifty lines of *Paradise Lost.* But it is one thing to state such a theme, quite another to realize it for the imagination. To evaluate Milton's achievement as an artist, one must look at his *imaginative* treatment of these materials at their three great *foci*—in Hell, in Heaven, on earth.

Hell

Milton's Hell is a triumphant solution of a difficult problem. The problem was to portray a Hell that should be a place without ceasing to be an idea: positive enough to win our imaginative assent as the scene of dramatic action, but impalpable enough to suggest, in symbol, that evil is negative—the absence of good. Milton attacks this problem in various ways. For one thing, he makes Hell, in its darkness, vagueness, and discord, an inversion of the bright clear harmony of Heaven, as we realize more fully in the third book: Hell is less itself than a poor parody of something else. Again, he makes his fallen angels sound repeatedly the note of loss; they are keenly conscious of what they once were and are not now—speaking of this again and again in their addresses to each other: "But oh how fallen, how chang'd" (84); "Heaven, once yours, now lost" (316); "Far other once beheld in bliss" (607). The negativism of evil comes out in a third way in the character of the fallen angels' program, which is itself negative—to obstruct God, "pervert that end,/And out of good still to find means of evil" (158 ff.). And it echoes in the poet's similes: the fallen angels are like fallen leaves, cut off from the source of life (301); or like great pines and oaks burnt out by lightning (611); or, best of all, like the sun in eclipse (594), which "darkened so, yet shone." The phrase is the very image of evil conceived as the loss or perversion of a good.

Perhaps the most subtle of Milton's ways of imagining Hell is a device of style.* It is exemplified repeatedly in the first two books of the poem, in phrases like "bottomless perdition," "darkness visible," "huge affliction," "hideous ruin," "bad eminence," "palpable obscure," "vast abrupt," "black fire and horror." What it amounts to is a fusion of concrete with abstract, or imaginable with unimaginable, or moral quality with physical, which never lets us forget that Hell is concept as well as place. Thus Hell has "regions" in it, but not regions as we usually think of them, spatially; they are "regions of sorrow." It has "shades" in it, but not from objects; from mental states: "doleful shades." It is such a place that "hope that comes to all" never comes there (again a logical impossibility). And its fire is not fire, but flood, or whirlwind, or even a solid resembling land (77, 227).

By a variant of this method, taking away with one hand what he gives with the other, Milton also constructs his allegory of Sin and

---

* I suspect my attention was drawn to this point in conversations with my colleagues—especially Mr. W. K. Wimsatt.

Death, and his still more tenuous allegory of Chaos and old Night, in the second book. Death, for instance, is sufficiently embodied to shake "a dreadful dart" and wear a crown; yet he is also that "other shape,/ If shape it might be called that shape had none,/ . . . Or substance might be called that shadow seemed"(666)—and his crown is only the "likeness" of a crown on "what seemed his head." In Chaos the projections of discord that Satan meets are not even shapeless shapes, but disembodied names: "the dreaded name of Demogorgon; Rumour next and Chance,/And Tumult and Confusion"—as nightmarish and indeterminate in texture as Chaos itself, through which Satan "swims, or sinks, or wades, or creeps, or flies" (950).

In handling the fallen angels, Milton has to achieve a somewhat similar balance between the power and grandeur that belong to them as actors in an epic poem (and particularly as antagonists of God) and the abjectness and repulsiveness which are theirs as representatives of evil. To fill our consciousness with their grandeur, he relies heavily on the similes that strew these two books, comparisons insisting either on number—autumn leaves, Red Sea sedge, locusts, barbarian hordes, all the armies of Thebes, Troy, Arthur, Charlemagne; or else on heroic size—Briareus, Typhon, Leviathan, gigantic trees, moons, suns. This grandeur is extended in the second book by the opulence and dignity of the fallen angels' "great consult" and the Ciceronian eloquence of their orations.

But directly athwart these associations, Milton throws others of an antithetical kind, like the catalogue of demons in Book I. Here these apparently heroic angels are identified with the false gods of the Old Testament, and their names are packed full of associations of idolatry, lust, greed, cruelty, murder, human sacrifice—all that the Old Testament writers sum up in the term "abomination." Once established, these associations can be reinvoked by the poet at will, and many of them are brought back to us even during the great consult, as we detect beneath the persuasive surface of the oratory, brutality, cowardice, obtuseness, arrogance, and deceit. There is no one of these speakers, as C. S. Lewis has cogently said, who is not foolish or vicious or both at once. Moloch has a simple-minded instinct to destroy Omnipotence; Belial cringes from the facts toward illusory quiescence; Mammon is content to deceive himself with substitutes for heaven; Beelzebub, though not deluded, is vindictive, malicious, and ignoble; and Satan, magnificently courageous, is courageous only through his pride. In all these personages, Milton brings together the despicable and the grand.

Heaven

Structurally, *Paradise Lost* is founded on a series of contrasts. The largest over-all contrast is that between destruction and creation—the sin of the angels compensated by the creation of the world and man; the sin of man, by Christ's atonement and the ultimate creation of "new Heaven and Earth." Within this inclusive contrast, which is really an opposition of principles, Milton sets the contrast of Heaven and Hell as places, and develops it in several ways. Partly in images of light *versus* darkness: hence his opening hymn to light in Book III. Partly in terms of sharp outlines—given to objects in Heaven, to the speeches of the celestial persons, and even to the style of the third book—*versus* the vague incertitudes (mental as well as physical) that typify Hell. And partly too in terms of unity *versus* division, concord *versus* discord. Hell, we notice, has divided counsels; Heaven has unanimity. Hell has many rivers; Heaven has one. Hell is filled with disorders, confusions, miscellaneous activities; in Heaven there is only one act: joy in the presence of the Lord. When citizens of Hell debate such relationships as that of free will and foreknowledge, they find (like men) "no end, in wandering mazes lost"; but in Heaven these relations are understood: they are expounded, with precision, by the One whose understanding causes them to exist.

Still further inside this nest of contrasts lies a dramatic opposition of Satan and the Son—and more obliquely, of the three persons of the heavenly Trinity to the hellish trinity of Satan, Sin, and Death. In Book III, the Son's self-renouncing plan to save man is plainly to be balanced against Satan's self-aggrandizing scheme to destroy him. Later, in Book VII, the Son is shown creating with ease in the same Chaos through which we have watched Satan make his way with so much toil. Still later, in Book X, the Son is delegated by his Father to judge the sin of Adam and Eve, as Satan delegates Sin and Death to rule over the world he has ruined. When Satan announces his triumph in Hell, he is greeted with hisses; when Christ's ultimate victory is announced in Heaven, there is song.

But though in all these ways Milton gives a tincture of dramatic color to his celestial persons, they remain less adequate to our imaginations than those of Hell. It is not simply, as is sometimes argued, that good is always less interesting than evil—or that in heaven, where all is union, there can be no drama. The real difficulties were rooted in Milton's theme. Since he conceived it as a story of conflict, a warfare of good and evil, it was almost bound to overstress the bellicose side of God. Since it required him to present the Persons of the Trinity as speaking characters, Divine Justice in the Father was almost certain to become imaginatively dissociated from Divine Mercy in the Son: hence Milton's God appears unduly rigorous. Moreover, since God was to explain his scheme of free will and justify it, he was put in the unfortunate position of celebrating his own perfections and rebutting implied objections—as Pope put it, "like a school divine."

All these are different ways of stating the artistic fact that God cannot be effectively represented in literature as a speaking character. Milton is most successful when he turns, as in the latter third of Book III, from God as speaker to His reflection in the orderly architecture of the created world; or when he takes a leaf from Dante's book and allows his poetry simply to *point* at a mystery and glory: "About him all the Sanctities of Heaven stood thick as stars, and from his sight received Beatitude past utterance."—"Dark with excessive bright thy skirts appear." Passages like these do more, artistically, to justify God's ways to man than all the explanations Milton places in his mouth. It was an unfortunate requirement of Milton's epic scheme that any *human* word should be so highly placed.

Eden

To understand Eden before the Fall, it is necessary to see it as an achievement in the art of "distancing." After the Fall, Eden can be like any other garden, as Adam and Eve can be like any other man and woman. Before the Fall, Eden must be different. This is because it is Milton's chief symbol for projecting imaginatively the unimaginable: a state of perfect spiritual innocence.

Milton uses, in passing, many other means to this end. He gives a grandeur to his description of Adam and Eve on our first meeting with them that is heroic like the descriptions of the fallen angels, but simple, luminous, uncomplicated—"innocent"—as those are not: "Two of far nobler shape erect and tall, Godlike erect, with native Honour clad." He also enhances their distance from us by enveloping them in patterns of high ceremony. In ritualistic salutations: "Daughter of God and Man, accomplisht Eve." Or solemn thanksgivings: "Thou also mad'st the night, Maker Omnipotent, and thou the Day." Or measured intricacies of verse, as in Eve's nuptial song, "Sweet is the breath of morn, her rising sweet," or the poet's own formal hymn to wedded love. Moreover, he is careful to enrich their dignified simplicity with associations stemming from cultures yet unborn (Eve is lovelier than Pandora, Proserpina, Pomona, Flora) and with images of natural harmony reflecting the harmonies of grace in heaven. Thus by day they walk in the garden hand in hand; by night they are "imparadised" in each other's arms; and about them always is music (Milton's favorite symbol of perfect union) from celestial voices.

Yet the great imaginative image of perfection is the garden, which, like Milton's ideal of spiritual life, is both luxuriant and disciplined. Its flowers are not disposed—Milton says (with a glance at prevailing landscape fashions)—in "Beds and curious Knots," but are such as "Nature boon poured forth profuse on Hill and Dale and Plain." Yet obviously it remains a garden (God's garden, in fact); has a design; is not a wilderness. It brings together, like the ideal Commonwealth in *Areopagitica,* variety and unity. Its individual leaves and airs are all "attuned." Its Universal Pan is "knit" with the Graces and the Hours in dance. Its waters are dispersed in "many a rill"— "diverse, wandering"—flowing "with mazy error"; yet they all spring from one source and often, "in a lake," reunite their streams.

To this scene of concord, Milton brings a dramatic tension that was not available to him in treating Heaven. For in the midst of all this unison in Eden, evil threatens; here is an order it *can* destroy. We are reminded of the impending doom by Satan's presence. But it is hinted also in the comparisons of Eve—to Proserpina, to Pandora. It accents her story of the reflection she fell in love with at the pool—a reflected vanity that will be her ruin. It insinuates itself into the description of the serpent. It is anticipated in every allusion to the forbidden tree.

But most of all, for the seventeenth-century reader, it was present by implication in the references to "degree." The notion of all life as organized in a great hierarchy of beings ranging down from God the Creator to the least created thing—each class of beings having its appointed function to fulfill in its appointed place—governs *Paradise Lost* everywhere, as it governed seventeenth-century thought. Satan fell, he tells us here, because he aspired above his appointed place; his plan for Adam and Eve is to make them do likewise; and the forbidden tree, as Adam himself emphasizes, is (in one way of looking at it) the sign of their acceptance of subordination and degree—"The only sign of our obedience left/Among so many signs of power and rule."

Degree reigns also in the relationship of Adam and Eve with each other. Man is woman's superior in *Paradise Lost,* and though this fact is sometimes mistaken today for Miltonic arrogance, it is extremely well founded in the general outlook of Milton's age. "Married folks," said a seventeenth-century preacher bluntly, "are either husband or wife. The husband is he which hath authority over the wife." "In the dignity and power of man over a woman," said another, "the glory of God shineth clearly." This inequality of Adam and Eve is equally well founded in the poem. It is quite clear, when the totality of Milton's references to them is examined, that he thinks of Adam as embodying primarily reason and of Eve as embodying primarily desire. Milton's complete projection of ideal humanity is in a sense neither Adam nor Eve, but both—reason and desire wedded, with reason in control. This is simply the variety-in-uniformity of the garden, expressed in human terms.

The Fall

The Fall in *Paradise Lost* is double. In its successive episodes— first Eve, then Adam—it illustrates the two ways in which, according to seventeenth-century psychology, man could be seduced by evil. Either through reason's being deceived, and so mistaking a lower for a higher good: the case of Eve. Or else through reason's yielding, not deceived, to the tug of passion: this is Adam's case.

Eve's fall, the crucial one because the first, is unfolded gradually in several stages. First there is Eve's ominous self-will in "breaking union" and going off independently on the morning of the Tempta- tion, appropriately symbolized in the withdrawn handclasp. Then there is the approach of Satan disguised as serpent. The point that Milton makes with this is that evil in the psychology of the sinner never looks like itself, but always like something else: "pleasing was his shape/And lovely." After this comes Satan's flattering address to Eve. The flattery is important. It is Milton's way of saying that the nature of temptation is an inclination to see not only the evil object as something other than it is, but ourselves as something other than we are—as "a goddess among gods," for instance, to use Satan's phrase. Furthermore, this rise in self-esteem is usually accompanied by decreased respect for our superiors. Thus while Eve is graded upward by Satan's glozing words—"Celestial Beauty," "Empress," "Queen of the Universe"—the Creator is graded downward. From having been "thy Maker fair" (538), he becomes first "the Threat- ener," then a being motivated by selfishness and envy (703, 729), and finally, in Eve's own mouth after she has fallen, "our great For- bidder." The gospel of innocence, as the prayers and hymns of the fourth book show, was a gospel that enlarged God and limited man. Satan's gospel enlarges man and limits God.

Adam's fall is the complement of Eve's. He sees what she has done and with his eyes wide open does it too. Even at his first sight of her, there is a premonition of Eden lost in "the faded roses shed" from the garland wreathed for her; another premonition echoes in the "defaced, deflowered" of his anguished opening words. But precisely while he is uttering these words, Milton lets us perceive the inner reversal of values of which his actual eating is to be only the concrete manifestation: "O fairest of Creation, last and best Of all God's works." Eve may be the fairest and last of God's works, but Adam knows that she is not the best: "He for God only, she for God in him"; to put Eve before God is to displace the highest good with a lower. Having made the reversal, however—which amounts to an act of idolatry on his part, like Eve's earlier idolatry of the tree (795) —Adam has no alternative but to eat and share Eve's fate. If we have grown used today to approving such highflown romantic renunciations, it is only because we have grown so sentimental that we fail to make distinctions. Renunciation is good, like the Son's, when it is creative. Adam's renunciation is destructive: it is a good perverted, Milton's culminating symbol of what evil is.

Adam and Eve have both now violated the hierarchy of right values. For this reason, the psychological hierarchy within their own natures is disturbed. Reason, in other words, becomes subject instead of sovereign of passion: "For Understanding ruled not, and the Will Heard not her lore, both in subjection now To sensual appetite." Human nature, whose distinguishing character has been rationality, sinks in the scale of being toward the animal level: Adam and his wife become intoxicated; they copulate in lust. Majestic once in nakedness, they shrink now to a pair of savages in loin cloths, such as of late "Columbus found th' American." And they fall from the fine courtesies of their conversation in innocence to domestic bickering. Meantime, other hierarchical relationships disintegrate. The stars are blasted, the influences of the moon and planets become noxious, storms appear, together with the changes of the seasons, and plagues; the beasts of the field begin to war on each other. Above all, the harmony of man with the processes of nature is broken: childbirth will become painful, livelihood must be got with toil, immortality on earth has been forfeited—and so of course has Eden. These are among the privative effects of knowing both good and evil: "Good [is] lost and Evil got."

But there is also a reconstitutive movement. Adam and Eve are gradually repentant and reconciled; in the closing lines of the poem, as they are driven from the garden together, their handclasp has been restored. Moreover, there is the hope springing from Christ's atonement—a plan already revealed to us, and in the final books revealed to Adam. Furthermore, through the course of history, in the vast panorama of the future that these final books unfold, there is always a saving remnant of good men: Noah, Abraham, Moses, to be followed at last by Christ. But the most important feature in this reconstitutive movement is the new definition of man's heroic aspect, which the whole poem has proposed. The old definition is the one that Milton explicitly rejects at the opening of Book IX; the hero defined as conqueror, heroism defined as great deeds performed for glory in the public arenas of life. This is the version of the hero that is also created and repudiated in Satan. In Hell, which is all self-centered, Satan's philosophy of lawless individualism looks impressive. After we have seen unison in Heaven, and more especially (because Milton is not wholly successful with Heaven) after we have seen it in Eden, we realize that such individualism is merely destructive. Milton emphasizes this in the sordid disguises in which, from the fourth book on, Satan appears. And when the fall of Eve is accomplished—the assault of a self-styled military hero on a frail woman, carried out not even with impressive might but only low cunning—the heroic aura of Satan is all gone: "Back to the thicket slunk The guilty serpent." Significantly, our last view of him is still as serpent, "on his belly prone," chewing ashes.

Meantime, the new version of the heroic, painfully illustrated in Eve's and Adam's failure to possess it, but grasped by Adam in his final vision, is the heroism of inner spiritual and moral *self*-conquest: to suffer for the cause of God and yet stand firm. "Henceforth I learn, that to obey is best, And love with fear the only God . . . ; that suffering for Truth's sake Is fortitude to highest victory, And to the faithful death the gate of life." Here (Milton seems to say) is a heroism of wayfaring and warfaring which is available not simply to political leaders and men of great place, but to all.

Conclusion

Paradise Lost is the great "long poem" of the English language. Considered as a nexus of ideas, it is a remarkable blend of the contemporary and universal. It glows throughout with the heroic energy of "reformation," the Puritan spirit of moral warfare, spiritual knight-errantry. It reflects too a typically Protestant and especially a Puritan rationality: its metaphysical universe is a universe known, conquered, mapped out, explicated. (It has often been said that there is little of the mystical sense in Milton, and this is as true of him as it is of radical Protestantism generally; though it is grotesque to go on to say, as some have done, that *Paradise Lost* betrays an "utter disbelief in the fundamental tenets" of Christianity.) Moreover, the whole poem may be regarded as an extended metaphor of what had happened in England under Milton's eyes. The holy community of sects that in *Areopagitica* Milton saw building—out of "many moderate varieties and brotherly dissimilitudes"—a goodly and graceful structure (forecast of the variety-in-unity of Heaven and Eden) had been lost like Eden through the passions of men. He now saw clearly, after nearly two decades of disappointed hope, that this community was not realizable in material terms or by the old kind of "public" heroism—not even that of a conquering Cromwell, or a Milton. It had to be reconstructed by the new heroism and in different terms: "A paradise within thee, happier far."

Yet these very contemporaneities are what make *Paradise Lost* universal too. Puritan "reformation" was after all simply a phase of the eternal human desire to shatter and reform; Puritan rationality, a reflection of everyone's wish to face up to an intelligible world. More important, in its central story of loss—the loss of spiritual innocence, the loss also of an external Utopia—accompanied by a story of regeneration and hope, Milton's epic became a vast parable of both the inner and outer history of mankind.

Considered, on the other hand, as a work of art, *Paradise Lost* is an equally remarkable blend. The nature of the blend may be suggested in such pairs of terms as Renaissance and Reformation, classical and Christian, opulent and austere; but perhaps best of all in variety-in-unity. For what impresses us if we look at the poem's fiction is the way in which a simple Biblical narrative has been fleshed out into an image of the whole range of man's experiences: love, war, adventure, fidelity, frailty, egoism, theology, mythology, history, and a hundred more—without ever losing its salience as narrative. And if we look at the style, we are impressed with something very similar. It is an impersonal style, carefully detemporized and distanced from idiomatic speech in order to make it suitable to an heroic and timeless theme. Yet from this fact it derives a marked particularity and personality: it could have been written in no other time and by no other man. Likewise, it is an assimilative style, constantly reaching out like fingers of lava and drawing in new territories of names, analogies, similes, allusions—or new patterns of syntax—or new ways of playing pentameter as a metrical unit across the drift of the sense. But again, the fact complementary to this is the style's sturdy, impervious, ongoing movement. It persistently asserts its own main lines of meaning. It heaps up nouns and epithets and verbs of parallel sense to do this (note in the following the italicized phrases): "Too well I see and rue the *dire event,*/That with *sad overthrow* and *foul defeat*/Hath *lost us Heaven* and all this mighty host/In *horrible destruction laid thus low*." Even the variety of the style, as it twists and turns along, is simultaneously a device of iteration. Often through internal rhyme: "Rocks, caves, lakes, *fens,* bogs, *dens.*" Or half-rhyme: "Abomin*able,* inutter*able.*" Or repetition: "Of *fierce extremes, extremes* by change more *fierce.*" Or (and this especially) modulation of word forms: "whom I could *pity* thus forlorn/Though I *unpitied*"; "Not to *know* me argues yourselves *unknown.*"

In its strangeness, inclusiveness, richness—but at the same time, in its essential simplicity, onwardness, sameness—the style is a good symbol of the poet's management of his narrative (its diversity yet perspicuity), and of his implicit theme: the luxuriance of nature held firm in the grasp of grace.

SAMSON AGONISTES

Samson Agonistes (probably Milton's last poem, though *Paradise Regained* may have been finished at about the same time) echoes with motifs from the poet's earlier work. Its story is in part the story of a false god's rout and hence linked with *On the Morning of Christ's Nativity.* Its central episodes, taking the form of temptations, underscore its affinities with *Comus* and also with *Paradise Lost.* Dalila's enticements are described by Samson in terms that parallel the central situation in *Comus:* "Thy fair enchanted cup and warbling charms"; her baneful influence on Samson resembles Eve's influence on Adam, except that Eve genuinely repents; and Milton had already stressed in *Paradise Lost* the likeness of Adam and Eve fallen to Samson shorn: "So rose the Danite strong, Herculean Samson from the Harlot-lap Of Philistean Dalilah, and waked Shorn of his strength; they destitute and bare Of all their virtue." This image, which seems to have haunted Milton's imagination, appears in his prose writings too, notably in a passage already quoted from *Areopagitica:* "Methinks I see in my mind a noble and puissant nation rousing herself like a strong man after sleep and shaking her invincible locks."

There is a suggestive difference in the image as used in these two instances. When Milton wrote *Areopagitica,* he had not yet been shorn of his dream of a kingdom of heaven on earth. Nor had he suffered yet the loss of sight commemorated in the sonnet "On His Blindness." This sonnet contains already in miniature much the same central conflict as *Samson.* Its speaker is "Milton *Agonistes*"— his own talent of poetry that he had dedicated to the service of his Maker now seemingly lodged with him useless like Samson's strength; though in Milton's case through no fault of his own. The poem also contrasts (like the Chorus in *Samson,* 1268 ff.) two ways of life, the active and the contemplative, with only the latter apparently now available to the poet: "They also serve who only stand and wait." But the poem is most like *Samson* in passing from a mood of complaint and impatience to one of faith and resignation. This is dramatized in the sonnet by the shift of emphasis from self-concern to the grandeur of God—from "I" and "me" to "he" and "his." In *Samson,* it is effected through the various episodes, or visitations of the hero, which gradually take him out of himself.

For the materials of *Samson,* Milton drew on the Biblical account in Judges, but its form and total artistic effect are largely Greek. This is what differentiates it from a play like *King Lear.* Elizabethan tragedy is expansive and exuberant. Greek tragedy is restrained and concentrative. It confines the story more often than not to one locality and a limited duration—the celebrated unities of time and place. It focuses exclusively on a single hero's fate and especially on a climactic or final episode in his career. It treats a story completely familiar to the audience in its general outlines, so that the source of interest lies not in *what* catastrophe will take place, but how it will take place. Its action is centered in psychological rather than in physical experience, and it carefully refrains from developing characters who, like Falstaff, are more "individual" than the thematic significance of the play can digest.

In all these respects, Milton's *Samson* re-creates Greek tragedy. It does so also in the wise use of messenger and chorus. The Chorus in *Samson* functions to remind the audience of circumstances and events prior to those which are the poet's present subject; its comments serve too as a kind of screen on which can be reflected the hero's changing emotions and psychological states; and it helps interpret the significance and oftentimes the growth of the action. The functional value of the messenger convention is also well illustrated by Milton's practice. The danger of showing violence on the stage, as in Gloucester's blinding, is that the inner meaning of the event may be lost in the horror it produces, its artistic purpose in pure physical effect. In the Elizabethan style of tragedy, this would have been Milton's difficulty with the pulling down of the temple, even if it were possible to re-produce such an event convincingly on the stage. In the Greek style, he can dispose of the problem easily through the messenger, who, in recounting what has happened, puts the emphasis on what it means, and so initiates the transition from the sufferings of the hero to their place in a larger plan.

The psychological movement in Milton's tragedy is from restlessness to peace. It begins with Samson's at first unavailing effort on Dagon's holiday "to find some ease" (17), and ends on a mood of peace and consolation—"calm of mind, all passion spent." The stages in this change are the subject of the intervening episodes. In the first, Samson and the Chorus, we find the hero, as we should expect, *agonistes*—that is to say, contesting: at this point only with himself. He utters various doubts about the justice of God's dealings with him, but also seeks to dispel these doubts. He manages to persuade the Chorus that his sin lay neither in marrying alien wives, for this was God's prompting, nor in failing to effect the liberation of his people, for this was their own fault in preferring "bondage with ease" to "strenuous liberty." His sin was his betrayal of God's secret to Dalila. The net effect of these revelations is to vindicate God, and the episode closes with the Chorus praising divine justice.

The second episode, Samson and Manoa and Chorus, shows Samson's father restating Samson's complaints against God in such a way that Samson wants to disown them. Here the hero takes the whole blame for his situation on himself, and in his anxiety to convince his father that the freedom he wishes is spiritual freedom and that the ransom he craves is ransom from sin, he falls into despair: he wants to die. This is the lowest point of the play, and the Chorus reflects it by singing now of the way in which God brings suffering on good as well as bad. "For oft alike, both come to evil end." It is important to notice, however, that Manoa, in his suggestion of ransom, has posed unwittingly a temptation, an easy way out, and Samson has resisted it. Furthermore, the assumption of total guilt that leads to Samson's despair is a necessary step; regeneration was impossible so long as he questioned God's fairness.

With the coming of Dalila and Harapha, in the third and fourth episodes, we have two further psychological stages. Dalila's appeal is a re-enactment of what Samson succumbed to before. Her words are filled with reminders of weakness, both his and hers. In rejecting her, therefore, Samson symbolically rejects his former frailty. Moreover, in uncovering each one of her specious arguments, Samson shows that he has now gained the wisdom he once lacked. Thinking of his fault, he had earlier exclaimed: "O impotence of mind, in body strong!" Now this impotence of mind is gone, and the following episode with Harapha shows that he has lost none of his physical potency. Both episodes, enkindling Samson's spirit, tease him out of his self-preoccupation. It is therefore an easy step to his acceptance of the officer's command in the fifth episode—accepted not in its character of compulsion from without, but by an act of the free will because it agrees with an impulse from within.

Following Harapha's departure, the Chorus has raised the question as to what kind of *agonistes* ("contestant") Samson is finally to be— active or contemplative. This question is answered in the remainder of the poem. Samson becomes a contestant, and in a very special sense the victor, of the Philistine games. So his final achievement is active. But both the participation and the victory issue from Samson's prior contest with and victory over himself, so the achievement is also contemplative. Here, as so often in Milton, we encounter the reconciliation of two competing ideals.

And there is still another reconciliation in the poem, one that sums up everything that has been said in these pages of Milton's work. If we look back at the dual conceptions of grace and nature sketched at the beginning, we can see that the order of grace asserts God and his claims; the order of nature, man and his. In *Samson,* Milton makes what is probably his profoundest acknowledgment of both. At one level, the play is occupied with man's sufferings, and man's questionings of divine justice, of his own powers, of the worth of life. Nothing is glossed over here, and there is no claim made, even in the closing chorus, that "all is best" for man as an individual. Least of all is any emotional claim made, for our emotions are all engaged with Samson, who, whatever he may have accomplished, is *dead*. At the same time, however, there is another level on which we see that the play is occupied with a spiritual regeneration, a victory over evil, a good made to grow out of evil, and a fulfillment of a divine plan— the latter all the more emphatic when we realize that for Milton and his contemporaries Samson's career prefigured Christ's. Philosophically, then, we may say that the play enables us to see man's fate from the outside, the position of grace, where what counts is what it all *means;* while emotionally it requires us to see it from within, the position of nature, where what counts is how it *feels*. This double vision, even where, as in Shakespeare, the position of grace is rarely given any precise religious definition, is essentially the vision of all great tragedies, and it is Milton's final word on the two worlds whose reconciliation had exercised his imagination all his life.

❧

A Note on the Texts

The texts contained in this volume are based on the following original editions: those of the *Nativity Ode, Comus,* and *Lycidas,* on the edition of 1645 (the Ode corrected by the edition of 1673); that of *Areopagitica* on the first edition of 1644; that of *Paradise Lost* on the revised second edition of 1674; and that of *Samson Agonistes* on the first edition of 1671.

Spelling, punctuation, and capitalization (to a large extent) have been modernized.

Minor Poems

Minor Poems

On the Morning of Christ's Nativity

(*Composed* 1629)

I

This is the month, and this the happy morn,
Wherein the Son of Heaven's eternal King,
Of wedded maid and virgin mother born,
Our great redemption from above did bring;
For so the holy sages once did sing,   5
   That he our deadly forfeit should release,
And with his Father work us a perpetual peace.

II

That glorious form, that light unsufferable,
And that far-beaming blaze of majesty,
Wherewith he wont at Heaven's high council-table   10
To sit the midst of Trinal Unity,
He laid aside, and, here with us to be,
   Forsook the courts of everlasting day,
And chose with us a darksome house of mortal clay.

III

Say, Heavenly Muse, shall not thy sacred vein   15
Afford a present to the Infant God,
Hast thou no verse, no hymn, or solemn strain,
To welcome him to this his new abode,

---

5. *holy sages:* Old Testament prophets. 6. *deadly forfeit:* penalties (including death) of the Fall.

Now while the heaven, by the Sun's team untrod,
   Hath took no print of the approaching light,   20
And all the spangled host keep watch in squadrons bright?

IV

See how from far upon the eastern road
The star-led wizards haste with odours sweet!
Oh! run; prevent them with thy humble ode,
And lay it lowly at his blessèd feet;   25
Have thou the honour first thy Lord to greet,
   And join thy voice unto the Angel Quire,
From out his secret altar touched with hallowed fire.

THE HYMN

I

   It was the winter wild,
   While the heaven-born child   30
All meanly wrapt in the rude manger lies;
   Nature, in awe to him,
   Had doffed her gaudy trim,
With her great Master so to sympathize:
It was no season then for her   35
To wanton with the Sun, her lusty paramour.

II

   Only with speeches fair
   She woos the gentle air
To hide her guilty front with innocent snow,
   And on her naked shame,   40
   Pollute with sinful blame,
The saintly veil of maiden white to throw;
Confounded, that her Maker's eyes
Should look so near upon her foul deformities.

III

   But he, her fears to cease,   45
   Sent down the meek-eyed Peace:
She, crowned with olive green, came softly sliding
   Down through the turning sphere,
   His ready harbinger,
With turtle wing the amorous clouds dividing;   50

21. *spangled host:* stars. 23. *wizards:* the three wise men. 24. *prevent:* anticipate. 41. *pollute:* polluted. 45. *cease:* allay.

And, waving wide her myrtle wand,
She strikes a universal peace through sea and land.

IV

    No war, or battle's sound,
    Was heard the world around;
The idle spear and shield were high uphung;   55
    The hookèd chariot stood,
    Unstained with hostile blood;
The trumpet spake not to the armèd throng;
And kings sat still with awful eye,
As if they surely knew their sovran Lord was by.   60

V

    But peaceful was the night
    Wherein the Prince of Light
His reign of peace upon the earth began.
    The winds, with wonder whist,
    Smoothly the waters kissed,   65
Whispering new joys to the mild Ocean,
Who now hath quite forgot to rave,
While birds of calm sit brooding on the charmèd wave.

VI

    The stars, with deep amaze,
    Stand fixed in steadfast gaze,   70
Bending one way their precious influence,
    And will not take their flight,
    For all the morning light,
Or Lucifer that often warned them thence;
But in their glimmering orbs did glow,   75
Until their Lord himself bespake, and bid them go.

VII

    And, though the shady gloom
    Had given day her room,
The Sun himself withheld his wonted speed,
    And hid his head for shame,   80
    As his inferior flame
The new-enlightened world no more should need:

---

56. *hookèd:* barbed. 59. *awful:* full of awe. 64. *whist:* hushed. 68. It was believed that halcyons nested on the sea in late December, at which time the seas grew quiet. 71. *influence:* see *Par. Lost,* iv 667-73. 73. *for:* despite. 74. *Lucifer:* name of the morning-star and of the sun. 81. *As:* as if.

He saw a greater Sun appear
Than his bright throne or burning axletree could bear.

VIII

    The shepherds on the lawn,   85
    Or ere the point of dawn,
Sat simply chatting in a rustic row;
    Full little thought they than
    That the mighty Pan
Was kindly come to live with them below: 90
Perhaps their loves, or else their sheep,
Was all that did their silly thoughts so busy keep.

IX

    When such music sweet
    Their hearts and ears did greet
As never was by mortal finger strook,   95
    Divinely-warbled voice
    Answering the stringèd noise,
As all their souls in blissful rapture took:
The air, such pleasure loath to lose,
With thousand echoes still prolongs each heavenly close.   100

X

    Nature, that heard such sound
    Beneath the hollow round
Of Cynthia's seat the Airy region thrilling,
    Now was almost won
    To think her part was done,   105
And that her reign had here its last fulfilling:
She knew such harmony alone
Could hold all Heaven and Earth in happier union.

XI

    At last surrounds their sight
    A globe of circular light,   110
That with long beams the shamefaced Night arrayed;
    The helmèd cherubim
    And sworded seraphim
Are seen in glittering ranks with wings displayed,
Harping in loud and solemn quire,   115
With unexpressive notes, to Heaven's new-born Heir.

---

88. *than:* then. 89. *Pan:* Greek spirit of nature and guardian of flocks, often identified (as here) with Christ. 100. *close:* cadence. 116. *unexpressive:* inexpressible.

XII

Such music (as 'tis said)
Before was never made,
But when of old the Sons of Morning sung,
    While the Creator great   120
    His constellations set,
And the well-balanced World on hinges hung,
And cast the dark foundations deep,
And bid the weltering waves their oozy channel keep.

XIII

Ring out, ye crystal spheres!   125
Once bless our human ears,
If ye have power to touch our senses so;
    And let your silver chime
    Move in melodious time;
And let the bass of heaven's deep organ blow;   130
And with your ninefold harmony
Make up full consort to th' angelic symphony.

XIV

For, if such holy song
Enwrap our fancy long,
Time will run back and fetch the Age of Gold;   135
    And speckled Vanity
    Will sicken soon and die,
And leprous Sin will melt from earthly mould;
And Hell itself will pass away,
And leave her dolorous mansions to the peering day.   140

XV

Yea, Truth and Justice then
Will down return to men,
Orbed in a rainbow; and, like glories wearing,
    Mercy will sit between,
    Throned in celestial sheen,   145
With radiant feet the tissued clouds down steering;
And Heaven, as at some festival,
Will open wide the gates of her high palace-hall.

---

119. *But when . . . the Sons of Morning:* Cf. the description of Creation
in Job (38 : 6-7), "When the morning stars sang together, and all the sons
of God shouted for joy." 124. *weltering:* tossing. 125-7. The divine harmony of the spheres, believed inaudible to men since the Fall. 136. *Vanity:*
Man's general unregeneracy.

XVI

But wisest Fate says No,
  This must not yet be so;
    The Babe lies yet in smiling infancy   150
    That on the bitter cross
    Must redeem our loss,
  So both himself and us to glorify:
Yet first, to those ychained in sleep,   155
The wakeful trump of doom must thunder through the deep.

XVII

With such a horrid clang
  As on Mount Sinai rang,
    While the red fire and smouldering clouds outbrake:
    The agèd Earth, aghast   160
    With terror of that blast,
  Shall from the surface to the centre shake,
When, at the world's last session,
The dreadful Judge in middle air shall spread his throne.

XVIII

And then at last our bliss   165
  Full and perfect is,
    But now begins; for from this happy day
    Th' Old Dragon under ground,
    In straiter limits bound,
  Not half so far casts his usurpèd sway,   170
And, wroth to see his kingdom fail,
Swinges the scaly horror of his folded tail.

XIX

The Oracles are dumb;
  No voice or hideous hum
    Runs through the archèd roof in words deceiving.   175
    Apollo from his shrine
    Can no more divine,
  With hollow shriek the steep of Delphos leaving.
No nightly trance, or breathèd spell,
Inspires the pale-eyed priest from the prophetic cell.   180

---

153. *loss:* ruin. 158-9. Thunder, lightning, and "the voice of the trumpet exceeding loud" accompanied Moses's receiving the Ten Commandments on Sinai (Exodus 19 : 16). 163. *session:* a judge's "session." 168-72. "And the great dragon was cast out . . . called the Devil and Satan." (Revelation 12 : 9). 178. Apollo's oracle at Delphi.

XX

The lonely mountains o'er,
And the resounding shore,
A voice of weeping heard and loud lament;
From haunted spring, and dale
Edged with poplar pale,   185
The parting Genius is with sighing sent;
With flower-inwoven tresses torn
The Nymphs in twilight shade of tangled thickets mourn.

XXI

In consecrated earth,
And on the holy hearth,   190
The Lars and Lemures moan with midnight plaint;
In urns, and altars round,
A drear and dying sound
Affrights the flamens at their service quaint;
And the chill marble seems to sweat,   195
While each peculiar power forgoes his wonted seat.

XXII

Peor and Baälim
Forsake their temples dim,
With that twice-battered god of Palestine;
And moonèd Ashtaroth,   200
Heaven's queen and mother both,
Now sits not girt with tapers' holy shine:
The Libyc Hammon shrinks his horn;
In vain the Tyrian maids their wounded Thammuz mourn.

XXIII

And sullen Moloch, fled,   205
Hath left in shadows dread
His burning idol all of blackest hue;

---

186. *Genius:* any local god. 191. *Lars: Lares,* gods of families. *Lemures:* spirits of the dead. 194. *flamens:* priests. 197. *Peor:* Baal, chief god of the Canaanites, called Peor from his great shrine at Mt. Peor. *Baalim:* plural of Baal, used here to mean other minor pagan deities. 199. Dagon, god of the Philistines, whose idol was twice broken (cf. I Samuel 5). 200. *Ashtaroth:* Ashtoreth (Astarte), a fertility goddess associated with the moon. Cf. *Par. Lost* I 438-9. 203. *Hammon:* the Egyptian ram-god (hence his *horn*), whose chief temple was in Libya (*Libyc*). 204. *Thammuz:* the Phoenician (*Tyrian*) version of the Greek Adonis. Cf. *Par. Lost* I 446-7. 205. *Moloch:* a brutal god worshipped with human sacrifices (cf. 2 Kings 23 : 10).

In vain with cymbals' ring
    They call the grisly king,
  In dismal dance about the furnace blue;   210
The brutish gods of Nile as fast,
Isis, and Orus, and the dog Anubis, haste.

XXIV

Nor is Osiris seen
    In Memphian grove or green,
  Trampling the unshowered grass with lowings loud;   215
    Nor can he be at rest
    Within his sacred chest;
  Nought but profoundest Hell can be his shroud;
In vain, with timbreled anthems dark,
The sable-stolèd sorcerers bear his worshipped ark.   220

XXV

He feels from Juda's land
    The dreaded Infant's hand;
  The rays of Bethlehem blind his dusky eyn;
    Nor all the gods beside
    Longer dare abide,   225
  Not Typhon huge ending in snaky twine;
Our Babe, to show his Godhead true,
Can in his swaddling bands control the damnèd crew.

XXVI

So, when the sun in bed,
    Curtained with cloudy red,   230
  Pillows his chin upon an orient wave,
    The flocking shadows pale
    Troop to the infernal jail,
  Each fettered ghost slips to his several grave,
And the yellow-skirted fays   235
Fly after the night-steeds, leaving their moon-loved maze.

XXVII

But see! the Virgin blest
    Hath laid her Babe to rest.

---

211. *brutish*: because depicted with animal attributes: Isis with cow's horns, Horus with a hawk's head, Anubis with a jackal's face, Osiris (whose shrine was at Memphis) as a bull. 220. *sable-stolèd*: black-robed. 226. *Typhon*: a monster, half-man, half-snake, slain by Hercules. 227-8. Hercules was said as an infant to have strangled two serpents which threatened to devour him. Because he was a friend to mankind, a conqueror of evil, and was finally translated to heaven by Zeus, he was often associated with Christ. 235. *fays*: fairies. 236. *maze*: intricate dance.

Time is our tedious song should here have ending:
   Heaven's youngest-teemèd star   240
   Hath fixed her polished car,
Her sleeping Lord with handmaid lamp attending;
And all about the courtly stable
Bright-harnessed Angels sit in order serviceable.

Comus

(Performed 1634, published 1637)

THE PERSONS

THE ATTENDANT SPIRIT, *afterwards*	FIRST BROTHER
in the habit of THYRSIS	SECOND BROTHER
COMUS, *with his Crew*	SABRINA, *the Nymph*
THE LADY	

The first Scene discovers a wild wood.

[*The* ATTENDANT SPIRIT *descends or enters.*]

Before the starry threshold of Jove's court
My mansion is, where those immortal shapes
Of bright aerial spirits live insphered
In regions mild of calm and serene air,
Above the smoke and stir of this dim spot   5
Which men call Earth, and, with low-thoughted care,
Confined and pestered in this pinfold here,
Strive to keep up a frail and feverish being,
Unmindful of the crown that Virtue gives,
After this mortal change, to her true servants   10
Amongst the enthroned gods on sainted seats.
Yet some there be that by due steps aspire
To lay their just hands on that golden key
That opes the palace of eternity.
To such my errand is; and, but for such,   15
I would not soil these pure ambrosial weeds
With the rank vapours of this sin-worn mould.

---

240. *teemèd:* born. 244. *Bright-harnessed:* bright-armoured.
  1. *Jove:* used synonymously for "God." 7. *pinfold:* pound (for animals).
16. *ambrosial weeds:* heavenly garments. 17. *sin-worn mould:* sinful (human) flesh.

But to my task. Neptune, besides the sway
Of every salt flood and each ebbing stream,
Took in by lot 'twixt high and nether Jove   20
Imperial rule of all the sea-girt isles
That like to rich and various gems inlay
The unadornèd bosom of the deep;
Which he, to grace his tributary gods,
By course commits to several government,   25
And gives them leave to wear their sapphire crowns
And wield their little tridents. But this Isle,
The greatest and the best of all the main,
He quarters to his blue-haired deities;
And all this tract that fronts the falling sun   30
A noble Peer of mickle trust and power
Has in his charge, with tempered awe to guide
An old and haughty nation, proud in arms:
Where his fair offspring, nursed in princely lore,
Are coming to attend their father's state,   35
And new-entrusted sceptre. But their way
Lies through the perplexed paths of this drear wood,
The nodding horror of whose shady brows
Threats the forlorn and wandering passenger;
And here their tender age might suffer peril,   40
But that, by quick command from sovran Jove,
I was despatched for their defence and guard!
And listen why; for I will tell you now
What never yet was heard in tale or song,
From old or modern bard, in hall or bower.   45
   Bacchus, that first from out the purple grape
Crushed the sweet poison of misusèd wine,
After the Tuscan mariners transformed,
Coasting the Tyrrhene shore, as the winds listed,
On Circe's island fell. (Who knows not Circe,   50
The daughter of the Sun, whose charmèd cup
Whoever tasted lost his upright shape,
And downward fell into a grovelling swine?)
This Nymph, that gazed upon his clustering locks,
With ivy berries wreathed, and his blithe youth,   55

18-20. Homer represents the universe as divided among Neptune (sea), Jove
(sky), and Pluto, i.e., "nether Jove" (underworld). 29. *quarters to:* divides
among. 31. *mickle:* much. 33. A compliment to the Welsh. 35. *state:*
position (as Lord President of Wales). 37. *perplexed:* tangled. 48. Kid-
napped by pirates, Bacchus *transformed* his captors to dolphins, their ships
to a grape-arbor. 49. *Tyrrhene:* Italy's southwest shore.

Had by him, ere he parted thence, a son
Much like his father, but his mother more,
Whom therefore she brought up, and Comus named:
Who, ripe and frolic of his full-grown age,
Roving the Celtic and Iberian fields,   60
At last betakes him to this ominous wood,
And, in thick shelter of black shades imbowered,
Excels his mother at her mighty art;
Offering to every weary traveller
His orient liquor in a crystal glass,   65
To quench the drouth of Phœbus; which as they taste
(For most do taste through fond intemperate thirst),
Soon as the potion works, their human count'nance,
The express resemblance of the gods, is changed
Into some brutish form of wolf or bear,   70
Or ounce or tiger, hog, or bearded goat,
All other parts remaining as they were.
And they, so perfect in their misery,
Not once perceive their foul disfigurement,
But boast themselves more comely than before,   75
And all their friends and native home forget,
To roll with pleasure in a sensual sty.
Therefore, when any favoured of high Jove
Chances to pass through this adventurous glade,
Swift as the sparkle of a glancing star   80
I shoot from heaven, to give him safe convoy,
As now I do. But first I must put off
These my sky-robes, spun out of Iris' woof,
And take the weeds and likeness of a swain
That to the service of this house belongs,   85
Who, with his soft pipe and smooth-dittied song,
Well knows to still the wild winds when they roar,
And hush the waving woods; nor of less faith,
And in this office of his mountain watch
Likeliest, and nearest to the present aid   90
Of this occasion. But I hear the tread
Of hateful steps; I must be viewless now.

---

60. *Iberian:* Spanish. 65. *orient:* shining (i.e., like the day, which rises in
the East). 66. *the . . . Phoebus:* thirst occasioned by the sun. 71. *ounce:*
lynx. 83. *Iris:* the rainbow goddess. 84. *swain:* countryman. 87-8. *still,
hush:* effects traditionally attributed to Orpheus's music and hence here a
great compliment to Lawes's. 88. *nor . . . faith:* just as reliable in character as able in music. 90. *Likeliest:* best fitted.

[COMUS *enters, with a charming-rod in one hand, his glass in the other; with him a rout of monsters, headed like sundry sorts of wild beasts, but otherwise like men and women, their apparel glistening. They come in making a riotous and unruly noise, with torches in their hands.*]

COMUS. The star that bids the shepherd fold
Now the top of heaven doth hold;
And the gilded car of day   95
His glowing axle doth allay
In the steep Atlantic stream:
And the slope sun his upward beam
Shoots against the dusky pole,
Pacing toward the other goal   100
Of his chamber in the east.
Meanwhile, welcome joy and feast,
Midnight shout and revelry,
Tipsy dance and jollity.
Braid your locks with rosy twine,   105
Dropping odours, dropping wine.
Rigour now is gone to bed;
And Advice with scrupulous head,
Strict Age, and sour Severity,
With their grave saws, in slumber lie.   110
We, that are of purer fire,
Imitate the starry quire,
Who, in their nightly watchful spheres,
Lead in swift round the months and years.
The sounds and seas, with all their finny drove,   115
Now to the moon in wavering morrice move;
And on the tawny sands and shelves
Trip the pert fairies and the dapper elves.
By dimpled brook and fountain-brim,
The wood-nymphs, decked with daisies trim,   120
Their merry wakes and pastimes keep:
What hath night to do with sleep?
Night hath better sweets to prove;
Venus now wakes, and wakens Love.

---

93. Hesperus, the evening star, signal to shepherds to put their flocks in fold. 95. The sun, conceived as a chariot. 105. *rosy twine:* garlands twined of flowers. 110. *saws:* maxims. 111. We who are spirits and thus made *of purer fire* than men, who are mostly "earth" (cf. l. 17). 116. *morrice:* grotesque dance.

Come, let us our rites begin; 125
'Tis only daylight that makes sin,
Which these dun shades will ne'er report.
Hail, goddess of nocturnal sport,
Dark-veiled Cotytto, to whom the secret flame
Of midnight torches burns! mysterious dame, 130
That ne'er art called but when the dragon womb
Of Stygian darkness spets her thickest gloom,
And makes one blot of all the air!
Stay thy cloudy ebon chair,
Wherein thou rid'st with Hecat', and befriend 135
Us thy vowed priests, till utmost end
Of all thy dues be done, and none left out
Ere the blabbing eastern scout,
The nice Morn on the Indian steep,
From her cabined loop-hole peep, 140
And to the tell-tale Sun descry
Our concealed solemnity.
Come, knit hands, and beat the ground
In a light fantastic round.

The Measure

Break off, break off! I feel the different pace 145
Of some chaste footing near about this ground.
Run to your shrouds within these brakes and trees;
Our number may affright. Some virgin sure
(For so I can distinguish by mine art)
Benighted in these woods! Now to my charms, 150
And to my wily trains: I shall ere long
Be well stocked with as fair a herd as grazed
About my mother Circe. Thus I hurl
My dazzling spells into the spongy air,
Of power to cheat the eye with blear illusion, 155
And give it false presentments, lest the place
And my quaint habits breed astonishment,

---

129. *Cotytto:* Thracian goddess associated with obscene rites. 132. *Stygian darkness:* darkness like that around the river Styx in hell. *spets:* spits. 134. *ebon:* black like ebony. 135. *Hecat':* Hecate, mistress of witches. 139. *nice:* priggish. 142. *solemnity:* service of worship (to Cotytto). 144. *round:* round-dance. S.d. *The Measure:* The "round" is here danced by Comus and his crew. 147. *brakes:* thickets. 151. *trains:* lures. 154. *spongy:* absorbent (of the charms). 156. *false presentments:* illusions.

And put the damsel to suspicious flight;
Which must not be, for that's against my course.
I, under fair pretence of friendly ends,   160
And well-placed words of glozing courtesy,
Baited with reasons not unplausible,
Wind me into the easy-hearted man,
And hug him into snares. When once her eye
Hath met the virtue of this magic dust   165
I shall appear some harmless villager,
Whom thrift keeps up about his country gear.
But here she comes; I fairly step aside,
And hearken, if I may her business hear.

[THE LADY *enters.*]

LADY. This way the noise was, if mine ear be true,   170
My best guide now. Methought it was the sound
Of riot and ill-managed merriment,
Such as the jocund flute or gamesome pipe
Stirs up among the loose unlettered hinds,
When, for their teeming flocks and granges full,   175
In wanton dance they praise the bounteous Pan,
And thank the gods amiss. I should be loth
To meet the rudeness and swilled insolence
Of such late wassailers; yet, oh! where else
Shall I inform my unacquainted feet   180
In the blind mazes of this tangled wood?
My brothers, when they saw me wearied out
With this long way, resolving here to lodge
Under the spreading favour of these pines,
Stepped, as they said, to the next thicket-side   185
To bring me berries, or such cooling fruit
As the kind hospitable woods provide.
They left me then when the grey-hooded Even,
Like a sad votarist in palmer's weed,
Rose from the hindmost wheels of Phœbus' wain.   190
But where they are, and why they came not back,
Is now the labour of my thoughts. 'Tis likeliest

---

160. *ends:* aims. 161. *glozing:* flattering. 163. *Wind me:* insinuate myself.
165. *virtue:* power. 167. *gear:* duties. 175. *teeming:* multiplying. *granges:*
barns. 176. *Pan:* shepherd-god. 177. *amiss:* in the wrong way. 178. *swilled:*
drunken. 179. *wassailers:* merrymakers. 189. *sad . . . weed:* grave pilgrim
in pilgrim dress. 190. *wain:* car.

They had engaged their wandering steps too far;
And envious darkness, ere they could return,
Had stole them from me. Else, O thievish Night, 195
Why shouldst thou, but for some felonious end,
In thy dark lantern thus close up the stars
That Nature hung in heaven, and filled their lamps
With everlasting oil, to give due light
To the misled and lonely traveller? 200
This is the place, as well as I may guess,
Whence even now the tumult of loud mirth
Was rife, and perfect in my listening ear;
Yet nought but single darkness do I find.
What might this be? A thousand fantasies 205
Begin to throng into my memory,
Of calling shapes, and beckoning shadows dire,
And airy tongues that syllable men's names
On sands and shores and desert wildernesses.
These thoughts may startle well, but not astound 210
The virtuous mind, that ever walks attended
By a strong siding champion, Conscience.—
O, welcome, pure-eyed Faith, white-handed Hope,
Thou hovering angel girt with golden wings,
And thou unblemished form of Chastity! 215
I see ye visibly, and now believe
That He, the Supreme Good, to whom all things ill
Are but as slavish officers of vengeance,
Would send a glistering guardian, if need were,
To keep my life and honour unassailed.— 220
Was I deceived, or did a sable cloud
Turn forth her silver lining on the night?
I did not err: there does a sable cloud
Turn forth her silver lining on the night,
And casts a gleam over this tufted grove. 225
I cannot hallo to my brothers, but
Such noise as I can make to be heard farthest
I'll venture, for my new-enlivened spirits
Prompt me; and they perhaps are not far off.

---

203. *perfect:* perfectly clear. 204. *single:* total. 213-15. *Faith, Hope, and* (instead of Charity, i.e., Love) *Chastity.* Here Milton is thinking of Chastity in Plato's terms as a spiritual love of the Supreme Good, transcending physical love.

Song

Sweet Echo, sweetest nymph, that liv'st unseen   230
    Within thy airy shell
   By slow Meander's margent green,
And in the violet-embroidered vale
   Where the love-lorn nightingale
Nightly to thee her sad song mourneth well: 235
Canst thou not tell me of a gentle pair
    That likest thy Narcissus are?
     O, if thou have
   Hid them in some flowery cave,
    Tell me but where,   240
  Sweet Queen of Parley, Daughter of the Sphere!
  So may'st thou be translated to the skies,
And give resounding grace to all Heaven's harmonies!

comus. Can any mortal mixture of earth's mould
Breathe such divine enchanting ravishment?   245
Sure something holy lodges in that breast,
And with these raptures moves the vocal air
To testify his hidden residence.
How sweetly did they float upon the wings
Of silence, through the empty-vaulted night,   250
At every fall smoothing the raven down
Of darkness till it smiled! I have oft heard
My mother Circe with the Sirens three,
Amidst the flowery-kirtled Naiades,
Culling their potent herbs and baleful drugs,   255
Who, as they sung, would take the prisoned soul,
And lap it in Elysium: Scylla wept,
And chid her barking waves into attention,
And fell Charybdis murmured soft applause.
Yet they in pleasing slumber lulled the sense,   260
And in sweet madness robbed it of itself;
But such a sacred and home-felt delight,

---

232. *Meander:* a river. 237. *Narcissus:* Echo's lover. 241. *Queen of Parley* because a great "talker"; *Daughter of the Sphere* because she "echoes" to the vault (*sphere*) of the sky. 243. *resounding:* both resounding and resounding. 246. *something holy:* e.g., an angel. 251. *raven down:* dark feathers. 253. *Sirens:* the women whose singing lured ships to their destruction. 254. *Naiades:* water-nymphs. 256. *prisoned:* captivated. 257. *Elysium:* bliss—as in the Elysian Fields. 257-60. *Scylla, Charybdis:* the Sicilian straits, represented in the *Odyssey* as a group of ragged rocks on one side, a sucking whirlpool on the other.

Such sober certainty of waking bliss,
I never heard till now. I'll speak to her,
And she shall be my queen.—Hail, foreign wonder!   265
Whom certain these rough shades did never breed,
Unless the goddess that in rural shrine
Dwell'st here with Pan or Sylvan, by blest song
Forbidding every bleak unkindly fog
To touch the prosperous growth of this tall wood.   270
   LADY. Nay, gentle shepherd, ill is lost that praise
That is addressed to unattending ears.
Not any boast of skill, but extreme shift
How to regain my severed company,
Compelled me to awake the courteous Echo   275
To give me answer from her mossy couch.
   COMUS. What chance, good Lady, hath bereft you thus?
   LADY. Dim darkness and this leavy labyrinth.
   COMUS. Could that divide you from near-ushering guides?
   LADY. They left me weary on a grassy turf.   280
   COMUS. By falsehood, or discourtesy, or why?
   LADY. To seek i' the valley some cool friendly spring.
   COMUS. And left your fair side all unguarded, Lady?
   LADY. They were but twain, and purposed quick return.
   COMUS. Perhaps forestalling night prevented them.   285
   LADY. How easy my misfortune is to hit!
   COMUS. Imports their loss, beside the present need?
   LADY. No less than if I should my brothers lose.
   COMUS. Were they of manly prime, or youthful bloom?
   LADY. As smooth as Hebe's their unrazored lips.   290
   COMUS. Two such I saw, what time the laboured ox
In his loose traces from the furrow came,
And the swinked hedger at his supper sat.
I saw them under a green mantling vine,
That crawls along the side of yon small hill,   295
Plucking ripe clusters from the tender shoots;
Their port was more than human, as they stood.
I took it for a faery vision
Of some gay creatures of the element,
That in the colours of the rainbow live,   300
And play i' the plighted clouds. I was awe-strook,
And, as I passed, I worshiped. If those you seek,

---

267. *Unless:* unless you are. 268. *Sylvan:* Sylvanus, a wood-god. 273. I.e.,
no wish to show off, but real concern. 290. *Hebe:* goddess of youth. 293.
swinked hedger: tired hedgemaker. 299. *element:* air. 301. *plighted:* folded,
or interwoven.

It were a journey like the path to Heaven
To help you find them.
  LADY.   Gentle villager,
What readiest way would bring me to that place?   305
  COMUS. Due west it rises from this shrubby point.
  LADY. To find out that, good shepherd, I suppose,
In such a scant allowance of star-light,
Would overtask the best land-pilot's art,
Without the sure guess of well-practised feet.   310
  COMUS. I know each lane, and every alley green,
Dingle, or bushy dell, of this wild wood,
And every bosky bourn from side to side,
My daily walks and ancient neighbourhood;
And, if your stray attendance be yet lodged,   315
Or shroud within these limits, I shall know
Ere morrow wake, or the low-roosted lark
From her thatched pallet rouse. If otherwise,
I can conduct you, Lady, to a low
But loyal cottage, where you may be safe   320
Till further quest.
  LADY.   Shepherd, I take thy word,
And trust thy honest-offered courtesy,
Which oft is sooner found in lowly sheds,
With smoky rafters, than in tap'stry halls
And courts of princes, where it first was named,   325
And yet is most pretended. In a place
Less warranted than this, or less secure,
I cannot be, that I should fear to change it.
Eye me, blest Providence, and square my trial
To my proportioned strength! Shepherd, lead on.—   330

[THE TWO BROTHERS.]

  ELD. BRO. Unmuffle, ye faint stars; and thou, fair moon,
That wont'st to love the traveller's benison,
Stoop thy pale visage through an amber cloud,
And disinherit Chaos, that reigns here
In double night of darkness and of shades;   335
Or, if your influence be quite dammed up
With black usurping mists, some gentle taper,

---

312. *Dingle:* hollow between hills. 313. *bosky bourn:* bush-hung brook.
316. *shroud:* shelter. 318. *thatched pallet:* straw nest. 327. *warranted:*
protected. 329. *square:* suit. 332. *benison:* blessing.

Though a rush-candle from the wicker hole
Of some clay habitation, visit us
With thy long levelled rule of streaming light,   340
And thou shalt be our star of Arcady,
Or Tyrian Cynosure.
    SEC. BRO.   Or, if our eyes
Be barred that happiness, might we but hear
The folded flocks, penned in their wattled cotes,
Or sound of pastoral reed with oaten stops,   345
Or whistle from the lodge, or village cock
Count the night-watches to his feathery dames,
'Twould be some solace yet, some little cheering,
In this close dungeon of innumerous boughs.
But, oh, that hapless virgin, our lost sister!   350
Where may she wander now, whither betake her
From the chill dew, amongst rude burrs and thistles?
Perhaps some cold bank is her bolster now,
Or 'gainst the rugged bark of some broad elm
Leans her unpillowed head, fraught with sad fears.   355
What if in wild amazement and affright,
Or, while we speak, within the direful grasp
Of savage hunger, or of savage heat!
    ELD. BRO. Peace, brother: be not over-exquisite
To cast the fashion of uncertain evils;   360
For, grant they be so, while they rest unknown,
What need a man forestall his date of grief,
And run to meet what he would most avoid?
Or, if they be but false alarms of fear,
How bitter is such self-delusion!   365
I do not think my sister so to seek,
Or so unprincipled in virtue's book,
And the sweet peace that goodness bosoms ever,
As that the single want of light and noise
(Not being in danger, as I trust she is not)   370
Could stir the constant mood of her calm thoughts,
And put them into misbecoming plight.

341-2. *star . . . Cynosure:* Callisto of Arcadia was translated to the skies
as the Great Bear; while her son became the Little Bear, also called *Cyno-
sura,* guide to Phoenician (*Tyrian*) navigators, as the Great Bear was to
the Greeks. 344. *wattled cotes:* sheepfolds of woven boughs. 345. Oaten
stalk, traditional shepherd's instrument in English verse. 355. *fraught:*
filled. 358. *heat:* lust. 359. *exquisite:* curious. 362. *forestall:* anticipate.
366. *so to seek:* so at a loss. 368. *bosoms:* has in its bosom.

Virtue could see to do what Virtue would
By her own radiant light, though sun and moon
Were in the flat sea sunk. And Wisdom's self   375
Oft seeks to sweet retirèd solitude,
Where, with her best nurse, Contemplation,
She plumes her feathers, and lets grow her wings,
That, in the various bustle of resort,
Were all to-ruffled, and sometimes impaired.   380
He that has light within his own clear breast
May sit i' the centre, and enjoy bright day:
But he that hides a dark soul and foul thoughts
Benighted walks under the mid-day sun;
Himself is his own dungeon.
  SEC. BRO.   'Tis most true   385
That musing Meditation most affects
The pensive secrecy of desert cell,
Far from the cheerful haunt of men and herds,
And sits as safe as in a senate-house;
For who would rob a hermit of his weeds,   390
His few books, or his beads, or maple dish,
Or do his grey hairs any violence?
But Beauty, like the fair Hesperian tree
Laden with blooming gold, had need the guard
Of dragon-watch with unenchanted eye   395
To save her blossoms, and defend her fruit,
From the rash hand of bold Incontinence.
You may as well spread out the unsunned heaps
Of miser's treasure by an outlaw's den,
And tell me it is safe, as bid me hope   400
Danger will wink on Opportunity,
And let a single helpless maiden pass
Uninjured in this wild surrounding waste.
Of night or loneliness it recks me not;
I fear the dread events that dog them both,   405
Lest some ill-greeting touch attempt the person
Of our unownèd sister.
  ELD. BRO.   I do not, brother,
Infer as if I thought my sister's state
Secure without all doubt or controversy;

---

382. *centre:* i.e., of the earth. 391. *beads:* rosary. 393. *Hesperian tree:* the
golden-fruited tree in the Garden of the Hesperides, watched by a dragon.
407. *unownèd:* unescorted.

Yet, where an equal poise of hope and fear 410
Does arbitrate the event, my nature is
That I incline to hope rather than fear,
And gladly banish squint suspicion.
My sister is not so defenceless left
As you imagine; she has a hidden strength, 415
Which you remember not.
 SEC. BRO.   What hidden strength,
Unless the strength of Heaven, if you mean that?
 ELD. BRO. I mean that too, but yet a hidden strength,
Which, if Heaven gave it, may be termed her own.
'Tis chastity, my brother, chastity: 420
She that has that is clad in complete steel,
And, like a quivered nymph with arrows keen,
May trace huge forests, and unharboured heaths,
Infamous hills, and sandy perilous wilds;
Where, through the sacred rays of chastity, 425
No savage fierce, bandit, or mountaineer,
Will dare to soil her virgin purity.
Yea, there where very desolation dwells,
By grots and caverns shagged with horrid shades,
She may pass on with unblenched majesty, 430
Be it not done in pride, or in presumption.
Some say no evil thing that walks by night,
In fog or fire, by lake or moorish fen,
Blue meagre hag, or stubborn unlaid ghost,
That breaks his magic chains at curfew time, 435
No goblin or swart faery of the mine,
Hath hurtful power o'er true virginity.
Do ye believe me yet, or shall I call
Antiquity from the old schools of Greece
To testify the arms of chastity? 440
Hence had the huntress Dian her dread bow,
Fair silver-shafted queen for ever chaste,
Wherewith she tamed the brinded lioness
And spotted mountain-pard, but set at nought
The frivolous bolt of Cupid; gods and men 445

---

422. *quivered:* i.e., a follower of the huntress Diana, patroness of chastity.
429. *horrid:* bristling. 430. *unblenched:* unterrified. 435. Spirits walk only
after curfew. 436. *swart:* black (dirtied by mining). 441 ff. Diana's mastery, as the huntress goddess, over wild beasts becomes here an allegory of
her mastery, as the goddess of chastity, over wild passions. 445. *bolt:* arrow.

Feared her stern frown, and she was queen o' the woods.
What was that snaky-headed Gorgon shield
That wise Minerva wore, unconquered virgin,
Wherewith she freezed her foes to congealed stone,
But rigid looks of chaste austerity,   450
And noble grace that dashed brute violence
With sudden adoration and blank awe?
So dear to Heaven is saintly chastity
That, when a soul is found sincerely so,
A thousand liveried angels lackey her,   455
Driving far off each thing of sin and guilt,
And in clear dream and solemn vision
Tell her of things that no gross ear can hear;
Till oft converse with heavenly habitants
Begin to cast a beam on the outward shape,   460
The unpolluted temple of the mind,
And turns it by degrees to the soul's essence,
Till all be made immortal. But, when lust,
By unchaste looks, loose gestures, and foul talk,
But most by lewd and lavish act of sin,   465
Lets in defilement to the inward parts,
The soul grows clotted by contagion,
Imbodies, and imbrutes, till she quite lose
The divine property of her first being.
Such are those thick and gloomy shadows damp   470
Oft seen in charnel-vaults and sepulchres,
Lingering and sitting by a new-made grave,
As loth to leave the body that it loved,
And linked itself by carnal sensuality
To a degenerate and degraded state.   475
    SEC. BRO. How charming is divine Philosophy!
Not harsh and crabbèd, as dull fools suppose,
But musical as is Apollo's lute,
And a perpetual feast of nectared sweets,
Where no crude surfeit reigns.
    ELD. BRO.   List! list! I hear   480
Some far-off hallo break the silent air.

447-52. On the shield of Minerva, goddess of wisdom, was depicted the head
of the Gorgon, Medusa, the sight of whom turned men to stone: this power
also is allegorized as chastity. 455. *lackey:* attend. 459-69. The Platonic idea
that the soul may "spiritualize" the body, or the body "imbrute" the soul.
477. *crabbèd:* sour. 480. *crude surfeit:* undigested excess.

SEC. BRO. Methought so too; what should it be?
ELD. BRO.   For certain,
Either some one, like us, night-foundered here,
Or else some neighbour woodman, or, at worst,
Some roving robber calling to his fellows.   485
SEC. BRO. Heaven keep my sister! Again, again, and near!
Best draw, and stand upon our guard.
ELD. BRO.   I'll hallo.
If he be friendly, he comes well: if not,
Defence is a good cause, and Heaven be for us!

[*The* ATTENDANT SPIRIT, *habited like a shepherd.*]

That hallo I should know. What are you? speak.   490
Come not too near; you fall on iron stakes else.
  SPIR. What voice is that? my young Lord? speak again.
  SEC. BRO. O brother, 'tis my father's Shepherd, sure.
  ELD. BRO. Thyrsis? whose artful strains have oft delayed
The huddling brook to hear his madrigal,   495
And sweetened every musk-rose of the dale.
How cam'st thou here, good swain? Hath any ram
Slipped from the fold, or young kid lost his dam,
Or straggling wether the pent flock forsook?
How couldst thou find this dark sequestered nook?   500
  SPIR. O my loved master's heir, and his next joy,
I came not here on such a trivial toy
As a strayed ewe, or to pursue the stealth
Of pilfering wolf; not all the fleecy wealth
That doth enrich these downs is worth a thought   505
To this my errand, and the care it brought.
But, oh! my virgin Lady, where is she?
How chance she is not in your company?
  ELD. BRO. To tell thee sadly, Shepherd, without blame
Or our neglect, we lost her as we came.   510
  SPIR. Ay me unhappy! then my fears are true.
  ELD. BRO. What fears, good Thyrsis? Prithee briefly shew.
  SPIR. I'll tell ye. 'Tis not vain or fabulous
(Though so esteemed by shallow ignorance)
What the sage poets, taught by the heavenly Muse,   515
Storied of old in high immortal verse
Of dire Chimeras and enchanted isles,

---

491. *iron stakes:* swords. 495. *The . . . hear:* brook crowding to hear. 499. *pent:* penned up.

And rifted rocks whose entrance leads to Hell;
For such there be, but unbelief is blind.
   Within the navel of this hideous wood,   520
Immured in cypress shades, a sorcerer dwells,
Of Bacchus and of Circe born, great Comus,
Deep skilled in all his mother's witcheries,
And here to every thirsty wanderer
By sly enticement gives his baneful cup,   525
With many murmurs mixed, whose pleasing poison
The visage quite transforms of him that drinks,
And the inglorious likeness of a beast
Fixes instead, unmoulding reason's mintage
Charactered in the face. This have I learnt   530
Tending my flocks hard by i' the hilly crofts
That brow this bottom glade; whence night by night
He and his monstrous rout are heard to howl
Like stabled wolves, or tigers at their prey,
Doing abhorrèd rites to Hecate   535
In their obscurèd haunts of inmost bowers.
Yet have they many baits and guileful spells
To inveigle and invite the unwary sense
Of them that pass unweeting by the way.
This evening late, by then the chewing flocks   540
Had ta'en their supper on the savoury herb
Of knot-grass dew-besprent, and were in fold,
I sat me down to watch upon a bank
With ivy canopied, and interwove
With flaunting honeysuckle, and began,   545
Wrapt in a pleasing fit of melancholy,
To meditate my rural minstrelsy,
Till fancy had her fill. But ere a close
The wonted roar was up amidst the woods,
And filled the air with barbarous dissonance;   550
At which I ceased, and listened them a while,
Till an unusual stop of sudden silence
Gave respite to the drowsy-flighted steeds
That draw the litter of close-curtained Sleep.
At last a soft and solemn-breathing sound   555

---

526. *murmurs:* incantations. 530. *Charactered:* engraved. 531. *crofts:* fields.
532. *brow:* overlook. 539. *unweeting:* unaware. 547. I.e., to improvise a
tune on my shepherd's pipe. 548. *close:* closing cadence. 549. *wonted:* usual.

Rose like a steam of rich distilled perfumes,
And stole upon the air, that even Silence
Was took ere she was ware, and wished she might
Deny her nature, and be never more,
Still to be so displaced. I was all ear, 560
And took in strains that might create a soul
Under the ribs of Death. But, oh! ere long
Too well I did perceive it was the voice
Of my most honoured Lady, your dear sister.
Amazed I stood, harrowed with grief and fear; 565
And 'O poor hapless nightingale,' thought I,
'How sweet thou sing'st, how near the deadly snare!'
Then down the lawns I ran with headlong haste,
Through paths and turnings often trod by day,
Till, guided by mine ear, I found the place 570
Where that damned wizard, hid in sly disguise
(For so by certain signs I knew), had met
Already, ere my best speed could prevent,
The aidless innocent lady, his wished prey;
Who gently asked if he had seen such two, 575
Supposing him some neighbour villager.
Longer I durst not stay, but soon I guessed
Ye were the two she meant; with that I sprung
Into swift flight, till I had found you here;
But further know I not.

    SEC. BRO. O night and shades, 580
How are ye joined with hell in triple knot
Against the unarmed weakness of one virgin,
Alone and helpless! Is this the confidence
You gave me, brother?

    ELD. BRO. Yes, and keep it still;
Lean on it safely; not a period 585
Shall be unsaid for me. Against the threats
Of malice or of sorcery, or that power
Which erring men call Chance, this I hold firm:
Virtue may be assailed, but never hurt,
Surprised by unjust force, but not enthralled; 590
Yea, even that which Mischief meant most harm
Shall in the happy trial prove most glory.

---

560. *Still . . . displaced:* provided her place would always be supplied by
such music. 585. *period:* sentence. 586. *for me:* for my part. 591-2. I.e.,
evil shall be made to produce good.

But evil on itself shall back recoil,
And mix no more with goodness, when at last,
Gathered like scum, and settled to itself,   595
It shall be in eternal restless change
Self-fed and self-consumed. If this fail,
The pillared firmament is rottenness,
And earth's base built on stubble. But come, let's on.
Against the opposing will and arm of Heaven   600
May never this just sword be lifted up;
But, for that damned magician, let him be girt
With all the grisly legions that troop
Under the sooty flag of Acheron,
Harpies and Hydras, or all the monstrous forms   605
'Twixt Africa and Ind, I'll find him out,
And force him to return his purchase back,
Or drag him by the curls to a foul death,
Cursed as his life.

SPIR.   Alas! good venturous youth,
I love thy courage yet, and bold emprise;   610
But here thy sword can do thee little stead.
Far other arms and other weapons must
Be those that quell the might of hellish charms.
He with his bare wand can unthread thy joints,
And crumble all thy sinews.

ELD. BRO.   Why, prithee, Shepherd,   615
How durst thou then thyself approach so near
As to make this relation?

SPIR.   Care and utmost shifts
How to secure the Lady from surprisal
Brought to my mind a certain shepherd lad,
Of small regard to see to, yet well skilled   620
In every virtuous plant and healing herb
That spreads her verdant leaf to the morning ray.
He loved me well, and oft would beg me sing;
Which when I did, he on the tender grass
Would sit, and hearken even to ecstasy,   625
And in requital ope his leathern scrip,
And show me simples of a thousand names,
Telling their strange and vigorous faculties.

---

604. *Acheron:* Hell. 605. *Harpies and Hydras:* used as symbols of all
threatening monsters. 607. *purchase:* prey. 610. *emprise:* spirit. 620. *to see
to:* to look at. 621. *virtuous:* full of healing "virtues." 626. *scrip:* bag.
627. *simples:* medicinal plants.

Amongst the rest a small unsightly root,
But of divine effect, he culled me out.   630
The leaf was darkish, and had prickles on it,
But in another country, as he said,
Bore a bright golden flower, but not in this soil:
Unknown, and like esteemed, and the dull swain
Treads on it daily with his clouted shoon;   635
And yet more med'cinal is it than that Moly
That Hermes once to wise Ulysses gave.
He called it Hæmony, and gave it me,
And bade me keep it as of sovran use
'Gainst all enchantments, mildew blast, or damp,   640
Or ghastly Furies' apparitïon.
I pursed it up, but little reckoning made,
Till now that this extremity compelled.
But now I find it true; for by this means
I knew the foul enchanter, though disguised,   645
Entered the very lime-twigs of his spells,
And yet came off. If you have this about you
(As I will give you when we go) you may
Boldly assault the necromancer's hall;
Where if he be, with dauntless hardihood   650
And brandished blade rush on him: break his glass,
And shed the luscious liquor on the ground;
But seize his wand. Though he and his curst crew
Fierce sign of battle make, and menace high,
Or, like the sons of Vulcan, vomit smoke,   655
Yet will they soon retire, if he but shrink.
    ELD. BRO. Thyrsis, lead on apace; I'll follow thee;
And some good angel bear a shield before us!

[*The Scene changes to a stately palace, set out with all manner of de-
    liciousness: soft music, tables spread with all dainties.* COMUS *ap-
    pears with his rabble, and* THE LADY *set in an enchanted chair: to
    whom he offers his glass; which she puts by, and goes about to
    rise.*]

---

634. *like esteemed:* i.e., unvalued. 635. *clouted shoon:* hobnailed shoes. 637.
I.e., to immunize Odysseus against the charms of Circe, Comus's mother,
which also turned men to brutes. 642. I.e., I accepted it but ignored it.
646. *lime-twigs:* traps (i.e., twigs covered with sticky bird-lime to capture
birds). 649. *necromancer:* magician. 655. *Vulcan:* God of fire and forge.

COMUS. Nay, Lady, sit. If I but wave this wand,
Your nerves are all chained up in alabaster,   660
And you a statue; or as Daphne was,
Root-bound, that fled Apollo.
    LADY.   Fool, do not boast.
Thou canst not touch the freedom of my mind
With all thy charms, although this corporal rind
Thou hast immanacled, while Heaven sees good.   665
    COMUS. Why are you vexed, Lady? why do you frown?
Here dwell no frowns, nor anger; from these gates
Sorrow flies far. See, here be all the pleasures
That fancy can beget on youthful thoughts,
When the fresh blood grows lively, and returns   670
Brisk as the April buds in primrose season.
And first behold this cordial julep here,
That flames and dances in his crystal bounds,
With spirits of balm and fragrant syrups mixed.
Not that Nepenthes which the wife of Thone   675
In Egypt gave to Jove-born Helena
Is of such power to stir up joy as this,
To life so friendly, or so cool to thirst.
Why should you be so cruel to yourself,
And to those dainty limbs, which Nature lent   680
For gentle usage and soft delicacy?
But you invert the covenants of her trust,
And harshly deal, like an ill borrower,
With that which you received on other terms,
Scorning the unexempt condition   685
By which all mortal frailty must subsist,
Refreshment after toil, ease after pain,
That have been tired all day without repast,
And timely rest have wanted. But, fair virgin,
This will restore all soon.
    LADY.   'Twill not, false traitor!   690
'Twill not restore the truth and honesty
That thou hast banished from thy tongue with lies.
Was this the cottage and the safe abode

661-2. Daphne escaped the embraces of Apollo by becoming a laurel tree.
664. *corporal rind*: i.e., body. 675. *Nepenthes*: a drug banishing all grief,
administered to Helen and Menelaus on their way home from Troy by
Polydamna, wife of Thone. 682-7. I.e., with your physical self, lent by
Nature on condition that you treat it well, you deal harshly, scornfully
ignoring the fact that all physical life requires sustenance and rest.

Thou told'st me of? What grim aspects are these,
These ugly-headed monsters? Mercy guard me! 695
Hence with thy brewed enchantments, foul deceiver!
Hast thou betrayed my credulous innocence
With vizored falsehood and base forgery?
And wouldst thou seek again to trap me here
With lickerish baits, fit to ensnare a brute? 700
Were it a draught for Juno when she banquets,
I would not taste thy treasonous offer. None
But such as are good men can give good things;
And that which is not good is not delicious
To a well-governed and wise appetite. 705
   comus. O foolishness of men! that lend their ears
To those budge doctors of the Stoic fur,
And fetch their precepts from the Cynic tub,
Praising the lean and sallow Abstinence!
Wherefore did Nature pour her bounties forth 710
With such a full and unwithdrawing hand,
Covering the earth with odours, fruits, and flocks,
Thronging the seas with spawn innumerable,
But all to please and sate the curious taste?
And set to work millions of spinning worms, 715
That in their green shops weave the smooth-haired silk,
To deck her sons; and, that no corner might
Be vacant of her plenty, in her own loins
She hutched the all-worshiped ore and precious gems,
To store her children with. If all the world 720
Should, in a pet of temperance, feed on pulse,
Drink the clear stream, and nothing wear but frieze,
Th' All-giver would be unthanked, would be unpraised,
Not half his riches known, and yet despised;
And we should serve him as a grudging master, 725
As a penurious niggard of his wealth,
And live like Nature's bastards, not her sons,
Who would be quite surcharged with her own weight,
And strangled with her waste fertility:
The earth cumbered, and the winged air darked with plumes, 730
The herds would over-multitude their lords;

---

698. *vizored:* masked. 700. *lickerish:* sensual. 707. *budge:* fur trim on academic gowns. *Stoic:* The Stoics taught suppression of the appetites. 708.
The Cynic philosophers also taught ascetic doctrines; the most famous of
them, Diogenes, lived in a tub to illustrate them. 719. *hutched:* enclosed.
721. *pulse:* edible seeds. 722. *frieze:* coarse cloth.

The sea o'erfraught would swell, and the unsought diamonds
Would so emblaze the forehead of the deep,
And so bestud with stars, that they below
Would grow inured to light, and come at last   735
To gaze upon the sun with shameless brows.
List, Lady; be not coy, and be not cozened
With that same vaunted name, Virginity.
Beauty is Nature's coin, must not be hoarded,
But must be current, and the good thereof   740
Consists in mutual and partaken bliss,
Unsavoury in the enjoyment of itself.
If you let slip time, like a neglected rose
It withers on the stalk with languished head.
Beauty is Nature's brag, and must be shown   745
In courts, at feasts, and high solemnities,
Where most may wonder at the workmanship.
It is for homely features to keep home;
They had their name thence: coarse complexiöns
And cheeks of sorry grain will serve to ply   750
The sampler, and to tease the huswife's wool.
What need a vermeil-tinctured lip for that,
Love-darting eyes, or tresses like the morn?
There was another meaning in these gifts;
Think what, and be advised; you are but young yet.   755
    LADY. I had not thought to have unlocked my lips
In this unhallowed air, but that this juggler
Would think to charm my judgment, as mine eyes,
Obtruding false rules pranked in reason's garb.
I hate when vice can bolt her arguments   760
And virtue has no tongue to check her pride.—
Imposter! do not charge most innocent Nature,
As if she would her children should be riotous
With her abundance. She, good cateress,
Means her provision only to the good,   765
That live according to her sober laws,
And holy dictate of spare Temperance.

732-6. I.e., as more and more diamonds "grew" in the earth by the sun's
influence (this was the old theory of the formation of all gems and metals),
the spirits who inhabited there (cf. 436) would become so acclimated to
light that at last they could live on top of the earth. 737. *cozened*: misled.
750. *grain*: hue. *ply*: work at. 751. *tease*: comb out. 754. I.e., they were
given to be used. 757. *juggler*: magician. 759. *pranked*: dressed up. 760.
bolt: sift.

f every just man that now pines with want
Had but a moderate and beseeming share
Of that which lewdly-pampered Luxury   770
Now heaps upon some few with vast excess,
Nature's full blessings would be well-dispensed
In unsuperfluous even proportion,
And she no whit encumbered with her store;
And then the Giver would be better thanked,   775
His praise due paid: for swinish gluttony
Ne'er looks to Heaven amidst his gorgeous feast,
But with besotted base ingratitude
Crams, and blasphemes his Feeder. Shall I go on?
Or have I said enow? To him that dares   780
Arm his profane tongue with contemptuous words
Against the sun-clad power of chastity
Fain would I something say—yet to what end?
Thou hast nor ear, nor soul, to apprehend
The sublime notion and high mystery   785
That must be uttered to unfold the sage
And serious doctrine of Virginity;
And thou art worthy that thou shouldst not know
More happiness than this thy present lot.
Enjoy your dear wit, and gay rhetoric,   790
That hath so well been taught her dazzling fence;
Thou art not fit to hear thyself convinced.
Yet, should I try, the uncontrollèd worth
Of this pure cause would kindle my rapt spirits
To such a flame of sacred vehemence   795
That dumb things would be moved to sympathize,
And the brute Earth would lend her nerves, and shake,
Till all thy magic structures, reared so high,
Were shattered into heaps o'er thy false head.
   COMUS. She fables not. I feel that I do fear   800
Her words set off by some superior power;
And, though not mortal, yet a cold shuddering dew
Dips me all o'er, as when the wrath of Jove
Speaks thunder and the chains of Erebus
To some of Saturn's crew. I must dissemble,   805

---

73. I.e., enough for each, excess for none. 775. *Giver:* God. 785. *mystery:*
i.e., a doctrine revealed supernaturally. 791. *fence:* art of parrying, debating.
93. *uncontrollèd:* unlimited. 804. I.e., both thunders and sentences to Hell
(*Erebus*). 805. *Saturn's crew:* the Titans whom Zeus overthrew.

And try her yet more strongly.—Come, no more!
This is mere moral babble, and direct
Against the canon laws of our foundation.
I must not suffer this, yet 'tis but the lees
And settlings of a melancholy blood.   81(

But this will cure all straight; one sip of this
Will bathe the drooping spirits in delight
Beyond the bliss of dreams. Be wise, and taste.

[*The* BROTHERS *rush in with swords drawn, wrest his glass out of hi*
   hand, and break it against the ground: his rout make sign of re
   sistance, but are all driven in. The ATTENDANT SPIRIT *comes in.*

SPIR. What! have you let the false enchanter scape?
O ye mistook; ye should have snatched his wand,   81(
And bound him fast. Without his rod reversed,
And backward mutters of dissevering power,
We cannot free the Lady that sits here
In stony fetters fixed and motionless.

Yet stay: be not disturbed; now I bethink me,   82(
Some other means I have which may be used,
Which once of Melibœus old I learnt,
The soothest shepherd that e'er piped on plains.

   There is a gentle Nymph not far from hence,
That with moist curb sways the smooth Severn stream: 82
Sabrina is her name: a virgin pure;
Whilom she was the daughter of Locrine,
That had the sceptre from his father Brute.
She, guiltless damsel, flying the mad pursuit
Of her enragèd stepdame, Guendolen,   83(
Commended her fair innocence to the flood
That stayed her flight with his cross-flowing course.
The water-nymphs, that in the bottom played,
Held up their pearlèd wrists, and took her in,
Bearing her straight to agèd Nereus' hall;   83
Who, piteous of her woes, reared her lank head,

816-17. I.e., unless you reverse his rod and say backwards his incantation
822. *Meliboeus:* a shepherd-name, used here for Spenser, who tells the ta
of Sabrina in *Faerie Queene,* II x 4-9. 825. *curb:* curb-bit (used to contro
a spirited horse). 826 ff. Sabrina is given an origin among the legendar
kings of Britain (Brute, mythical grandson of Aeneas, was reputed to hav
founded the nation) and an Ovidian metamorphosis into the river Severn
827. *Whilom:* formerly. 835. *Nereus:* a sea-god.

And gave her to his daughters to imbathe
In nectared lavers strewed with asphodil,
And through the porch and inlet of each sense
Dropt in ambrosial oils, till she revived,   840
And underwent a quick immortal change,
Made Goddess of the river. Still she retains
Her maiden gentleness, and oft at eve
Visits the herds along the twilight meadows,
Helping all urchin blasts, and ill-luck signs   845
That the shrewd meddling elf delights to make,
Which she with precious vialed liquors heals:
For which the shepherds, at their festivals,
Carol her goodness loud in rustic lays,
And throw sweet garland wreaths into her stream   850
Of pansies, pinks, and gaudy daffodils.
And, as the old swain said, she can unlock
The clasping charm, and thaw the numbing spell,
If she be right invoked in warbled song;
For maidenhood she loves, and will be swift   855
To aid a virgin, such as was herself,
In hard-besetting need. This will I try,
And add the power of some adjuring verse.

Song

Sabrina fair,
    Listen where thou art sitting   860
Under the glassy, cool, translucent wave,
    In twisted braids of lilies knitting
The loose train of thy amber-dropping hair;
    Listen for dear honour's sake,
    Goddess of the silver lake,   865
        Listen and save!

Listen, and appear to us,
In name of great Oceanus,
By the earth-shaking Neptune's mace,
And Tethys' grave majestic pace;   870
By hoary Nereus' wrinkled look,
And the Carpathian wizard's hook;

---

838. *lavers:* vessels. *asphodil:* flower of immortality. 845. *urchin blasts:* injuries caused by evil spirits. 870. *Tethys:* wife of the ocean-god Oceanus and mother of the rivers. 871. *Nereus:* father of the sea-nymphs or Nereids. 872. Proteus, the Old Man of the Sea, shepherd of sea-beasts, carries a sheep-hook.

By scaly Triton's winding shell,
And old soothsaying Glaucus' spell;
By Leucothea's lovely hands,   875
And her son that rules the strands;
By Thetis' tinsel-slippered feet,
And the songs of Sirens sweet;
By dead Parthenope's dear tomb,
And fair Ligea's golden comb,   880
Wherewith she sits on diamond rocks
Sleeking her soft alluring locks;
By all the nymphs that nightly dance
Upon thy streams with wily glance;
Rise, rise, and heave thy rosy head   885
From thy coral-paven bed,
And bridle in thy headlong wave,
Till thou our summons answered have.

                                    Listen and save!

[SABRINA *rises, attended by Water-nymphs, and sings.*]

By the rushy-fringèd bank,   890
Where grows the willow and the osier dank,
    My sliding chariot stays,
Thick set with agate, and the azurn sheen
Of turkis blue, and emerald green,
    That in the channel strays: 895
Whilst from off the waters fleet
Thus I set my printless feet
O'er the cowslip's velvet head,
    That bends not as I tread.
Gentle swain, at thy request   900
    I am here!

SPIR. Goddess dear,
We implore thy powerful hand

---

873. *Triton,* Neptune's herald, announces his edicts through a conch-shell.
874. *Glaucus:* a sea-wizard. 875. *Leucothea:* sea-goddess often associated
with Aurora, the "rosy-fingered" dawn-goddess: hence perhaps her "lovely
hands." 877. *Thetis:* a Nereid whom Homer called "silver-footed" (cf.
tinsel-slippered). 878. *Sirens:* cf. 253n. 879. *Parthenope:* a Siren whose
dear tomb was reputedly at Naples and after whose name that city was
anciently called. 880. *Ligea:* another Siren. 894. *turkis:* turquoise.

To undo the charmèd band
Of true virgin here distressed 905
Through the force and through the wile
Of unblessed enchanter vile.

   SABR. Shepherd, 'tis my office best
To help ensnarèd chastity.
Brightest Lady, look on me. 910
Thus I sprinkle on thy breast
Drops that from my fountain pure
I have kept of precious cure;
Thrice upon thy finger's tip,
Thrice upon thy rubied lip: 915
Next this marble venomed seat,
Smeared with gums of glutinous heat,
I touch with chaste palms moist and cold.
Now the spell hath lost his hold;
And I must haste ere morning hour 920
To wait in Amphitrite's bower.

[SABRINA *descends, and* THE LADY *rises out of her seat.*]

   SPIR. Virgin, daughter of Locrine,
Sprung of old Anchises' line,
May thy brimmèd waves for this
Their full tribute never miss 925
From a thousand petty rills,
That tumble down the snowy hills:
Summer drouth or singèd air
Never scorch thy tresses fair,
Nor wet October's torrent flood 930
Thy molten crystal fill with mud;
May thy billows roll ashore
The beryl and the golden ore;
May thy lofty head be crowned
With many a tower and terrace round, 935
And here and there thy banks upon
With groves of myrrh and cinnamon.
   Come, Lady, while Heaven lends us grace,
Let us fly this cursèd place,
Lest the sorcerer us entice 940

---

921. *Amphitrite:* Neptune's wife. 923. *Anchises:* father of Aeneas, and
hence great grandfather of Brute, who is, in turn, grandfather of Sabrina:
cf. 827-8. 933. *beryl:* a mineral of which the aquamarine and the emerald
are varieties.

With some other new device.
Not a waste or needless sound
Till we come to holier ground.
I shall be your faithful guide
Through this gloomy covert wide;   945
And not many furlongs thence
Is your Father's residence,
Where this night are met in state
Many a friend to gratulate
His wished presence, and beside   950
All the swains that there abide
With jigs and rural dance resort.
We shall catch them at their sport,
And our sudden coming there
Will double all their mirth and cheer.   955
Come, let us haste; the stars grow high,
But Night sits monarch yet in the mid sky.

[*The Scene changes, presenting Ludlow Town, and the President's
Castle: then come in Country Dancers; after them the* ATTENDANT
SPIRIT, *with the two* BROTHERS *and* THE LADY.]

Song

SPIR. Back, shepherds, back! Enough your play
Till next sun-shine holiday.
Here be without duck or nod   960
Other trippings to be trod
Of lighter toes, and such Court guise
As Mercury did first devise
With the mincing Dryades
On the lawns and on the leas.   965

[*This second Song presents them to their Father and Mother.*]

Noble Lord and Lady bright,
I have brought ye new delight.
Here behold so goodly grown
Three fair branches of your own.
Heaven hath timely tried their youth,   970

---

945. *covert:* woods. 949. *gratulate:* rejoice in. 958 ff. I.e., the country-dance
called for by the stage direction must give way to a courtly dance by the
Earl of Bridgewater's guests as soon as the performance of *Comus* ends.
960. *duck:* a clumsy country curtsy. 963-4. Mercury is traditionally the
leader of the dancing nymphs (here the *Dryades* or wood-nymphs).

Their faith, their patience, and their truth,
And sent them here through hard assays
With a crown of deathless praise,
To triumph in victorious dance
O'er sensual folly and intemperance.   975

[*The dances ended, the* SPIR *epilogizes.*]

SPIR. To the ocean now I fly,
And those happy climes that lie
Where day never shuts his eye,
Up in the broad fields of the sky.
There I suck the liquid air,   980
All amidst the gardens fair
Of Hesperus, and his daughters three
That sing about the golden tree.
Along the crispèd shades and bowers
Revels the spruce and jocund Spring;   985
The Graces and the rosy-bosomed Hours
Thither all their bounties bring.
There eternal Summer dwells,
And west winds with musky wing
About the cedarn alleys fling   990
Nard and cassia's balmy smells.
Iris there with humid bow
Waters the odorous banks, that blow
Flowers of more mingled hue
Than her purfled scarf can shew,   995
And drenches with Elysian dew
(List, mortals, if your ears be true)
Beds of hyacinth and roses,
Where young Adonis oft reposes,
Waxing well of his deep wound,   1000

---

976 ff. A description of the vaguely located "mansion" (cf. 2) from which
the Spirit has come and where the life of grace (virtue) is one with the
life of nature (sensuous delight). 991. Spicy scents of spikenard and cinnamon. 993. *blow:* cause to bloom. 995. *purfled:* varied. Her scarf is the
rainbow. 999-1002. The beautiful youth Adonis, fatally wounded while
boar-hunting, was mourned by Venus (*the Assyrian Queen*) and through
her intercession allowed to return from the underworld for half the year.
The story can thus be used as a symbol of (1) the immortality of love; (2)
the annual death and rebirth of nature; (3) the consequences of the Fall
(i.e., Adonis's or Nature's *deep wound*) redeemed. Milton's context seems
to invite all three interpretations.

In slumber soft, and on the ground
Sadly sits the Assyrian queen.
But far above, in spangled sheen,
Celestial Cupid, her famed son, advanced
Holds his dear Psyche, sweet entranced   1005
After her wandering labours long,
Till free consent the gods among
Make her his eternal bride,
And from her fair unspotted side
Two blissful twins are to be born,   1010
Youth and Joy; so Jove hath sworn.

But now my task is smoothly done:
I can fly, or I can run
Quickly to the green earth's end,
Where the bowed welkin slow doth bend,   1015
And from thence can soar as soon
To the corners of the moon.
Mortals, that would follow me,
Love Virtue; she alone is free,
She can teach ye how to climb   1020
Higher than the sphery chime;
Or, if Virtue feeble were,
Heaven itself would stoop to her.

❧

1003-1011. The story of the lovers Cupid and Psyche, united by the consent of the gods after many trials, seems to be allegorized here into an
image of "celestial" love (counterpart at the level of grace of the love
between Venus and Adonis), which will finally produce eternal youth and
joy. 1015. *welkin:* sky. 1021. I.e., beyond the music of the spheres—the
limits of the universe—to the throne of God.

Lycidas

(1637)

In this Monody the Author bewails a learned Friend, unfortunately drowned in his passage from Chester on the Irish Seas, 1637; and, by occasion, foretells the ruin of our corrupted Clergy, then in their height.

Yet once more, O ye laurels, and once more,
Ye myrtles brown, with ivy never sere,
I come to pluck your berries harsh and crude,
And with forced fingers rude
Shatter your leaves before the mellowing year.   5
Bitter constraint and sad occasion dear
Compels me to disturb your season due;
For Lycidas is dead, dead ere his prime,
Young Lycidas, and hath not left his peer.
Who would not sing for Lycidas? he knew   10
Himself to sing, and build the lofty rhyme.
He must not float upon his watery bier
Unwept, and welter to the parching wind,
Without the meed of some melodious tear.
    Begin, then, Sisters of the sacred well   15
That from beneath the seat of Jove doth spring;
Begin, and somewhat loudly sweep the string.
Hence with denial vain and coy excuse:
So may some gentle Muse
With lucky words favour *my* destined urn,   20

---

1 ff. *Laurels, myrtles,* and *ivy* are the evergreens sacred to the inspirers of poetry (Apollo, Venus, and Bacchus) and traditionally used for poets' crowns. In saying that he comes to gather these prematurely, Milton is saying that King's death has obliged him to break his silence (study at Horton) and try to practise an art for which he does not yet feel "ripe." 2. *sere:* withered. 3. *harsh and crude:* unripe. 5. *before . . . year:* before the year has mellowed them. 7. *your season due:* your proper season. 10-11. *he . . . sing:* he himself knew how to sing. 13. *welter:* toss. 14. *meed:* recompense. *melodious tear:* conventional phrase for "poetic lament." 15. *Sisters:* the nine Muses—*the sacred well* being (probably) the Pierian spring at the base of Mt. Olympus, *the seat of Jove* (16). Invoking the Muse, though a convention, implies that the poet speaks for men in general —supra-personally. 19. *Muse:* i.e., poet. 20. *lucky:* propitious.

And as he passes turn,
And bid fair peace be to my sable shroud!
   For we were nursed upon the self-same hill,
Fed the same flock, by fountain, shade, and rill;
Together both, ere the high lawns appeared   25
Under the opening eyelids of the Morn,
We drove a-field, and both together heard
What time the grey-fly winds her sultry horn,
Batt'ning our flocks with the fresh dews of night,
Oft till the star that rose at evening bright   30
Toward heaven's descent had sloped his westering wheel.
Meanwhile the rural ditties were not mute;
Tempered to the oaten flute
Rough Satyrs danced, and Fauns with cloven heel
From the glad sound would not be absent long;   35
And old Damœtas loved to hear our song.
   But, oh! the heavy change, now thou art gone,
Now thou art gone and never must return!
Thee, Shepherd, thee the woods and desert caves,
With wild thyme and the gadding vine o'ergrown,   40
And all their echoes, mourn.
The willows, and the hazel copses green,
Shall now no more be seen
Fanning their joyous leaves to thy soft lays.
As killing as the canker to the rose,   45
Or taint-worm to the weanling herds that graze,
Or frost to flowers, that their gay wardrobe wear,
When first the white-thorn blows;
Such, Lycidas, thy loss to shepherd's ear.
   Where were ye, Nymphs, when the remorseless deep   50
Closed o'er the head of your loved Lycidas?
For neither were ye playing on the steep

23-36. A pastoral version of Milton's and King's life at Cambridge: in
25-31, their strenuous studies; in 32-36 their lighter pursuits. 28. I.e., mid-
day, when insects sing in the heat. 30. *star:* i.e., Hesperus, which appeared
(*rose*) in the western sky at sunset and then soon sank below the horizon
(*heaven's descent*). 33. *tempered to:* harmonized with. 34-6. In terms of
Milton's and King's life at Cambridge, the satyrs and fauns (minor deities
of the field and wood) are undergraduates who enjoyed their poetry, as the
shepherd Damoetas is evidently a tutor who encouraged it. 40. *gadding:*
wandering. 45. *canker:* cankerworm. 50. *Nymphs:* the deities of the waters,
whose usual haunts (near the site of King's shipwreck) are named in 52-5.
52. *the steep:* probably Holyhead on the Welsh coast, a place associated
with the ancient priestly poets, *the famous Druids* (53).

Where your old bards, the famous Druids, lie,
Nor on the shaggy top of Mona high,
Nor yet where Deva spreads her wizard-stream.   55
Ay me! I fondly dream
"Had ye been there," . . . for what could that have done?
What could the Muse herself that Orpheus bore,
The Muse herself, for her enchanting son,
Whom universal nature did lament,   60
When, by the rout that made the hideous roar,
His gory visage down the stream was sent,
Down the swift Hebrus to the Lesbian shore?
    Alas! what boots it with uncessant care
To tend the homely, slighted, shepherd's trade,   65
And strictly meditate the thankless Muse?
Were it not better done, as others use,
To sport with Amaryllis in the shade,
Or with the tangles of Neæra's hair?
Fame is the spur that the clear spirit doth raise   70
(That last infirmity of noble mind)
To scorn delights and live laborious days;
But the fair guerdon when we hope to find,
And think to burst out into sudden blaze,
Comes the blind Fury with the abhorrèd shears,   75
And slits the thin-spun life. "But not the praise,"
Phœbus replied, and touched my trembling ears:
"Fame is no plant that grows on mortal soil,

---

54. *Mona:* an island off Wales. 55. *Deva:* the Welsh river Dee, whose *stream* is *wizard* because it was said to prophesy the future by the position of its fords. 58. *the Muse herself:* Calliope, chief of the Muses and Muse of epic poetry, mother of the great mythical poet Orpheus, who was torn to pieces by a group of maniacal women whose celebration of the wild rites of Bacchus he had refused to join. His severed head was said to have floated down the river Hebrus to the isle of Lesbos, and so enchanted it that it became the birthplace of many poets. 65. *shepherd's:* poet's. 66. *meditate . . . Muse:* study the art of poetry, which is powerless to recompense one (as the fate of Orpheus has shown). 73. *guerdon:* recompense. 74. *blaze:* i.e., of fame. 75. *blind Fury:* Atropos (one of the three Fates), who cuts the thread of life spun by Clotho and drawn out by Lachesis— here called a *blind Fury* to stress the arbitrary and vindictive character of her choices. 77. Apollo, god of poetry, breaks into the poem to rebuke Milton for doubting the justice of God, reminding him that when Midas was similarly stupid (preferring Pan's music to Apollo's) he was punished with ass's ears. 78-80. I.e., true fame does not consist in brilliant show (like a gem set off with a *glistering* leaf of *foil*), nor in popular adulation (*broad rumor*).

Nor in the glistering foil
Set off to the world, nor in broad rumour lies,   80
But lives and spreads aloft by those pure eyes
And perfect witness of all-judging Jove;
As he pronounces lastly on each deed,
Of so much fame in heaven expect thy meed."

O fountain Arethuse, and thou honoured flood,   85
Smooth-sliding Mincius, crowned with vocal reeds,
That strain I heard was of a higher mood.
But now my oat proceeds,
And listens to the Herald of the Sea,
That came in Neptune's plea.   90
He asked the waves, and asked the felon winds,
What hard mishap hath doomed this gentle swain?
And questioned every gust of rugged wings
That blows from off each beakèd promontory.
They knew not of his story;   95
And sage Hippotades their answer brings,
That not a blast was from his dungeon strayed:
The air was calm, and on the level brine
Sleek Panope with all her sisters played.
It was that fatal and perfidious bark,   100
Built in the eclipse, and rigged with curses dark,
That sunk so low that sacred head of thine.
Next, Camus, reverend sire, went footing slow,
His mantle hairy, and his bonnet sedge,

85-86. *Arethuse, Mincius:* Sicilian fountain associated with Theocritus's birthplace, and Italian river associated with Virgil's. Here used to typify the pastoral vein which has been interrupted by the *higher mood* of Apollo's rebuke. 87. *mood:* (1) state of feeling, (2) musical scale or "mode." 89. *Herald of the Sea:* Triton: cf. Comus, 873. 90. *plea:* i.e., a legal inquiry into the facts of the drowning. 96. *Hippotades:* Aeolus, god of the winds, who keeps them locked in his *dungeon.* 99. *Panope . . . sisters:* the sea-nymphs. 101. Literally the line suggests that King's ship was foredoomed to sink by malign supernatural influences. Figuratively, there is perhaps an oblique allusion in *bark* to King's natural body, and in *eclipse* and *curses,* to the Fall and its consequences—the chief consequence being the subjection (which King's death illustrates) of the realm of nature to change and death. 103. *Camus:* god of the river Cam which flows through Cambridge (here representing the university). The god is so described as to suggest the attributes of a *reverend* scholar: *footing slow, mantle, bonnet;* and also the river: *hairy* (i.e., the floating river weeds) and *sedge* (the grass along the banks).

Inwrought with figures dim, and on the edge   105
Like to that sanguine flower inscribed with woe.
"Ah! who hath reft," quoth he, "my dearest pledge?"
Last came, and last did go,
The Pilot of the Galilean Lake;
Two massy keys he bore of metals twain   110
(The golden opes, the iron shuts amain).
He shook his mitred locks, and stern bespake:—
"How well could I have spared for thee, young swain,
Enow of such as, for their bellies' sake,
Creep, and intrude, and climb into the fold!   115
Of other care they little reckoning make
Than how to scramble at the shearers' feast,
And shove away the worthy bidden guest.
Blind mouths! that scarce themselves know how to hold
A sheep-hook, or have learnt aught else the least   120
That to the faithful herdman's art belongs!
What recks it them? What need they? They are sped;
And, when they list, their lean and flashy songs
Grate on their scrannel pipes of wretched straw;
The hungry sheep look up, and are not fed,   125
But, swoln with wind and the rank mist they draw,
Rot inwardly, and foul contagion spread;
Besides what the grim Wolf with privy paw
Daily devours apace, and nothing said.

---

106. *that . . . woe:* i.e., the Greek hyacinth, a *sanguine flower* because
made from the blood of the boy Hyacinthus whom Apollo killed accidentally with his discus, and *inscribed with woe* because on its petals
Apollo set the Greek letters AI, meaning "alas!" 107. *pledge:* child. 109.
I.e., St. Peter who holds the keys of Heaven (one for admitting the
righteous, the other for locking out the wicked), and, as first bishop of
Rome, wears a mitre. 111. *amain:* "powerfully" and "at once." 113 ff. St.
Peter's denunciation of the corrupt clergy is assimilated to the pastoral
pattern through the meaning of *pastor* as both shepherd and priest. It
is based on such passages from the Bible as Ezekiel 34:2: "Woe be to the
shepherds of Israel that do feed themselves! should not the shepherds feed
the flocks?" and 1 Peter 5:2: "Feed the flock of God . . . not for filthy lucre,
but of a ready mind"; and John 10:1: "He that entereth not by the door
into the sheepfold, but climbeth up some other way . . . is a thief and a
robber." 119. *Blind mouths:* The force of this paradoxical phrase lies in
the fact that "bishop" meant originally "one who sees," and "pastor," "one
who feeds." 122. *What . . . them:* What do *they* care? *sped:* provided
for. 123. *songs:* i.e., sermons. 124. *scrannel:* thin and harsh. 126. *wind . . .
mist:* i.e., hollow and false teachings. 128. *grim wolf:* possibly the Devil,
possibly Roman Catholicism.

But that two-handed engine at the door   130
Stands ready to smite once, and smite no more."
    Return, Alpheus; the dread voice is past
That shrunk thy streams; return, Sicilian Muse,
And call the vales, and bid them hither cast
Their bells and flowerets of a thousand hues.   135
Ye valleys low, where the mild whispers use
Of shades, and wanton winds, and gushing brooks,
On whose fresh lap the swart star sparely looks,
Throw hither all your quaint enamelled eyes,
That on the green turf suck the honeyed showers,   140
And purple all the ground with vernal flowers.
Bring the rathe primrose that forsaken dies,
The tufted crow-toe, and pale jessamine,
The white pink, and the pansy freaked with jet,
The glowing violet,   145
The musk-rose, and the well-attired woodbine,
With cowslips wan that hang the pensive head,
And every flower that sad embroidery wears;
Bid amaranthus all his beauty shed,
And daffadillies fill their cups with tears,   150
To strew the laureate hearse where Lycid lies.
For so, to interpose a little ease,
Let our frail thoughts dally with false surmise.
Ay me! whilst thee the shores and sounding seas
Wash far away, where'er thy bones are hurled;   155
Whether beyond the stormy Hebrides,
Where thou perhaps under the whelming tide
Visit'st the bottom of the monstrous world;

---

130. *two-handed . . . door:* an allusion never satisfactorily explained, though it clearly refers to retribution—and possibly to the sword of (God's) justice. 132-3. A reinvocation of the pastoral vein, as in 85-6, after another passage in *higher mood.* 136. *use:* inhabit. 138. *the . . . star:* Sirius, the dog-star, called *swart* (i.e., black) because supposed to have a malign influence and also to blacken vegetation. *sparely:* not fully. 139. *eyes:* i.e., flowers. 142. *the . . . dies:* i.e., the early primrose, which, opening to its lover the sun, dies soon forsaken by him. 144. *freaked:* spotted. 149. *amaranthus:* a fabulous unfading flower, symbol of immortality. 151. *laureate hearse:* i.e., King's bier, thought of as laurel-crowned (and perhaps as covered with memorial verses). 153. *frail thoughts:* i.e., such mortal frailties as concern for the body of the dead—which, with a comforting *false surmise,* the poet has imagined lying on a bier covered with flowers. 156. *Hebrides:* islands west of Scotland. 158. *monstrous world:* world of sea-monsters.

Or whether thou, to our moist vows denied,
Sleep'st by the fable of Bellerus old,   160
Where the great Vision of the guarded mount
Looks toward Namancos and Bayona's hold.
Look homeward, Angel, now, and melt with ruth:
And, O ye dolphins, waft the hapless youth.

Weep no more, woeful shepherds, weep no more,   165
For Lycidas, your sorrow, is not dead,
Sunk though he be beneath the watery floor.
So sinks the day-star in the ocean bed,
And yet anon repairs his drooping head,
And tricks his beams, and with new-spangled ore   170
Flames in the forehead of the morning sky:
So Lycidas sunk low, but mounted high,
Through the dear might of Him that walked the waves,
Where, other groves and other streams along,
With nectar pure his oozy locks he laves,   175
And hears the unexpressive nuptial song,
In the blest kingdoms meek of joy and love.
There entertain him all the Saints above,
In solemn troops, and sweet societies,
That sing, and singing in their glory move,   180
And wipe the tears for ever from his eyes.
Now, Lycidas, the shepherds weep no more;
Henceforth thou art the Genius of the shore,

---

159. *moist vows:* tearful prayers. 160. *the . . . Bellerus:* i.e., the place
(Land's End in Cornwall) named for the fabulous personage Bellerus.
161-2. Near Land's End is St. Michael's Mount, on which tradition has it
that the angel Michael sits looking in defiance toward the coast (*Namancos*
and *Bayona's* fortress) of Spain. 163-4. Milton urges the angel to look
homeward (where the source of evil now is) with pity for England's
loss, and urges the dolphins to bring Lycidas's body back to land. The
latter is probably a telescoped reference to both the Greek poet Arion, saved
from drowning by dolphins because they loved his music; and also
Melicertes, whose drowned body was miraculously brought to Corinth by
a dolphin, and who was transformed by a compassionate Neptune into
the sea-deity Palaemon, patron of sailors. Compare with Lycidas's becoming
the *Genius of the shore* (183). 168. *day-star:* sun. 170. *tricks:* i.e., adorns
his beams with renewed radiance (with a play on "or," heraldic term for
gold). 176. *unexpressive nuptial song:* inexpressible (i.e., mystical) song
at "the marriage supper of the Lamb" (Revelation 19:9). 181. Revelation
7:17: "And God shall wipe away all tears from their eyes." 183. *Genius:*
i.e., a deity, protector of mariners.

In thy large recompense, and shalt be good
To all that wander in that perilous flood.   185

     Thus sang the uncouth swain to th' oaks and rills,
While the still morn went out with sandals grey:
He touched the tender stops of various quills,
With eager thought warbling his Doric lay:
And now the sun had stretched out all the hills,   190
And now was dropt into the western bay.
At last he rose, and twitched his mantle blue:
To-morrow to fresh woods, and pastures new.

On His Blindness

When I consider how my light is spent   3
     Ere half my days in this dark world and wide,
     And that one talent which is death to hide
     Lodged with me useless, though my soul more bent
To serve therewith my Maker, and present   5
     My true account, lest He returning chide,
     "Doth God exact day-labour, light denied?"
     I fondly ask. But Patience, to prevent
That murmur, soon replies, "God doth not need
     Either man's work or his own gifts. Who best   10

---

184. *recompense:* the answer to 64 ff. 186. *uncouth swain:* i.e., unlearned and also unknown shepherd. 188. *quills:* reed pipes. 189. *Doric:* i.e., pastoral (because Doric had been the dialect of the classical pastoral poets, Theocritus, Bion, and Moschus). 193. *fresh . . . new:* i.e., other non-pastoral kinds of poetry.

ON HIS BLINDNESS: *Title:* Milton became totally blind in 1651. 1. *light . . . spent:* possibly an allusion to the parable of the wise and foolish virgins which in Matthew immediately precedes the parable of the talents to which Milton refers in 3-6. 3 ff. In the parable of the talents (Matthew 25:14 ff.), the good servants are those who put to use what their lord has entrusted to them, the bad servant is the one who hides it. 4. *useless:* (1) unusable, (2) returning no interest (as in the parable of the talents). 10. *his . . . gifts:* the gifts he bestows on men—e.g., Milton's gifts as a poet.

Bear his mild yoke, they serve him best. His state
Is kingly: thousands at his bidding speed,
And post o'er land and ocean without rest;
They also serve who only stand and wait."

On the Late Massacre in Piedmont

Avenge, O Lord, thy slaughtered saints, whose bones
Lie scattered on the Alpine mountains cold;
Even them who kept thy truth so pure of old,
When all our fathers worshiped stocks and stones,
Forget not: in thy book record their groans   5
Who were thy sheep, and in their ancient fold
Slain by the bloody Piemontese, that rolled
Mother with infant down the rocks. Their moans
The vales redoubled to the hills, and they
To heaven. Their martyred blood and ashes sow   10
O'er all the Italian fields, where still doth sway
The triple Tyrant; that from these may grow
A hundredfold, who, having learnt thy way,
Early may fly the Babylonian woe.

1. *mild yoke:* with reference to Christ's statement (Matthew 11:30) that "my yoke is easy and my burden is light." In his Biblical references, as in the sonnet as a whole, Milton sets side by side two halves of a central Christian paradox: (1) that God insists on man's engaging in the work of His kingdom, (2) that God *needs* nothing man can do or give. 12. *thousands:* i.e., of angels. 14. The highest orders of angels were those who served God in contemplation. *wait:* in the two senses of "stay expectant" and "attend."

ON THE LATE MASSACRE: *Title:* On April 24, 1655, soldiers under orders of the Catholic Marquis of Pianezza slaughtered three hundred Waldensian Protestants who lived in the province of Piedmont (in Alpine Italy). The Waldensian sect was supposed to have preserved the simple uncorrupted rites of the early church. 12. *the . . . Tyrant:* the Pope. 14. *the . . . woe:* i.e., the Roman Church, which, for what Puritanism alleged to be its oppressions and corruptions, was often compared to wicked Babylon.

Areopagitica read

A SPEECH FOR THE LIBERTY OF UNLICENSED PRINTING, TO THE PARLIAMENT OF ENGLAND

(1644)

. . . This is not the liberty which we can hope, that no grievance ever should arise in the Commonwealth—that let no man in this world expect; but when complaints are freely heard, deeply considered, and speedily reformed, then is the utmost bound of civil liberty attained that wise men look for. . . . [5

If ye be thus resolved, as it were injury to think ye were not, I know not what should withhold me from presenting ye with a fit instance wherein to show both that love of truth which ye eminently profess, and that uprightness of your judgment which is not wont to be partial to yourselves; by judging over again that Order which ye have [10 ordained *to regulate Printing: that no book, pamphlet, or paper shall be henceforth printed, unless the same be first approved and licensed by such,* or at least one of such as shall be thereto appointed. For that part which preserves justly every man's copy to himself, or provides for the poor, I touch not, only wish they be not made pre- [15 tences to abuse and persecute honest and painful men, who offend not in either of these particulars. But that other clause of licensing books, which we thought had died . . . when the prelates expired, I shall now attend with such a homily as shall lay before ye, first, the inventors of it to be those whom ye will be loath to own; next, what is to [20

6. *thus:* i.e., to hear complaints and make reforms. 14. *copy:* copyright.
16. *painful:* painstaking. 18. *expired:* lost their control. 19. *attend:* supply.
20. *it:* i.e., licensing or censorship. *to own:* to have on your side.

be thought in general of reading, whatever sort the books be; and
that this Order avails nothing to the suppressing of scandalous, sedi-
tious, and libellous books, which were mainly intended to be suppressed. Last, that it will be primely to the discouragement of all
learning, and the stop of truth, not only by disexercising and   [25
blunting our abilities in what we know already, but by hindering
and cropping the discovery that might be yet further made both in
religious and civil wisdom.

I deny not but that it is of greatest concernment in the Church
and Commonwealth to have a vigilant eye how books demean   [30
themselves as well as men; and thereafter to confine, imprison, and
do sharpest justice on them as malefactors. For books are not absolutely dead things, but do contain a potency of life in them to be as
active as that soul was whose progeny they are; nay, they do preserve
as in a vial the purest efficacy and extraction of that living   [35
intellect that bred them. I know they are as lively, and as vigorously
productive, as those fabulous dragon's teeth; and being sown up and
down, may chance to spring up armed men. And yet, on the other
hand, unless wariness be used, as good almost kill a man as kill a good
book: who kills a man kills a reasonable creature, God's   [40
image; but he who destroys a good book, kills reason itself, kills the
image of God, as it were, in the eye. Many a man lives a burden
to the earth; but a good book is the precious life-blood of a master
spirit, embalmed and treasured up on purpose to a life beyond life.
'Tis true, no age can restore a life, whereof perhaps there is no   [45
great loss; and revolutions of ages do not oft recover the loss of a
rejected truth, for the want of which whole nations fare the worse.
We should be wary, therefore, what persecution we raise against the
living labors of public men, how we spill that seasoned life of man,
preserved and stored up in books; since we see a kind of homi-   [50
cide may be thus committed, sometimes a martyrdom; and if it extend
to the whole impression, a kind of massacre, whereof the execution
ends not in the slaying of an elemental life, but strikes at that ethereal
and fifth essence, the breath of reason itself, slays an immortality
rather than a life. But lest I should be condemned of intro-   [55
ducing licence, while I oppose licensing, I refuse not the pains to be

---

30. *demean:* behave. 35. *the . . . extraction:* the very essence. 37-8. *those
. . . men:* Cadmus, founder of Thebes, sowed the teeth of a dragon he had
killed, and they sprang up armed men. 51-2. *if . . . impression:* if we
suppress the whole edition. 53. *elemental:* composed of the four elements.
53-4. *that . . . essence:* a fifth substance over and above the four elements,
supposed in Milton's time to be the primal energy or principle of things—
hence to strike at *it* is to *slay an immortality*.

so much historical as will serve to show what hath been done by
ancient and famous commonwealths against this disorder, till the very
time that this project of licensing crept out of the Inquisition. . . .

And that the primitive councils and bishops were wont only   [60
to declare what books were not commendable, passing no further, but
leaving it to each one's conscience to read or to lay by, till after the
year 800, is observed already by Padre Paolo, the great unmasker of
the Trentine Council. After which time the Popes of Rome, engrossing what they pleased of political rule into their own hands,   [65
extended their dominion over men's eyes, as they had before over their
judgments, burning and prohibiting to be read what they fancied not;
yet sparing in their censures, and the books not many which they
so dealt with. . . . Which course Leo X and his successors followed,
until the Council of Trent and the Spanish Inquisition, engen-   [70
dering together, brought forth, or perfected those catalogues, and
expurging indexes, that rake through the entrails of many an old good
author, with a violation worse than any could be offered to his tomb.

Nor did they stay in matters heretical, but any subject that was not
to their palate, they either condemned in a prohibition, or had   [75
it straight into the new purgatory of an Index. To fill up the measure
of encroachment, their last invention was to ordain that no book,
pamphlet, or paper should be printed (as if St. Peter had bequeathed
them the keys of the press also out of Paradise) unless it were approved and licensed under the hands of two or three glutton   [80
friars. . . .

And thus ye have the inventors and the original of book-licensing
ripped up and drawn as lineally as any pedigree. We have it not, that
can be heard of, from any ancient state, or polity, or church, nor by
any statute left us by our ancestors elder or later; nor from the   [85
modern custom of any reformed city or church abroad; but from the
most anti-christian council and the most tyrannous inquisition that
ever inquired.

Till then books were ever as freely admitted into the world as any
other birth; the issue of the brain was no more stifled than the   [90
issue of the womb; no envious Juno sat cross-legged over the nativity

63. *Paolo:* i.e., Paolo Sarpi, historian of the Council of Trent, which con-
cluded its eighteen-year effort (1545-63) to reconcile Protestant with
Catholic doctrines by reaffirming the latter. 64-5. *engrossing:* monopolizing.
72. *expurging indexes:* indexes to the passages in books which are not to
be read, like the *Index Expurgatorius* of the Roman church. 76-7. *To . . .
encroachment:* i.e., to add the last straw. 91. *Juno:* To prevent Alcmena
from giving birth to Jove's child, Juno required the goddess of childbirth
to sit cross-legged beside Alcmena, closing (by example and) by her spells
Alcmena's womb.

of any man's intellectual offspring; but if it proved a monster, who denies but that it was justly burnt, or sunk into the sea. But that a book, in worse condition than a peccant soul, should be to stand before a jury ere it be born to the world, and undergo yet in darkness   [95 the judgment of Radamanth and his colleagues, ere it can pass the ferry backward into light, was never heard before, till that mysterious iniquity, provoked and troubled at the first entrance of reformation, sought out new limbos and new hells wherein they might include our books also within the number of their damned. . . .   [100

But some will say, what though the inventors were bad, the thing for all that may be good. It may be so; yet if that thing be no such deep invention, but obvious and easy for any man to light on, and yet best and wisest commonwealths through all ages and occasions have forborne to use it, and falsest seducers and oppressors of men   [105 were the first who took it up, and to no other purpose but to obstruct and hinder the first approach of reformation; I am of those who believe it will be a harder alchymy than Lullius ever knew to sublimate any good use out of such an invention. Yet this only is what I request to gain from this reason, that it may be held a dan-   [110 gerous and suspicious fruit, as certainly it deserves, for the tree that bore it, until I can dissect one by one the properties it has. But I have first to finish, as was propounded, what is to be thought in general of reading books, whatever sort they be, and whether be more the benefit or the harm that thence proceeds? . . .   [115

Good and evil we know in the field of this world grow up together almost inseparably; and the knowledge of good is so involved and interwoven with the knowledge of evil, and in so many cunning re-semblances hardly to be discerned, that those confused seeds which were imposed upon Psyche as an incessant labor to cull out,   [120 and sort asunder, were not more intermixed. It was from out the rind of one apple tasted, that the knowledge of good and evil, as two twins cleaving together, leaped forth into the world. And perhaps this is that doom which Adam fell into of knowing good and evil, that is to say, of knowing good by evil.   [125

---

94. *peccant:* sinful. 96. *Rhadamanth . . . colleagues:* Rhadamanthus, Minos, and Aeacus, the three judges of the souls of the dead. 98. *iniquity:* apparently a reference to the Roman church as a whole, but with special emphasis on the Inquisition. 99. *limbos:* ante-rooms to hell. 108. *Lullius:* Raymond Lully (1234-1315), noted for his alchemical learning. *sublimate:* transform a base metal to gold. 110. *it:* licensing. 120-1. Irritated by Cupid's love for Psyche, Venus set her the task of sorting out the different kinds of grain in a huge mixed heap.

As therefore the state of man now is, what wisdom can there be to choose, what continence to forbear without the knowledge of evil? He that can apprehend and consider vice with all her baits and seeming pleasures, and yet abstain, and yet distinguish, and yet prefer that which is truly better, he is the true wayfaring Christian. I   [130 cannot praise a fugitive and cloistered virtue, unexercised and unbreathed, that never sallies out and sees her adversary, but slinks out of the race where that immortal garland is to be run for, not without dust and heat. Assuredly we bring not innocence into the world, we bring impurity much rather: that which purifies us is trial,   [135 and trial is by what is contrary. That virtue therefore which is but a youngling in the contemplation of evil, and knows not the utmost that vice promises to her followers, and rejects it, is but a blank virtue, not a pure; her whiteness is but an excremental whiteness; which was the reason why our sage and serious poet Spenser, whom I dare   [140 be known to think a better teacher than Scotus or Aquinas, describing true temperance under the person of Guion, brings him in with his palmer through the cave of Mammon and the bower of earthly bliss, that he might see and know, and yet abstain.

Since therefore, the knowledge and survey of vice is in this   [145 world so necessary to the constituting of human virtue, and the scanning of error to the confirmation of truth, how can we more safely, and with less danger, scout into the regions of sin and falsity, than by reading all manner of tractates and hearing all manner of reason? And this is the benefit which may be had of books promiscu-   [150 ously read. . . .

Seeing, therefore, that those books, and those in great abundance, which are likeliest to taint both life and doctrine, cannot be suppressed without the fall of learning, and of all ability in disputation; and that these books of either sort are most and soonest catching to   [155 the learned, from whom to the common people whatever is heretical or dissolute may quickly be conveyed; and that evil manners are as perfectly learned without books a thousand other ways which cannot be stopped; and evil doctrine not with books can propagate, except a teacher guide, which he might also do without writing, and   [160 so beyond prohibiting: I am not able to unfold how this cautelous

---

131. *fugitive:* i.e., which flees life.   133. *that . . . garland:* immortality. 139. *excremental:* surface.   141. *Scotus or Aquinas:* John Duns Scotus (1265?-1308) and St. Thomas Aquinas (1225?-74), two of the great scholastic philosophers.   141-4. *describing . . . abstain:* Cf. *Faerie Queene,* II viii-xii.   149. *tractates:* treatises.   159. *except:* unless.   161. *so:* so be. *cautelous:* ticklish.

enterprise of licensing can be exempted from the number of vain and impossible attempts. And he who were pleasantly disposed, could not well avoid to liken it to the exploit of that gallant man who thought to pound up the crows by shutting his park gate.   [165

Besides another inconvenience, if learned men be the first receivers out of books and dispreaders both of vice and error, how shall the licensers themselves be confided in, unless we can confer upon them, or they assume to themselves above all others in the land, the grace of infallibility and uncorruptedness? And again, if it be true   [170 that a wise man, like a good refiner, can gather gold out of the drossiest volume, and that a fool will be a fool with the best book, yea or without book, here is no reason that we should deprive a wise man of any advantage to his wisdom, while we seek to restrain from a fool that which being restrained will be no hindrance to his folly.   [175 For if there should be so much exactness always used to keep that from him which is unfit for his reading, we should, in the judgment of Aristotle not only, but of Solomon and of our Saviour, not vouchsafe him good precepts, and by consequence not willingly admit him to good books; as being certain that a wise man will make   [180 better use of an idle pamphlet than a fool will do of sacred Scripture.

'Tis next alleged we must not expose ourselves to temptations without necessity, and, next to that, not employ our time in vain things. To both these objections one answer will serve, out of the grounds already laid; that to all men such books are not temptations   [185 nor vanities, but useful drugs and materials wherewith to temper and compose effective and strong medicines which man's life cannot want. The rest, as children and childish men, who have not the art to qualify and prepare these working minerals, well may be exhorted to forbear, but hindered forcibly they cannot be by all the licensing that   [190 sainted Inquisition could ever yet contrive. Which is what I promised to deliver next: that this order of licensing conduces nothing to the end for which it was framed. . . .

If we think to regulate printing, thereby to rectify manners, we must regulate all recreations and pastimes, all that is delight-   [195 ful to man. No music must be heard, no song be set or sung, but what is grave and Doric. There must be licensing dancers, that no gesture,

---

178. *Aristotle, Solomon, our Saviour:* Aristotle notes in his *Nicomachean Ethics* (X viii 3) that the ordinary man is unaffected by ethical study; Proverbs, attributed to Solomon, states (17:24) that the eyes of the fool are always elsewhere than on wisdom; and Christ's advice in Matthew (7:6) is "Neither cast ye your pearls before swine." 187. *want:* do without. 188. *qualify:* compound. 197. *Doric:* Cf. *Lycidas,* 189. Doric music was held by Plato and Aristotle to have a tonic moral effect.

motion, or deportment be taught our youth, but what by their allowance shall be thought honest; . . . It will ask more than the work of twenty licensers to examine all the lutes, the violins, and the guitars [200 in every house; they must not be suffered to prattle as they do, but must be licensed what they may say. And who shall silence all the airs and madrigals that whisper softness in chambers? The windows also, and the balconies must be thought on; there are shrewd books, with dangerous frontispieces, set to sale; who shall prohibit [205 them? Shall twenty licensers? The villages also must have their visitors to inquire what lectures the bagpipe and the rebeck reads even to the ballatry, and the gamut of every municipal fiddler, for these are the countryman's Arcadias, and his Monte Mayors.

Next, what more national corruption, for which England [210 hears ill abroad, than household gluttony? Who shall be the rectors of our daily rioting? And what shall be done to inhibit the multitudes that frequent those houses where drunkenness is sold and harbored? Our garments also should be referred to the licensing of some more sober workmasters, to see them cut into a less wanton garb. [215 Who shall regulate all the mixed conversation of our youth, male and female together, as is the fashion of this country? Who shall still appoint what shall be discoursed, what presumed, and no further? Lastly, who shall forbid and separate all idle resort, all evil company? These things will be, and must be; but how they shall be [220 least hurtful, how least enticing, herein consists the grave and governing wisdom of a state. . . .

Impunity and remissness, for certain, are the bane of a commonwealth; but here the great art lies, to discern in what the law is to bid restraint and punishment, and in what things persuasion [225 only is to work. If every action which is good or evil in man at ripe years, were to be under pittance and prescription and compulsion, what were virtue but a name, what praise could be then due to welldoing, what gramercy to be sober, just, or continent?

Many there be that complain of divine Providence for suf- [230

---

198. *their:* the licensers'. 199. *honest:* decent. 204. *shrewd:* wicked. 205. *frontispiece:* used in its architectural sense (the façade of a building) as well as its book-making sense. 207. *visitors:* inspectors. *rebeck:* kind of violin. 207-8. *even . . . ballatry:* as accompaniment to ballads. 208. *and the gamut:* i.e., the inspectors must inquire about the gamut (range). 209-10. *for . . . Monte Mayors:* i.e., these are the countryman's substitutes for the pastoral romances that appeal to the courtier. The reference is to works like Sir Philip Sidney's *Arcadia* (1590) and Jorge de Montemayor's *Diana Enamorada* (Engl. trans. 1598). 211. *rectors:* regulators. 219. *resort:* i.e., gathering together. 227. *pittance:* ration. 229. *gramercy:* thanks.

fering Adam to transgress. Foolish tongues! when God gave him reason, he gave him freedom to choose, for reason is but choosing; he had been else a mere artificial Adam, such an Adam as he is in the motions. We ourselves esteem not of that obedience, or love, or gift, which is of force. God, therefore, left him free, set before   [235 him a provoking object, ever almost in his eyes; herein consisted his merit, herein the right of his reward, the praise of his abstinence. Wherefore did he create passions within us, pleasures round about us, but that these rightly tempered are the very ingredients of virtue? They are not skilful considerers of human things, who   [240 imagine to remove sin by removing the matter of sin. For, besides that it is a huge heap increasing under the very act of diminishing, though some part of it may for a time be withdrawn from some persons, it cannot from all, in such a universal thing as books are; and when this is done, yet the sin remains entire. Though ye   [245 take from a covetous man all his treasure, he has yet one jewel left— ye cannot bereave him of his covetousness. Banish all objects of lust, shut up all youth into the severest discipline that can be exercised in any hermitage, ye cannot make them chaste, that came not thither so: such great care and wisdom is required to the right manag-   [250 ing of this point.

Suppose we could expel sin by this means; look how much we thus expel of sin, so much we expel of virtue: for the matter of them both is the same; remove that, and ye remove them both alike. This justifies the high providence of God, who, though he command   [255 us temperance, justice, continence, yet pours out before us, even to a profuseness, all desirable things, and gives us minds that can wander beyond all limit and satiety. Why should we then affect a rigor contrary to the manner of God and of nature, by abridging or scanting those means which books freely permitted are, both to the   [260 trial of virtue, and the exercise of truth?

It would be better done to learn that the law must needs be frivolous which goes to restrain things uncertainly and yet equally working to good and to evil. And were I the chooser, a dram of well-doing should be preferred before many times as much the   [265 forcible hindrance of evil-doing. For God sure esteems the growth and completing of one virtuous person more than the restraint of ten vicious. And albeit whatever thing we hear or see, sitting, walking, travelling, or conversing, may be fitly called our book, and is of the same effect that writings are; yet grant the thing to be pro-   [270

233. *artificial*: i.e., made by "art," not created by God.   234. *motions*: puppet shows.   254-8. Cf. *Comus*, 705-79.

hibited were only books, it appears that this order hitherto is far insufficient to the end which it intends. Do we not see—not once or oftener, but weekly—that continued court-libel against the Parliament and City printed, as the wet sheets can witness, and dispersed among us, for all that licensing can do? Yet this is the prime service [275 a man would think, wherein this Order should give proof of itself. If it were executed, you'll say. But certain, if execution be remiss or blindfold now, and in this particular, what will it be hereafter and in other books?

If then the Order shall not be vain and frustrate, behold a [280 new labor, Lords and Commons. Ye must repeal and proscribe all scandalous and unlicensed books already printed and divulged (after ye have drawn them up into a list, that all may know which are condemned and which not) and ordain that no foreign books be delivered out of custody, till they have been read over. This office will [285 require the whole time of not a few overseers, and those no vulgar men. There be also books which are partly useful and excellent, partly culpable and pernicious; this work will ask as many more officials, to make expurgations and expunctions, that the commonwealth of learning be not damnified. In fine, when the multitude of [290 books increase upon their hands, ye must be fain to catalogue all those printers who are found frequently offending, and forbid the importation of their whole suspected typography. In a word, that this your Order may be exact and not deficient, ye must reform it perfectly according to the model of Trent and Seville, which I know [295 ye abhor to do.

Yet, though ye should condescend to this, which God forbid, the Order still would be but fruitless and defective to that end whereto ye meant it. If to prevent sects and schisms, who is so unread or so uncatechized in story that hath not heard of many sects refus- [300 ing books as a hindrance, and preserving their doctrine unmixed for many ages, only by unwritten traditions? The Christian faith, for that was once a schism, is not unknown to have spread all over Asia, ere any Gospel or Epistle was seen in writing. If the amendment of manners be aimed at, look into Italy and Spain, whether [305 those places be one scruple the better, the honester, the wiser, the chaster, since all the inquisitional rigor that hath been executed upon books. . . .

---

273. *court-libel:* the weekly journal—*Mercurius Aulicus*—published by the Cavalier party. 282. *divulged:* disseminated. 289. *expunctions:* expungings. 290. *In fine:* In conclusion. 295. *Seville:* alluding to the strict inquisitorial censorship established in Spain. 299-300. *so . . . story:* so ignorant of history.

I lastly proceed from the no good it can do, to the manifest hurt it causes in being first the greatest discouragement and affront   [310 that can be offered to learning and to learned men. . . .

What advantage is it to be a man over it is to be a boy at school, if we have only scaped the ferula to come under the fescue of an Imprimatur; if serious and elaborate writings, as if they were no more than the theme of a grammar-lad under his pedagogue, must   [315 not be uttered without the cursory eyes of a temporizing and extemporizing licenser? He who is not trusted with his own actions, his drift not being known to be evil, and standing to the hazard of law and penalty, has no great argument to think himself reputed, in the commonwealth wherein he was born, for other than a fool   [320 or a foreigner.

When a man writes to the world, he summons up all his reason and deliberation to assist him; he searches, meditates, is industrious, and likely consults and confers with his judicious friends, after all which done he takes himself to be informed in what he writes, as   [325 well as any that writ before him. If in this the most consummate act of his fidelity and ripeness, no years, no industry, no former proof of his abilities can bring him to that state of maturity as not to be still mistrusted and suspected (unless he carry all his considerate diligence, all his midnight watchings, and expense of Palladian oil, to   [330 the hasty view of an unleisured licenser, perhaps much his younger, perhaps far his inferior in judgment, perhaps one who never knew the labor of book-writing), and if he be not repulsed, or slighted, must appear in print like a puny with his guardian, and his censor's hand on the back of his title to be his bail and surety that he is no   [335 idiot, or seducer; it cannot be but a dishonor and derogation to the author, to the book, to the privilege and dignity of learning.

And what if the author shall be one so copious of fancy as to have many things well worth the adding, come into his mind after licensing, while the book is yet under the press, which not seldom   [340 happens to the best and diligentest writers; and that perhaps a dozen times in one book. The printer dares not go beyond his licensed copy. So often then must the author trudge to his leave-giver, that those his new insertions may be viewed, and many a jaunt will be made, ere that licenser, for it must be the same man, can either be   [345

---

312. *it is to be:* being. 313. *ferula:* rod. *fescue:* a schoolmaster's pointer. 314. *Imprimatur:* the Latin for "Let it be printed" affixed by the censor; hence it here means the whole system of censorship. 316. *uttered:* published. *cursory:* hasty. 316-17. *temporizing and extemporizing:* compliant and offhand. 318. *standing . . . of:* liable to. 330. *Palladian oil:* oil of Pallas Athene, i.e., of wisdom. 334. *a puny:* a minor.

found, or found at leisure. Meanwhile, either the press must stand still, which is no small damage, or the author lose his accuratest thoughts, and send the book forth worse than he had made it, which to a diligent writer is the greatest melancholy and vexation that can befall. [350

And how can a man teach with authority, which is the life of teaching, how can he be a doctor in his book as he ought to be, or else had better be silent, whenas all he teaches, all he delivers, is but under the tuition, under the correction of his partriarchal licenser to blot or alter what precisely accords not with the hide-bound humor [355 which he calls his judgment? When every acute reader upon the first sight of a pedantic license, will be ready with these like words to ding the book a quoit's distance from him: "I hate a pupil teacher, I endure not an instructor that comes to me under the wardship of an over-seeing fist. I know nothing of the licenser, but that I have his [360 own hand here for his arrogance; who shall warrant me his judgment?". . .

Nay, which is more lamentable, if the work of any deceased author, though never so famous in his lifetime, and even to this day, come to their hands for licence to be printed, or reprinted; if there be [365 found in his book one sentence of a venturous edge, uttered in the height of zeal, and who knows whether it might not be the dictate of a divine spirit, yet not suiting with every low, decrepit humor of their own, though it were Knox himself, the reformer of a kingdom, that spake it, they will not pardon him their dash; the sense of [370 that great man shall to all posterity be lost, for the fearfulness, or the presumptuous rashness, of a perfunctory licenser. . . .

Yet if these things be not resented seriously and timely by them who have the remedy in their power, but that such iron-moulds as these shall have authority to gnaw out the choicest periods of [375 exquisitest books, and to commit such a treacherous fraud against the orphan remainders of worthiest men after death, the more sorrow will belong to that hapless race of men whose misfortune it is to have understanding. Henceforth, let no man care to learn, or care to be more than worldly wise; for certainly in higher matters to [380 be ignorant and slothful, to be a common steadfast dunce, will be the only pleasant life, and only in request.

---

354. *patriarchal:* belonging to a patriarchate, i.e., an archbishopric. 357-8. *ding . . . distance:* toss as far as one tosses a quoit (in a game of quoits). 359. *wardship:* guardianship. 369. *Knox:* John Knox (1505-72), leader of the Scottish Presbyterians. 370. *dash:* i.e., with the censoring pen. 374. *iron-moulds:* stains, i.e., expungers. 377. *remainders:* i.e., books.

And as it is a particular disesteem of every knowing person alive,
and most injurious to the written labors and monuments of the dead,
so to me it seems an undervaluing and vilifying of the whole   [385
nation. I cannot set so light by all the invention, the art, the wit, the
grave and solid judgment which is in England, as that it can be com-
prehended in any twenty capacities how good soever; much less that
it should not pass except their superintendence be over it, except it be
sifted and strained with their strainers; that it should be   [390
uncurrent without their manual stamp. Truth and understanding are
not such wares as to be monopolised and traded in by tickets and
statutes and standards. We must not think to make a staple com-
modity of all the knowledge in the land, to mark and license it like
our broadcloth and our woolpacks. What is it but a servi-   [395
tude like that imposed by the Philistines, not to be allowed the sharpening of our own axes and coulters, but we must repair from all
quarters to twenty licensing forges.

Had any one written and divulged erroneous things and scandalous
to honest life, misusing and forfeiting the esteem had of his   [400
reason among men; if, after conviction, this only censure were adjudged him, that he should never henceforth write, but what were
first examined by an appointed officer, whose hand should be annexed
to pass his credit for him, that now he might be safely read; it could
not be apprehended less than a disgraceful punishment.   [405

Whence, to include the whole nation, and those that never yet thus
offended, under such a diffident and suspectful prohibition, may
plainly be understood what a disparagement it is. So much the more,
whenas debtors and delinquents may walk abroad without a keeper,
but unoffensive books must not stir forth without a visible   [410
jailor in their title. Nor is it to the common people less than a reproach; for if we be so jealous over them as that we dare not trust
them with an English pamphlet, what do we but censure them for
a giddy, vicious, and ungrounded people; in such a sick and weak
state of faith and discretion, as to be able to take nothing   [415
down but through the pipe of a licenser. . . .

And in conclusion, it reflects to the disrepute of our ministers also,
of whose labors we should hope better, and of the proficiency which
their flock reaps by them, than that after all this light of the Gospel

---

386. *set . . . by:* value so little. *invention:* creative imagination. 388. *in
. . . capacities:* i.e., by twenty censors. 391. *uncurrent:* invalid. 392. *tickets:* permits. 395-8. Cf. 1 Samuel, 13:20. The Philistines prohibited forges
among the Jews and made them sharpen their tools at the forges of the
Philistines. 403. *whose . . . annexed:* i.e., whose permission should be
affixed. 407. *diffident:* untrusting. 416. *pipe:* feeding-tube.

which is and is to be, and all this continual preaching, they   [420
should be still frequented with such an unprincipled, unedified, and
laic rabble, as that the whiff of every new pamphlet should stagger
them out of their catechism and Christian walking. This may have
much reason to discourage the ministers, when such a low conceit is
had of all their exhortations and the benefiting of their hear-   [425
ers, as that they are not thought fit to be turned loose to three sheets
of paper without a licenser; that all the sermons, all the lectures
preached, printed, vented in such numbers, and such volumes, as have
now well-nigh made all other books unsaleable, should not be armor
enough against one single enchiridion, without the castle of   [430
St. Angelo of an Imprimatur.

And lest some should persuade ye, Lords and Commons, that these
arguments of learned men's discouragement at this your Order are
mere flourishes, and not real, I could recount what I have seen and
heard in other countries where this kind of inquisition tyran-   [435
nizes; when I have sat among their learned men, for that honor I had,
and been counted happy to be born in such a place of philosophic
freedom as they supposed England was, while themselves did nothing
but bemoan the servile condition into which learning amongst them
was brought; that this was it which had damped the glory   [440
of Italian wits; that nothing had been there written now these many
years but flattery and fustian. There it was that I found and visited
the famous Galileo, grown old, a prisoner to the Inquisition for thinking in astronomy otherwise than the Franciscan and Dominican licensers thought. . . .   [445

That this is not, therefore, the disburdening of a particular fancy,
but the common grievance of all those who had prepared their minds
and studies above the vulgar pitch to advance truth in others, and
from others to entertain it, thus much may satisfy. And in their name
I shall for neither friend nor foe conceal what the general   [450
murmur is; that if it come to inquisitioning again and licensing, and
that we are so timorous of ourselves and so suspicious of all men as
to fear each book and the shaking of every leaf, before we know what
the contents are; if some who but of late were little better than
silenced from preaching, shall come now to silence us from   [455
reading, except what they please, it cannot be guessed what is intended

---

422. *laic:* belonging to the laity; hence "untaught." 428. *vented:* (1) published; (2) sold. 430. *enchiridion:* hand-book. 430-1. *without . . . Imprimatur:* i.e., without an Imprimatur, which is comparable to the Castle of St.
Angelo in Rome, the Popes' prison. 442. *fustian:* exaggerated nonsense.
443. *Galileo:* Milton had visited him in person in Florence during his
Italian journey (1638-9). 448. *the . . . pitch:* the ordinary.

by some but a second tyranny over learning; and will soon put it out of controversy that bishops and presbyters are the same to us both name and thing. . . .

But now, the bishops abrogated and voided out of the   [460 Church, as if our reformation sought no more, but to make room for others into their seats under another name, the episcopal arts begin to bud again; the cruse of truth must run no more oil; liberty of printing must be enthralled again under a prelatical commission of twenty, the privilege of the people nullified; and, which is worse, the   [465 freedom of learning must groan again, and to her old fetters: all this the Parliament yet sitting. Although their own late arguments and defences against the prelates might remember them that this obstructing violence meets for the most part with an event utterly opposite to the end which it drives at; instead of suppressing sects and   [470 schisms, it raises them and invests them with a reputation: "The punishing of wits enhances their authority," saith the Viscount St. Albans, "and a forbidden writing is thought to be a certain spark of truth that flies up in the faces of them who seek to tread it out."

This Order, therefore, may prove a nursing mother to   [475 sects, but I shall easily show how it will be a step-dame to Truth; and first by disenabling us to the maintenance of what is known already.

Well knows he who uses to consider, that our faith and knowledge thrives by exercise, as well as our limbs and complexion. Truth is compared in Scripture to a streaming fountain; if her waters   [480 flow not in a perpetual progression, they sicken into a muddy pool of conformity and tradition. A man may be a heretic in the truth; and if he believe things only because his pastor says so, or the Assembly so determines, without knowing other reason, though his belief be true, yet the very truth he holds becomes his heresy. There is not   [485 any burden that some would gladlier post off to another than the charge and care of their religion. There be, who knows not that there be, of Protestants and professors who live and die in as arrant an implicit faith, as any lay Papist of Loretto.

A wealthy man addicted to his pleasure and to his profits,   [490 finds religion to be a traffic so entangled, and of so many piddling

<hr>

457. *some:* the Presbyterians. 460. *abrogated and voided:* annulled and expelled. 463. *cruse:* vessel. 464. *enthralled:* enslaved. *prelatical:* i.e., like the commissions formerly appointed by the prelates. 467. *their:* the Presbyterians'. 469. *event:* result. 472-3. *Viscount St. Albans:* Francis Bacon, whose *Advertisement Touching the Controversies of the Church of England* Milton quotes here. 477. *to:* for. 480. *Scripture:* Psalms 85:11. 483. *Assembly:* the assembly of Puritan ministers, mainly Presbyterians, which was in session at Westminster when Milton wrote. 486. *post off:* delegate. 488. *professors:* persons professing religious faith. 489. *Loretto:* site of a famous Roman Catholic shrine. 491. *traffic:* commerce.

accounts, that of all mysteries he cannot skill to keep a stock going upon that trade. What should he do? Fain he would have the name to be religious, fain he would bear up with his neighbors in that. What does he, therefore, but resolves to give over toiling,   [495 and to find himself out some factor to whose care and credit he may commit the whole managing of his religious affairs; some Divine of note and estimation that must be. To him he adheres, resigns the whole warehouse of his religion, with all the locks and keys into his custody; and indeed makes the very person of that man his   [500 religion; esteems his associating with him a sufficient evidence and commendatory of his own piety. So that a man may say his religion is now no more within himself, but is become a dividual movable, and goes and comes near him, according as that good man frequents the house. He entertains him, gives him gifts, feasts him, lodges   [505 him. His religion comes home at night, prays, is liberally supped, and sumptuously laid to sleep, rises, is saluted, and after the malmsey, or some well-spiced brewage, and better breakfasted than he whose morning appetite would have gladly fed on green figs between Bethany and Jerusalem, his religion walks abroad at eight, and leaves his   [510 kind entertainer in the shop trading all day without his religion.

Another sort there be, who, when they hear that all things shall be ordered, all things regulated and settled, nothing written but what passes through the custom-house of certain publicans that have the tonnaging and poundaging of all free-spoken truth, will   [515 straight give themselves up into your hands, make 'em and cut 'em out what religion ye please. There be delights, there be recreations and jolly pastimes that will fetch the day about from sun to sun, and rock the tedious year as in a delightful dream. What need they torture their heads with that which others have taken so strictly,   [520 and so unalterably into their own purveying? These are the fruits which a dull ease and cessation of our knowledge will bring forth among the people. How goodly, and how to be wished, were such an obedient unanimity as this, what a fine conformity would it starch us all into! Doubtless a staunch and solid piece of framework,   [525 as any January could freeze together. . . .

For if we be sure we are in the right, and do not hold the truth guiltily—which becomes not—, if we ourselves condemn not our own

---

492. *mysteries:* a term applied to trades or skills and here used with over-tones from its religious sense. *skill:* learn how. 494. *bear:* keep. 496. *factor:* agent. 502. *commendatory:* testimonial. 503. *dividual:* separable. 507. *malmsey:* wine. 508. *he:* i.e., Christ, who being hungry and searching a fig tree found only leaves (Mark 11: 12-13). 514. *publicans:* tax collectors, who collect the foreign and poundage taxes referred to. 521. *purveying:* pro-viding. 528. *which . . . not:* which is unbecoming.

weak and frivolous teaching, and the people for an untaught and
irreligious, gadding rout, what can be more fair than when   [530
a man judicious, learned, and of a conscience, for aught we know,
as good as theirs that taught us what we know, shall not privily from
house to house, which is more dangerous, but openly by writing, publish to the world what his opinion is, what his reasons, and where-
for that which is now thought cannot be sound? Christ   [535
urged it as wherewith to justify himself that he preached in public; yet
writing is more public than preaching; and more easy to refutation, if
need be, there being so many whose business and profession merely it
is, to be the champions of truth; which if they neglect, what can be
imputed but their sloth, or unability? . . .   [540

There is yet behind of what I purposed to lay open, the incredible loss
and detriment that this plot of licensing puts us to. More than if some
enemy at sea should stop up all our havens, and ports, and creeks, it hinders and retards the importation of our richest merchandise, truth. . . .

Truth indeed came once into the world with her divine   [545
Master, and was a perfect shape most glorious to look on. But when
he ascended, and his apostles after him were laid asleep, then straight
arose a wicked race of deceivers, who, as that story goes of the Egyptian Typhon with his conspirators, how they dealt with the good
Osiris, took the virgin Truth, hewed her lovely form into   [550
a thousand pieces, and scattered them to the four winds. From that
time ever since, the sad friends of Truth, such as durst appear, imitat-
ing the careful search that Isis made for the mangled body of Osiris,
went up and down gathering up limb by limb still as they could find
them. We have not yet found them all, Lords and Com-   [555
mons, nor ever shall do, till her Master's second coming. He shall
bring together every joint and member, and shall mould them into an
immortal feature of loveliness and perfection. Suffer not these licensing prohibitions to stand at every place of opportunity, forbidding and
disturbing them that continue seeking, that continue to do   [560
our obsequies to the torn body of our martyred saint. . . .

Lords and Commons of England, consider what nation it is whereof
ye are, and whereof ye are the governors; a nation not slow and dull,
but of a quick, ingenious, and piercing spirit, acute to invent, subtle
and sinewy to discourse, not beneath the reach of any point   [565
the highest that human capacity can soar to. Therefore the studies of

---

535-6. Cf. John 18:20. 548-51. *Typhon,* having murdered his brother Osiris,
mangled the body and scattered the pieces; *Isis,* Osiris's wife, painstakingly
sought them out again. In his *Isis and Osiris,* Plutarch makes the story
into an allegory of the ceaseless fragmentation and reassembling of divine
truth. 561. *obsequies:* acts of veneration.

learning in her deepest sciences have been so ancient and so eminent among us, that writers of good antiquity and ablest judgment have been persuaded that even the school of Pythagoras and the Persian wisdom, took beginning from the old philosophy of this   [570 island. And that wise and civil Roman, Julius Agricola, who governed once here for Cæsar, preferred the natural wits of Britain before the labored studies of the French. Nor is it for nothing that the grave and frugal Transylvanian sends out yearly from as far as the mountainous borders of Russia and beyond the Hercynian   [575 wilderness, not their youth but their staid men, to learn our language and our theologic arts.

Yet that which is above all this, the favor and the love of Heaven, we have great argument to think in a peculiar manner propitious and propending towards us. Why else was this nation chosen   [580 before any other, that out of her as out of Sion should be proclaimed and sounded forth the first tidings and trumpet of reformation to all Europe? And had it not been the obstinate perverseness of our prelates against the divine and admirable spirit of Wyclif, to suppress him as a schismatic and innovator, perhaps neither the Bohemian   [585 Huss and Jerome, no, nor the name of Luther, or of Calvin, had been ever known; the glory of reforming all our neighbors had been completely ours. But now, as our obdurate clergy have with violence demeaned the matter, we are become hitherto the latest and the backwardest scholars, of whom God offered to have made us the   [590 teachers.

Now once again by all concurrence of signs, and by the general instinct of holy and devout men, as they daily and solemnly express their thoughts, God is decreeing to begin some new and great period in his Church, even to the reforming of reformation itself.   [595 What does he then but reveal himself to his servants, and, as his manner is, first to his Englishmen; I say as his manner is, first to us, though we mark not the method of his counsels, and are unworthy. Behold now this vast city, a city of refuge, the mansion house of liberty, encompassed and surrounded with his protection. The   [600 shop of war hath not there more anvils and hammers waking, to

---

569. *Pythagoras:* a Greek philosopher of the sixth century B. C. *Persian:* Persia is the legendary cradle of all learning. 571. *Agricola:* Roman governor of Britain, 78-85 B. C. 574. *Transylvanian:* Transylvania, occupying much of the present territory of Romania, was an independent Protestant state. 575. *Hercynian:* used vaguely with reference to the mountains and wilds of middle Europe. 580. *propending:* inclining. 581. *Sion:* Jerusalem. 564. *Wyclif:* English reformer. 586. *Huss and Jerome:* John Huss and Jerome of Prague, Bohemian reformers. 589. *demeaned:* managed.

fashion out the plates and instruments of armed justice in defence of beleaguered truth, than there be pens and heads there, sitting by their studious lamps, musing, searching, revolving new notions and ideas wherewith to present, as with their homage and their fealty, [605 the approaching reformation; others as fast reading, trying all things, assenting to the force of reason and convincement.

What could a man require more from a nation so pliant and so prone to seek after knowledge? What wants there to such a towardly and pregnant soil, but wise and faithful laborers, to make a [610 knowing people, a nation of prophets, of sages, and of worthies? We reckon more than five months yet to harvest; there need not be five weeks, had we but eyes to lift up; the fields are white already. Where there is much desire to learn, there of necessity will be much arguing, much writing, many opinions; for opinion in good men is [615 but knowledge in the making. Under these fantastic terrors of sect and schism, we wrong the earnest and zealous thirst after knowledge and understanding which God hath stirred up in this city.

What some lament of, we rather should rejoice at, should rather praise this pious forwardness among men, to reassume the [620 ill-deputed care of their religion into their own hands again. A little generous prudence, a little forbearance of one another, and some grain of charity might win all these diligences to join and unite into one general and brotherly search after truth. . . .

Yet these are the men cried out against for schismatics and [625 sectaries; as if, while the temple of the Lord was building, some cutting, some squaring the marble, others hewing the cedars, there should be a sort of irrational men who could not consider there must be many schisms and many dissections made in the quarry and in the timber, ere the house of God can be built. And when [630 every stone is laid artfully together, it cannot be united into a continuity, it can but be contiguous in this world; neither can every piece of the building be of one form; nay rather the perfection consists in this, that out of many moderate varieties and brotherly dissimilitudes that are not vastly disproportional, arises the goodly and the [635 graceful symmetry that commends the whole pile and structure.

Let us, therefore, be more considerate builders, more wise in spiritual architecture, when great reformation is expected. For now the time seems come, wherein Moses, the great prophet, may sit in heaven

---

602. *plates:* i.e., armor. 613. Cf. John 4:35. "Say not ye, There are yet four months [till harvest]? behold, I say unto you, Lift up your eyes . . . ; for [the fields] are white already. . . . 629. *schisms:* a pun on the literal sense, cutting.

rejoicing to see that memorable and glorious wish of his ful-   [640
filled, when not only our seventy elders, but all the Lord's people, are
become prophets. No marvel then though some men, and some good
men, too, perhaps, but young in goodness, as Joshua then was, envy
them. They fret, and out of their own weakness are in agony, lest
these divisions and subdivisions will undo us. The adversary   [645
again applauds, and waits the hour. When they have branched themselves out, saith he, small enough into parties and partitions, then will
be our time. Fool! he sees not the firm root, out of which we all grow,
though into branches; nor will beware until he see our small divided
maniples cutting through at every angle of his ill-united and   [650
unwieldy brigade. And that we are to hope better of all these supposed sects and schisms, and that we shall not need that solicitude,
honest perhaps, though over-timorous, of them that vex in this behalf,
but shall laugh in the end at those malicious applauders of our differences, I have these reasons to persuade me.   [655
   First, when a city shall be as it were besieged and blocked about,
her navigable river infested, inroads and incursions round, defiance
and battle oft rumored to be marching up even to her walls and
suburb trenches; that then the people, or the greater part, more than
at other times, wholly taken up with the study of highest and   [660
most important matters to be reformed, should be disputing, reasoning, reading, inventing, discoursing, even to a rarity and admiration,
things not before discoursed or written of, argues first a singular good-
will, contentedness and confidence in your prudent foresight, and safe
government, Lords and Commons; and from thence derives   [665
itself to a gallant bravery and well grounded contempt of their enemies, as if there were no small number of as great spirits among us,
as his was, who, when Rome was nigh besieged by Hannibal, being
in the city, bought that piece of ground at no cheap rate whereon
Hannibal himself encamped his own regiment.   [670
   Next, it is a lively and cheerful presage of our happy success and
victory. For as in a body, when the blood is fresh, the spirits pure and
vigorous not only to vital but to rational faculties, and those in the
acutest and the pertest operations of wit and subtlety, it argues in
what good plight and constitution the body is; so when the   [675
cheerfulness of the people is so sprightly up, as that it has not only
wherewith to guard well its own freedom and safety, but to spare, and

---

640. *wish:* Cf. Numbers 11:29. 650. *maniples:* platoons. 653. *vex:* worry.
656 ff. A description of London as it was in late 1643, with the royalists
encircling it. 668-70. For this story, cf. Livy's *History of Rome* (XXVI
xi). 672. *the spirits:* and when the spirits are.

to bestow upon the solidest and sublimest points of controversy and new invention, it betokens us not degenerated nor drooping to a fatal decay, but casting off the old and wrinkled skin of corrup-   [680 tion to outlive these pangs, and wax young again, entering the glorious ways of truth and prosperous virtue, destined to become great and honorable in these latter ages.

Methinks I see in my mind a noble and puissant nation rousing herself like a strong man after sleep, and shaking her invincible   [685 locks. Methinks I see her as an eagle newing her mighty youth, and kindling her undazzled eyes at the full midday beam; purging and unscaling her long-abused sight at the fountain itself of heavenly radiance; while the whole noise of timorous and flocking birds, with those also that love the twilight, flutter about, amazed at what she   [690 means, and in their envious gabble would prognosticate a year of sects and schisms.

What should ye do then, should ye suppress all this flowery crop of knowledge and new light sprung up and yet springing daily in this city? Should ye set an oligarchy of twenty engrossers over it,   [695 to bring a famine upon our minds again, when we shall know nothing but what is measured to us by their bushel? Believe it, Lords and Commons, they who counsel ye to such a suppressing, do as good as bid ye suppress yourselves; and I will soon show how.

If it be desired to know the immediate cause of all this free   [700 writing and free speaking, there cannot be assigned a truer than your own mild and free and humane government. It is the liberty, Lords and Commons, which your own valorous and happy counsels have purchased us, liberty which is the nurse of all great wits. This is that which hath rarefied and enlightened our spirits like the influ-   [705 ence of heaven; this is that which hath enfranchised, enlarged, and lifted up our apprehensions degrees above themselves. Ye cannot make us now less capable, less knowing, less eagerly pursuing of the truth, unless ye first make yourselves, that made us so, less the lovers, less the founders of our true liberty. We can grow ignorant   [710 again, brutish, formal, and slavish, as ye found us; but you then must first become that which ye cannot be, oppressive, arbitrary, and tyrannous, as they were from whom ye have freed us. That our hearts are now more capacious, our thoughts more erected to the search and expectation of greatest and exactest things, is the issue of   [715

---

687. *undazzled:* The eagle was reputed to be able to behold the sun without going blind. 689. *timorous . . . birds:* for instance, the Presbyterians (who are, Milton implies, afraid of uncensored publishing). 695. *engrossers:* monopolists.

your own virtue propagated in us. Ye cannot suppress that unless ye reinforce an abrogated and merciless law, that fathers may despatch at will their own children. And who shall then stick closest to ye, and excite others? not he who takes up arms for coat and conduct, and his four nobles of Danegelt. Although I dispraise not   [720 the defence of just immunities, yet love my peace better, if that were all. Give me the liberty to know, to utter, and to argue freely according to conscience, above all liberties. . . .

And now the time in special is, by privilege to write and speak what may help to the further discussing of matters in agitation. The   [725 temple of Janus with his two controversal faces might now not unsignificantly be set open. And though all the winds of doctrine were let loose to play upon the earth, so Truth be in the field, we do injuriously by licensing and prohibiting to misdoubt her strength. Let her and Falsehood grapple; who ever knew Truth put to the   [730 worse, in a free and open encounter. . . .

For who knows not that Truth is strong, next to the Almighty. She needs no policies, nor stratagems, nor licensings to make her victorious—those are the shifts and the defences that error uses against her power. . . .   [735

In the meanwhile, if any one would write and bring his helpful hand to the slow-moving reformation which we labor under, if truth have spoken to him before others, or but seemed at least to speak, who hath so bejesuited us that we should trouble that man with asking license to do so worthy a deed? And not consider this, that   [740 if it come to prohibiting, there is not aught more likely to be prohibited than truth itself; whose first appearance to our eyes bleared and dimmed with prejudice and custom, is more unsightly and unplausible than many errors, even as the person is of many a great man slight and contemptible to see to. And what do they tell   [745 us vainly of new opinions, when this very opinion of theirs, that none must be heard but whom they like, is the worst and newest opinion of all others; and is the chief cause why sects and schisms do so much abound, and true knowledge is kept at distance from us; besides yet a greater danger which is in it. For when God shakes a   [750 kingdom with strong and healthful commotions to a general reforming, 'tis not untrue that many sectaries and false teachers are then busiest in seducing; but yet more true it is that God then raises to his

719-20. _for . . . Danegelt:_ i.e., to resist illegal taxation by the Crown (with reference to some ancient taxes arbitrarily revised by Charles I in his contest with Parliament. 726-7. _open:_ i.e., as they were in Rome in time of war; for this too is a time of war, between falsehood and truth. 745. _see to:_ look at.

own work men of rare abilities, and more than common industry, not only to look back and revise what hath been taught hereto-   [755 fore, but to gain further and go on, some new enlightened steps in the discovery of truth. . . .

And if the men be erroneous who appear to be the leading schismatics, what withholds us but our sloth, our self-will, and distrust in the right cause, that we do not give them gentle meetings   [760 and gentle dismissions, that we debate not and examine the matter thoroughly with liberal and frequent audience; if not for their sakes, yet for our own? Seeing no man who hath tasted learning but will confess the many ways of profiting by those who, not contented with stale receipts, are able to manage and set forth new positions   [765 to the world. And were they but as the dust and cinders of our feet, so long as in that notion they may yet serve to polish and brighten the armory of Truth, even for that respect they were not utterly to be cast away. But if they be of those whom God hath fitted for the special use of these times with eminent and ample gifts—and   [770 those perhaps neither among the priests, nor among the pharisees— and we in the haste of a precipitant zeal shall make no distinction, but resolve to stop their mouths because we fear they come with new and dangerous opinions (as we commonly forejudge them ere we understand them); no less than woe to us while, thinking thus   [775 to defend the Gospel, we are found the persecutors. . . .

This I know, that errors in a good government and in a bad are equally almost incident; for what magistrate may not be misinformed and much the sooner, if liberty of printing be reduced into the power of a few; but to redress willingly and speeedily what hath   [780 been erred, and in highest authority to esteem a plain advertisement more than others have done a sumptuous bribe, is a virtue, honored Lords and Commons, answerable to your highest actions, and whereof none can participate but greatest and wisest men.

⟨~❧⟩

---

781. *erred:* done wrong. *advertisement:* notice (like this treatise).

Major Poems

HEAVEN or the EMPYREAN

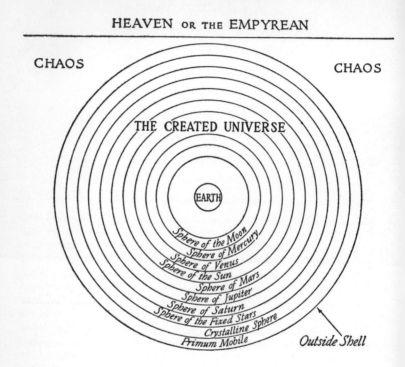

CHAOS

CHAOS

THE CREATED UNIVERSE

EARTH

Sphere of the Moon
Sphere of Mercury
Sphere of Venus
Sphere of the Sun
Sphere of Mars
Sphere of Jupiter
Sphere of Saturn
Sphere of the Fixed Stars
Crystalline Sphere
Primum Mobile

Outside Shell

CHAOS

CHAOS

A Diagram of Milton's Universe

Major Poems

Paradise Lost

(1667)

BOOK I

THE ARGUMENT

This First Book proposes, first in brief, the whole subject—Man's disobedience, and the loss thereupon of Paradise, wherein he was placed: then touches the prime cause of his fall—the Serpent, or rather Satan in the Serpent; who, revolting from God, and drawing to his side many legions of Angels, was, by the command of God, driven out of Heaven, with all his crew, into the great Deep. Which action passed over, the Poem hastens into the midst of things; presenting Satan, with his Angels, now fallen into Hell—described here not in the Centre (for heaven and earth may be supposed as yet not made, certainly not yet accursed), but in a place of utter darkness, fitliest called Chaos. Here Satan, with his Angels lying on the burning lake, thunderstruck and astonished, after a certain space recovers, as from confusion; calls up him who, next in order and dignity, lay by him: they confer of their miserable fall. Satan awakens all his legions, who lay till then in the same manner confounded. They rise: their numbers; array of battle; their chief leaders named, according to the idols known afterwards in Canaan and the countries adjoining. To these Satan directs his speech; comforts them with hope yet of regaining Heaven; but tells them, lastly, of a new world and new kind of creature to be created, according to an ancient prophecy, or report, in Heaven—for that Angels were long before this visible creation was

---

Title: The Genesis story on which Milton founds his poem is given in the Appendix.

the opinion of many ancient Fathers. To find out the truth of this
prophecy, and what to determine thereon, he refers to a full council.
What his associates thence attempt. Pandemonium, the palace of
Satan, rises, suddenly built out of the Deep: the infernal Peers there
sit in council.

O F man's first disobedience, and the fruit
Of that forbidden tree whose mortal taste
Brought death into the World, and all our woe,
With loss of Eden, till one greater Man
Restore us, and regain the blissful seat,   5
Sing, Heavenly Muse, that, on the secret top
Of Oreb, or of Sinai, didst inspire
That shepherd who first taught the chosen seed
In the beginning how the heavens and earth
Rose out of Chaos: or, if Sion hill   10
Delight thee more, and Siloa's brook that flowed
Fast by the oracle of God, I thence
Invoke thy aid to my adventurous song,
That with no middle flight intends to soar
Above the Aonian mount, while it pursues   15
Things unattempted yet in prose or rhyme.
And chiefly Thou, O Spirit, that dost prefer
Before all temples the upright heart and pure,
Instruct me, for Thou know'st; Thou from the first
Wast present, and, with mighty wings outspread,   20
Dove-like sat'st brooding on the vast Abyss,
And mad'st it pregnant: what in me is dark
Illumine, what is low raise and support;
That, to the highth of this great argument,
I may assert Eternal Providence,   25
And justify the ways of God to men.
    Say first—for Heaven hides nothing from thy view,
Nor the deep tract of Hell—say first what cause

---

4. *Man:* i.e., Christ. 6-11. Milton Christianizes the epic Muse—invoking the
power which spoke to Moses from the burning bush on Horeb, gave him
the Ten Commandments on Sinai, inspired the account of the Creation
(which is in the part of the Old Testament traditionally ascribed to Moses)
and dwelt in the Temple on Mt. Sion above the brook Siloam. 14. *no . . .*
flight: i.e., Milton's poem is to be in the "high" or epic style. 15. *the . . .*
mount: Helicon, home of the pagan Muses and thus the inspirer of pagan
epics, which Milton's Christian epic is to surpass. 17. *Spirit:* the Holy Spirit.
21. *Abyss:* Chaos.

Moved our grand Parents, in that happy state,
Favoured of Heaven so highly, to fall off   30
From their Creator, and transgress his will
For one restraint, lords of the World besides.
Who first seduced them to that foul revolt?
The infernal Serpent; he it was whose guile,
Stirred up with envy and revenge, deceived   35
The mother of mankind, what time his pride
Had cast him out from Heaven, with all his host
Of rebel Angels, by whose aid, aspiring
To set himself in glory above his peers,
He trusted to have equalled the Most High,   40
If he opposed, and, with ambitious aim
Against the throne and monarchy of God,
Raised impious war in Heaven and battle proud,
With vain attempt. Him the Almighty Power
Hurled headlong flaming from the ethereal sky,   45
With hideous ruin and combustion down
To bottomless perdition, there to dwell
In adamantine chains and penal fire,
Who durst defy the Omnipotent to arms.
    Nine times the space that measures day and night   50
To mortal men, he with his horrid crew
Lay vanquished, rolling in the fiery gulf
Confounded though immortal. But his doom
Reserved him to more wrath; for now the thought
Both of lost happiness and lasting pain   55
Torments him: round he throws his baleful eyes,
That witnessed huge affliction and dismay,
Mixed with obdurate pride and steadfast hate.
At once, as far as Angel's ken, he views
The dismal situation waste and wild.   60
A dungeon horrible, on all sides round,
As one great furnace flamed; yet from those flames
No light, but rather darkness visible
Served only to discover sights of woe,
Regions of sorrow, doleful shades, where peace   65
And rest can never dwell, hope never comes

---

36. *what time:* after. 56. *baleful:* full of evil. 57. *witnessed:* bore witness to.
59. *as . . . ken:* as far as angels' vision extends. 66-7. *hope . . . all:* cf.
Dante's "All hope abandon, ye who enter here" (*Inferno* III, 9).

That comes to all; but torture without end
Still urges, and a fiery deluge, fed
With ever-burning sulphur unconsumed.
Such place Eternal Justice had prepared   70
For those rebellious, here their prison ordained
In utter darkness, and their portion set,
As far removed from God and light of Heaven
As from the centre thrice to the utmost pole.
Oh how unlike the place from whence they fell!   75
There the companions of his fall, o'erwhelmed
With floods and whirlwinds of tempestuous fire,
He soon discerns; and, weltering by his side,
One next himself in power, and next in crime,
Long after known in Palestine, and named   80
Beëlzebub. To whom the Arch-Enemy,
And thence in Heaven called Satan, with bold words
Breaking the horrid silence, thus began:
   "If thou beest he—but oh how fallen! how changed
From him! who in the happy realms of light   85
Clothed with transcendent brightness didst outshine
Myriads though bright—if he whom mutual league,
United thoughts and counsels, equal hope
And hazard in the glorious enterprise,
Joined with me once, now misery hath joined   90
In equal ruin; into what pit thou seest
From what highth fallen: so much the stronger proved
He with his thunder: and till then who knew
The force of those dire arms? Yet not for those,
Nor what the potent Victor in his rage   95
Can else inflict, do I repent, or change,
Though changed in outward lustre, that fixed mind,
And high disdain from sense of injured merit,
That with the Mightiest raised me to contend,
And to the fierce contention brought along   100
Innumerable force of Spirits armed,
That durst dislike his reign, and, me preferring,
His utmost power with adverse power opposed

---

72. *utter:* outer. 74. *centre:* earth. 84 ff. *If . . . arms:* The introductory
conditional clause extends to *ruin* in 91; the rest of the sentence is not
logically related to this clause: Satan keeps breaking off to try to account
for the faded appearance of Beëlzebub and the unexpected defeat. 87. *if he:*
if you are he. 90. *now:* and now.

In dubious battle on the plains of Heaven,
And shook his throne. What though the field be lost?   105
All is not lost—the unconquerable will,
And study of revenge, immortal hate,
And courage never to submit or yield:
And what is else not to be overcome.
That glory never shall his wrath or might   110
Extort from me. To bow and sue for grace
With suppliant knee, and deify his power
Who, from the terror of this arm, so late
Doubted his empire—that were low indeed;
That were an ignominy and shame beneath   115
This downfall; since, by fate, the strength of Gods,
And this empyreal substance, cannot fail;
Since, through experience of this great event,
In arms not worse, in foresight much advanced,
We may with more successful hope resolve   120
To wage by force or guile eternal war,
Irreconcilable to our grand Foe,
Who now triúmphs, and in the excess of joy
Sole reigning holds the tyranny of Heaven."
    So spake the apostate Angel, though in pain,   125
Vaunting aloud, but racked with deep despair;
And him thus answered soon his bold compeer:
    "O Prince, O Chief of many thronèd Powers
That led the embattled Seraphim to war
Under thy conduct, and, in dreadful deeds   130
Fearless, endangered Heaven's perpetual King,
And put to proof his high supremacy,
Whether upheld by strength, or chance, or fate!
Too well I see and rue the dire event
That, with sad overthrow and foul defeat,   135
Hath lost us Heaven, and all this mighty host
In horrible destruction laid thus low,
As far as Gods and Heavenly Essences
Can perish: for the mind and spirit remains
Invincible, and vigour soon returns,   140

---

110. *That glory:* i.e., submission. 114. *Doubted:* feared for. 116. *fate:* Satan
often evades the facts of his situation by imagining powers like "fate" or
"chance" to which even God is subject. 124. *tyranny:* Tyranny is rule over
one's *equals.* It is a sign of Satan's sin that he does not recognize God to
be his and the other angels' superior and hence rightfully their ruler. 129.
Seraphim: Hebrew plural of *Seraph.*

Though all our glory extinct, and happy state
Here swallowed up in endless misery.
But what if He our Conqueror (whom I now
Of force believe almighty, since no less
Than such could have o'erpowered such force as ours)   145
Have left us this our spirit and strength entire,
Strongly to suffer and support our pains,
That we may so suffice his vengeful ire,
Or do him mightier service as his thralls
By right of war, whate'er his business be,   150
Here in the heart of Hell to work in fire,
Or do his errands in the gloomy Deep?
What can it then avail though yet we feel
Strength undiminished, or eternal being
To undergo eternal punishment?"   155
     Whereto with speedy words the Arch-Fiend replied:
"Fallen Cherub, to be weak is miserable,
Doing or suffering: but of this be sure—
To do aught good never will be our task,
But ever to do ill our sole delight,   160
As being the contrary to His high will
Whom we resist. If then his providence
Out of our evil seek to bring forth good,
Our labour must be to pervert that end,
And out of good still to find means of evil;   165
Which ofttimes may succeed so as perhaps
Shall grieve him, if I fail not, and disturb
His inmost counsels from their destined aim.
But see! the angry Victor hath recalled
His minsters of vengeance and pursuit   170
Back to the gates of Heaven: the sulphurous hail,
Shot after us in storm, o'erblown hath laid
The fiery surge that from the precipice
Of Heaven received us falling; and the thunder,
Winged with red lightning and impetuous rage,   175
Perhaps hath spent his shafts, and ceases now
To bellow through the vast and boundless Deep.
Let us not slip the occasion, whether scorn
Or satiate fury yield it from our Foe.
Seest thou yon dreary plain, forlorn and wild,   180

---

141. *extinct:* be extinct. 148-50. *That . . . war:* that we may satisfy his desire for vengeance, or serve him as slave labor. 158. *Doing or suffering:* whether one is active or passive. 178. *slip:* let slip.

The seat of desolation, void of light,
Save what the glimmering of these livid flames
Casts pale and dreadful? Thither let us tend
From off the tossing of these fiery waves;
There rest, if any rest can harbour there;   185
And, reassembling our afflicted powers,
Consult how we may henceforth most offend
Our enemy, our own loss how repair,
How overcome this dire calamity,
What reinforcement we may gain from hope,   190
If not what resolution from despair."
    Thus Satan, talking to his nearest mate,
With head uplift above the wave, and eyes
That sparkling blazed; his other parts besides
Prone on the flood, extended long and large,   195
Lay floating many a rood, in bulk as huge
As whom the fables name of monstrous size,
Titanian or Earth-born, that warred on Jove,
Briareos or Typhon, whom the den
By ancient Tarsus held, or that sea-beast   200
Leviathan, which God of all his works
Created hugest that swim the ocean-stream.
Him, haply slumbering on the Norway foam,
The pilot of some small night-foundered skiff,
Deeming some island, oft, as seamen tell,   205
With fixèd anchor in his scaly rind,
Moors by his side under the lee, while night
Invests the sea, and wishèd morn delays.
So stretched out huge in length the Arch-Fiend lay,
Chained on the burning lake; nor ever thence   210
Had risen, or heaved his head, but that the will
And high permission of all-ruling Heaven
Left him at large to his own dark designs,
That with reiterated crimes he might
Heap on himself damnation, while he sought   215
Evil to others, and enraged might see

---

186. *powers:* armies. 196-8. *as . . . Jove:* Satan is compared here to the
Titans not simply because they too were gigantic, but because they also
warred against Heaven. These pagan stories were thought in Milton's day
to be corrupt versions of those in Scripture. 200 ff. The whale, owing to its
identification with the mysterious Leviathan of the Old Testament, became
a traditional emblem of Satan or evil (cf. Melville's *Moby Dick*). The
simile stresses the ease with which evil can be mistaken for something safe
and sheltering—like the island. 208. *invests:* covers.

How all his malice served but to bring forth
Infinite goodness, grace, and mercy, shewn
On Man by him seduced, but on himself
Treble confusion, wrath, and vengeance poured.   220
    Forthwith upright he rears from off the pool
His mighty stature; on each hand the flames
Driven backward slope their pointing spires, and, rolled
In billows, leave i' the midst a horrid vale.
Then with expanded wings he steers his flight   225
Aloft, incumbent on the dusky air,
That felt unusual weight; till on dry land
He lights—if it were land that ever burned
With solid, as the lake with liquid fire,
And such appeared in hue as when the force   230
Of subterranean wind transports a hill
Torn from Pelorus, or the shattered side
Of thundering Ætna, whose combustible
And fueled entrails, thence conceiving fire,
Sublimed with mineral fury, aid the winds,   235
And leave a singèd bottom all involved
With stench and smoke. Such resting found the sole
Of unblest feet. Him followed his next mate;
Both glorying to have scaped the Stygian flood
As gods, and by their own recovered strength,   240
Not by the sufferance of supernal power.
    "Is this the region, this the soil, the clime,"
Said then the lost Archangel, "this the seat
That we must change for Heaven, this mournful gloom
For that celestial light? Be it so, since He   245
Who now is sovran can dispose and bid
What shall be right: farthest from Him is best,
Whom reason hath equaled, force hath made supreme
Above his equals. Farewell, happy fields,
Where joy for ever dwells! Hail, horrors! hail,   250
Infernal World! and thou, profoundest Hell,
Receive thy new possessor—one who brings
A mind not to be changed by place or time.

232. *Pelorus:* Sicilian promontory near Aetna. 235. *sublimed:* transformed
from solids to gases. 245-7. *He . . . right:* Satan characteristically sees
might as maker of right. 248-9. *Whom . . . Above:* i.e., who in his reason
equals, in his force surpasses. Again Satan tries to evade the recognition
that God is better (not merely stronger).

The mind is its own place, and in itself
Can make a Heaven of Hell, a Hell of Heaven.   255
What matter where, if I be still the same,
And what I should be, all but less than he
Whom thunder hath made greater? Here at least
We shall be free; the Almighty hath not built
Here for his envy, will not drive us hence: 260
Here we may reign secure; and, in my choice,
To reign is worth ambition, though in Hell:
Better to reign in Hell than serve in Heaven.
But wherefore let we then our faithful friends,
The associates and co-partners of our loss,   265
Lie thus astonished on the oblivious pool,
And call them not to share with us their part
In this unhappy mansion, or once more
With rallied arms to try what may be yet
Regained in Heaven, or what more lost in Hell?"   270
    So Satan spake; and him Beëlzebub
Thus answered: "Leader of those armies bright
Which, but the Omnipotent, none could have foiled!
If once they hear that voice, their liveliest pledge
Of hope in fears and dangers—heard so oft   275
In worst extremes, and on the perilous edge
Of battle, when it raged, in all assaults
Their surest signal—they will soon resume
New courage and revive, though now they lie
Groveling and prostrate on yon lake of fire,   280
As we erstwhile, astounded and amazed;
No wonder, fallen such a pernicious highth!"
    He scarce had ceased when the superior Fiend
Was moving toward the shore; his ponderous shield,
Ethereal temper, massy, large, and round,   285
Behind him cast; the broad circumference
Hung on his shoulders like the moon, whose orb
Through optic glass the Tuscan artist views
At evening, from the top of Fesolè,
'Or in Valdarno, to descry new lands,   290

---

266. *astonished . . . pool:* stunned on the pool that causes forgetfulness.
285. *Ethereal temper:* alluding to the shield's heavenly substance and manu-
facture. 288-91. A reference to Galileo, whom Milton had visited at Fiesole
(*Fesolè*) overlooking the valley of the Arno (*Valdarno*) during his Italian
journey in 1638.

Rivers, or mountains, in her spotty globe.
His spear—to equal which the tallest pine
Hewn on Norwegian hills, to be the mast
Of some great ammiral, were but a wand—
He walked with, to support uneasy steps   295
Over the burning marl, not like those steps
On Heaven's azure; and the torrid clime
Smote on him sore besides, vaulted with fire.
Nathless he so endured, till on the beach
Of that inflamèd sea he stood, and called   300
His legions—Angel Forms, who lay entranced
Thick as autumnal leaves that strow the brooks
In Vallombrosa, where the Etrurian shades
High over-arched embower; or scattered sedge
Afloat, when with fierce winds Orion armed   305
Hath vexed the Red-Sea coast, whose waves o'erthrew
Busiris and his Memphian chivalry,
While with perfidious hatred they pursued
The sojourners of Goshen, who beheld
From the safe shore their floating carcasses   310
And broken chariot-wheels: so thick bestrown,
Abject and lost, lay these, covering the flood,
Under amazement of their hideous change.
He called so loud that all the hollow deep
Of Hell resounded: "Princes, Potentates,   315
Warriors, the Flower of Heaven—once yours; now lost,
If such astonishment as this can seize
Eternal Spirits! Or have ye chosen this place
After the toil of battle to repose
Your wearied virtue, for the ease you find   320
To slumber here, as in the vales of Heaven?
Or in this abject posture have ye sworn
To adore the Conqueror, who now beholds
Cherub and Seraph rolling in the flood
With scattered arms and ensigns, till anon   325

---

294. *ammiral:* chief ship of the fleet. 296. *marl:* clay. 299. *Nathless:* never-theless. 302-4. *Thick . . . embower:* a memory of Milton's autumn journey from Florence through the valley of Vallombrosa (in English, "Shady Vale"). 303. *shades:* forests. 305-6. *when . . . coast:* i.e., when the constellation Orion brings autumn storms. 307-11. *Busiris* is wrongly named as the Pharaoh who pursued the Hebrews (*sojourners of Goshen*) with all his Egyptian cavalry (*Memphian chivalry*) and was drowned. 316. *once . . . lost:* The phrases modify *Heaven.*

His swift pursuers from Heaven-gates discern
The advantage, and, descending, tread us down
Thus drooping, or with linkèd thunderbolts
Transfix us to the bottom of this gulf?—
Awake, arise, or be for ever fallen!"   330
    They heard, and were abashed, and up they sprung
Upon the wing, as when men wont to watch,
On duty sleeping found by whom they dread,
Rouse and bestir themselves ere well awake.
Nor did they not perceive the evil plight   335
In which they were, or the fierce pains not feel;
Yet to their General's voice they soon obeyed
Innumerable. As when the potent rod
Of Amram's son, in Egypt's evil day
Waved round the coast, up-called a pitchy cloud   340
Of locusts, warping on the eastern wind,
That o'er the realm of impious Pharaoh hung
Like Night, and darkened all the land of Nile;
So numberless were those bad Angels seen
Hovering on wing under the cope of Hell,   345
'Twixt upper, nether, and surrounding fires;
Till, as a signal given, the uplifted spear
Of their great Sultan waving to direct
Their course, in even balance down they light
On the firm brimstone, and fill all the plain: 350
A multitude like which the populous North
Poured never from her frozen loins to pass
Rhene or the Danaw, when her barbarous sons
Came like a deluge on the South, and spread
Beneath Gibraltar to the Libyan sands.   355
Forthwith, from every squadron and each band,
The heads and leaders thither haste where stood
Their great Commander—godlike shapes and forms
Excelling human; princely Dignities;
And Powers that erst in Heaven sat on thrones,   360
Though of their names in Heavenly records now
Be no memorial, blotted out and rased
By their rebellion from the Books of Life.

---

333. *whom:* one whom. 339. *Amram's son:* Moses, who called up the
plague of locusts. 341. *warping:* flying with a curving flight. 345. *cope:*
vault. 351-5. A comparison of the fallen angels to the barbarian hordes
which invaded Europe in the fifth to seventh centuries.

Nor had they yet among the sons of Eve
Got them new names, till, wandering o'er the earth,   365
Through God's high sufferance for the trial of man,
By falsities and lies the greatest part
Of mankind they corrupted to forsake
God their Creator, and the invisible
Glory of Him that made them, to transform   370
Oft to the image of a brute, adorned
With gay religions full of pomp and gold,
And devils to adore for deities:
Then were they known to men by various names,
And various idols through the Heathen World.   375
    Say, Muse, their names then known, who first, who last,
Roused from the slumber on that fiery couch,
At their great Emperor's call, as next in worth
Came singly where he stood on the bare strand,
While the promiscuous crowd stood yet aloof.   380
    The chief were those who, from the pit of Hell
Roaming to seek their prey on Earth, durst fix
Their seats, long after, next the seat of God,
Their altars by His altar, gods adored
Among the nations round, and durst abide   385
Jehovah thundering out of Sion, throned
Between the Cherubim; yea, often placed
Within His sanctuary itself their shrines,
Abominations; and with cursèd things
His holy rites and solemn feasts profaned,   390
And with their darkness durst affront His light.
First, *Moloch,* horrid king, besmeared with blood
Of human sacrifice, and parents' tears;
Though, for the noise of drums and timbrels loud,
Their children's cries unheard that passed through fire   395
To his grim idol. Him the Ammonite

364-75. I.e., the fallen angels are the idols and false gods of the Old Testament and Greek myth. In 392 ff. Milton invokes around them the atmosphere of "abomination" in which they are viewed in Old Testament history. 366. *sufferance:* permission. 380. *promiscuous:* miscellaneous. 387. *Between . . . Cherubim:* Psalm 80:1 addresses God as "Thou that dwellest between the Cherubim." 394. *for:* because of. 395. *unheard:* were unheard. 396 ff. Most of the places named in the next 100 lines are sites where Jehovah helped the Israelites overcome their enemies, and / or they repudiated him for false gods.

Worshiped in Rabba and her watery plain,
In Argob and in Basan, to the stream
Of utmost Arnon. Nor content with such
Audacious neighbourhood, the wisest heart   400
Of Solomon he led by fraud to build
His temple right against the temple of God
On that opprobrious hill, and made his grove
The pleasant valley of Hinnom, Tophet thence
And black Gehenna called, the type of Hell.   405
Next *Chemos,* the obscene dread of Moab's sons,
From Aroar to Nebo and the wild
Of southmost Abarim; in Hesebon
And Horonaim, Seon's realm, beyond
The flowery dale of Sibma clad with vines,   410
And Elealè to the Asphaltic Pool:
Peor his other name, when he enticed
Israel in Sittim, on their march from Nile,
To do him wanton rites, which cost them woe.
Yet thence his lustful orgies he enlarged   415
Even to that hill of scandal, by the grove
Of Moloch homicide, lust hard by hate,
Till good Josiah drove them thence to Hell.
With these came they who, from the bordering flood
Of old Euphrates to the brook that parts   420
Egypt from Syrian ground, had general names
Of *Baalim* and *Ashtaroth*—those male,
These feminine. For Spirits, when they please,
Can either sex assume, or both; so soft
And uncompounded is their essence pure,   425

397-9. *Rabba* was the Ammonites' capital city; *Argob* and *Basan* were districts in their territory, which was bounded by the stream *Arnon.* 400-2. *the . . . temple:* Solomon built "an high place . . . for Moloch, the abomination of . . . Ammon." (1 Kings 11:7). 403. *opprobrious hill:* shameful hill—the Mount of Olives: cf. 416 and 443 below. 404-5. *Gehenna* is the Greek name for the valley of Hinnom (a part of which was called Tophet), associated by Jeremiah with human sacrifice (7:30-2). 405. *type:* prefiguration. 406. *Chemos:* god of the Moabites, known also as Baal-Peor (412). 407-11. *Aroar, Hesebon,* and *Elealè* are towns in Moab; *Nebo* is a mountain and *Abarim* a mountain range; *Seon* is a vanquished Amorite king; and the *Asphaltic Pool* is the Dead Sea. 412. *Peor:* i.e., Baal-Peor. See the *Nativity Ode,* 197. 412-14. *when . . . woe:* when certain Israelites began to worship Baal-Peor, Moses had them executed (Numbers, 25:1-5). 417. *homicide:* referring to human sacrifices in his honor. 418. *Josiah:* the reforming king of Judah (cf. 2 Kings 22). 422. *Baalim, Ashtaroth:* plural forms of Baal and Astoreth (438).

Not tied or manacled with joint or limb,
Nor founded on the brittle strength of bones,
Like cumbrous flesh; but, in what shape they choose,
Dilated or condensed, bright or obscure,
Can execute their aery purposes,   430
And works of love or enmity fulfil.
For those the race of Israel oft forsook
Their Living Strength, and unfrequented left
His righteous altar, bowing lowly down
To bestial gods; for which their heads, as low   435
Bowed down in battle, sunk before the spear
Of despicable foes. With these in troop
Came *Astoreth,* whom the Phoenicians called
Astarte, queen of heaven, with crescent horns;
To whose bright image nightly by the moon   440
Sidonian virgins paid their vows and songs;
In Sion also not unsung, where stood
Her temple on the offensive mountain, built
By that uxorious king whose heart, though large,
Beguiled by fair idolatresses, fell   445
To idols foul. *Thammuz* came next behind,
Whose annual wound in Lebanon allured
The Syrian damsels to lament his fate   *how pleasant*
In amorous ditties all a summer's day, ➤ *vice is*
While smooth Adonis from his native rock   450
Ran purple to the sea, supposed with blood
Of Thammuz yearly wounded: the love-tale
Infected Sion's daughters with like heat,
Whose wanton passions in the sacred porch
Ezekiel saw, when, by the vision led,   455
His eye surveyed the dark idolatries
Of alienated Judah. Next came one
Who mourned in earnest, when the captive ark
Maimed his brute image, head and hands lopt off,
In his own temple, on the grunsel-edge,   460

---

438. *Ashtoreth:* Astarte, Phoenician Aphrodite and moon-goddess. 444. *king:* Solomon. 446. *Thammuz:* Syrian counterpart of Adonis, whose *annual wound* and revival represent the death and rebirth of the year. A river in Lebanon is also named Adonis (450). 454-5. Cf. Ezekiel 8: 13-14. 457-60. *one . . . edge:* When the Philistines lodged the captive Hebrews' ark of God in the temple of their idol Dagon, "on the morrow morning, behold, Dagon was fallen upon his face to the ground before the ark of the Lord; and the head of Dagon and both the palms of his hands were cut off upon the threshold" (1 Samuel 5:4), i.e., *on the grunsel* (460).

Where he fell flat and shamed his worshipers:
Dagon his name, sea-monster, upward man
And downward fish; yet had his temple high
Reared in Azotus, dreaded through the coast
Of Palestine, in Gath and Ascalon,   465
And Accaron and Gaza's frontier bounds.
Him followed *Rimmon,* whose delightful seat
Was fair Damascus, on the fertile banks
Of Abbana and Pharphar, lucid streams.
He also against the house of God was bold: 470
A leper once he lost, and gained a king—
Ahaz, his sottish conqueror, whom he drew
God's altar to disparage and displace
For one of Syrian mode, whereon to burn
His odious offerings, and adore the gods   475
Whom he had vanquished. After these appeared
A crew who, under names of old renown—
Osiris, Isis, Orus, and their train—
With monstrous shapes and sorceries abused
Fanatic Egypt and her priests to seek   480
Their wandering gods disguised in brutish forms
Rather than human. Nor did Israel scape
The infection, when their borrowed gold composed
The calf in Oreb; and the rebel king
Doubled that sin in Bethel and in Dan,   485
Likening his Maker to the grazèd ox—
Jehovah, who, in one night, when he passed
From Egypt marching, equaled with one stroke
Both her first-born and all her bleating gods.
Belial came last, than whom a Spirit more lewd   490

464-6. The five names belong to Philistine cities. 471. Referring to the
Syrian general Naaman, who was converted to the worship of Jehovah on
being cured of his leprosy by Elisha (2 Kings 5); and the Hebrew king
Ahaz, who, having overcome Rimmon's *delightful seat,* was converted to
his worship (2 Kings 16). 477-82. *A . . . human:* Egyptian animal-gods:
cf. *Nativity Ode,* 211 ff. 482-4. *Nor . . . Oreb:* Exodus 32:4. 484-89. *and
. . . gods:* Jeroboam, taking control of the northern half of the Hebrew
kingdom after Solomon's death, feared his people would become disaffected
if they went to Jerusalem (capital of the southern half of the kingdom) to
worship; and so he set up golden calves at Bethel and Dan in the north,
telling the people it was these gods "which brought thee up out of Egypt"
(1 Kings 12:28). With these gods, in 487-9, Milton contrasts the God
who *did* bring them out of Egypt. 488. *equalled:* (1) was equal to, (2)
made equal (in their deaths). 490. *Belial:* the Hebrew word for worth-
lessness.

Fell not from Heaven, or more gross to love
Vice for itself. To him no temple stood
Or altar smoked; yet who more oft than he
In temples and at altars, when the priest
Turns atheist, as did Eli's sons, who filled   495
With lust and violence the house of God?
In courts and palaces he also reigns,
And in luxurious cities, where the noise
Of riot ascends above their loftiest towers,
And injury and outrage; and, when night   500
Darkens the streets, then wander forth the sons
Of Belial, flown with insolence and wine.
Witness the streets of Sodom, and that night
In Gibeah, when the hospitable door
Exposed a matron, to avoid worse rape.   505
  These were the prime in order and in might:
The rest were long to tell; though far renowned
The Ionian gods—of Javan's issue held
Gods, yet confessed later than Heaven and Earth,
Their boasted parents;—*Titan,* Heaven's first-born,   510
With his enormous brood, and birthright seized
By younger *Saturn:* he from mightier Jove,
His own and Rhea's son, like measure found;
So *Jove* usurping reigned. These, first in Crete
And Ida known, thence on the snowy top   515
Of cold Olympus ruled the middle air,
Their highest heaven; or on the Delphian cliff,
Or in Dodona, and through all the bounds
Of Doric land; or who with Saturn old
Fled over Adria to the Hesperian fields,   520
And o'er the Celtic roamed the utmost Isles.

494-6. *when . . . God:* The sons of the priest Eli "knew not the Lord," took
by force part of the temple offerings, and "lay with the women who assembled at the door" (1 Samuel 2:12-25). 501-2. *sons of Belial:* the name
given to Eli's sons (1 Samuel 2:12) and here to all licentious persons. 503-5.
witness . . . rape: Cf. Genesis 19:1-11; Judges 19:22-30: two instances when
the privacy of a home was violated by "sons of Belial." 508. *Javan's issue:*
i.e., the Greeks. 509. *Heaven and Earth:* supposed to be the parents of the
first gods, the Titans. 510-14. *Titan . . . reigned:* Titan, first king of the
gods, was overthrown by his younger brother Saturn, and Saturn by his
son, Zeus or Jove. 514-21. These lines describe the dissemination of the worship of the Greek gods: from Crete through the mainland of Greece and
then across the Adriatic to Italy (*Hesperian fields*) and over France (*Celtic*
fields) to Britain (*utmost Isles*).

All these and more came flocking; but with looks
Downcast and damp; yet such wherein appeared
Obscure some glimpse of joy to have found their Chief
Not in despair, to have found themselves not lost   525
In loss itself; which on his countenance cast
Like doubtful hue. But he, his wonted pride
Soon recollecting, with high words, that bore
Semblance of worth, not substance, gently raised
Their fainting courage, and dispelled their fears: 530
Then straight commands that, at the warlike sound
Of trumpets loud and clarions, be upreared
His mighty standard. That proud honour claimed
Azazel as his right, a Cherub tall:
Who forthwith from the glittering staff unfurled   535
The imperial ensign; which, full high advanced,
Shone like a meteor streaming to the wind,
With gems and golden lustre rich emblazed,
Seraphic arms and trophies; all the while
Sonorous metal blowing martial sounds: 540
At which the universal host up-sent
A shout that tore Hell's concave, and beyond
Frighted the reign of Chaos and old Night.
All in a moment through the gloom were seen
Ten thousand banners rise into the air,   545
With orient colours waving: with them rose
A forest huge of spears; and thronging helms
Appeared, and serried shields in thick array
Of depth immeasurable. Anon they move
In perfect phalanx to the Dorian mood   550
Of flutes and soft recorders—such as raised
To highth of noblest temper heroes old
Arming to battle, and instead of rage
Deliberate valour breathed, firm, and unmoved
With dread of death to flight or foul retreat;   555
Nor wanting power to mitigate and swage
With solemn touches troubled thoughts, and chase
Anguish and doubt and fear and sorrow and pain
From mortal or immortal minds. Thus they,
Breathing united force with fixèd thought,   560

---

523. *such wherein:* i.e., looks in which. 534. *Azazel:* an occult name for the
element earth. 548. *serried:* crowded. 550. *Dorian mood:* Cf. *Lycidas,* 189.
556. *swage:* assuage.

Moved on in silence to soft pipes that charmed
Their painful steps o'er the burnt soil. And now
Advanced in view they stand—a horrid front
Of dreadful length and dazzling arms, in guise
Of warriors old, with ordered spear and shield,   565
Awaiting what command their mighty Chief
Had to impose. He through the armèd files
Darts his experienced eye, and soon traverse
The whole battalion views—their order due,
Their visages and stature as of gods;   570
Their number last he sums. And now his heart
Distends with pride, and, hardening in his strength,
Glories: for never, since created Man,
Met such embodied force as, named with these,
Could merit more than that small infantry   575
Warred on by cranes—though all the giant brood
Of Phlegra with the heroic race were joined
That fought at Thebes and Ilium, on each side
Mixed with auxiliar gods; and what resounds
In fable or romance of Uther's son,   580
Begirt with British and Armoric knights;
And all who since, baptized or infidel,
Jousted in Aspramont, or Montalban,
Damasco, or Marocco, or Trebisond,
Or whom Biserta sent from Afric shore   585
When Charlemain with all his peerage fell
By Fontarabbia. Thus far these beyond
Compare of mortal prowess, yet observed
Their dread Commander. He, above the rest
In shape and gesture proudly eminent,   590
Stood like a tower. His form had yet not lost
All her original brightness, nor appeared
Less than Archangel ruined, and the excess
Of glory obscured: as when the sun new-risen

---

565. *warriors old:* warriors of antiquity. 568. *traverse:* crosswise. 574.
named: compared. 575. *that . . . infantry:* the Pygmies, said by Homer
(*Iliad,* III 1-5) to be the victims of migrating cranes; *infantry* puns on "infant." 576-7. *giant . . . Phlegra:* the Titans. 578. *That . . . Ilium:* i.e.,
the heroes of the expedition of the Seven against Thebes, and of the Trojan
War. 580-1. *Uther's . . . knights:* King Arthur and both his British and
his Breton knights. 583-5. *Aspramont . . . Biserta:* The names refer to battles, sieges, and jousts in Italian verse romances. 587. *Fontarabbia:* scene of
the death of Roland (in the *Song of Roland*).

Looks through the horizontal misty air   595
Shorn of his beams, or, from behind the moon,
In dim eclipse, disastrous twilight sheds
On half the nations, and with fear of change
Perplexes monarchs. Darkened so, yet shone
Above them all the Archangel: but his face   600
Deep scars of thunder had intrenched, and care
Sat on his faded cheek, but under brows
Of dauntless courage, and considerate pride
Waiting revenge. Cruel his eye, but cast
Signs of remorse and passion, to behold   605
The fellows of his crime, the followers rather
(Far other once beheld in bliss), condemned
For ever now to have their lot in pain—
Millions of Spirits for his fault amerced
Of Heaven, and from eternal splendours flung   610
For his revolt—yet faithful how they stood,
Their glory withered; as, when heaven's fire
Hath scathed the forest oaks or mountain pines,
With singèd top their stately growth, though bare,
Stands on the blasted heath. He now prepared   615
To speak; whereat their doubled ranks they bend
From wing to wing, and half enclose him round
With all his peers: Attention held them mute.
Thrice he assayed, and thrice, in spite of scorn,
Tears, such as Angels weep, burst forth: at last   620
Words interwove with sighs found out their way:
   "O myriads of immortal Spirits! O Powers
Matchless, but with the Almighty!—and that strife
Was not inglorious, though the event was dire,
As this place testifies, and this dire change,   625
Hateful to utter. But what power of mind,
Foreseeing or presaging, from the depth
Of knowledge past or present, could have feared
How such united force of gods, how such
As stood like these, could ever know repulse?   630
For who can yet believe, though after loss,
That all these puissant legions, whose exíle
Hath emptied Heaven, shall fail to re-ascend,
Self-raised, and re-possess their native seat?

597. *disastrous . . . monarchs:* i.e., because a portent of evil. 603. *con-siderate:* considered, deliberate. 609. *amerced:* deprived. 623. *but:* except.

For me, be witness all the host of Heaven,   635
If counsels different, or danger shunned
By me, have lost our hopes. But he who reigns
Monarch in Heaven till then as one secure
Sat on his throne, upheld by old repute,
Consent or custom, and his regal state   640
Put forth at full, but still his strength concealed—
Which tempted our attempt, and wrought our fall.
Henceforth his might we know, and know our own,
So as not either to provoke, or dread
New war provoked: our better part remains   645
To work in close design, by fraud or guile,
What force effected not; that he no less
At length from us may find, Who overcomes
By force hath overcome but half his foe.
Space may produce new Worlds; whereof so rife   650
There went a fame in Heaven that He ere long
Intended to create, and therein plant
A generation whom his choice regard
Should favour equal to the Sons of Heaven.
Thither, if but to pry, shall be perhaps   655
Our first eruption—thither, or elsewhere;
For this infernal pit shall never hold
Celestial Spirits in bondage, nor the Abyss
Long under darkness cover. But these thoughts
Full counsel must mature. Peace is despaired;   660
For who can think submission? War, then, war
Open or understood, must be resolved."
      He spake; and, to confirm his words, out-flew
Millions of flaming swords, drawn from the thighs
Of mighty Cherubim; the sudden blaze   665
Far round illumined Hell. Highly they raged
Against the Highest, and fierce with graspèd arms
Clashed on their sounding shields the din of war,
Hurling defiance toward the vault of Heaven.
      There stood a hill not far, whose grisly top   670
Belched fire and rolling smoke; the rest entire
Shone with a glossy scurf—undoubted sign
That in his womb was hid metallic ore,
The work of sulphur. Thither, winged with speed,

---

645. *better part:* best course. 650. *rife:* i.e., current, common. 651. *fame:*
rumor. 673-4. All metals were believed to be forms of *sulphur*.

A numerous brígad hastened: as when bands   675
Of píoners with spade and pickaxe armed
Forerun the royal camp, to trench a field,
Or cast a rampart. Mammon led them on—
Mammon, the least erected Spirit that fell
From Heaven; for even in Heaven his looks and thoughts   680
Were always downward bent, admiring more
The riches of Heaven's pavement, trodden gold,
Than aught divine or holy else enjoyed
In vision beatific. By him first
Men also, and by his suggestion taught,   685
Ransacked the Centre, and with impious hands
Rifled the bowels of their mother Earth
For treasures better hid. Soon had his crew
Opened into the hill a spacious wound,
And digged out ribs of gold. Let none admire   690
That riches grow in Hell; that soil may best
Deserve the precious bane. And here let those
Who boast in mortal things, and wondering tell
Of Babel, and the works of Memphian kings,
Learn how their greatest monuments of fame,   695
And strength, and art, are easily outdone
By Spirits reprobate, and in an hour
What in an age they, with incessant toil
And hands innumerable, scarce perform.
Nigh on the plain, in many cells prepared,   700
That underneath had veins of liquid fire
Sluiced from the lake, a second multitude
With wondrous art founded the massy ore,
Severing each kind, and scummed the bullion-dross.
A third as soon had formed within the ground   705
A various mould, and from the boiling cells
By strange conveyance filled each hollow nook;
As in an organ, from one blast of wind,
To many a row of pipes the sound-board breathes.
Anon out of the earth a fabric huge   710
Rose like an exhalation, with the sound
Of dulcet symphonies and voices sweet—
Built like a temple, where pilasters round

---

676. *píoners:* soldiers detailed to construction and excavation duty. 684.
beatific: blessed. 692. *bane:* curse. 694. I.e., Babylon and Memphis, famous
for their buildings. 703. *founded:* melted and poured.

Were set, and Doric pillars overlaid
With golden architrave; nor did there want   715
Cornice or frieze, with bossy sculptures graven:
The roof was fretted gold. Not Babylon
Nor great Alcairo such magnificence
Equaled in all their glories, to enshrine
Belus or Serapis their gods, or seat   720
Their kings, when Egypt with Assyria strove
In wealth and luxury. The ascending pile
Stood fixed her stately highth; and straight the doors,
Opening their brazen folds, discover, wide
Within, her ample spaces o'er the smooth   725
And level pavement: from the archèd roof,
Pendent by subtle magic, many a row
Of starry lamps and blazing cressets, fed
With naphtha and asphaltus, yielded light
As from a sky. The hasty multitude   730
Admiring entered; and the work some praise,
And some the architect. His hand was known
In Heaven by many a towered structure high,
Where sceptred Angels held their residence,
And sat as Princes, whom the supreme King   735
Exalted to such power, and gave to rule,
Each in his hierarchy, the Orders bright.
Nor was his name unheard or unadored
In ancient Greece; and in Ausonian land
Men called him Mulciber; and how he fell   740
From Heaven they fabled, thrown by angry Jove
Sheer o'er the crystal battlements: from morn
To noon he fell, from noon to dewy eve,
A summer's day, and with the setting sun
Dropt from the zenith, like a falling star,   745
On Lemnos, the Ægæan isle. Thus they relate,
Erring; for he with this rebellious rout
Fell long before; nor aught availed him now
To have built in Heaven high towers; nor did he scape
By all his engines, but was headlong sent,   750
With his industrious crew, to build in Hell.

---

716. *bossy:* projecting. 718. *Alcairo:* Cairo. 720. *Belus* is a variant form of
Baal; *Serapis,* a variant name for Osiris. 728. *cressets:* fire-pots. 737. The
angels were traditionally classified into nine ranks or *orders:* Seraphim,
Cherubim, Thrones, Dominions, Virtues, Powers, Principalities, Archangels,
Angels. 739. *Ausonian:* Italian. 740-51. Milton sees in the Greek story of
Mulciber's fall (Homer's Iliad, I 588-95) a reflection of the Christian story
of the fall of the rebel angels.

Meanwhile the wingèd Heralds, by command
Of sovran power, with awful ceremony
And trumpets' sound, throughout the host proclaim
A solemn council forthwith to be held   755
At Pandemonium, the high capital
Of Satan and his peers. Their summons called
From every band and squarèd regiment
By place or choice the worthiest: they anon
With hundreds and with thousands trooping came   760
Attended. All access was thronged; the gates
And porches wide, but chief the spacious hall
(Though like a covered field, where champions bold
Wont ride in armed, and at the Soldan's chair
Defied the best of Paynim chivalry   765
To mortal combat, or career with lance),
Thick swarmed, both on the ground and in the air,
Brushed with the hiss of rustling wings. As bees
In spring-time, when the Sun with Taurus rides,
Pour forth their populous youth about the hive   770
In clusters; they among fresh dews and flowers
Fly to and fro, or on the smoothèd plank,
The suburb of their straw-built citadel,
New rubbed with balm, expatiate, and confer
Their state-affairs: so thick the aery crowd   775
Swarmed and were straitened; till, the signal given,
Behold a wonder! They but now who seemed
In bigness to surpass Earth's giant sons,
Now less than smallest dwarfs, in narrow room
Throng numberless—like that pygmean race   780
Beyond the Indian mount; or faery elves,
Whose midnight revels, by a forest-side
Or fountain, some belated peasant sees,
Or dreams he sees, while overhead the Moon
Sits arbitress, and nearer to the Earth   785
Wheels her pale course: they, on their mirth and dance

---

756. *Pandemonium:* i.e., Milton's coinage from the Greek words for "all"
and "spirit." 758. *squared:* in square formation. 761. *All access:* every approach. 764-6. Referring to the Crusaders' tournaments with pagan
(*Paynim*) knights before the Sultan (*Soldan*). 764. *Wont:* used to. 769.
Taurus: the sign of the Bull in the Zodiac. 774. *expatiate:* walk about. A
simile of crowds and bees was almost an expected feature in epic, but
Milton here employs it to rationalize the transformation of the angels from
gigantic to Pygmean stature. 780-1. *that . . . mount:* The pigmies of 575,
reputed to dwell beyond the Himalayas.

Intent, with jocund music charm his ear;
At once with joy and fear his heart rebounds.
Thus incorporeal Spirits to smallest forms
Reduced their shapes immense, and were at large,   790
Though without number still, amidst the hall
Of that infernal court. But far within,
And in their own dimensions like themselves,
The great Seraphic Lords and Cherubim
In close recess and secret conclave sat,   795
A thousand demi-gods on golden seats,
Frequent and full. After short silence then,
And summons read, the great consult began.

THE END OF THE FIRST BOOK

❧

BOOK II

THE ARGUMENT

*The consultation begun, Satan debates whether another battle be to
be hazarded for the recovery of Heaven: some advise it, others dissuade. A third proposal is preferred, mentioned before by Satan—to
search the truth of that prophecy or tradition in Heaven concerning
another world, and another kind of creature, equal, or not much inferior, to themselves, about this time to be created. Their doubt who
shall be sent on this difficult search: Satan, their chief, undertakes
alone the voyage; is honoured and applauded. The council thus ended,
the rest betake them several ways and to several employments, as their
inclinations lead them, to entertain the time till Satan return. He passes
on his journey to Hell-gates; finds them shut, and who sat there to
guard them; by whom at length they are opened, and discover to him
the great gulf between Hell and Heaven. With what difficulty he
passes through, directed by Chaos, the Power of that place, to the sight
of this new World which he sought.*

Hɪɢʜ on a throne of royal state, which far
Outshone the wealth of Ormus and of Ind,

---

797. *frequent:* crowded.

    2. *Ormus:* trading centre on the Persian gulf, supposed in Milton's day to
be fabulously opulent.

Or where the gorgeous East with richest hand
Showers on her kings barbaric pearl and gold,
Satan exalted sat, by merit raised   5
To that bad eminence; and, from despair
Thus high uplifted beyond hope, aspires
Beyond thus high, insatiate to pursue
Vain war with Heaven; and, by success untaught,
His proud imaginations thus displayed: 10
    "Powers and Dominions, Deities of Heaven!—
For, since no deep within her gulf can hold
Immortal vigour, though oppressed and fallen,
I give not Heaven for lost: from this descent
Celestial Virtues rising will appear   15
More glorious and more dread than from no fall,
And trust themselves to fear no second fate!—
Me, though just right, and the fixed laws of Heaven,
Did first create your leader—next, free choice,
With what besides in council or in fight   20
Hath been achieved of merit—yet this loss,
Thus far at least recovered, hath much more
Established in a safe, unenvied throne,
Yielded with full consent. The happier state
In Heaven, which follows dignity, might draw   25
Envy from each inferior; but who here
Will envy whom the highest place exposes
Foremost to stand against the Thunderer's aim
Your bulwark, and condemns to greatest share
Of endless pain? Where there is, then, no good   30
For which to strive, no strife can grow up there
From faction: for none sure will claim in Hell
Precedence; none whose portion is so small
Of present pain that with ambitious mind
Will covet more! With this advantage, then,   35
To union, and firm faith, and firm accord,
More than can be in Heaven, we now return
To claim our just inheritance of old,
Surer to prosper than prosperity
Could have assured us; and by what best way,   40
Whether of open war or covert guile,

---

9. *success:* consequence. 12 ff. Satan explains why he still calls the fallen
angels *Deities of Heaven.* 15. *Virtues:* i.e., the angelic rank of that name.
19-24. Satan's justification for assuming leadership. 25. *which . . . dignity:*
which results from merit.

We now debate. Who can advise, may speak."
    He ceased; and next him Moloch, sceptred king,
Stood up—the strongest and the fiercest Spirit
That fought in Heaven, now fiercer by despair.   45
His trust was with the Eternal to be deemed
Equal in strength, and rather than be less
Cared not to be at all; with that care lost
Went all his fear: of God, or Hell, or worse,
He recked not, and these words thereafter spake: 50
    "My sentence is for open war. Of wiles,
More unexpert, I boast not: them let those
Contrive who need, or when they need; not now.
For, while they sit contriving, shall the rest—
Millions that stand in arms, and longing wait   55
The signal to ascend—sit lingering here,
Heaven's fugitives, and for their dwelling-place
Accept this dark opprobrious den of shame,
The prison of His tyranny who reigns
By our delay? No! let us rather choose,   60
Armed with Hell-flames and fury, all at once
O'er Heaven's high towers to force resistless way,
Turning our tortures into horrid arms
Against the Torturer; when, to meet the noise
Of his almighty engine, he shall hear   65
Infernal thunder, and, for lightning, see
Black fire and horror shot with equal rage
Among his Angels, and his throne itself
Mixed with Tartarean sulphur and strange fire,
His own invented torments. But perhaps   70
The way seems difficult, and steep to scale
With upright wing against a higher foe!
Let such bethink them, if the sleepy drench
Of that forgetful lake benumb not still,
That in our proper motion we ascend   75
Up to our native seat; descent and fall
To us is adverse. Who but felt of late,
When the fierce foe hung on our broken rear
Insulting, and pursued us through the Deep,

63-4. *Turning . . . Torturer:* Failure to show just how this is to be accomplished is one of the many deficiencies in Moloch's program. 69. *Tartarean:* i.e., "Hellish"—from Tartarus, one of the Greek names for hell. 73-4. *if . . . still:* Cf. I 266. 77. *adverse:* i.e., a contradiction of our natures.

With what compulsion and laborious flight   80
We sunk thus low? The ascent is easy, then;
The event is feared! Should we again provoke
Our stronger, some worse way his wrath may find
To our destruction, if there be in Hell
Fear to be worse destroyed! What can be worse   85
Than to dwell here, driven out from bliss, condemned
In this abhorrèd deep to utter woe;
Where pain of unextinguishable fire
Must exercise us without hope of end
The vassals of his anger, when the scourge   90
Inexorably, and the torturing hour,
Calls us to penance? More destroyed than thus,
We should be quite abolished, and expire.
What fear we then? what doubt we to incense
His utmost ire? which, to the highth enraged,   95
Will either quite consume us, and reduce
To nothing this essential—happier far
Than miserable to have eternal being!—
Or, if our substance be indeed divine,
And cannot cease to be, we are at worst   100
On this side nothing; and by proof we feel
Our power sufficient to disturb his Heaven,
And with perpetual inroads to alarm,
Though inaccessible, his fatal throne:
Which, if not victory, is yet revenge."   105
   He ended frowning, and his look denounced
Desperate revenge, and battle dangerous
To less than gods. On the other side up rose
Belial, in act more graceful and humane.
A fairer person lost not Heaven; he seemed   110
For dignity composed, and high exploit.
But all was false and hollow; though his tongue
Dropt manna, and could make the worse appear
The better reason, to perplex and dash
Maturest counsels: for his thoughts were low—   115
To vice industrious, but to nobler deeds
Timorous and slothful. Yet he pleased the ear,
And with persuasive accent thus began:

---

82. *event:* outcome. 97. *essential:* i.e., substance of which we are made. 104.
fatal: The fallen angels like to think God dependent on "fate." Cf. I 116.

"I should be much for open war, O Peers,
As not behind in hate, if what was urged   120
Main reason to persuade immediate war
Did not dissuade me most, and seem to cast
Ominous conjecture on the whole success;
When he who most excels in fact of arms,
In what he counsels and in what excels   125
Mistrustful, grounds his courage on despair
And utter dissolution, as the scope
Of all his aim, after some dire revenge.
First, what revenge? The towers of Heaven are filled
With armèd watch, that render all access   130
Impregnable: oft on the bordering Deep
Encamp their legions, or with obscure wing
Scout far and wide into the realm of Night,
Scorning surprise. Or, could we break our way
By force, and at our heels all Hell should rise   135
With blackest insurrection to confound
Heaven's purest light, yet our great Enemy,
All incorruptible, would on his throne
Sit unpolluted, and the ethereal mould,
Incapable of stain, would soon expel   140
Her mischief, and purge off the baser fire,
Victorious. Thus repulsed, our final hope
Is flat despair: we must exasperate
The Almighty Victor to spend all his rage;
And that must end us; that must be our cure—   145
To be no more. Sad cure! for who would lose,
Though full of pain, this intellectual being,
Those thoughts that wander through eternity,
To perish rather, swallowed up and lost
In the wide womb of uncreated Night,   150
Devoid of sense and motion? And who knows,
Let this be good, whether our angry Foe
Can give it, or will ever? How he can
Is doubtful; that he never will is sure.
Will He, so wise, let loose at once his ire,   155
Belike through impotence or unaware,
To give his enemies their wish, and end
Them in his anger whom his anger saves
To punish endless? 'Wherefore cease we, then?'

_____

124. *fact:* deeds. 139. *mould:* substance. 152. *Let this be:* even admitting
that this is.

Say they who counsel war; 'we are decreed, 160
Reserved, and destined to eternal woe;
Whatever doing, what can we suffer more,
What can we suffer worse?' Is this, then, worst—
Thus sitting, thus consulting, thus in arms?
What when we fled amain, pursued and strook 165
With Heaven's afflicting thunder, and besought
The Deep to shelter us? This Hell then seemed
A refuge from those wounds. Or when we lay
Chained on the burning lake? That sure was worse.
What if the breath that kindled those grim fires, 170
Awaked, should blow them into sevenfold rage,
And plunge us in the flames; or from above
Should intermitted vengeance arm again
His red right hand to plague us? What if all
Her stores were opened, and this firmament 175
Of Hell should spout her cataracts of fire,
Impendent horrors, threatening hideous fall
One day upon our heads; while we perhaps,
Designing or exhorting glorious war,
Caught in a fiery tempest, shall be hurled, 180
Each on his rock transfixed, the sport and prey
Of racking whirlwinds, or for ever sunk
Under yon boiling ocean, wrapt in chains,
There to converse with everlasting groans,
Unrespited, unpitied, unreprieved, 185
Ages of hopeless end? This would be worse.
War, therefore, open or concealed, alike
My voice dissuades; for what can force or guile
With Him, or who deceive His mind, whose eye
Views all things at one view? He from Heaven's highth 190
All these our motions vain sees and derides,
Not more almighty to resist our might
Than wise to frustrate all our plots and wiles.
Shall we, then, live thus vile—the race of Heaven
Thus trampled, thus expelled, to suffer here 195
Chains and these torments? Better these than worse,
By my advice; since fate inevitable
Subdues us, and omnipotent decree,
The Victor's will. To suffer, as to do,
Our strength is equal; nor the law unjust 200

---

165. *What when:* was it not then worse when. 177. *Impendent:* hanging.
188. *what can:* what good is.

That so ordains. This was at first resolved,
If we were wise, against so great a foe
Contending, and so doubtful what might fall.
I laugh when those who at the spear are bold
And venturous, if that fail them, shrink, and fear   205
What yet they know must follow—to endure
Exile, or ignominy, or bonds, or pain,
The sentence of their conqueror. This is now
Our doom; which if we can sustain and bear,
Our Supreme Foe in time may much remit   210
His anger, and perhaps, thus far removed,
Not mind us not offending, satisfied
With what is punished; whence these raging fires
Will slacken, if his breath stir not their flames.
Our purer essence then will overcome   215
Their noxious vapour; or, inured, not feel;
Or, changed at length, and to the place conformed
In temper and in nature, will receive
Familiar the fierce heat; and, void of pain,
This horror will grow mild, this darkness light;   220
Besides what hope the never-ending flight
Of future days may bring, what chance, what change
Worth waiting—since our present lot appears
For happy though but ill, for ill not worst,
If we procure not to ourselves more woe."   225
   Thus Belial, with words clothed in reason's garb,
Counselled ignoble ease and peaceful sloth,
Not peace; and after him thus Mammon spake:
   "Either to disenthrone the King of Heaven
We war, if war be best, or to regain   230
Our own right lost. Him to unthrone we then
May hope, when everlasting Fate shall yield
To fickle Chance, and Chaos judge the strife.
The former, vain to hope, argues as vain
The latter; for what place can be for us   235
Within Heaven's bound, unless Heaven's Lord Supreme
We overpower? Suppose he should relent,
And publish grace to all, on promise made
Of new subjection; with what eyes could we
Stand in his presence humble, and receive   240
Strict laws imposed, to celebrate his throne

---

201. *This . . . resolved:* this was to be expected. 216. *inured:* grown accustomed to it. 232-3. Cf. 104 n.

With warbled hymns, and to his Godhead sing
Forced Halleluiahs, while he lordly sits
Our envied sovran, and his altar breathes
Ambrosial odours and ambrosial flowers,   245
Our servile offerings? This must be our task
In Heaven, this our delight. How wearisome
Eternity so spent in worship paid
To whom we hate! Let us not then pursue,
By force impossible, by leave obtained   250
Unácceptable, though in Heaven, our state
Of splendid vassalage; but rather seek
Our own good from ourselves, and from our own
Live to ourselves, though in this vast recess,
Free and to none accountable, preferring   255
Hard liberty before the easy yoke
Of servile pomp. Our greatness will appear
Then most conspicuous when great things of small,
Useful of hurtful, prosperous of adverse,
We can create, and in what place soe'er   260
Thrive under evil, and work ease out of pain
Through labour and endurance. This deep world
Of darkness do we dread? How oft amidst
Thick clouds and dark doth Heaven's all-ruling Sire
Choose to reside, his glory unobscured,   265
And with the majesty of darkness round
Covers his throne, from whence deep thunders roar,
Mustering their rage, and Heaven resembles Hell!
As He our darkness, cannot we His light
Imitate when we please? This desert soil   270
Wants not her hidden lustre, gems and gold;
Nor want we skill or art from whence to raise
Magnificence; and what can Heaven show more?
Our torments also may, in length of time,
Become our elements, these piercing fires   275
As soft as now severe, our temper changed
Into their temper; which must needs remove
The sensible of pain. All things invite

---

244. *envied:* That the fallen angels envy God is the measure of their sin of
pride. 249-52. *Let . . . vassalage:* i.e., let us not seek a return to Heaven
(*vassalage*), which would be impossible to achieve by force, and unac-
ceptable if achieved by God's permission. 278. *The sensible of:* Capacity
for feeling.

To peaceful counsels, and the settled state
Of order, how in safety best we may   280
Compose our present evils, with regard
Of what we are and where, dismissing quite
All thoughts of war. Ye have what I advise."
    He scarce had finished, when such murmur filled
The assembly as when hollow rocks retain   285
The sound of blustering winds, which all night long
Had roused the sea, now with hoarse cadence lull
Seafaring men o'erwatched, whose bark by chance,
Or pinnace, anchors in a craggy bay
After the tempest. Such applause was heard   290
As Mammon ended, and his sentence pleased,
Advising peace: for such another field
They dreaded worse than Hell; so much the fear
Of thunder and the sword of Michaël
Wrought still within them; and no less desire   295
To found this nether empire, which might rise,
By policy and long process of time,
In emulation opposite to Heaven.
Which when Beëlzebub perceived—than whom,
Satan except, none higher sat—with grave   300
Aspect he rose, and in his rising seemed
A pillar of state. Deep on his front engraven
Deliberation sat, and public care;
And princely counsel in his face yet shone,
Majestic, though in ruin. Sage he stood,   305
With Atlantean shoulders, fit to bear
The weight of mightiest monarchies; his look
Drew audience and attention still as night
Or summer's noontide air, while thus he spake:
    "Thrones and Imperial Powers, Offspring of Heaven,   310
Ethereal Virtues! or these titles now
Must we renounce, and, changing style, be called
Princes of Hell? for so the popular vote
Inclines—here to continue, and build up here
A growing empire; doubtless! while we dream,   315
And know not that the King of Heaven hath doomed

---

288. *o'erwatched:* tired from keeping their watches. 297. *policy:* statesman-
ship. 306. *Atlantean:* i.e., like those of Atlas. 312. *style:* i.e., our formal
title.

This place our dungeon—not our safe retreat
Beyond his potent arm, to live exempt
From Heaven's high jurisdiction, in new league
Banded against his throne, but to remain   320
In strictest bondage, though thus far removed,
Under the inevitable curb, reserved
His captive multitude. For He, be sure,
In highth or depth, still first and last will reign
Sole king, and of his kingdom lose no part   325
By our revolt, but over Hell extend
His empire, and with iron sceptre rule
Us here, as with his golden those in Heaven.
What sit we then projecting peace and war?
War hath determined us and foiled with loss   330
Irreparable; terms of peace yet none
Voutsafed or sought; for what peace will be given
To us enslaved, but custody severe,
And stripes, and arbitrary punishment
Inflicted? and what peace can we return,   335
But, to our power, hostility and hate,
Untamed reluctance, and revenge, though slow,
Yet ever plotting how the Conqueror least
May reap his conquest, and may least rejoice
In doing what we most in suffering feel?   340
Nor will occasion want, nor shall we need
With dangerous expedition to invade
Heaven, whose high walls fear no assault or siege,
Or ambush from the Deep. What if we find
Some easier enterprise? There is a place   345
(If ancient and prophetic fame in Heaven
Err not)—another World, the happy seat
Of some new race, called Man, about this time
To be created like to us, though less
In power and excellence, but favoured more   350
Of Him who rules above; so was His will
Pronounced among the gods, and by an oath
That shook Heaven's whole circumference confirmed.
Thither let us bend all our thoughts, to learn

327-8. *iron, golden:* a contrast with many associations: e.g., the Iron Age
and the Golden Age; iron as emblem of hate, gold as emblem of friendship;
etc. 334. *stripes:* lashings. 336. *But . . . power:* except (to the extent of our
power).

What creatures there inhabit, of what mould   355
Or substance, how endued, and what their power
And where their weakness: how attempted best,
By force or subtlety. Though Heaven be shut,
And Heaven's high Arbitrator sit secure
In his own strength, this place may lie exposed,   360
The utmost border of his kingdom, left
To their defence who hold it: here, perhaps,
Some advantageous act may be achieved
By sudden onset—either with Hell-fire
To waste his whole creation, or possess   365
All as our own, and drive, as we are driven,
The puny habitants; or, if not drive,
Seduce them to our party, that their God
May prove their foe, and with repenting hand
Abolish his own works. This would surpass   370
Common revenge, and interrupt His joy
In our confusion, and our joy upraise
In His disturbance; when his darling sons,
Hurled headlong to partake with us, shall curse
Their frail original, and faded bliss—   375
Faded so soon! Advise if this be worth
Attempting, or to sit in darkness here
Hatching vain empires." Thus Beëlzebub
Pleaded his devilish counsel—first devised
By Satan, and in part proposed: for whence,   380
But from the author of all ill, could spring
So deep a malice, to confound the race
Of mankind in one root, and Earth with Hell
To mingle and involve, done all to spite
The great Creator? But their spite still serves   385
His glory to augment. The bold design
Pleased highly those Infernal States, and joy
Sparkled in all their eyes: with full assent
They vote: whereat his speech he thus renews:
"Well have ye judged, well ended long debate,   390
Synod of Gods, and, like to what ye are,
Great things resolved, which from the lowest deep
Will once more lift us up, in spite of fate,
Nearer our ancient seat—perhaps in view
Of those bright confines, whence, with neighbouring arms,   395

---

380. Cf. I 650 ff.   387. *States:* estates—like the three estates, Lords, Clergy, and Commons of the English parliament.   393. *fate:* Cf. 104 n.

And opportune excursion, we may chance
Re-enter Heaven; or else in some mild zone
Dwell, not unvisited of Heaven's fair light,
Secure, and at the brightening orient beam
Purge off this gloom: the soft delicious air,   400
To heal the scar of these corrosive fires,
Shall breathe her balm. But, first, whom shall we send
In search of this new World? whom shall we find
Sufficient? who shall tempt with wandering feet
The dark, unbottomed, infinite Abyss,   405
And through the palpable obscure find out
His uncouth way, or spread his aery flight,
Borne up with indefatigable wings
Over the vast abrupt, ere he arrive
The happy Isle? What strength, what art, can then   410
Suffice, or what evasion bear him safe
Through the strict senteries and stations thick
Of Angels watching round? Here he had need
All circumspection: and we now no less
Choice in our suffrage; for on whom we send   415
The weight of all, and our last hope, relies."
     This said, he sat; and expectation held
His look suspense, awaiting who appeared
To second, or oppose, or undertake
The perilous attempt. But all sat mute,   420
Pondering the danger with deep thoughts; and each
In other's countenance read his own dismay,
Astonished. None among the choice and prime
Of those Heaven-warring champions could be found
So hardy as to proffer or accept,   425
Alone, the dreadful voyage; till at last
Satan, whom now transcendent glory raised
Above his fellows, with monarchal pride
Conscious of highest worth, unmoved thus spake:
     "O Progeny of Heaven! Empyreal Thrones!   430
With reason hath deep silence and demur
Seized us, though undismayed. Long is the way
And hard, that out of Hell leads up to Light.

---

405. *Abyss:* Chaos. 407. *uncouth:* (1) unknown (2) wild. 409. *abrupt:* gap,
fissure. 410. *Isle:* i.e., the ordered Universe is an island surrounded by
Chaos. 412. *senteries:* Variant of "sentries." 415. *suffrage:* selection. 431.
demur: hesitation.

Our prison strong, this huge convex of fire,
Outrageous to devour, immures us round
Ninefold; and gates of burning adamant,   435
Barred over us, prohibit all egress.
These passed, if any pass, the void profound
Of unessential Night receives him next,
Wide-gaping, and with utter loss of being   440
Threatens him, plunged in that abortive gulf.
If thence he scape, into whatever world,
Or unknown region, what remains him less
Than unknown dangers, and as hard escape?
But I should ill become this throne, O Peers,   445
And this imperial sovranty, adorned
With splendour, armed with power, if aught proposed
And judged of public moment in the shape
Of difficulty or danger, could deter
Me from attempting. Wherefore do I assume   450
These royalties, and not refuse to reign,
Refusing to accept as great a share
Of hazard as of honour, due alike
To him who reigns, and so much to him due
Of hazard more as he above the rest   455
High honoured sits? Go, therefore, mighty Powers,
Terror of Heaven, though fallen; intend at home,
While here shall be our home, what best may ease
The present misery, and render Hell
More tolerable; if there be cure or charm   460
To respite, or deceive, or slack the pain
Of this ill mansion: intermit no watch
Against a wakeful foe, while I abroad
Through all the coasts of dark destruction seek
Deliverance for us all. This enterprise   465
None shall partake with me." Thus saying, rose
The Monarch, and prevented all reply;
Prudent lest, from his resolution raised,
Others among the chief might offer now,
Certain to be refused, what erst they feared,   470
And, so refused, might in opinion stand
His rivals, winning cheap the high repute

---

434. *convex:* sphere. 439. *unessential:* insubstantial. 441. *abortive:* (1)
dead, (2) deadly, (3) monstrous. 457. *intend:* attend to. 468. *raised:* heartened. 470. *what . . . feared:* the grammatical object of *offer,* 469.

Which he through hazard huge must earn. But they
Dreaded not more the adventure than his voice
Forbidding; and at once with him they rose.   475
Their rising all at once was as the sound
Of thunder heard remote. Towards him they bend
With awful reverence prone, and as a God
Extol him equal to the Highest in Heaven.
Nor failed they to express how much they praised   480
That for the general safety he despised
His own: for neither do the Spirits damned
Lose all their virtue; lest bad men should boast
Their specious deeds on earth, which glory excites,
Or close ambition varnished o'er with zeal.   485
   Thus they their doubtful consultations dark
Ended, rejoicing in their matchless Chief:
As, when from mountain-tops the dusky clouds
Ascending, while the North-wind sleeps, o'erspread
Heaven's cheerful face, the louring element   490
Scowls o'er the darkened landskip snow or shower,
If chance the radiant sun, with farewell sweet,
Extend his evening beam, the fields revive,
The birds their notes renew, and bleating herds
Attest their joy, that hill and valley rings.   495
O shame to men! Devil with devil damned
Firm concord holds; men only disagree
Of creatures rational, though under hope
Of heavenly grace, and, God proclaiming peace,
Yet live in hatred, enmity, and strife   500
Among themselves, and levy cruel wars
Wasting the earth, each other to destroy:
As if (which might induce us to accord)
Man had not hellish foes enow besides,
That day and night for his destruction wait!   505
   The Stygian council thus dissolved; and forth
In order came the grand Infernal Peers:
Midst came their mighty Paramount, and seemed
Alone the antagonist of Heaven, nor less
Than Hell's dread Emperor, with pomp supreme,   510

482-5. I.e., it is possible to have some virtue and still be damned; hence bad
men who show some virtue (caused by desire of glory or ambition) cannot
boast that they are really good (i.e., not damned). 508. *Paramount:* over-
lord.

And God-like imitated state: him round
A globe of fiery Seraphim enclosed
With bright emblazonry, and horrent arms.
Then of their session ended they bid cry
With trumpet's regal sound the great result: 515
Toward the four winds four speedy Cherubim
Put to their mouths the sounding alchymy,
By herald's voice explained; the hollow Abyss
Heard far and wide, and all the host of Hell
With deafening shout returned them loud acclaim.   520
Thence more at ease their minds, and somewhat raised
By false presumptuous hope, the rangèd Powers
Disband; and, wandering, each his several way
Pursues, as inclination or sad choice
Leads him perplexed, where he may likeliest find   525
Truce to his restless thoughts, and entertain
The irksome hours, till his great Chief return.
Part on the plain, or in the air sublime,
Upon the wing or in swift race contend,
As at the Olympian games or Pythian fields;   530
Part curb their fiery steeds, or shun the goal
With rapid wheels, or fronted brigads form:
As when, to warn proud cities, war appears
Waged in the troubled sky, and armies rush
To battle in the clouds; before each van   535
Prick forth the aery knights, and couch their spears,
Till thickest legions close; with feats of arms
From either end of heaven the welkin burns.
Others, with vast Typhœan rage, more fell,
Rend up both rocks and hills, and ride the air   540
In whirlwind; Hell scarce holds the wild uproar:
As when Alcides, from Oechalia crowned
With conquest, felt the envenomed robe, and tore
Through pain up by the roots Thessalian pines,
And Lichas from the top of Oeta threw   545
Into the Euboic sea. Others, more mild,
Retreated in a silent valley, sing

---

513. *horrent:* bristling. 517. *alchymy:* "alchemy gold," i.e., brass. 530. *Pythian:* Greek games were held at Delphi (Pytho) as well as at Olympia. 531-2. *shun . . . with:* swing their teams around the end-post in a chariot race. 538. *welkin:* sky. 539. *Typhœan:* from "Typhon"—a giant Titan. 542-6. Coming victorious from Oechalia, Hercules was ignorantly given by his friend Lichas a poisoned robe; 544-6 describe his death agonies.

With notes angelical to many a harp
Their own heroic deeds, and hapless fall
By doom of battle, and complain that Fate   550
Free Virtue should enthrall to Force or Chance.
Their song was partial; but the harmony
(What could it less when Spirits immortal sing?)
Suspended Hell, and took with ravishment
The thronging audience. In discourse more sweet   555
(For Eloquence the Soul, Song charms the Sense)
Others apart sat on a hill retired,
In thoughts more elevate, and reasoned high
Of Providence, Foreknowledge, Will, and Fate—
Fixed fate, free will, foreknowledge absolute—   560
And found no end, in wandering mazes lost.
Of good and evil much they argued then,
Of happiness and final misery,
Passion and apathy, and glory and shame:
Vain wisdom all, and false philosophy!—   565
Yet, with a pleasing sorcery, could charm
Pain for a while or anguish, and excite
Fallacious hope, or arm the obdurèd breast
With stubborn patience as with triple steel.
Another part, in squadrons and gross bands,   570
On bold adventure to discover wide
That dismal world, if any clime perhaps
Might yield them easier habitation, bend
Four ways their flying march, along the banks
Of four infernal rivers, that disgorge   575
Into the burning lake their baleful streams—
Abhorrèd Styx, the flood of deadly hate;
Sad Acheron of sorrow, black and deep;
Cocytus, named of lamentation loud
Heard on the rueful stream; fierce Phlegeton,   580
Whose waves of torrent fire inflame with rage.
Far off from these, a slow and silent stream,
Lethe, the river of oblivion, rolls
Her watery labyrinth, whereof who drinks
Forthwith his former state and being forgets—   585

---

550. Cf. 104 n. 552. *partial:* i.e., in their own favor. 564. The relations
between passion, suppression of passion (*apathy*), love of fame, sense of
shame—and virtue—were favorite topics of pagan ethics, and hence from
Milton's Christian view, *Vain wisdom all.* 568. *obdured:* obdurate.

Forgets both joy and grief, pleasure and pain.
Beyond this flood a frozen continent
Lies dark and wild, beat with perpetual storms
Of whirlwind and dire hail, which on firm land
Thaws not, but gathers heap, and ruin seems   590
Of ancient pile; all else deep snow and ice,
A gulf profound as that Serbonian bog
Betwixt Damiata and Mount Casius old,
Where armies whole have sunk: the parching air
Burns frore, and cold performs the effect of fire.   595
Thither, by harpy-footed Furies haled,
At certain revolutions all the damned
Are brought; and feel by turns the bitter change
Of fierce extremes, extremes by change more fierce,
From beds of raging fire to starve in ice   600
Their soft ethereal warmth, and there to pine
Immovable, infixed, and frozen round,
Periods of time,—thence hurried back to fire.
They ferry over this Lethean sound
Both to and fro, their sorrow to augment,   605
And wish and struggle, as they pass, to reach
The tempting stream, with one small drop to lose
In sweet forgetfulness all pain and woe,
All in one moment, and so near the brink;
But Fate withstands, and, to oppose the attempt,   610
Medusa with Gorgonian terror guards
The ford, and of itself the water flies
All taste of living wight, as once it fled
The lip of Tantalus. Thus roving on
In confused march forlorn, the adventurous bands,   615
With shuddering horror pale, and eyes aghast,
Viewed first their lamentable lot, and found
No rest. Through many a dark and dreary vale
They passed, and many a region dolorous,
O'er many a frozen, many a fiery Alp,   620
Rocks, caves, lakes, fens, bogs, dens, and shades of death—

---

590. *gathers heap:* accumulates. 591. *pile:* building. 592. *bog:* Lake Ser-
bonis (now dried up) in northeast Egypt between Damietta and Mt. Casius.
595. *frore:* frosty. 596. *harpy-footed:* with taloned feet like those of the
Harpies, who were half woman and half bird. 600. *starve:* destroy. 604.
sound: narrow stretch of water. 611. *Medusa:* one of the three Gorgons in
Greek myth. 614. *Tantalus:* punished (in the Greek hell) for his greed by
being placed in a stream which he could not bend down to drink.

A universe of death, which God by curse
Created evil, for evil only good;
Where all life dies, death lives, and Nature breeds,
Perverse, all monstrous, all prodigious things,   625
Abominable, inutterable, and worse
Than fables yet have feigned or fear conceived,
Gorgons, and Hydras, and Chimeras dire.

   Meanwhile the Adversary of God and Man,
Satan, with thoughts inflamed of highest design,   630
Puts on swift wings, and toward the gates of Hell
Explores his solitary flight: sometimes
He scours the right hand coast, sometimes the left;
Now shaves with level wing the deep, then soars
Up to the fiery concave towering high.   635
As when far off at sea a fleet descried
Hangs in the clouds, by equinoctial winds
Close sailing from Bengala, or the isles
Of Ternate and Tidore, whence merchants bring
Their spicy drugs; they on the trading flood,   640
Through the wide Ethiopian to the Cape,
Ply stemming nightly toward the pole: so seemed
Far off the flying Fiend. At last appear
Hell-bounds, high reaching to the horrid roof,
And thrice threefold the gates; three folds were brass,   645
Three iron, three of adamantine rock,
Impenetrable, impaled with circling fire,
Yet unconsumed. Before the gates there sat
On either side a formidable Shape.
The one seemed woman to the waist, and fair,   650
But ended foul in many a scaly fold,
Voluminous and vast—a serpent armed
With mortal sting. About her middle round
A cry of Hell-hounds never-ceasing barked
With wide Cerberean mouths full loud, and rung   655
A hideous peal; yet, when they list, would creep,
If aught disturbed their noise, into her womb,
And kennel there; yet there still barked and howled

---

628. I.e., all kinds of monsters. 635. *concave:* the *convex* of 434, but now
conceived from within. 638. *Bengala:* India. 639. *Ternate and Tidore:*
islands in the Moluccas. 641. Through the Indian Ocean to the Cape of
Good Hope. 642. *stemming:* making headway. 655. *Cerberean:* like those
of Cerberus, the three-headed hound of the Greek hell.

Within unseen. Far less abhorred than these
Vexed Scylla, bathing in the sea that parts   660
Calabria from the hoarse Trinacrian shore;
Nor uglier follow the night-hag, when, called
In secret, riding through the air she comes,
Lured with the smell of infant blood, to dance
With Lapland witches, while the labouring moon   665
Eclipses at their charms. The other Shape—
If shape it might be called that shape had none
Distinguishable in member, joint, or limb;
Or substance might be called that shadow seemed,
For each seemed either—black it stood as Night,   670
Fierce as ten Furies, terrible as Hell,
And shook a dreadful dart: what seemed his head
The likeness of a kingly crown had on.
Satan was now at hand, and from his seat
The monster moving onward came as fast   675
With horrid strides; Hell trembled as he strode.
The undaunted Fiend what this might be admired—
Admired, not feared (God and his Son except,
Created thing naught valued he nor shunned),
And with disdainful look thus first began: 680
    "Whence and what art thou, execrable Shape,
That dar'st, though grim and terrible, advance
Thy miscreated front athwart my way
To yonder gates? Through them I mean to pass,
That be assured, without leave asked of thee.   685
Retire; or taste thy folly, and learn by proof,
Hell-born, not to contend with Spirits of Heaven."
    To whom the Goblin, full of wrath, replied:
"Art thou that Traitor-Angel, art thou he,
Who first broke peace in Heaven and faith, till then   690
Unbroken, and in proud rebellious arms
Drew after him the third part of Heaven's sons,
Conjured against the Highest—for which both thou
And they, outcast from God, are here condemned
To waste eternal days in woe and pain?   695
And reckon'st thou thyself with Spirits of Heaven,

---

660. *Scylla:* cf. *Comus,* 257 n. 661. I.e., Italy from Sicily. 662. *the night-hag:*
Hecate, queen of witches. 677. *admired:* wondered. 693. *Conjured:* sworn
(in a plot).

Hell-doomed, and breath'st defiance here and scorn,
Where I reign king, and, to enrage thee more,
Thy king and lord? Back to thy punishment,
False fugitive; and to thy speed add wings,   700
Lest with a whip of scorpions I pursue
Thy lingering, or with one stroke of this dart
Strange horror seize thee, and pangs unfelt before."
    So spake the grisly Terror, and in shape,
So speaking and so threatening, grew tenfold   705
More dreadful and deform. On the other side,
Incensed with indignation, Satan stood
Unterrified, and like a comet burned,
That fires the length of Ophiuchus huge
In the arctic sky, and from his horrid hair   710
Shakes pestilence and war. Each at the head
Levelled his deadly aim; their fatal hands
No second stroke intend; and such a frown
Each cast at the other as when two black clouds,
With heaven's artillery fraught, come rattling on   715
Over the Caspian,—then stand front to front
Hovering a space, till winds the signal blow
To join their dark encounter in mid-air.
So frowned the mighty combatants that Hell
Grew darker at their frown; so matched they stood;   720
For never but once more was either like
To meet so great a foe. And now great deeds
Had been achieved, whereof all Hell had rung,
Had not the snaky Sorceress, that sat
Fast by Hell-gate and kept the fatal key,   725
Risen, and with hideous outcry rushed between.
    "O father, what intends thy hand," she cried,
"Against thy only son? What fury, O son,
Possesses thee to bend that mortal dart
Against thy father's head? And know'st for whom?   730
For Him who sits above, and laughs the while
At thee, ordained his drudge to execute
Whate'er his wrath, which He calls justice, bids—
His wrath, which one day will destroy ye both!"
    She spake, and at her words the hellish Pest   735
Forbore: then these to her Satan returned:

---

709. *Ophiuchus:* the constellation called "the Serpent-Bearer." 710. *horrid:*
bristling. 721-2. I.e., at the second coming of Christ.

"So strange thy outcry, and thy words so strange
Thou interposest, that my sudden hand,
Prevented, spares to tell thee yet by deeds
What it intends, till first I know of thee   740
What thing thou art, thus double-formed, and why,
In this infernal vale first met, thou call'st
Me father, and that phantasm call'st my son.
I know thee not, nor ever saw till now
Sight more detestable than him and thee."   745
      To whom thus the Portress of Hell-gate replied:
"Hast thou forgot me, then; and do I seem
Now in thine eye so foul?—once deemed so fair
In Heaven, when at the assembly, and in sight
Of all the Seraphim with thee combined   750
In bold conspiracy against Heaven's King,
All on a sudden miserable pain
Surprised thee, dim thine eyes, and dizzy swum
In darkness, while thy head flames thick and fast
Threw forth, till on the left side opening wide,   755
Likest to thee in shape and countenance bright,
Then shining heavenly fair, a goddess armed,
Out of thy head I sprung. Amazement seized
All the host of Heaven; back they recoiled afraid
At first, and called me *Sin,* and for a sign   760
Portentous held me; but, familiar grown,
I pleased, and with attractive graces won
The most averse—thee chiefly, who, full oft
Thyself in me thy perfect image viewing,
Becam'st enamoured; and such joy thou took'st   765
With me in secret that my womb conceived
A growing burden. Meanwhile war arose,
And fields were fought in Heaven: wherein remained
(For what could else?) to our Almighty Foe
Clear victory; to our part loss and rout   770
Through all the Empyrean. Down they fell,
Driven headlong from the pitch of Heaven, down
Into this Deep; and in the general fall
I also: at which time this powerful key
Into my hands was given, with charge to keep   775

---

747 ff. This passage allegorizes James 1:15: "When lust hath conceived, it
bringeth forth sin: and sin, when it is finished, bringeth forth death." 752-8.
Sin springs from Satan's head as, in the Greek stories, Athene (i.e., wisdom) from Zeus's. 771. *Empyrean:* Heaven.

These gates for ever shut, which none can pass
Without my opening. Pensive here I sat
Alone; but long I sat not, till my womb,
Pregnant by thee, and now excessive grown,
Prodigious motion felt and rueful throes.   780
At last this odious offspring whom thou seest,
Thine own begotten, breaking violent way,
Tore through my entrails, that, with fear and pain
Distorted, all my nether shape thus grew
Transformed: but he my inbred enemy   785
Forth issued, brandishing his fatal dart,
Made to destroy. I fled, and cried out *Death!*
Hell trembled at the hideous name, and sighed
From all her caves, and back resounded *Death!*
I fled; but he pursued (though more it seems,   790
Inflamed with lust than rage), and, swifter far,
Me overtook, his mother, all dismayed,
And, in embraces forcible and foul
Engendering with me, of that rape begot
These yelling monsters, that with ceaseless cry   795
Surround me, as thou saw'st—hourly conceived
And hourly born, with sorrow infinite
To me: for, when they list, into the womb
That bred them they return, and howl, and gnaw
My bowels, their repast; then, bursting forth   800
Afresh, with conscious terrors vex me round,
That rest or intermission none I find.
Before mine eyes in opposition sits
Grim Death, my son and foe, who sets them on,
And me, his parent, would full soon devour   805
For want of other prey, but that he knows
His end with mine involved, and knows that I
Should prove a bitter morsel, and his bane,
Whenever that shall be: so Fate pronounced.
But thou, O father, I forewarn thee, shun   810
His deadly arrow; neither vainly hope
To be invulnerable in those bright arms,
Though tempered heavenly; for that mortal dint,
Save He who reigns above, none can resist."
  She finished; and the subtle Fiend his lore   815
Soon learned, now milder, and thus answered smooth:

---

815. *lore:* lesson.

"Dear daughter—since thou claim'st me for thy sire,
And my fair son here show'st me, the dear pledge
Of dalliance had with thee in Heaven, and joys
Then sweet, now sad to mention, through dire change   820
Befallen us unforeseen, unthought-of—know
I come no enemy, but to set free
From out this dark and dismal house of pain
Both him and thee, and all the Heavenly host
Of Spirits that, in our just pretences armed,   825
Fell with us from on high. From them I go
This uncouth errand sole, and one for all
Myself expose, with lonely steps to tread
The unfounded Deep, and through the void immense
To search, with wandering quest, a place foretold   830
Should be—and, by concurring signs, ere now
Created vast and round—a place of bliss
In the purlieus of Heaven; and therein placed
A race of upstart creatures, to supply
Perhaps our vacant room, though more removed,   835
Lest Heaven, surcharged with potent multitude,
Might hap to move new broils. Be this, or aught
Than this more secret, now designed, I haste
To know; and, this once known, shall soon return,
And bring ye to the place where thou and Death   840
Shall dwell at ease, and up and down unseen
Wing silently the buxom air, embalmed
With odours. There ye shall be fed and filled
Immeasurably; all things shall be your prey."
    He ceased; for both seemed highly pleased, and Death   845
Grinned horrible a ghastly smile, to hear
His famine should be filled, and blessed his maw
Destined to that good hour. No less rejoiced
His mother bad, and thus bespake her sire:
    "The key of this infernal Pit, by due   850
And by command of Heaven's all-powerful King,
I keep, by Him forbidden to unlock
These adamantine gates; against all force
Death ready stands to interpose his dart,
Fearless to be o'ermatched by living might.   855
But what owe I to His commands above,
Who hates me, and hath hither thrust me down

---

829. *unfounded:* bottomless. 833. *purlieus:* borders. 842. *buxom:* yielding.

Into this gloom of Tartarus profound,
To sit in hateful office here confined,
Inhabitant of Heaven and heavenly-born—   860
Here in perpetual agony and pain,
With terrors and with clamours compassed round
Of mine own brood, that on my bowels feed?
Thou art my father, thou art my author, thou
My being gav'st me; whom should I obey   865
But thee? whom follow? Thou wilt bring me soon
To that new world of light and bliss, among
The gods who live at ease, where I shall reign
At thy right hand voluptuous, as beseems
Thy daughter and thy darling, without end."   870
    Thus saying, from her side the fatal key,
Sad instrument of all our woe, she took;
And, towards the gate rolling her bestial **train**,
Forthwith the huge portcullis high up-drew,
Which, but herself, not all the Stygian Powers   875
Could once have moved; then in the key-hole **turns**
The intricate wards, and every bolt and bar
Of massy iron or solid rock with ease
Unfastens. On a sudden open fly,
With impetuous recoil and jarring sound,   880
The infernal doors, and on their hinges grate
Harsh thunder, that the lowest bottom shook
Of Erebus. She opened; but to shut
Excelled her power: the gates wide open stood,
That with extended wings a bannered host,   885
Under spread ensigns marching, might pass through
With horse and chariots ranked in loose array;
So wide they stood, and like a furnace-mouth
Cast forth redounding smoke and ruddy flame.
Before their eyes in sudden view appear   890
The secrets of the hoary Deep—a dark
Illimitable ocean, without bound,
Without dimension; where length, breadth, and highth,
And time, and place, are lost; where eldest Night
And Chaos, ancestors of Nature, hold   895
Eternal anarchy, amidst the noise

---

869. *At . . . hand:* Sin will sit at the right hand of Satan, as Christ sits at
the right hand of God. 883. *Erebus:* Hell. 889. *redounding:* overflowing.
891. *Deep:* Milton treats this (i.e., Chaos) as both place and person.

Of endless wars, and by confusion stand.
For Hot, Cold, Moist, and Dry, four champions fierce,
Strive here for mastery, and to battle bring
Their embryon atoms: they around the flag   900
Of each his faction, in their several clans,
Light-armed or heavy, sharp, smooth, swift, or slow,
Swarm populous, unnumbered as the sands
Of Barca or Cyrene's torrid soil,
Levied to side with warring winds, and poise   905
Their lighter wings. To whom these most adhere
He rules a moment: Chaos umpire sits,
And by decision more embroils the fray
By which he reigns: next him, high arbiter,
Chance governs all. Into this wild Abyss,   910
The womb of Nature, and perhaps her grave,
Of neither Sea, nor Shore, nor Air, nor Fire,
But all these in their pregnant causes mixed
Confusedly, and which thus must ever fight,
Unless the Almighty Maker them ordain   915
His dark materials to create more worlds—
Into this wild Abyss the wary Fiend
Stood on the brink of Hell and looked a while,
Pondering his voyage; for no narrow frith
He had to cross. Nor was his ear less pealed   920
With noises loud and ruinous (to compare
Great things with small) than when Bellona storms
With all her battering engines, bent to rase
Some capital city; or less than if this frame
Of heaven were falling, and these elements   925
In mutiny had from her axle torn
The steadfast Earth. At last his sail-broad vans
He spreads for flight, and in the surging smoke
Uplifted spurns the ground; thence many a league
As in a cloudy chair ascending rides   930
Audacious; but, that seat soon failing, meets
A vast vacuity: all unawares,
Fluttering his pennons vain, plumb-down he drops
Ten thousand fathom deep, and to this hour

---

898 ff. In Chaos the war of the four elements, which is reconciled in the "created" universe, continues unabated. 904. I.e., the deserts of North Africa. 919. *frith*: firth. 920. *pealed*: assailed. 922. *Bellona*: goddess of war. 924. *less*: refers back to *less pealed* in 920. 933. *pennons*: wings.

Down had been falling, had not, by ill chance,   935
The strong rebuff of some tumultuous cloud,
Instinct with fire and nitre, hurried him
As many miles aloft. That fury stayed—
Quenched in a boggy Syrtis, neither sea,
Nor good dry land—nigh foundered, on he fares,   940
Treading the crude consistence, half on foot,
Half flying; behoves him now both oar and sail.
As when a gryphon through the wilderness
With wingèd course, o'er hill or moory dale,
Pursues the Arimaspian, who by stealth   945
Had from his wakeful custody purloined
The guarded gold; so eagerly the Fiend
O'er bog or steep, through strait, rough, dense, or rare,
With head, hands, wings, or feet, pursues his way,
And swims, or sinks, or wades, or creeps, or flies.   950
At length a universal hubbub wild
Of stunning sounds, and voices all confused,
Borne through the hollow dark, assaults his ear
With loudest vehemence. Thither he plies
Undaunted, to meet there whatever Power   955
Or Spirit of the nethermost Abyss
Might in that noise reside, of whom to ask
Which way the nearest coast of darkness lies
Bordering on light; when straight behold the throne
Of Chaos, and his dark pavilion spread   960
Wide on the wasteful Deep! With him enthroned
Sat sable-vested Night, eldest of things,
The consort of his reign; and by them stood
Orcus and Ades, and the dreaded name
Of Demogorgon; Rumour next, and Chance,   965
And Tumult, and Confusion, all embroiled,
And Discord with a thousand various mouths.
    To whom Satan, turning boldly, thus: "Ye Powers
And Spirits of this nethermost Abyss,
Chaos and ancient Night, I come no spy   970
With purpose to explore or to disturb
The secrets of your realm; but, by constraint

---

939. *Syrtis:* i.e., quicksand (from an African gulf renowned for quicksand). 942. *behoves him:* he needs. 943-7. According to Herodotus (III 16), the Arimaspians were a people who stole gold from the griffins. 964. *Orcus and Ades:* classical names for hell, here used as names of presiding spirits in Chaos.

Wandering this darksome desert, as my way
Lies through your spacious empire up to light,
Alone and without guide, half lost, I seek   975
What readiest path leads where your gloomy bounds
Confine with Heaven; or, if some other place,
From your dominion won, the Ethereal King
Possesses lately, thither to arrive
I travel this profound. Direct my course: 980
Directed, no mean recompense it brings
To your behoof, if I that region lost,
All usurpation thence expelled, reduce
To her original darkness and your sway
(Which is my present journey), and once more   985
Erect the standard there of ancient Night.
Yours be the advantage all, mine the revenge!"
    Thus Satan; and him thus the Anarch old,
With faltering speech and visage incomposed,
Answered: "I know thee, stranger, who thou art—   990
That mighty leading Angel, who of late
Made head against Heaven's King, though overthrown.
I saw and heard; for such a numerous host
Fled not in silence through the frighted Deep,
With ruin upon ruin, rout on rout,   995
Confusion worse confounded; and Heaven-gates
Poured out by millions her victorious bands
Pursuing. I upon my frontiers here
Keep residence; if all I can will serve
That little which is left so to defend,   1000
Encroached on still through our intestine broils
Weakening the sceptre of old Night: first, Hell,
Your dungeon, stretching far and wide beneath;
Now lately Heaven and Earth, another world
Hung o'er my realm, linked in a golden chain   1005
To that side Heaven from whence your legions fell.
If that way be your walk, you have not far;
So much the nearer danger. Go, and speed;
Havoc and spoil and ruin are my gain."
    He ceased; and Satan staid not to reply,   1010

---

977. *Confine with:* border on. 980. *profound:* depth. 982. *behoof:* advantage. *lost:* i.e., carved from, and so lost to, Chaos. 989. *incomposed:* because nothing is composed or fixed in Chaos. 999. *can:* can do. 1004. *Heaven and Earth:* i.e., the universe recently created for man—not God's Heaven (1006), which is created from all eternity.

But glad that now his sea should find a shore,
With fresh alacrity and force renewed
Springs upward like a pyramid of fire
Into the wild expanse, and through the shock
Of fighting elements, on all sides round   1015
Environed, wins his way; harder beset
And more endangered than when Argo passed
Through Bosporus betwixt the justling rocks,
Or when Ulysses on the larboard shunned
Charybdis, and by the other Whirlpool steered.   1020
So he with difficulty and labour hard
Moved on, with difficulty and labour he;
But he once passed, soon after, when Man fell,
Strange alteration! Sin and Death amain,
Following his track (such was the will of Heaven)   1025
Paved after him a broad and beaten way
Over the dark Abyss, whose boiling gulf
Tamely endured a bridge of wondrous length,
From Hell continued, reaching the utmost Orb
Of this frail World; by which the Spirits perverse   1030
With easy intercourse pass to and fro
To tempt or punish mortals, except whom
God and good Angels guard by special grace.
    But now at last the sacred influence
Of light appears, and from the walls of Heaven   1035
Shoots far into the bosom of dim Night
A glimmering dawn. Here Nature first begins
Her farthest verge, and Chaos to retire,
As from her outmost works, a broken foe,
With tumult less and with less hostile din;   1040
That Satan with less toil, and now with ease,
Wafts on the calmer wave by dubious light,
And, like a weather-beaten vessel, holds
Gladly the port, though shrouds and tackle torn;
Or in the emptier waste, resembling air,   1045
Weighs his spread wings, at leisure to behold
Far off the empyreal Heaven, extended wide
In circuit, undetermined square or round,

1017. *Argo:* the ship in which Jason sought the Golden Fleece and safely
passed the straits of the Bosporus. 1019-20. Referring to Odysseus's safe
passing between Scylla and Charybdis. 1041. *That:* so that. 1048. *undetermined . . . round:* i.e., its shape is undefined.

With opal towers and battlements adorned
Of living sapphire, once his native seat,   1050
And, fast by, hanging in a golden chain,
This pendent World, in bigness as a star
Of smallest magnitude close by the moon.
Thither, full fraught with mischievous revenge,
Accurst, and in a cursèd hour, he hies.   1055

THE END OF THE SECOND BOOK

❧

BOOK III

THE ARGUMENT

   God, sitting on his throne, sees Satan flying towards this World, then newly created; shows him to the Son, who sat at his right hand; foretells the success of Satan in perverting mankind; clears his own justice and wisdom from all imputation, having created Man free, and able enough to have withstood his Tempter; yet declares his purpose of grace towards him, in regard he fell not of his own malice, as did Satan, but by him seduced. The Son of God renders praises to his Father for the manifestation of his gracious purpose towards Man: but God again declares that grace cannot be extended towards Man without the satisfaction of Divine Justice; Man hath offended the majesty of God by aspiring to Godhead, and therefore, with all his progeny, devoted to death, must die, unless some one can be found sufficient to answer for his offence, and undergo his punishment. The Son of God freely offers himself a ransom for Man: the Father accepts him, ordains his incarnation, pronounces his exaltation above all names in Heaven and Earth; commands all the Angels to adore him. They obey, and, hymning to their harps in full quire, celebrate the Father and the Son. Meanwhile Satan alights upon the bare convex of this World's outermost orb; where wandering he first finds a place since called the Limbo of Vanity; what persons and things fly up thither: thence comes to the gate of Heaven, described ascending by stairs, and the waters above the firmament that flow about it. His passage thence to the orb of the Sun: he finds there Uriel, the regent of that orb, but first changes himself into the shape of a meaner Angel, and, pretending a zealous desire to behold the new Creation, and Man whom God had placed here, inquires of him the place of his habitation, and is directed: alights first on Mount Niphates.

*H*AIL, holy Light, offspring of Heaven first-born!
Or of the Eternal coeternal beam
May I express thee unblamed? since God is light,
And never but in unapproachèd light
Dwelt from eternity—dwelt then in thee,   5
Bright effluence of bright essence increate!
Or hear'st thou rather pure Ethereal stream,
Whose fountain who shall tell? Before the Sun,
Before the Heavens, thou wert, and at the voice
Of God, as with a mantle, didst invest   10
The rising World of waters dark and deep,
Won from the void and formless Infinite!
Thee I revisit now with bolder wing,
Escaped the Stygian Pool, though long detained
In that obscure sojourn, while in my flight,   15
Through utter and through middle Darkness borne,
With other notes than to the Orphean lyre
I sung of Chaos and eternal Night,
Taught by the Heavenly Muse to venture down
The dark descent, and up to reascend,   20
Though hard and rare. Thee I revisit safe,
And feel thy sovran vital lamp; but thou
Revisit'st not these eyes, that roll in vain
To find thy piercing ray, and find no dawn;
So thick a drop serene hath quenched their orbs,   25
Or dim suffusion veiled. Yet not the more
Cease I to wander where the Muses haunt
Clear spring, or shady grove, or sunny hill,
Smit with the love of sacred song; but chief
Thee, Sion, and the flowery brooks beneath,   30
That wash thy hallowed feet, and warbling flow,
Nightly I visit: nor sometimes forget

---

3. *express . . . unblamed:* i.e., call thee without falling into a theological error. 6. *increate:* uncreated. 7. *hear'st . . . rather:* wouldst thou prefer to be called. 8-11 Milton refers to the creation of light as described in Genesis 1:3-5. 8. *Whose . . . tell:* i.e., of mysterious origin. 16. *utter, middle Darkness:* i.e., Hell and Chaos. 17. *Orpheus,* as the Renaissance interpreted him, was a great harmonizing and ordering influence; hence his kind of song would have been inappropriate to the theme of Hell and Chaos, but is now appropriate in treating Heaven. (Thus Milton remembers Orpheus again when he begins to describe the Creation, VII 32 ff.) 25. *drop serene:* English for *gutta serena,* a blindness in which the eye keeps its normal appearance. 26-32. I.e., Milton still loves and studies all poetry, but most the inspired poetry of Scripture.

Those other two equaled with me in fate,
So were I equaled with them in renown,
Blind Thamyris and blind Mæonides,   35
And Tiresias and Phineus, prophets old:
Then feed on thoughts that voluntary move
Harmonious numbers; as the wakeful bird
Sings darkling, and, in shadiest covert hid,
Tunes her nocturnal note. Thus with the year   40
Seasons return; but not to me returns
Day, or the sweet approach of even or morn,
Or sight of vernal bloom, or summer's rose,
Or flocks, or herds, or human face divine;
But cloud instead and ever-during dark   45
Surrounds me, from the cheerful ways of men
Cut off, and, for the book of knowledge fair,
Presented with a universal blank
Of Nature's works, to me expunged and rased,
And wisdom at one entrance quite shut out.   50
So much the rather thou, Celestial Light,
Shine inward, and the mind through all her powers
Irradiate; there plant eyes; all mist from thence
Purge and disperse, that I may see and tell
Of things invisible to mortal sight.   55
  Now had the Almighty Father from above,
From the pure Empyrean where He sits
High throned above all highth, bent down his eye,
His own works and their works at once to view:
About him all the Sanctities of Heaven   60
Stood thick as stars, and from his sight received
Beatitude past utterance; on his right
The radiant image of his glory sat,
His only Son. On Earth he first beheld
Our two first parents, yet the only two   65
Of mankind, in the Happy Garden placed,
Reaping immortal fruits of joy and love,
Uninterrupted joy, unrivaled love,
In blissful solitude. He then surveyed

---

34. So . . . I: would I were. 35. *Thamyris* is a legendary epic poet;
Maeonides is Homer; *Tiresias* and *Phineus* are legendary prophets, the
former appearing in Sophocles's *Oedipus Rex* and *Antigone,* and in Mr.
T. S. Eliot's *Waste Land.* 38. *numbers:* poetry. 39. *darkling:* in darkness.
60. *Sanctities:* ranks of angels.

Hell and the gulf between, and Satan there   70
Coasting the wall of Heaven on this side Night,
In the dun air sublime, and ready now
To stoop, with wearied wings and willing feet,
On the bare outside of this World, that seemed
Firm land imbosomed without firmament,   75
Uncertain which, in ocean or in air.
Him God beholding from his prospect high,
Wherein past, present, future, he beholds,
Thus to His only Son foreseeing spake:
"Only-begotten Son, seest thou what rage   80
Transports our Adversary? whom no bounds
Prescribed, no bars of Hell, nor all the chains
Heaped on him there, nor yet the main Abyss
Wide interrupt, can hold; so bent he seems
On desperate revenge, that shall redound   85
Upon his own rebellious head. And now,
Through all restraint broke loose, he wings his way
Not far off Heaven, in the precincts of light,
Directly towards the new-created World,
And Man there placed, with purpose to assay   90
If him by force he can destroy, or, worse,
By some false guile pervert: And shall pervert;
For Man will hearken to his glozing lies,
And easily transgress the sole command,
Sole pledge of his obedience: so will fall   95
He and his faithless progeny. Whose fault?
Whose but his own? Ingrate, he had of me
All he could have; I made him just and right,
Sufficient to have stood, though free to fall.
Such I created all the Ethereal Powers   100
And Spirits, both them who stood and them who failed;
Freely they stood who stood, and fell who fell.
Not free, what proof could they have given sincere
Of true allegiance, constant faith, or love,
Where only what they needs must do appeared,   105
Not what they would? What praise could they receive,
What pleasure I, from such obedience paid,

---

72. *sublime:* aloft. 74. *World:* the universe, not the earth. 84. *interrupt:*
i.e., "broken between" Hell and Earth. 97. *Ingrate:* ungrateful. 103-111.
I.e., if men were so made by God that they could act *only* virtuously, they
would be servants of "Necessity," not His servants.

When Will and Reason (Reason also is Choice),
Useless and vain, of freedom both despoiled,
Made passive both, had served Necessity,   110
Not Me? They, therefore, as to right belonged
So were created, nor can justly accuse
Their Maker, or their making, or their fate,
As if Predestination overruled
Their will, disposed by absolute decree   115
Or high foreknowledge. They themselves decreed
Their own revolt, not I. If I foreknew,
Foreknowledge had no influence on their fault,
Which had no less proved certain unforeknown.
So without least impulse or shadow of fate,   120
Or aught by me immutably foreseen,
They trespass, authors to themselves in all,
Both what they judge and what they choose; for so
I formed them free, and free they must remain
Till they enthrall themselves: I else must change   125
Their nature, and revoke the high decree
Unchangeable, eternal, which ordained
Their freedom; they themselves ordained their fall.
The first sort by their own suggestion fell,
Self-tempted, self-depraved; Man falls, deceived   130
By the other first: Man, therefore, shall find grace;
The other, none. In mercy and justice both,
Through Heaven and Earth, so shall my glory excel;
But mercy, first and last, shall brightest shine."
    Thus while God spake ambrosial fragrance filled   135
All Heaven, and in the blessed Spirits elect
Sense of new joy ineffable diffused.
Beyond compare the Son of God was seen
Most glorious; in him all his Father shone
Substantially expressed; and in his face   140
Divine compassion visibly appeared,
Love without end, and without measure grace;
Which uttering, thus He to his Father spake:
    "O Father, gracious was that word which closed
Thy sovran sentence, that Man should find grace;   145
For which both Heaven and Earth shall high extol
Thy praises, with the innumerable sound
Of hymns and sacred songs, wherewith thy throne

---

129. *The . . . sort:* the angels. *suggestion:* temptation. 131. *grace:* i.e., an
opportunity for redemption through God's mercy.

Encompassed shall resound thee ever blest.
For should Man finally be lost—should Man,   150
Thy creature late so loved, thy youngest son,
Fall circumvented thus by fraud, though joined
With his own folly? that be from thee far,
That far be from thee, Father, who art judge
Of all things made, and judgest only right!   155
Or shall the Adversary thus obtain
His end, and frustrate thine? shall he fulfil
His malice, and thy goodness bring to naught,
Or proud return, though to his heavier doom
Yet with revenge accomplished, and to Hell   160
Draw after him the whole race of mankind,
By him corrupted? Or wilt thou thyself
Abolish thy creation, and unmake,
For him, what for thy glory thou hast made?
So should thy goodness and thy greatness both   165
Be questioned and blasphemed without defence."
    To whom the great Creator thus replied:
"O Son, in whom my soul hath chief delight,
Son of my bosom, Son who art alone
My word, my wisdom, and effectual might,   170
All hast thou spoken as my thoughts are, all
As my eternal purpose hath decreed.
Man shall not quite be lost, but saved who will;
Yet not of will in him, but grace in me
Freely voutsafed. Once more I will renew   175
His lapsèd powers, though forfeit, and enthralled
By sin to foul exorbitant desires:
Upheld by me, yet once more he shall stand
On even ground against his mortal foe—
By me upheld, that he may know how frail   180
His fallen condition is, and to me owe
All his deliverance, and to none but me.
Some I have chosen of peculiar grace,
Elect above the rest; so is my will:
The rest shall hear me call, and oft be warned   185
Their sinful state, and to appease betimes

---

176. *lapsèd:* fallen. 183-90. Milton modifies the doctrine of election from its extreme form (according to which an individual's salvation depends on God's arbitrary choice of him) to a form in which it can be reconciled with free will—i.e., the number of the "peculiarly elect" is only a small proportion of the total number who can be saved if they seek grace.

The incensèd Deity, while offered grace
Invites; for I will clear their senses dark
What may suffice, and soften stony hearts
To pray, repent, and bring obedience due.   190
To prayer, repentance, and obedience due,
Though but endeavoured with sincere intent,
Mine ear shall not be slow, mine eye not shut.
And I will place within them as a guide
My umpire Conscience; whom if they will hear,   195
Light after light well used they shall attain,
And to the end persisting safe arrive.
This my long sufferance, and my day of grace,
They who neglect and scorn shall never taste;
But hard be hardened, blind be blinded more,   200
That they may stumble on, and deeper fall;
And none but such from mercy I exclude.—
But yet all is not done. Man disobeying,
Disloyal, breaks his fealty, and sins
Against the high supremacy of Heaven,   205
Affecting Godhead, and, so losing all,
To expiate his treason hath naught left,
But, to destruction sacred and devote,
He with his whole posterity must die:—
Die he or Justice must; unless for him   210
Some other, able, and as willing, pay
The rigid satisfaction, death for death.
Say, Heavenly Powers, where shall we find such love?
Which of ye will be mortal, to redeem
Man's mortal crime, and just, the unjust to save?   215
Dwells in all Heaven charity so dear?"
    He asked, but all the Heavenly Quire stood mute,
And silence was in Heaven: on Man's behalf
Patron or intercessor none appeared—
Much less that durst upon his own head draw   220
The deadly forfeiture, and ransom set.
And now without redemption all mankind
Must have been lost, adjudged to Death and Hell
By doom severe, had not the Son of God,
In whom the fulness dwells of love divine,   225
His dearest mediation thus renewed:
    "Father, thy word is passed, Man shall find grace;
And shall Grace not find means, that finds her way,

---

216. *charity:* i.e., love, as in the New Testament generally.

The speediest of thy wingèd messengers,
To visit all thy creatures, and to all   230
Comes unprevented, unimplored, unsought?
Happy for Man, so coming! He her aid
Can never seek, once dead in sins and lost—
Atonement for himself, or offering meet,
Indebted and undone, hath none to bring.   235
Behold *me,* then: me for him, life for life,
I offer; on me let thine anger fall;
Account me Man: I for his sake will leave
Thy bosom, and this glory next to thee
Freely put off, and for him lastly die   240
Well pleased; on me let Death wreak all his rage.
Under his gloomy power I shall not long
Lie vanquished. Thou hast given me to possess
Life in myself for ever; by thee I live;
Though now to Death I yield, and am his due,   245
All that of me can die, yet, that debt paid,
Thou wilt not leave me in the loathsome grave
His prey, nor suffer my unspotted soul
For ever with corruption there to dwell;
But I shall rise victorious, and subdue   250
My vanquisher, spoiled of his vaunted spoil.
Death his death's wound shall then receive, and stoop
Inglorious, of his mortal sting disarmed;
I through the ample air in triumph high
Shall lead Hell captive maugre Hell, and show   255
The powers of Darkness bound. Thou, at the sight
Pleased, out of Heaven shalt look down and smile,
While, by thee raised, I ruin all my foes—
Death last, and with his carcas glut the grave;
Then, with the multitude of my redeemed,   260
Shall enter Heaven, long absent, and return,
Father, to see thy face, wherein no cloud
Of anger shall remain, but peace assured
And reconcilement: wrath shall be no more
Thenceforth, but in thy presence joy entire."   265
    His words here ended; but his meek aspèct
Silent yet spake, and breathed immortal love
To mortal men, above which only shone
Filial obedience: as a sacrifice
Glad to be offered, he attends the will   270

---

231. *unprevented:* unanticipated. 234. *meet:* suitable. 255. *maugre:* despite.

Of his great Father. Admiration seized
All Heaven, what this might mean, and whither tend,
Wondering; but soon the Almighty thus replied:
  "O thou in Heaven and Earth the only peace
Found out for mankind under wrath, O thou   275
My sole complacence! well thou know'st how dear
To me are all my works; nor Man the least,
Though last created, that for him I spare
Thee from my bosom and right hand, to save,
By losing thee a while, the whole race lost!   280
Thou, therefore, whom thou only canst redeem,
Their nature also to thy nature join;
And be thyself Man among men on Earth,
Made flesh, when time shall be, of virgin seed,
By wondrous birth; be thou in Adam's room   285
The head of all mankind, though Adam's son.
As in him perish all men, so in thee,
As from a second root, shall be restored
As many as are restored; without thee, none.
His crime makes guilty all his sons; thy merit,   290
Imputed, shall absolve them who renounce
Their own both righteous and unrighteous deeds,
And live in thee transplanted, and from thee
Receive new life. So Man, as is most just,
Shall satisfy for Man, be judged and die,   295
And dying rise, and rising with him raise
His brethren, ransomed with his own dear life.
So Heavenly love shall outdo Hellish hate,
Giving to death, and dying to redeem,
So dearly to redeem what Hellish hate   300
So easily destroyed, and still destroys
In those who, when they may, accept not grace.
Nor shalt thou, by descending to assume
Man's nature, lessen or degrade thine own.
Because thou hast, though throned in highest bliss   305
Equal to God, and equally enjoying
God-like fruition, quitted all to save

---

276. *complacence:* pleasure—with allusion to "This is my beloved son in
whom I am well pleased" (Matthew 17:5). 281-2. Take on the nature, i.e.,
mortality, of those *whom thou only canst redeem.* 291. *imputed:* with
reference to the doctrine of imputed righteousness, i.e., the righteousness of
Christ *imputed* to—and so the cause of the salvation of—sinful man.

A world from utter loss, and hast been found
By merit more than birthright Son of God,—
Found worthiest to be so by being good,   310
Far more than great or high; because in thee
Love hath abounded more than glory abounds;
Therefore thy humiliation shall exalt
With thee thy manhood also to this throne:
Here shalt thou sit incarnate, here shalt reign   315
Both God and Man, Son both of God and Man,
Anointed universal King. All power
I give thee; reign for ever, and assume
Thy merits; under thee, as Head Supreme,
Thrones, Princedoms, Powers, Dominions, I reduce: 320
All knees to thee shall bow of them that bide
In Heaven, or Earth, or under Earth in Hell.
When thou, attended gloriously from Heaven,
Shalt in the sky appear, and from thee send
The summoning Archangels to proclaim   325
Thy dread tribunal, forthwith from all winds
The living, and forthwith the cited dead
Of all past ages, to the general doom
Shall hasten; such a peal shall rouse their sleep.
Then, all thy Saints assembled, thou shalt judge   330
Bad men and Angels; they arraigned shall sink
Beneath thy sentence; Hell, her numbers full,
Thenceforth shall be for ever shut. Meanwhile
The World shall burn, and from her ashes spring
New Heaven and Earth, wherein the just shall dwell,   335
And, after all their tribulations long,
See golden days, fruitful of golden deeds,
With Joy and Love triumphing, and fair Truth.
Then thou thy regal sceptre shalt lay by;
For regal sceptre then no more shall need,   340
God shall be all in all. But all ye gods,
Adore him who, to compass all this, dies;
Adore the Son, and honour him as me."
   No sooner had the Almighty ceased but—all
The multitude of Angels, with a shout   345
Loud as from numbers without number, sweet

320. I.e., all the angelic ranks (not merely the four named). 326. *winds:*
directions. 327. *cited:* summoned. 335. *New . . . Earth:* i.e., as predicted
in Revelation 21:1. 341. *gods:* i.e., angels.

As from blest voices, uttering joy—Heaven rung
With jubilee, and loud hosannas filled
The eternal regions. Lowly reverent
Towards either throne they bow, and to the ground　　350
With solemn adoration down they cast
Their crowns, inwove with amarant and gold,—
Immortal amarant, a flower which once
In Paradise, fast by the Tree of Life,
Began to bloom, but, soon for Man's offence　　355
To Heaven removed where first it grew, there grows
And flowers aloft, shading the Fount of Life,
And where the River of Bliss through midst of Heaven
Rolls o'er Elysian flowers her amber stream!
With these, that never fade, the Spirits elect　　360
Bind their resplendent locks, inwreathed with beams.
Now in loose garlands thick thrown off, the bright
Pavement, that like a sea of jasper shone,
Impurpled with celestial roses smiled.
Then, crowned again, their golden harps they took—　　365
Harps ever tuned, that glittering by their side
Like quivers hung; and with preamble sweet
Of charming symphony they introduce
Their sacred song, and waken raptures high:
No voice exempt, no voice but well could join　　370
Melodious part; such concord is in Heaven.
　　Thee, Father, first they sung, Omnipotent,
Immutable, Immortal, Infinite,
Eternal King; thee, Author of all being,
Fountain of light, thyself invisible　　375
Amidst the glorious brightness where thou sitt'st
Throned inaccessible, but when thou shad'st
The full blaze of thy beams, and through a cloud
Drawn round about thee like a radiant shrine
Dark with excessive bright thy skirts appear,　　380
Yet dazzle Heaven, that brightest Seraphim
Approach not, but with both wings veil their eyes.

---

352. *amarant and gold:* the mythical flower that never fades, and the "perfect" metal of the alchemists which nothing impairs. 358-9. Revelation 22:1: "And he shewed me a pure river of water of life, clear as crystal, proceeding out of the throne of God." 362. *Now . . . off:* i.e., owing to the thick-scattered garlanded crowns. 363. *that . . . shone:* Revelation 4:6—"And before the throne was a sea of glass." 371. *part:* i.e., as in "part-singing." 377. *but:* except.

Thee next they sang, of all creation first,
Begotten Son, Divine Similitude,
In whose conspicuous countenance, without cloud   385
Made visible, the Almighty Father shines,
Whom else no creature can behold: on thee
Impressed the effulgence of his glory abides;
Transfused on thee his ample Spirit rests.
He Heaven of Heavens, and all the Powers therein,   390
By thee created; and by thee threw down
The aspiring Dominations. Thou that day
Thy Father's dreadful thunder didst not spare,
Nor stop thy flaming chariot-wheels, that shook
Heaven's everlasting frame, while o'er the necks   395
Thou drov'st of warring Angels disarrayed.
Back from pursuit, thy Powers with loud acclaim
Thee only extolled, Son of thy Father's might,
To execute fierce vengeance on his foes.
Not so on Man: him, through their malice fallen,   400
Father of mercy and grace, thou didst not doom
So strictly, but much more to pity incline:
No sooner did thy dear and only Son
Perceive thee purposed not to doom frail Man
So strictly, but much more to pity inclined,   405
He, to appease thy wrath, and end the strife
Of mercy and justice in thy face discerned,
Regardless of the bliss wherein he sat
Second to thee, offered himself to die
For Man's offence. O unexampled love!   410
Love nowhere to be found less than Divine!
Hail, Son of God, Saviour of men! Thy name
Shall be the copious matter of my song
Henceforth, and never shall my harp thy praise
Forget, nor from thy Father's praise disjoin!   415
    Thus they in Heaven, above the Starry Sphere,
Their happy hours in joy and hymning spent.
Meanwhile, upon the firm opacous globe
Of this round World, whose first convex divides
The luminous inferior Orbs, enclosed   420
From Chaos and the inroad of Darkness old,

392. *Dominations:* the rebel angels. 418. *opacous:* not shining (with the
exception noted at 427-9). 418 ff. On Milton's "cosmos," see the drawing
on page 98.

Satan alighted walks. A globe far off
It seemed; now seems a boundless continent,
Dark, waste, and wild, under the frown of Night
Starless exposed, and ever-threatening storms
Of Chaos blustering round, inclement sky,   425
Save on that side which from the wall of Heaven,
Though distant far, some small reflection gains
Of glimmering air less vexed with tempest loud.
Here walked the Fiend at large in spacious field.   430
As when a vulture, on Imaus bred,
Whose snowy ridge the roving Tartar bounds,
Dislodging from a region scarce of prey,
To gorge the flesh of lambs or yeanling kids
On hills where flocks are fed, flies toward the springs   435
Of Ganges or Hydaspes, Indian streams,
But in his way lights on the barren plains
Of Sericana, where Chineses drive
With sails and wind their cany waggons light:
So, on this windy sea of land, the Fiend   440
Walked up and down alone, bent on his prey;
Alone, for other creature in this place,
Living or lifeless, to be found was none;—
None yet; but store hereafter from the Earth
Up hither like aerial vapours flew   445
Of all things transitory and vain, when Sin
With vanity had filled the works of men—
Both all things vain, and all who in vain things
Built their fond hopes of glory or lasting fame,
Or happiness in this or the other life.   450
All who have their reward on earth, the fruits
Of painful superstition and blind zeal,
Naught seeking but the praise of men, here find
Fit retribution, empty as their deeds;
All the unaccomplished works of Nature's hand,   455
Abortive, monstrous, or unkindly mixed,
Dissolved on Earth, fleet hither, and in vain,
Till final dissolution, wander here—
Not in the neighbouring Moon, as some have dreamed:

---

431. *Imaus:* A range of mountains in Afghanistan. 438. *Sericana:* Indo-
China. 442 ff. Milton's "Paradise of Fools"—partly an attack on Roman
Catholicism.

Those argent fields more likely habitants—   460
Translated Saints, or middle Spirits—hold
Betwixt the angelical and human kind.
Hither, of ill-joined sons and daughters born,
First from the ancient world those Giants came,
With many a vain exploit, though then renowned: 465
The builders next Babel on the plain
Of Sennaar, and still with vain design
New Babels, had they wherewithal, would build:
Others came single; he who, to be deemed
A god, leaped fondly into Ætna flames,   470
Empedocles; and he who, to enjoy
Plato's Elysium, leaped into the sea,
Cleombrotus; and many more, too long,
Embryos and idiots, eremites and friars,
White, black, and grey, with all their trumpery.   475
Here pilgrims roam, that strayed so far to seek
In Golgotha him dead who lives in Heaven;
And they who, to be sure of Paradise,
Dying put on the weeds of Dominic,
Or in Franciscan think to pass disguised.   480
They pass the planets seven, and pass the fixed,
And that crystalline sphere whose balance weighs
The trepidation talked, and that first moved;
And now Saint Peter at Heaven's wicket seems
To wait them with his keys, and now at foot   485
Of Heaven's ascent they lift their feet, when, lo!
A violent cross wind from either coast
Blows them transverse, ten thousand leagues awry,
Into the devious air. Then might ye see
Cowls, hoods, and habits, with their wearers, tost   490

---

460. *Those . . . fields:* i.e., the moon. 464. *Giants:* i.e., the giants of Genesis 6:1-4. 467. *Sennaar:* Shinar, where the Tower of Babel was built (Genesis 11:2). 470. *fondly:* foolishly (because he is reputed to have leaped in the vain hope of being thought a god). 471. *he:* Cleombrotus of Epirus is said to have committed suicide with this intent. 475. *White . . . grey:* i.e., the Carmelites, Dominicans, Franciscans, known by their habits as White Friars, Black Friars, and Grey Friars. 477. *Golgotha:* Christ's burial place. 481. *the fixed:* the fixed stars. 482-3. *whose . . . talked:* i.e., which oscillates (like a scale: *balance*) to make the *talked-of trepidation* (i.e., the movement by which the precession of the equinoxes used to be explained). 483. *first moved:* the *primum mobile,* outermost of the spheres, thought of as moving all the rest.

And fluttered into rags; then reliques, beads,
Indulgences, dispenses, pardons, bulls,
The sport of winds: all these, upwhirled aloft,
Fly o'er the backside of the World far off
Into a Limbo large and broad, since called   495
The Paradise of Fools; to few unknown
Long after, now unpeopled and untrod.
  All this dark globe the Fiend found as he passed;
And long he wandered, till at last a gleam
Of dawning light turned thitherward in haste   500
His travelled steps. Far distant he descries,
Ascending by degrees magnificent
Up to the wall of Heaven, a structure high;
At top whereof, but far more rich, appeared
The work as of a kingly palace-gate,   505
With frontispiece of diamond and gold
Embellished; thick with sparkling orient gems
The portal shone, inimitable on Earth
By model, or by shading pencil drawn.
The stairs were such as whereon Jacob saw   510
Angels ascending and descending, bands
Of guardians bright, when he from Esau fled
To Padan-Aram, in the field of Luz
Dreaming by night under the open sky,
And waking cried, *This is the gate of Heaven.*   515
Each stair mysteriously was meant, nor stood
There always, but drawn up to Heaven sometimes
Viewless; and underneath a bright sea flowed
Of jasper, or of liquid pearl, whereon
Who after came from Earth, sailing arrived,   520
Wafted by Angels, or flew o'er the lake
Rapt in a chariot drawn by fiery steeds.
The stairs were then let down, whether to dare
The Fiend by easy ascent, or aggravate
His sad exclusion from the doors of bliss: 525
Direct against which opened from beneath,

---

491. *beads:* prayer beads. 492. *dispenses:* dispensations from vows. 497.
now: i.e., at this early date. 502. *degrees:* steps (the *structure high* is like
Jacob's ladder). 506. *frontispiece:* façade. 510-15. Cf. Genesis 28:10-19.
520-2. The references are to Lazarus, translated "by the angels into Abraham's bosom," i.e., heaven (Luke 16:22); and to Elijah, who was carried to
heaven in "a chariot of fire" (2 Kings 2:11). 523. *Then:* at this time.

Just o'er the blissful seat of Paradise,
A passage down to the Earth—a passage wide;
Wider by far than that of after-times
Over Mount Sion, and, though that were large,   530
Over the Promised Land to God so dear,
By which, to visit oft those happy tribes,
On high behests his Angels to and fro
Passed frequent, and his eye with choice regard
From Paneas, the fount of Jordan's flood,   535
To Beërsaba, where the Holy Land
Borders on Egypt and the Arabian shore:
So wide the opening seemed, where bounds were set
To darkness, such as bound the ocean wave.
    Satan from hence, now on the lower stair,   540
That scaled by steps of gold to Heaven-gate,
Looks down with wonder at the sudden view
Of all this World at once. As when a scout,
Through dark and desert ways with peril gone
All night, at last by break of cheerful dawn   545
Obtains the brow of some high-climbing hill,
Which to his eye discovers unaware
The goodly prospect of some foreign land
First seen, or some renowned metropolis
With glistering spires and pinnacles adorned,   550
Which now the rising sun gilds with his beams;
Such wonder seized, though after Heaven seen,
The Spirit malign, but much more envy seized,
At sight of all this World beheld so fair.
Round he surveys (and well might, where he stood   555
So high above the circling canopy
Of Night's extended shade) from eastern point
Of Libra to the fleecy star that bears
Andromeda far off Atlantic seas
Beyond the horizon; then from pole to pole   560
He views in breadth,—and, without longer pause,
Down right into the World's first region throws

535-6. *From . . . Beërsaba:* from one end to the other—Paneas (or Dan)
being in the north and Beërsaba in the south. 534-7. *and . . . shore:* The
verb is "passed," understood after *eye.* 552. *though . . . seen:* even though
he had formerly seen the spheres of heaven. 557-9. *from . . . Andromeda:*
from the Zodiacal sign, the Scales, to the opposite sign, the Ram (*fleecy
star*), which is just under the constellation Andromeda and so can be represented as bearing "her" on its back.

His flight precipitant, and winds with ease
Through the pure marble air his oblique way
Amongst innumerable stars, that shone   565
Stars distant, but nigh-hand seemed other worlds.
Or other worlds they seemed, or happy isles,
Like those Hesperian Gardens famed of old,
Fortunate fields, and groves, and flowery vales;
Thrice happy isles! but who dwelt happy there   570
He staid not to inquire: above them all
The golden Sun, in splendour likest Heaven,
Allured his eye. Thither his course he bends,
Through the calm firmament (but up or down,
By centre or eccentric, hard to tell,   575
Or longitude) where the great luminary,
Aloof the vulgar constellations thick,
That from his lordly eye keep distance due,
Dispenses light from far. They, as they move
Their starry dance in numbers that compute   580
Days, months, and years, towards his all-cheering lamp
Turn swift their various motions, or are turned
By his magnetic beam, that gently warms
The Universe, and to each inward part
With gentle penetration, though unseen,   585
Shoots invisible virtue even to the Deep;
So wondrously was set his station bright.
    There lands the Fiend, a spot like which perhaps
Astronomer in the Sun's lucent orb
Through his glazed optic tube yet never saw.   590
The place he found beyond expression bright,
Compared with aught on Earth, metal or stone—
Not all parts like, but all alike informed
With radiant light, as glowing iron with fire.
If metal, part seemed gold, part silver clear;   595
If stone, carbuncle most or chrysolite,
Ruby or topaz, to the twelve that shone
In Aaron's breast-plate, and a stone besides,
Imagined rather oft than elsewhere seen—

---

564. *marble:* smooth as marble. 568. *Hesperian Gardens:* Cf. *Comus,* 393 n.
575. *By . . . eccentric:* i.e., whether toward earth or away from it. Cf.
IV 592-5 n. 577. *Aloof:* i.e., aloof from. 586. *virtue:* generative power.
588-90. *spot. . . . saw:* Sun spots had been detected by Galileo in 1609. 597.
to . . . twelve: including the twelve. Cf. Exodus 28:17-20.

That stone, or like to that, which here below   600
Philosophers in vain so long have sought;
In vain, though by their powerful art they bind
Volatile Hermes, and call up unbound
In various shapes old Proteus from the sea,
Drained through a limbec to his native form.   605
What wonder then if fields and regions here
Breathe forth elixir pure, and rivers run
Potable gold, when, with one virtuous touch,
The arch-chemic Sun, so far from us remote,
Produces, with terrestrial humour mixed,   610
Here in the dark so many precious things
Of colour glorious and effect so rare?
Here matter new to gaze the Devil met
Undazzled. Far and wide his eye commands;
For sight no obstacle found here, nor shade,   615
But all sunshine, as when his beams at noon
Culminate from the equator, as they now
Shot upward still direct, whence no way round
Shadow from body opaque can fall; and the air,
Nowhere so clear, sharpened his visual ray   620
To objects distant far, whereby he soon
Saw within ken a glorious Angel stand,
The same whom John saw also in the Sun.
His back was turned, but not his brightness hid;
Of beaming sunny rays a golden tiar   625
Circled his head, nor less his locks behind
Illustrious on his shoulders fledge with wings
Lay waving round: on some great charge employed

600-1. The "philosopher's stone," supposed in alchemy to be able to trans-
mute baser metals into gold. 603. *Hermes:* Mercury, i.e., quicksilver, of
which each other metal was believed by alchemists to be a special "fixation."
604. *Proteus:* Homer's Old Man of the Sea, who transforms himself into
many shapes to avoid being caught, became a suggestive Renaissance symbol, as here, of a mysterious primeval substance to which all forms of matter
could theoretically be reduced. 605. *limbec:* alembic, a distilling vessel.
607. *elixir:* the supposed "elixir of life" obtained from the "perfect metal,"
gold. 608. *virtuous:* Cf. *virtue* in 586. 610-12. *Produces . . . rare:* i.e., the
sun's rays mixing with earth's moisture form the gems and precious metals.
This was the standard theory of their origin. 617. *Culminate:* Reach their
highest altitude. 620. *ray:* His sight, thought of as a beam emitted from the
eye. 623. Cf. Revelation 19:17. 627. *illustrious:* shining. *fledge:* feathered.

He seemed, or fixed in cogitation deep.
Glad was the Spirit impure, as now in hope   630
To find who might direct his wandering flight
To Paradise, the happy seat of Man,
His journey's end, and our beginning woe.
But first he casts to change his proper shape,
Which else might work him danger or delay: 635
And now a stripling Cherub he appears,
Not of the prime, yet such as in his face
Youth smiled celestial, and to every limb
Suitable grace diffused; so well he feigned.
Under a coronet his flowing hair   640
In curls on either cheek played, wings he wore
Of many a coloured plume sprinkled with gold,
His habit fit for speed succinct, and held
Before his decent steps a silver wand.
He drew not nigh unheard; the Angel bright,   645
Ere he drew nigh, his radiant visage turned,
Admonished by his ear, and straight was known
The Archangel Uriel—one of the seven
Who in God's presence, nearest to his throne,
Stand ready at command, and are his eyes   650
That run through all the Heavens, or down to the Earth
Bear his swift errands over moist and dry,
O'er sea and land. Him Satan thus accosts:
   "Uriel! for thou of those seven Spirits that stand
In sight of God's high throne, gloriously bright,   655
The first art wont his great authentic will
Interpreter through highest Heaven to bring,
Where all his Sons thy embassy attend,
And here art likeliest by supreme decree
Like honour to obtain, and as his eye   660
To visit oft this new Creation round—
Unspeakable desire to see and know
All these his wondrous works, but chiefly Man,
His chief delight and favour, him for whom
All these his works so wondrous he ordained,   665
Hath brought me from the quires of Cherubim
Alone thus wandering. Brightest Seraph, tell

---

643. *succinct:* tucked up. 656-7. I.e., art accustomed to be the first to make
known God's commands throughout heaven and to interpret them. 659.
here: i.e., in the sun.

In which of all these shining orbs hath Man
His fixèd seat—or fixèd seat hath none,
But all these shining orbs his choice to dwell—   670
That I may find him, and with secret gaze
Or open admiration him behold
On whom the great Creator hath bestowed
Worlds, and on whom hath all these graces poured;
That both in him and all things, as is meet,   675
The Universal Maker we may praise;
Who justly hath driven out his rebel foes
To deepest Hell, and to repair that loss
Created this new happy race of Men
To serve him better: Wise are all his ways!"   680
    So spake the false dissembler unperceived;
For neither man nor angel can discern
Hypocrisy—the only evil that walks
Invisible, except to God alone,
By his permissive will, through Heaven and Earth;   685
And oft, though Wisdom wake, Suspicion sleeps
At Wisdom's gate, and to Simplicity
Resigns her charge, while Goodness thinks no ill
Where no ill seems: which now for once beguiled
Uriel, though Regent of the Sun, and held   690
The sharpest-sighted Spirit of all in Heaven;
Who to the fraudulent impostor foul,
In his uprightness, answer thus returned:
    "Fair Angel, thy desire, which tends to know
The works of God, thereby to glorify   695
The great Work-master, leads to no excess
That reaches blame, but rather merits praise
The more it seems excess, that led thee hither
From thy empyreal mansion thus alone,
To witness with thine eyes what some perhaps   700
Contented with report hear only in Heaven:
For wonderful indeed are all his works,
Pleasant to know, and worthiest to be all
Had in remembrance always with delight;
But what created mind can comprehend   705
Their number, or the wisdom infinite
That brought them forth, but hid their causes deep?
I saw when, at his Word, the formless mass,

---

685. *permissive:* i.e., God permits creatures of free will to do evil, but does
not cause them to do it. 694. *tends:* aims.

This World's material mould, came to a heap:
Confusion heard his voice, and wild Uproar   710
Stood ruled, stood vast Infinitude confined;
Till, at his second bidding, Darkness fled,
Light shone, and order from disorder sprung.
Swift to their several quarters hasted then
The cumbrous elements—Earth, Flood, Air, Fire;   715
And this ethereal quintessence of Heaven
Flew upward, spirited with various forms,
That rolled orbicular, and turned to stars
Numberless, as thou seest, and how they move:
Each had his place appointed, each his course;   720
The rest in circuit walls this Universe.
Look downward on that globe, whose hither side
With light from hence, though but reflected, shines:
That place is Earth, the seat of Man; that light
His day, which else, as the other hemisphere,   725
Night would invade; but there the neighbouring Moon
(So call that opposite fair star) her aid
Timely interposes, and, her monthly round
Still ending, still renewing, through mid-heaven,
With borrowed light her countenance triform   730
Hence fills and empties, to enlighten the Earth,
And in her pale dominion checks the night.
That spot to which I point is Paradise,
Adam's abode; those lofty shades his bower.
Thy way thou canst not miss; me mine requires."   735
   Thus said, he turned; and Satan, bowing low,
As to superior Spirits is wont in Heaven,
Where honour due and reverence none neglects,
Took leave, and toward the coast of Earth beneath,
Down from the ecliptic, sped with hoped success,   740
Throws his steep flight in many an aery wheel,
Nor staid till on Niphates' top he lights.

THE END OF THE THIRD BOOK

❧

716. *quintessence:* the fifth element of which the stars were supposed to be made. 717 *spirited:* the heavenly bodies were traditionally thought of as spiritual beings. 721. *rest:* of the quintessence. 730. *triform:* so-called owing to the three phases—crescent, full, and waning. 742. *Niphates:* a mountain in Mesopotamia, where Eden was usually supposed to have been situated.

BOOK IV

THE ARGUMENT

Satan, now in prospect of Eden, and nigh the place where he must now attempt the bold enterprise which he undertook alone against God and Man, falls into many doubts with himself, and many passions—fear, envy, and despair; but at length confirms himself in evil; journeys on to Paradise, whose outward prospect and situation is described; overleaps the bounds; sits, in the shape of a cormorant, on the Tree of Life, as highest in the Garden, to look about him. The Garden described; Satan's first sight of Adam and Eve; his wonder at their excellent form and happy state, but with resolution to work their fall; overhears their discourse; thence gathers that the Tree of Knowledge was forbidden them to eat of under penalty of death, and thereon intends to found his temptation by seducing them to transgress; then leaves them a while, to know further of their state by some other means. Meanwhile Uriel, descending on a sunbeam, warns Gabriel, who had in charge the gate of Paradise, that some evil Spirit had escaped the Deep, and passed at noon by his Sphere, in the shape of a good Angel, down to Paradise, discovered after by his furious gestures in the mount. Gabriel promises to find him ere morning. Night coming on, Adam and Eve discourse of going to their rest: their bower described; their evening worship. Gabriel, drawing forth his bands of night-watch to walk the rounds of Paradise, appoints two strong Angels to Adam's bower, lest the evil Spirit should be there doing some harm to Adam or Eve sleeping: there they find him at the ear of Eve, tempting her in a dream, and bring him, though unwilling, to Gabriel; by whom questioned, he scornfully answers; prepares resistance; but, hindered by a sign from Heaven, flies out of Paradise.

O FOR that warning voice, which he who saw
The Apocalypse heard cry in Heaven aloud,
Then when the Dragon, put to second rout,
Came furious down to be revenged on men,

1-2. *he . . . Apocalypse:* i.e., he who saw the visions recorded in Revelation. 3. *Dragon:* Revelation 12:9—"And the great Dragon was cast out, . . . called . . . Satan."

Woe to the inhabitants on Earth! that now,   5
While time was, our first parents had been warned
The coming of their secret foe, and scaped,
Haply so scaped, his mortal snare! For now
Satan, now first inflamed with rage, came down,
The tempter, ere the accuser, of mankind,   10
To wreak on innocent frail Man his loss
Of that first battle, and his flight to Hell.
Yet not rejoicing in his speed, though bold
Far off and fearless, nor with cause to boast,
Begins his dire attempt; which, nigh the birth   15
Now rolling, boils in his tumultuous breast,
And like a devilish engine back recoils
Upon himself. Horror and doubt distract
His troubled thoughts, and from the bottom stir
The hell within him; for within him Hell   20
He brings, and round about him, nor from Hell
One step, no more than from himself, can fly
By change of place. Now conscience wakes despair
That slumbered; wakes the bitter memory
Of what he was, what is, and what must be   25
Worse; of worse deeds worse sufferings must ensue!
Sometimes towards Eden, which now in his view
Lay pleasant, his grieved look he fixes sad;
Sometimes towards Heaven and the full-blazing Sun,
Which now sat high in his meridian tower: 30
Then, much revolving, thus in sighs began:
    "O thou that, with surpassing glory crowned,
Look'st from thy sole dominion like the god
Of this new World—at whose sight all the stars
Hide their diminished heads—to thee I call,   35
But with no friendly voice, and add thy name,
O Sun, to tell thee how I hate thy beams,
That bring to my remembrance from what state
I fell, how glorious once above thy sphere,
Till pride and worse ambition threw me down,   40
Warring in Heaven against Heaven's matchless King!
Ah, wherefore? He deserved no such return
From me, whom he created what I was

---

5. *Woe . . . Earth!* Revelation 12:10-12: "And I heard a loud voice . . .
in heaven, . . . 'Woe to the inhabiters of the earth and of the sea! for the
devil is come down unto you.'" 6. *While . . . was:* while there was still
time. 10. *accuser:* Satan is so called in Revelation 12:10.

In that bright eminence, and with his good
Upbraided none; nor was his service hard. 45
What could be less than to afford him praise,
The easiest recompense, and pay him thanks,
How due! Yet all his good proved ill in me,
And wrought but malice. Lifted up so high,
I 'sdained subjection, and thought one step higher 50
Would set me highest, and in a moment quit
The debt immense of endless gratitude,
So burdensome, still paying, still to owe;
Forgetful what from him I still received;
And understood not that a grateful mind 55
By owing owes not, but still pays, at once
Indebted and discharged—what burden then?
Oh, had his powerful destiny ordained
Me some inferior Angel, I had stood
Then happy; no unbounded hope had raised 60
Ambition. Yet why not? Some other Power
As great might have aspired, and me, though mean,
Drawn to his part. But other Powers as great
Fell not, but stand unshaken, from within
Or from without to all temptations armed! 65
Hadst thou the same free will and power to stand?
Thou hadst. Whom hast thou then, or what, to accuse,
But Heaven's free love dealt equally to all?
Be then his love accursed, since, love or hate,
To me alike it deals eternal woe. 70
Nay, cursed be thou; since against His thy will
Chose freely what it now so justly rues.
Me miserable! which way shall I fly — admits he is a crude.
Infinite wrath and infinite despair?
Which way I fly is Hell; myself am Hell; 75
And, in the lowest deep, a lower deep
Still threatening to devour me opens wide,
To which the Hell I suffer seems a Heaven.
O then at last relent! Is there no place
Left for repentance, none for pardon left? 80
None left but by submission; and that word,
Disdain forbids me, and my dread of shame
Among the Spirits beneath, whom I seduced
With other promises and other vaunts

---

44. *bright eminence:* Satan has only *bad eminence* in Hell (II 6). 51. *quit:*
free me from.

Than to submit, boasting I could subdue   85
The Omnipotent. Ay me! they little know
How dearly I abide that boast so vain,
Under what torments inwardly I groan.
While they adore me on the throne of Hell,
With diadem and sceptre high advanced,   90
The lower still I fall, only supreme
In misery: such joy ambition finds!
But say I could repent, and could obtain,
By act of grace, my former state; how soon
Would highth recall high thoughts, how soon unsay   95
What feigned submission swore! Ease would recant
Vows made in pain, as violent and void
(For never can true reconcilement grow
Where wounds of deadly hate have pierced so deep);
Which would but lead me to a worse relapse   100
And heavier fall: so should I purchase dear
Short intermission, bought with double smart.
This knows my Punisher, therefore as far
From granting He, as I from begging, peace.
All hope excluded thus, behold instead   105
Of us out-cast, exiled, his new delight,
Mankind, created, and for him this World.
So farewell hope, and with hope farewell fear,
Farewell remorse! All good to me is lost;
Evil, be thou my Good: by thee at least   110
Divided empire with Heaven's King I hold,
By thee, and more than half perhaps will reign;
As Man ere long, and this new World, shall know."
   Thus while he spake, each passion dimmed his face,
Thrice changed with pale—ire, envy, and despair;   115
Which marred his borrowed visage, and betrayed
Him counterfeit, if any eye beheld:
For Heavenly minds from such distempers foul
Are ever clear. Whereof he soon aware
Each perturbation smoothed with outward calm,   120
Artificer of fraud; and was the first
That practised falsehood under saintly show,
Deep malice to conceal, couched with revenge:

102. *intermission:* i.e., of pain. 115. *with pale:* with paleness (as each passion drained the blood from his face). 116. *borrowed visage:* Cf. III 634 ff.
123. *couched:* hidden away.

Yet not enough had practised to deceive
Uriel, once warned; whose eye pursued him down   125
The way he went, and on the Assyrian mount
Saw him disfigured, more than could befall
Spirit of happy sort: his gestures fierce
He marked and mad demeanour, then alone,
As he supposed, all unobserved, unseen.   130
    So on he fares, and to the border comes
Of Eden, where delicious Paradise,
Now nearer, crowns with her enclosure green,
As with a rural mound, the champaign head
Of a steep wilderness, whose hairy sides   135
With thicket overgrown, grotesque and wild,
Access denied; and overhead up-grew
Insuperable highth of loftiest shade,
Cedar, and pine, and fir, and branching palm,
A sylvan scene, and as the ranks ascend   140
Shade above shade, a woody theatre
Of stateliest view. Yet higher than their tops
The verdurous wall of Paradise up-sprung;
Which to our general sire gave prospect large
Into his nether empire neighbouring round.   145
And higher than that wall a circling row
Of goodliest trees, loaden with fairest fruit,
Blossoms and fruits at once of golden hue,
Appeared, with gay enamelled colours mixed;
On which the sun more glad impressed his beams   150
Than in fair evening cloud, or humid bow,
When God hath showered the earth: so lovely seemed
That landskip. And of pure now purer air
Meets his approach, and to the heart inspires
Vernal delight and joy, able to drive   155
All sadness but despair. Now gentle gales,
Fanning their odoriferous wings, dispense
Native perfumes, and whisper whence they stole
Those balmy spoils. As, when to them who sail
Beyond the Cape of Hope, and now are past   160
Mozambic, off at sea north-east winds blow
Sabean odours from the spicy shore

---

126. *Assyrian mount:* Niphates. 134. *champaign head:* level top. 144.
sire: Adam. 151. *humid bow:* rainbow. 161. *Mozambic:* Mozambique, an
island off Portuguese East Africa. 162. *Sabean:* Arabian.

Of Araby the Blest, with such delay
Well pleased they slack their course, and many a league
Cheered with the grateful smell old Ocean smiles: 165
So entertained those odorous sweets the Fiend
Who came their bane, though with them better pleased
Than Asmodëus with the fishy fume
That drove him, though enamoured, from the spouse
Of Tobit's son, and with a vengeance sent   170
From Media post to Egypt, there fast bound.
   Now to the ascent of that steep savage hill
Satan had journeyed on, pensive and slow;
But further way found none; so thick entwined,
As one continued brake, the undergrowth   175
Of shrubs and tangling bushes had perplexed
All path of man or beast that passed that way.
One gate there only was, and that looked east
On the other side: which when the Arch-Felon saw,
Due entrance he disdained, and, in contempt,   180
At one slight bound high overleaped all bound
Of hill or highest wall, and sheer within
Lights on his feet. As when a prowling wolf,
Whom hunger drives to seek new haunt for prey,
Watching where shepherds pen their flocks at eve,   185
In hurdled cotes amid the field secure,
Leaps o'er the fence with ease into the fold;
Or as a thief, bent to unhoard the cash
Of some rich burgher, whose substantial doors,
Cross-barred and bolted fast, fear no assault,   190
In at the window climbs, or o'er the tiles:
So clomb this first grand Thief into God's fold;
So since into his Church lewd hirelings climb.
Thence up he flew, and on the Tree of Life,
The middle tree and highest there that grew,   195
Sat like a cormorant; yet not true life
Thereby regained, but sat devising death
To them who lived; nor on the virtue thought
Of that life-giving plant, but only used

---

167. *bane:* destroyer. 168-71. *Tobit's son* Tobias, about to celebrate his
wedding night, was warned to save his life from the evil spirit Asmodëus
(who coveted the bride for himself) by burning a fish's heart and liver in
the room. The spirit fled from the *fishy fume* as far as Egypt. 175. *brake:*
thicket. 186. *In . . . cotes:* within fences made of interwoven boughs. 192.
Cf. *Lycidas,* 115.

For prospect what, well used, had been the pledge   200
Of immortality. So little knows
Any, but God alone, to value right
The good before him, but perverts best things
To worst abuse, or to their meanest use.
Beneath him, with new wonder, now he views,   205
To all delight of human sense exposed,
In narrow room Nature's whole wealth; yea more,
A Heaven on Earth: for blissful Paradise
Of God the garden was, by him in the east
Of Eden planted. Eden stretched her line   210
From Auran eastward to the royal towers
Of great Seleucia, built by Grecian kings,
Or where the sons of Eden long before
Dwelt in Telassar. In this pleasant soil
His far more pleasant garden God ordained.   215
Out of the fertile ground he caused to grow
All trees of noblest kind for sight, smell, taste;
And all amid them stood the Tree of Life,
High eminent, blooming ambrosial fruit
Of vegetable gold; and next to life,   220
Our death, the Tree of Knowledge, grew fast by—
Knowledge of good, bought dear by knowing ill.
Southward through Eden went a river large,
Nor changed his course, but through the shaggy hill
Passed underneath ingulfed; for God had thrown   225
That mountain, as his garden-mould, high raised
Upon the rapid current, which, through veins
Of porous earth with kindly thirst up-drawn,
Rose a fresh fountain, and with many a rill
Watered the garden; thence united fell   230
Down the steep glade, and met the nether flood,
Which from his darksome passage now appears,
And now, divided into four main streams,
Runs diverse, wandering many a famous realm
And country whereof here needs no account;   235
But rather to tell how, if Art could tell
How, from that sapphire fount the crispèd brooks,
Rolling on orient pearl and sands of gold,

---

200. *For prospect:* i.e., for looking around. 211-14. *Auran, Seleucia, Telassar:*
cities in or near the Mesopotamian region identified with Eden. 237.
crispèd: rippled.

With mazy error under pendent shades
Ran nectar, visiting each plant, and fed   240
Flowers worthy of Paradise, which not nice Art
In beds and curious knots, but Nature boon
Poured forth profuse on hill, and dale, and plain,
Both where the morning sun first warmly smote
The open field, and where the unpierced shade   245
Imbrowned the noontide bowers. Thus was this place,
A happy rural seat of various view:
Groves whose rich trees wept odorous gums and balm;
Others whose fruit, burnished with golden rind,
Hung amiable—Hesperian fables true,   250
If true, here only—and of delicious taste.
Betwixt them lawns, or level downs, and flocks
Grazing the tender herb, were interposed,
Or palmy hillock; or the flowery lap
Of some irriguous valley spread her store,   255
Flowers of all hue, and without thorn the rose.
Another side, umbrageous grots and caves
Of cool recess, o'er which the mantling vine
Lays forth her purple grape, and gently creeps
Luxuriant; meanwhile murmuring waters fall   260
Down the slope hills dispersed, or in a lake,
That to the fringèd bank with myrtle crowned
Her crystal mirror holds, unite their streams.
The birds their quire apply; airs, vernal airs,
Breathing the smell of field and grove, attune   265
The trembling leaves, while universal Pan,
Knit with the Graces and the Hours in dance,
Led on the eternal Spring. Not that fair field
Of Enna, where Proserpin gathering flowers,
Herself a fairer flower, by gloomy Dis   270

---

239. *error:* wandering. 242. *boon:* bountiful. 246. *Imbrowned:* darkened.
250-1. Milton dismisses, as usual, the pagan stories. 255. *irriguous:* well-
watered. 257. *umbrageous:* shadowy. 258. *mantling:* enveloping. 264.
quire: choir. 266. *Pan:* Underlying spirit of the life of the natural world,
(sometimes identified with the sun), and hence linked here with the beauty
of that world, (*the Graces*) and its maturing fruitfulness (*the Hours*).
268-72. Proserpina, goddess of the springtime fertility of earth, was kid-
napped at Enna in Sicily by *gloomy Dis,* god of the underworld, and sub-
sequently sought for through the whole earth by her mother, Ceres. The
simile is one of many premonitions in this book of Satan's *gathering* of
Eve in Book IX.

Was gathered—which cost Ceres all that pain
To seek her through the world; nor that sweet grove
Of Daphne, by Orontes and the inspired
Castalian spring, might with this Paradise
Of Eden strive; nor that Nyseian isle,   275
Girt with the river Triton, where old Cham,
Whom Gentiles Ammon call and Libyan Jove,
Hid Amalthea, and her florid son,
Young Bacchus, from his stepdame Rhea's eye;
Nor where Abassin kings their issue guard,   280
Mount Amara (though this by some supposed
True Paradise) under the Ethiop line
By Nilus' head, enclosed with shining rock,
A whole day's journey high, but wide remote
From this Assyrian garden, where the Fiend   285
Saw undelighted all delight, all kind
Of living creatures, new to sight and strange.
Two of far nobler shape, erect and tall,
God-like erect, with native honour clad
In naked majesty, seemed lords of all,   290
And worthy seemed; for in their looks divine
The image of their glorious Maker shone,
Truth, wisdom, sanctitude severe and pure—
Severe, but in true filial freedom placed,
Whence true authority in men; though both   295
Not equal, as their sex not equal seemed;
For contemplation he and valour formed,
For softness she and sweet attractive grace;
He for God only, she for God in him.

272-5. The gardens of Daphne on the Orontes River in Syria contained a
spring which was named for the Castalian spring situated on Mt. Parnassus,
and which was reputed, like it, to endow those who drank with prophetic
powers. 275-9. At Nysa, an island famous for its fertility (situated in the
Triton River in North Africa), Bacchus, the son of Jove and Amalthea, was
hidden by his mother from the vengeful eye of Rhea, Jove's wife. This
version of the story is told of *Lybian Jove,* i.e., the Egyptian god Ammon,
whom the Greeks and Romans identified with their own god as Jupiter-
Ammon, and whom the Christians identified with Ham (i.e., *old Cham*),
the son of Noah. (In the Greek and Roman versions, the name of Bacchus's
mother is Semele, and Jove's wife is Hera or Juno.) 280-4. Abyssinian kings
were said to rear their offspring in a sequestered palace on the top of Mt.
Amara (under the equatorial *line,* close to the *head* of the Nile), which was
supposed by some in Milton's time to have been the site of Paradise. 285.
this . . . garden: i.e., Milton's Paradise.

His fair large front and eye sublime declared   300
Absolute rule; and hyacinthine locks
Round from his parted forelock manly hung
Clustering, but not beneath his shoulders broad:
She, as a veil down to the slender waist,
Her unadornèd golden tresses wore   305
Dishevelled, but in wanton ringlets waved
As the vine curls her tendrils—which implied
Subjection, but required with gentle sway,
And by her yielded, by him best received,
Yielded with coy submission, modest pride,   310
And sweet, reluctant, amorous delay.
Nor those mysterious parts were then concealed,
Then was not guilty shame: dishonest shame
Of Nature's works, honour dishonourable,
Sin-bred, how have ye troubled all mankind   315
With shows instead, mere shows of seeming pure,
And banished from man's life his happiest life,
Simplicity and spotless innocence!
So passed they naked on, nor shunned the sight
Of God or Angel, for they thought no ill: 320
So hand in hand they passed, the loveliest pair
That ever since in love's embraces met—
Adam the goodliest man of men since born
His sons; the fairest of her daughters Eve.
Under a tuft of shade that on a green   325
Stood whispering soft, by a fresh fountain-side,
They sat them down; and, after no more toil
Of their sweet gardening labour than sufficed
To recommend cool Zephyr, and make ease
More easy, wholesome thirst and appetite   330
More grateful, to their supper-fruits they fell—
Nectarine fruits, which the compliant boughs
Yielded them, sidelong as they sat recline
On the soft downy bank damasked with flowers.
The savoury pulp they chew, and in the rind,   335
Still as they thirsted, scoop the brimming stream;

---

300. *front:* brow. *sublime:* i.e., upward (or heavenward) looking—traditionally regarded as a sign that man was a spiritual being. 301. *hyacinthine:* dark. 302-5. Milton follows I Corinthians 11: 14-15, where St. Paul says that in man long hair is "a shame unto him," but in woman, "a glory to her." 334. *damasked:* figured.

Nor gentle purpose, nor endearing smiles
Wanted, nor youthful dalliance, as beseems
Fair couple linked in happy nuptial league,
Alone as they. About them frisking played   340
All beasts of the earth, since wild, and of all chase
In wood or wilderness, forest or den.
Sporting the lion ramped, and in his paw
Dandled the kid; bears, tigers, ounces, pards,
Gambolled before them; the unwieldy elephant,   345
To make them mirth, used all his might, and wreathed
His lithe proboscis; close the serpent sly,
Insinuating, wove with Gordian twine
His braided train, and of his fatal guile
Gave proof unheeded. Others on the grass   350
Couched, and, now filled with pasture, gazing sat,
Or bedward ruminating; for the sun,
Declined, was hastening now with prone career
To the Ocean Isles, and in the ascending scale
Of Heaven the stars that usher evening rose: 355
When Satan, still in gaze as first he stood,
Scarce thus at length failed speech recovered sad:
    "O Hell! what do mine eyes with grief behold?
Into our room of bliss thus high advanced
Creatures of other mould—Earth-born perhaps,   360
Not Spirits, yet to Heavenly Spirits bright
Little inferior—whom my thoughts pursue
With wonder, and could love; so lively shines
In them divine resemblance, and such grace
The hand that formed them on their shape hath poured. 365
Ah! gentle pair, ye little think how nigh
Your change approaches, when all these delights
Will vanish, and deliver ye to woe—
More woe, the more your taste is now of joy:
Happy, but for so happy ill secured   370
Long to continue, and this high seat, your Heaven,
Ill fenced for Heaven to keep out such a foe
As now is entered; yet no purposed foe

---

337. *purpose:* talk. 341. *of all chase:* of every kind of hunting. 343. *ramped:* stood up and pawed. 344. *ounces, pards:* lynxes, leopards. 348. *with . . . twine:* with knottings of his body like those of the Gordian knot. 357. *failed . . . recovered:* recovered the speech that had failed him. 359. *our . . . bliss:* the happy position we once had.

To you, whom I could pity thus forlorn,
Though I unpitied: League with you I seek,   375
And mutual amity, so strait, so close,
That I with you must dwell, or you with me,
Henceforth. My dwelling haply may not please,
Like this fair Paradise, your sense, yet such
Accept your Maker's work; he gave it me,   380
Which I as freely give. Hell shall unfold,
To entertain you two, her widest gates,
And send forth all her kings; there will be room,
Not like these narrow limits, to receive
Your numerous offspring; if no better place,   385
Thank him who puts me, loath, to this revenge
On you, who wrong me not, for him who wronged.
And, should I at your harmless innocence
Melt, as I do, yet public reason just—
Honour and empire with revenge enlarged   390
By conquering this new World—compels me now
To do what else, though damned, I should abhor."
   So spake the Fiend, and with necessity,
The tyrant's plea, excused his devilish deeds.
Then from his lofty stand on that high tree   395
Down he alights among the sportful herd
Of those four-footed kinds, himself now one,
Now other, as their shape served best his end
Nearer to view his prey, and, unespied,
To mark what of their state he more might learn   400
By word or action marked. About them round
A lion now he stalks with fiery glare;
Then as a tiger, who by chance hath spied
In some purlieu two gentle fawns at play,
Straight crouches close; then rising, changes oft   405
His couchant watch, as one who chose his ground,
Whence rushing he might surest seize them both
Griped in each paw: when Adam, first of men,
To first of women, Eve, thus moving speech,
Turned him all ear to hear new utterance flow: 410
   "Sole partner and sole part of all these joys,
Dearer thyself than all, needs must the Power
That made us, and for us this ample World,

---

375. *Though I unpitied:* though I am myself unpitied (by God). 404. *purlieu:* forest's edge. 409. *moving speech:* beginning to speak.

Be infinitely good, and of his good
As liberal and free as infinite;   415
That raised us from the dust, and placed us here
In all this happiness, who at his hand
Have nothing merited, nor can perform
Aught whereof he hath need; he who requires
From us no other service than to keep   420
This one, this easy charge—of all the trees
In Paradise that bear delicious fruit
So various, not to taste that only Tree
Of Knowledge, planted by the Tree of Life;
So near grows Death to Life, whate'er Death is—   425
Some dreadful thing no doubt; for well thou know'st
God hath pronounced it Death to taste that Tree:
The only sign of our obedience left
Among so many signs of power and rule
Conferred upon us, and dominion given   430
Over all other creatures that possess
Earth, Air, and Sea. Then let us not think hard
One easy prohibition, who enjoy
Free leave so large to all things else, and choice
Unlimited of manifold delights;   435
But let us ever praise him, and extol
His bounty, following our delightful task,
To prune these growing plants, and tend these flowers;
Which, were it toilsome, yet with thee were sweet."
    To whom thus Eve replied: "O thou for whom   440
And from whom I was formed flesh of thy flesh,
And without whom am to no end, my guide
And head! what thou hast said is just and right.
For we to him, indeed, all praises owe,
And daily thanks—I chiefly, who enjoy   445
So far the happier lot, enjoying thee
Preëminent by so much odds, while thou
Like consort to thyself canst nowhere find.
That day I oft remember, when from sleep
I first awaked, and found myself reposed   450
Under a shade on flowers, much wondering where
And what I was, whence thither brought, and how.
Not distant far from thence a murmuring sound
Of waters issued from a cave, and spread

443. *head:* I Corinthians 11 : 3: "The head of the woman is the man."

Into a liquid plain, then stood unmoved,   455
Pure as the expanse of Heaven. I thither went
With unexperienced thought, and laid me down
On the green bank, to look into the clear
Smooth lake, that to me seemed another sky.
As I bent down to look, just opposite   460
A shape within the watery gleam appeared,
Bending to look on me. I started back,
It started back; but pleased I soon returned,
Pleased it returned as soon, with answering looks
Of sympathy and love. There I had fixed   465
Mine eyes till now, and pined with vain desire,
Had not a voice thus warned me: 'What thou seest,
What there thou seest, fair creature, is thyself;
With thee it came and goes: but follow me,
And I will bring thee where no shadow stays   470
Thy coming, and thy soft embraces—he
Whose image thou art; him thou shalt enjoy
Inseparably thine; to him shalt bear
Multitudes like thyself, and thence be called
Mother of human race.' What could I do,   475
But follow straight, invisibly thus led?
Till I espied thee, fair, indeed, and tall,
Under a platan; yet methought less fair,
Less winning soft, less amiably mild,
Than that smooth watery image. Back I turned;   480
Thou, following, cried'st aloud, 'Return, fair Eve;
Whom fliest thou? Whom thou fliest, of him thou art,
His flesh, his bone; to give thee being I lent
Out of my side to thee, nearest my heart,
Substantial life, to have thee by my side   485
Henceforth an individual solace dear:
Part of my soul I seek thee, and thee claim
My other half.' With that thy gentle hand
Seized mine: I yielded, and from that time see
How beauty is excelled by manly grace   490
And wisdom, which alone is truly fair."
    So spake our general mother, and, with eyes
Of conjugal attraction unreproved,
And meek surrender, half-embracing leaned

---

470. *where* . . . *stays:* i.e., where a real being, not a mere image in water,
awaits. 478. *platan:* plane tree. 486. *individual:* inseparable.

On our first father; half her swelling breast   495
Naked met his, under the flowing gold
Of her loose tresses hid. He, in delight
Both of her beauty and submissive charms,
Smiled with superior love, as Jupiter
On Juno smiles when he impregns the clouds   500
That shed May flowers, and pressed her matron lip
With kisses pure. Aside the Devil turned
For envy; yet with jealous leer malign
Eyed them askance, and to himself thus plained:
"Sight hateful, sight tormenting! Thus these two,   505
Imparadised in one another's arms,
The happier Eden, shall enjoy their fill
Of bliss on bliss; while I to Hell am thrust,
Where neither joy nor love, but fierce desire,
Among our other torments not the least,   510
Still unfulfilled, with pain of longing pines!
Yet let me not forget what I have gained
From their own mouths. All is not theirs, it seems;
One fatal tree there stands, of Knowledge called,
Forbidden them to taste. Knowledge forbidden?   515
Suspicious, reasonless! Why should their Lord
Envy them that? Can it be sin to know?
Can it be death? And do they only stand
By ignorance? Is that their happy state,
The proof of their obedience and their faith?   520
O fair foundation laid whereon to build
Their ruin! Hence I will excite their minds
With more desire to know, and to reject
Envious commands, invented with design
To keep them low, whom knowledge might exalt   525
Equal with gods. Aspiring to be such,
They taste and die: what likelier can ensue?
But first with narrow search I must walk round
This garden, and no corner leave unspied;
A chance but chance may lead where I may meet   530
Some wandering Spirit of Heaven, by fountain-side,
Or in thick shade retired, from him to draw
What further would be learned. Live while ye may,

499-501. Milton treats Jupiter and Juno as god and goddess, but also in
their allegorical characters, as aether, the creative principle, impregnating
the element of air. 504. *plained:* complained. 511. *pines:* makes me pine.

Yet happy pair; enjoy, till I return,
Short pleasures; for long woes are to succeed!"   535
　So saying, his proud step he scornful turned,
But with sly circumspection, and began
Through wood, through waste, o'er hill, o'er dale, his roam.
Meanwhile in utmost longitude, where Heaven
With Earth and Ocean meets, the setting Sun   540
Slowly descended, and with right aspect
Against the eastern gate of Paradise
Levelled his evening rays. It was a rock
Of alabaster, piled up to the clouds,
Conspicuous far, winding with one ascent   545
Accessible from Earth, one entrance high;
The rest was craggy cliff, that overhung
Still as it rose, impossible to climb.
Betwixt these rocky pillars Gabriel sat,
Chief of the angelic guards, awaiting night;   550
About him exercised heroic games
The unarmed youth of Heaven; but nigh at hand
Celestial armoury, shields, helms, and spears,
Hung high, with diamond flaming and with gold.
Thither came Uriel, gliding through the even   555
On a sunbeam, swift as a shooting star
In autumn thwarts the night, when vapours fired
Impress the air, and shows the mariner
From what point of his compass to beware
Impetuous winds. He thus began in haste: 560
　"Gabriel, to thee thy course by lot hath given
Charge and strict watch that to this happy place
No evil thing approach or enter in.
This day at highth of noon came to my sphere
A Spirit, zealous, as he seemed, to know   565
More of the Almighty's works, and chiefly Man,
God's latest image. I described his way
Bent all on speed, and marked his aery gait,
But in the mount that lies from Eden north,
Where he first lighted, soon discerned his looks   570
Alien from Heaven, with passions foul obscured.
Mine eye pursued him still, but under shade
Lost sight of him. One of the banished crew,

---

539. *utmost longitude:* extreme west. 541. *with . . . aspect:* i.e., facing
directly. 557. *thwarts:* cuts across. *fired:* burning.

I fear, hath ventured from the Deep, to raise
New troubles; him thy care must be to find."   575
   To whom the wingèd Warrior thus returned:
"Uriel, no wonder if thy perfect sight,
Amid the Sun's bright circle where thou sitt'st,
See far and wide. In at this gate none pass
The vigilance here placed, but such as come   580
Well known from Heaven; and since meridian hour
No creature thence. If Spirit of other sort,
So minded, have o'erleaped these earthy bounds
On purpose, hard thou know'st it to exclude
Spiritual substance with corporeal bar.   585
But, if within the circuit of these walks,
In whatsoever shape, he lurk of whom
Thou tell'st, by morrow dawning I shall know."
   So promised he; and Uriel to his charge
Returned on that bright beam, whose point now raised   590
Bore him slope downward to the Sun, now fallen
Beneath the Azores; whether the Prime Orb,
Incredible how swift, had thither rolled
Diurnal, or this less volúbil Earth,
By shorter flight to the east, had left him there   595
Arraying with reflected purple and gold
The clouds that on his western throne attend.
   Now came still Evening on, and Twilight gray
Had in her sober livery all things clad;
Silence accompanied; for beast and bird,   600
They to their grassy couch, these to their nests
Were slunk, all but the wakeful nightingale;
She all night long her amorous descant sung:
Silence was pleased. Now glowed the firmament
With living sapphires; Hesperus, that led   605
The starry host, rode brightest, till the Moon,
Rising in clouded majesty, at length
Apparent queen, unveiled her peerless light,
And o'er the dark her silver mantle threw.
   When Adam thus to Eve: "Fair consort, the hour   610

592-5. *whether . . . there:* Milton keeps his poem strictly impartial as
between the Ptolemaic and Copernican theories. 592. *Prime Orb:* sun.
594. *volúbil:* turnable. 601. *They, these:* i.e., beasts, birds. 603. *descant:*
song. 605. *Hesperus:* evening star. 608. *Apparent:* i.e., manifest queen (as
contrasted with her *clouded* state before).

Of night, and all things now retired to rest,
Mind us of like repose; since God hath set
Labour and rest, as day and night, to men
Successive, and the timely dew of sleep,
Now falling with soft slumbrous weight, inclines   615
Our eye-lids. Other creatures all day long
Rove idle, unemployed, and less need rest;
Man hath his daily work of body or mind
Appointed, which declares his dignity,
And the regard of Heaven on all his ways;   620
While other animals unactive range,
And of their doings God takes no account.
To-morrow, ere fresh morning streak the east
With first approach of light, we must be risen,
And at our pleasant labour, to reform   625
Yon flowery arbours, yonder alleys green,
Our walk at noon, with branches overgrown,
That mock our scant manuring, and require
More hands than ours to lop their wanton growth.
Those blossoms also, and those dropping gums,   630
That lie bestrewn, unsightly and unsmooth,
Ask riddance, if we mean to tread with ease.
Meanwhile, as Nature wills, Night bids us rest."
     To whom thus Eve, with perfect beauty adorned:
"My author and disposer, what thou bidd'st   635
Unargued I obey. So God ordains:
God is thy law, thou mine: to know no more
Is woman's happiest knowledge, and her praise.
With thee conversing, I forget all time,
All seasons, and their change; all please alike.   640
Sweet is the breath of Morn, her rising sweet,
With charm of earliest birds; pleasant the Sun,
When first on this delightful land he spreads
His orient beams, on herb, tree, fruit, and flower,
Glistering with dew; fragrant the fertile Earth   645
After soft showers; and sweet the coming-on
Of grateful Evening mild, then silent Night,
With this her solemn bird, and this fair Moon,
And these the gems of Heaven, her starry train:
But neither breath of Morn, when she ascends   650
With charm of earliest birds; nor rising Sun

---

642. *charm:* blended singing.

On this delightful land; nor herb, fruit, flower,
Glistering with dew; nor fragrance after showers;
Nor grateful Evening mild; nor silent Night,
With this her solemn bird; nor walk by moon,   655
Or glittering star-light, without thee is sweet.
But wherefore all night long shine these? for whom
This glorious sight, when sleep hath shut all eyes?"
    To whom our general ancestor replied:
"Daughter of God and Man, accomplished Eve,   660
Those have their course to finish round the Earth
By morrow evening, and from land to land
In order, though to nations yet unborn,
Ministering light prepared, they set and rise;
Lest total Darkness should by night regain   665
Her old possession, and extinguish life
In nature and all things; which these soft fires
Not only enlighten, but with kindly heat
Of various influence foment and warm,
Temper or nourish, or in part shed down   670
Their stellar virtue on all kinds that grow
On Earth, made hereby apter to receive
Perfection from the Sun's more potent ray.
These then, though unbeheld in deep of night,
Shine not in vain. Nor think, though men were none,   675
That Heaven would want spectators, God want praise.
Millions of spiritual creatures walk the Earth
Unseen, both when we wake, and when we sleep:
All these with ceaseless praise his works behold
Both day and night. How often, from the steep   680
Of echoing hill or thicket, have we heard
Celestial voices to the midnight air,
Sole, or responsive each to other's note,
Singing their great Creator! Oft in bands
While they keep watch, or nightly rounding walk,   685
With heavenly touch of instrumental sounds
In full harmonic number joined, their songs
Divide the night, and lift our thoughts to Heaven."
    Thus talking, hand in hand alone they passed
On to their blissful bower. It was a place   690
Chosen by the sovran Planter, when he framed
All things to Man's delightful use. The roof

---

657. *these:* the stars. 668-73. *but . . . ray:* The stars, like the sun, were
believed to shed "virtues" (i.e., benign potencies) on terrestrial things.

Of thickest covert was inwoven shade,
Laurel and myrtle, and what higher grew
Of firm and fragrant leaf; on either side   695
Acanthus, and each odorous bushy shrub,
Fenced up the verdant wall; each beauteous flower,
Iris all hues, roses, and jessamine,
Reared high their flourished heads between, and wrought
Mosaic; under foot the violet,   700
Crocus, and hyacinth, with rich inlay
Broidered the ground, more coloured than with stone
Of costliest emblem. Other creature here,
Beast, bird, insect, or worm, durst enter none;
Such was their awe of Man. In shadier bower   705
More sacred and sequestered, though but feigned,
Pan or Sylvanus never slept, nor Nymph
Nor Faunus haunted. Here, in close recess,
With flowers, garlands, and sweet-smelling herbs,
Espousèd Eve decked first her nuptial bed,   710
And heavenly choirs the hymenæan sung,
What day the genial Angel to our sire
Brought her, in naked beauty more adorned,
More lovely, than Pandora, whom the gods
Endowed with all their gifts; and, O! too like   715
In sad event, when to the unwiser son
Of Japhet brought by Hermes, she ensnared
Mankind with her fair looks, to be avenged
On him who had stole Jove's authentic fire.
    Thus at their shady lodge arrived, both stood,   720
Both turned, and under open sky adored
The God that made both Sky, Air, Earth, and Heaven,
Which they beheld, the Moon's resplendent globe,
And starry Pole: "Thou also mad'st the Night,
Maker Omnipotent; and thou the Day,   725
Which we in our appointed work employed

---

703. *Of . . . emblem:* i.e., inlaid with silver or gold. 707-8. *Sylvanus,
Faunus:* wood-sprites. 711. *hymenæan:* marriage-song. 714-19. A premonition of the disaster Eve will bring. To punish men for the act of Prometheus in stealing fire from heaven to help them, the gods sent him a
beautiful woman, *Pandora* (whose name means "all-gifted") bearing a
casket in which lay concealed all mortal ills. Prometheus rejected the gift,
but his *unwiser* brother Epimetheus (both were sons of the Titan, *Japhet*)
accepted it, and when he opened the casket, let all the ills loose upon mankind. 724. *Pole:* sky.

Have finished happy in our mutual help
And mutual love, the crown of all our bliss
Ordained by thee; and this delicious place,
For us too large, where thy abundance wants   730
Partakers, and uncropt falls to the ground.
But thou hast promised from us two a race
To fill the Earth, who shall with us extol
Thy goodness infinite, both when we wake,
And when we seek, as now, thy gift of sleep."   735
    This said unanimous, and other rites
Observing none, but adoration pure,
Which God likes best, into their inmost bower
Handed they went; and, eased the putting-off
These troublesome disguises which we wear,   740
Straight side by side were laid; nor turned, I ween,
Adam from his fair spouse, nor Eve the rites
Mysterious of connubial love refused:
Whatever hypocrites austerely talk
Of purity, and place, and innocence,   745
Defaming as impure what God declares
Pure, and commands to some, leaves free to all.
Our Maker bids increase; who bids abstain
But our destroyer, foe to God and Man?
Hail, wedded Love, mysterious law, true source   750
Of human offspring, sole propriety
In Paradise of all things common else!
By thee adulterous lust was driven from men
Among the bestial herds to range; by thee,
Founded in reason, loyal, just, and pure,   755
Relations dear, and all the charities
Of father, son, and brother, first were known.
Far be it that I should write thee sin or blame,
Or think thee unbefitting holiest place,
Perpetual fountain of domestic sweets,   760
Whose bed is undefiled and chaste pronounced,
Present, or past, as saints and patriarchs used.
Here Love his golden shafts employs, here lights
His constant lamp, and waves his purple wings,
Reigns here and revels; not in the bought smile   765

---

730. *wants:* lacks. 748. *increase:* Genesis 1 : 28: "Be fruitful and multiply."
751. *propriety:* proprietorship. 756. *Relations, charities:* Subjects of *were*
known in 757. 763. *golden:* Cupid was said to have a golden arrow which
caused love and a leaden arrow which banished it.

Of harlots—loveless, joyless, unendeared,
Casual fruition; nor in court amours,
Mixed dance, or wanton mask, or midnight ball,
Or serenate, which the starved lover sings
To his proud fair, best quitted with disdain.   770
These, lulled by nightingales, embracing slept,
And on their naked limbs the flowery roof
Showered roses, which the morn repaired. Sleep on,
Blest pair! and, O! yet happiest, if ye seek
No happier state, and know to know no more!   775
    Now had Night measured with her shadowy cone
Half-way up-hill this vast sublunar vault,
And from their ivory port the Cherubim
Forth issuing, at the accustomed hour, stood armed
To their night-watches in warlike parade;   780
When Gabriel to his next in power thus spake:
    "Uzziel, half these draw off, and coast the south
With strictest watch; these other wheel the north:
Our circuit meets full west." As flame they part,
Half wheeling to the shield, half to the spear.   785
From these, two strong and subtle Spirits he called
That near him stood, and gave them thus in charge:
    "Ithuriel and Zephon, with winged speed
Search through this Garden; leave unsearched no nook;
But chiefly where those two fair creatures lodge,   790
Now laid perhaps asleep, secure of harm.
This evening from the Sun's decline arrived
Who tells of some infernal Spirit seen
Hitherward bent (who could have thought?), escaped
The bars of Hell, on errand bad no doubt: 795
Such, where ye find, seize fast, and hither bring."
    So saying, on he led his radiant files,
Dazzling the moon; these to the bower direct
In search of whom they sought. Him there they found
Squat like a toad, close at the ear of Eve,   800
Assaying by his devilish art to reach
The organs of her fancy, and with them forge
Illusions as he list, phantasms and dreams;

---

769. *serenate:* serenade. 770. *quitted:* (1) requited, (2) abandoned. 773. *repaired:* replaced. 778. *port:* gate. 793. *Who:* one who. 798. *these:* Ithuriel and Zephon.

Or if, inspiring venom, he might taint
The animal spirits, that from pure blood arise   805
Like gentle breaths from rivers pure, thence raise
At least distempered, discontented thoughts,
Vain hopes, vain aims, inordinate desires,
Blown up with high conceits engendering pride.
Him thus intent Ithuriel with his spear   810
Touched lightly; for no falsehood can endure
Touch of celestial temper, but returns
Of force to its own likeness. Up he starts,
Discovered and surprised. As, when a spark
Lights on a heap of nitrous powder, laid   815
Fit for the tun, some magazine to store
Against a rumoured war, the smutty grain,
With sudden blaze diffused, inflames the air;
So started up in his own shape the Fiend.
Back stept those two fair Angels, half amazed   820
So sudden to behold the grisly King;
Yet thus, unmoved with fear, accost him soon:
    "Which of those rebel Spirits adjudged to Hell
Com'st thou, escaped thy prison? and, transformed,
Why sat'st thou like an enemy in wait,   825
Here watching at the head of these that sleep?"
    "Know ye not, then," said Satan, filled with scorn,
"Know ye not me? Ye knew me once no mate
For you, there sitting where ye durst not soar!
Not to know me argues yourselves unknown,   830
The lowest of your throng; or, if ye know,
Why ask ye, and superfluous begin
Your message, like to end as much in vain?"
    To whom thus Zephon, answering scorn with scorn:
"Think not, revolted Spirit, thy shape the same,   835
Or undiminished brightness, to be known
As when thou stood'st in Heaven upright and pure.
That glory then, when thou no more wast good,
Departed from thee; and thou resemblest now
Thy sin and place of doom obscure and foul.   840
But come; for thou, be sure, shalt give account

---

805. *animal spirits:* In the old physiology, these were thought to be distilled from the blood and to serve as agents of the brain. 813. *Of force:* compulsorily. 816. *tun:* storage barrel. 817. *Against:* in anticipation of.

To him who sent us, whose charge is to keep
This place inviolable, and these from harm."
    So spake the Cherub, and his grave rebuke,
Severe in youthful beauty, added grace   845
Invincible. Abashed the Devil stood,
And felt how awful goodness is, and saw
Virtue in her shape how lovely—saw, and pined
His loss; but chiefly to find here observed
His lustre visibly impaired; yet seemed   850
Undaunted. "If I must contend," said he,
"Best with the best—the sender, not the sent;
Or all at once: more glory will be won,
Or less be lost." "Thy fear," said Zephon bold,
"Will save us trial what the least can do   855
Single against thee wicked, and thence weak."
    The Fiend replied not, overcome with rage;
But, like a proud steed reined, went haughty on,
Champing his iron curb. To strive or fly
He held it vain; awe from above had quelled   860
His heart, not else dismayed. Now drew they nigh
The western point, where those half-rounding guards
Just met, and closing stood in squadron joined,
Awaiting next command. To whom their chief,
Gabriel, from the front thus called aloud: 865
    "O friends, I hear the tread of nimble feet
Hasting this way, and now by glimpse discern
Ithuriel and Zephon through the shade;
And with them comes a third, of regal port,
But faded splendour wan, who by his gait   870
And fierce demeanour seems the Prince of Hell—
Not likely to part hence without contest.
Stand firm, for in his look defiance lours."
    He scarce had ended, when those two approached,
And brief related whom they brought, where found,   875
How busied, in what form and posture couched.
To whom, with stern regard, thus Gabriel spake:
"Why hast thou, Satan, broke the bounds prescribed
To thy transgressions, and disturbed the charge
Of others, who approve not to transgress   880

---

843. *these:* Adam and Eve. 848. *pined:* pined because of. 852. *Best . . . best:* Best do it with the one in supreme command. 862. *half-rounding:* Cf. 782-4. 879. *charge:* i.e., Adam and Eve.

By thy example, but have power and right
To question thy bold entrance on this place;
Employed, it seems, to violate sleep, and those
Whose dwelling God hath planted here in bliss?"
   To whom thus Satan, with contemptuous brow: 885
"Gabriel, thou hadst in Heaven the esteem of wise;
And such I held thee; but this question asked
Puts me in doubt. Lives there who loves his pain?
Who would not, finding way, break loose from Hell,
Though thither doomed? Thou wouldst thyself, no doubt,   890
And boldly venture to whatever place
Farthest from pain, where thou mightst hope to change
Torment with ease, and soonest recompense
Dole with delight; which in this place I sought:
To thee no reason, who know'st only good,   895
But evil hast not tried. And wilt object
His will who bound us? Let him surer bar
His iron gates, if he intends our stay
In that dark durance. Thus much what was asked:
The rest is true; they found me where they say;   900
But that implies not violence or harm."
   Thus he in scorn. The warlike Angel moved,
Disdainfully half smiling, thus replied:
"O loss of one in Heaven to judge of wise,
Since Satan fell, whom folly overthrew,   905
And now returns him from his prison scaped,
Gravely in doubt whether to hold them wise
Or not, who ask what boldness brought him hither
Unlicensed from his bounds in Hell prescribed;
So wise he judges it to fly from pain   910
However, and to scape his punishment!
So judge thou still, presumptuous, till the wrath,
Which thou incurr'st by flying, meet thy flight
Sevenfold, and scourge that wisdom back to Hell,
Which taught thee yet no better that no pain   915
Can equal anger infinite provoked.
But wherefore thou alone? Wherefore with thee
Came not all Hell broke loose? Is pain to them

---

894. *dole:* dolour. 896. *wilt object:* And wilt thou raise as an objection (to
my argument)? 904. "O how sad that now no judge of wisdom is left in
heaven" (spoken sarcastically). 910. *wise:* thus wise (as illustrated by his
flight). 911. *However:* by any manner possible.

Less pain, less to be fled? or thou than they
Less hardy to endure? Courageous chief,   920
The first in flight from pain, hadst thou alleged
To thy deserted host this cause of flight,
Thou surely hadst not come sole fugitve."
  To which the Fiend thus answered, frowning stern:
"Not that I less endure, or shrink from pain,   925
Insulting Angel! well thou know'st I stood
Thy fiercest, when in battle to thy aid
The blasting volleyed thunder made all speed
And seconded thy else not dreaded spear.
But still thy words at random, as before,   930
Argue thy inexperience what behoves,
From hard assays and ill successes past,
A faithful leader—not to hazard all
Through ways of danger by himself untried.
I, therefore, I alone, first undertook   935
To wing the desolate Abyss, and spy
This new-created World, whereof in Hell
Fame is not silent, here in hope to find
Better abode, and my afflicted Powers
To settle here on Earth, or in mid Air;   940
Though for possession put to try once more
What thou and thy gay legions dare against;
Whose easier business were to serve their Lord
High up in Heaven, with songs to hymn his throne,
And practised distances to cringe, not fight."   945
  To whom the Warrior-Angel soon replied:
"To say and straight unsay, pretending first
Wise to fly pain, professing next the spy,
Argues no leader, but a liar traced,
Satan; and couldst thou 'faithful' add? O name,   950
O sacred name of faithfulness profaned!
Faithful to whom? to thy rebellious crew?
Army of fiends, fit body to fit head!
Was this your discipline and faith engaged,
Your military obedience, to dissolve   955
Allegiance to the acknowledged Power Supreme:
And thou, sly hypocrite, who now wouldst seem
Patron of liberty, who more than thou

---

931. Show your ignorance of what is suitable to (*a faithful leader*). 942.
against: against our enterprise.

Once fawned, and cringed, and servilely adored
Heaven's awful Monarch? wherefore, but in hope   960
To dispossess him, and thyself to reign?
But mark what I arede thee now: Avaunt!
Fly thither whence thou fledd'st. If from this hour
Within these hallowed limits thou appear,
Back to the Infernal Pit I drag thee chained,   965
And seal thee so as henceforth not to scorn
The facile gates of Hell too slightly barred."
   So threatened he; but Satan to no threats
Gave heed, but waxing more in rage, replied:
   "Then when I am thy captive, talk of chains,   970
Proud limitary Cherub! but ere then
Far heavier load thyself expect to feel
From my prevailing arm, though Heaven's King
Ride on thy wings, and thou with thy compeers,
Used to the yoke, draw'st his triumphant wheels   975
In progress through the road of Heaven star-paved."
   While thus he spake, the Angelic Squadron bright
Turned fiery red, sharpening in moonèd horns
Their phalanx, and began to hem him round
With ported spears, as thick as when a field   980
Of Ceres ripe for harvest waving bends
Her bearded grove of ears which way the wind
Sways them; the careful ploughman doubting stands
Lest on the threshing-floor his hopeful sheaves
Prove chaff. On the other side Satan alarmed   985
Collecting all his might dilated stood,
Like Teneriff or Atlas, unremoved:
His stature reached the sky, and on his crest
Sat Horror plumed; nor wanted in his grasp
What seemed both spear and shield. Now dreadful deeds   990
Might have ensued: nor only Paradise,
In this commotion, but the starry cope
Of Heaven perhaps, or all the Elements
At least, had gone to wrack, disturbed and torn
With violence of this conflict, had not soon   995
The Eternal, to prevent such horrid fray,

---

962. *arede:* advise. 971. *limitary:* (1) boundary-guarding, (2) limiting
Satan's activities. 980. *ported:* ready for use. 981. *Ceres:* i.e., grain. Cf.
268-72 n. 987. *Teneriff, Atlas:* A huge mountain in the Canaries; a mountain range in northwest Africa. 992. *cope:* covering.

Hung forth in Heaven his golden scales, yet seen
Betwixt Astræa and the Scorpion sign,
Wherein all things created first he weighed,
The pendulous round Earth with balanced air   1000
In counterpoise, now ponders all events,
Battles and realms. In these he put two weights,
The sequel each of parting and of fight:
The latter quick up flew, and kicked the beam;
Which Gabriel spying thus bespake the Fiend: 1005
    "Satan, I know thy strength, and thou know'st mine,
Neither our own, but given; what folly then
To boast what arms can do, since thine no more
Than Heaven permits, nor mine, though doubled now
To trample thee as mire. For proof look up,   1010
And read thy lot in yon celestial sign,
Where thou art weighed, and shown how light, how weak
If thou resist." The Fiend looked up, and knew
His mounted scale aloft: nor more; but fled
Murmuring; and with him fled the shades of Night.   1015

THE END OF THE FOURTH BOOK

❧

997-8. *yet . . . sign:* Milton identifies the scales with the Zodiacal sign of
Libra, the Scales, which stands between the signs of Astraea and the
Scorpion. 1001. *ponders:* weighs. 1003. *sequel:* consequence.

BOOK V

THE ARGUMENT

Morning approached, Eve relates to Adam her troublesome dream; he likes it not, yet comforts her: they come forth to their day labours: their morning hymn at the door of their bower. God, to render Man inexcusable, sends Raphael to admonish him of his obedience, of his free estate, of his enemy near at hand, who he is, and why his enemy, and whatever else may avail Adam to know. Raphael comes down to Paradise; his appearance described; his coming discerned by Adam afar off, sitting at the door of his bower; he goes out to meet him, brings him to his lodge, entertains him with the choicest fruits of Paradise, got together by Eve; their discourse at table. Raphael performs his message, minds Adam of his state and of his enemy; relates, at Adam's request, who that enemy is, and how he came to be so, beginning from his first revolt in Heaven, and the occasion thereof; how he drew his legions after him to the parts of the North, and there incited them to rebel with him, persuading all but only Abdiel, a seraph, who in argument dissuades and opposes him, then forsakes him.

BOOK VI

THE ARGUMENT

Raphael continues to relate how Michael and Gabriel were sent forth to battle against Satan and his Angels. The first fight described: Satan and his Powers retire under night. He calls a council; invents devilish engines, which, in the second day's fight, put Michael and his Angels to some disorder; but they at length, pulling up mountains, overwhelmed both the force and machines of Satan. Yet, the tumult not so ending, God, on the third day, sends Messiah his Son, for whom he had reserved the glory of that victory. He, in the power of his Father, coming to the place, and causing all his legions to stand still on either side, with his chariot and thunder driving into the midst of his enemies, pursues them, unable to resist, towards the wall of Heaven; which opening, they leap down with horror and confusion into the place of punishment prepared for them in the Deep. Messiah returns with triumph to his Father.

❧

BOOK VII

THE ARGUMENT

Raphael, at the request of Adam, relates how and wherefore this World was first created:—that God, after the expelling of Satan and his Angels out of Heaven, declared his pleasure to create another World, and other creatures to dwell therein; sends his Son with glory, and attendance of Angels, to perform the work of creation in six days: the Angels celebrate with hymns the performance thereof, and his reascension into Heaven.

❧

BOOK VIII

THE ARGUMENT

Adam inquires concerning celestial motions; is doubtfully answered, and exhorted to search rather things more worthy of knowledge. Adam assents, and, still desirous to detain Raphael, relates to him what he remembered since his own creation—his placing in Paradise; his talk with God concerning solitude and fit society; his first meeting and nuptials with Eve. His discourse with the Angel thereupon; who, after admonitions repeated, departs.

. . . .

So spake the godlike Power, and thus our Sire:
"For Man to tell how human life began   250
Is hard; for who himself beginning knew?
Desire with thee still longer to converse
Induced me. As new-waked from soundest sleep,
Soft on the flowery herb I found me laid,
In balmy sweat, which with his beams the Sun   255
Soon dried, and on the reeking moisture fed.
Straight toward Heaven my wondering eyes I turned,
And gazed a while the ample sky, till, raised
By quick instinctive motion, up I sprung,
As thitherward endeavouring, and upright   260
Stood on my feet. About me round I saw
Hill, dale, and shady woods, and sunny plains,
And liquid lapse of murmuring streams; by these,
Creatures that lived and moved, and walked or flew,
Birds on the branches warbling: all things smiled;   265
With fragrance and with joy my heart o'erflowed.
Myself I then perused, and limb by limb
Surveyed, and sometimes went, and sometimes ran
With supple joints, as lively vigour led;
But who I was, or where, or from what cause,   270
Knew not. To speak I tried, and forthwith spake;
My tongue obeyed, and readily could name
Whate'er I saw. 'Thou Sun,' said I, 'fair light,
And thou enlightened Earth, so fresh and gay,
Ye hills and dales, ye rivers, woods, and plains,   275
And ye that live and move, fair creatures, tell,
Tell, if ye saw, how come I thus, how here!
Not of myself; by some great Maker then,
In goodness and in power preëminent;
Tell me, how may I know him, how adore,   280
From whom I have that thus I move and live,
And feel that I am happier than I know!'

---

249 ff. Adam entertains his guest, the angel Raphael, with an account of
his own and Eve's creation. 249. *Power:* Raphael. 253. *Induced me:* i.e., led
me to suggest that I tell you of my creation. 258 ff. Man's upward look
and upright stature were taken as signs of his heavenly origin. 263. *lapse:*
flow. 268. *went:* walked. 281. *have . . . I:* have received the capacity to.

While thus I called, and strayed I knew not whither,
From where I first drew air, and first beheld
This happy light, when answer none returned,   285
On a green shady bank, profuse of flowers,
Pensive I sat me down. There gentle sleep
First found me, and with soft oppression seized
My drowsèd sense, untroubled, though I thought
I then was passing to my former state   290
Insensible, and forthwith to dissolve:
When suddenly stood at my head a dream,
Whose inward apparition gently moved
My fancy to believe I yet had being,
And lived. One came, methought, of shape divine,   295
And said, 'Thy mansion wants thee, Adam; rise,
First Man, of men innumerable ordained
First father! called by thee, I come thy guide
To the Garden of bliss, thy seat prepared.'
So saying, by the hand he took me, raised,   300
And over fields and waters, as in air
Smooth sliding without step, last led me up
A woody mountain, whose high top was plain,
A circuit wide, enclosed, with goodliest trees
Planted, with walks and bowers, that what I saw   305
Of Earth before scarce pleasant seemed. Each tree
Loaden with fairest fruit, that hung to the eye
Tempting, stirred in me sudden appetite
To pluck and eat; whereat I waked, and found
Before mine eyes all real, as the dream   310
Had lively shadowed. Here had new begun
My wandering, had not He who was my guide
Up hither from among the trees appeared,
Presence Divine. Rejoicing, but with awe,
In adoration at his feet I fell   315
Submiss. He reared me, and, 'Whom thou sought'st I am,'
Said mildly, 'Author of all this thou seest
Above, or round about thee, or beneath.
This Paradise I give thee; count it thine
To till and keep, and of the fruit to eat.   320
Of every tree that in the Garden grows
Eat freely with glad heart; fear here no dearth.
But of the tree whose operation brings
Knowledge of good and ill, which I have set,

The pledge of thy obedience and thy faith,   325
Amid the garden by the Tree of Life—
Remember what I warn thee—shun to taste,
And shun the bitter consequence: for know,
The day thou eat'st thereof, my sole command
Transgressed, inevitably thou shalt die,   330
From that day mortal, and this happy state
Shalt lose, expelled from hence into a world
Of woe and sorrow.' Sternly he pronounced
The rigid interdiction, which resounds
Yet dreadful in mine ear, though in my choice   335
Not to incur; but soon his clear aspéct
Returned, and gracious purpose thus renewed:
'Not only these fair bounds, but all the Earth
To thee and to thy race I give; as lords
Possess it, and all things that therein live,   340
Or live in sea or air, beast, fish, and fowl.
In sign whereof, each bird and beast behold
After their kinds; I bring them to receive
From thee their names, and pay thee fealty
With low subjection. Understand the same   345
Of fish within their watery residence,
Not hither summoned, since they cannot change
Their element to draw the thinner air.'
As thus he spake, each bird and beast behold
Approaching two and two—these cowering low   350
With blandishment; each bird stooped on his wing.
I named them as they passed, and understood
Their nature; with such knowledge God endued
My sudden apprehension. But in these
I found not what methought I wanted still,   355
And to the Heavenly Vision thus presumed:
   " 'O, by what name—for Thou above all these,
Above mankind, or aught than mankind higher,
Surpassest far my naming—how may I
Adore thee, Author of this Universe,   360
And all this good to Man, for whose well-being
So amply, and with hands so liberal,
Thou hast provided all things? But with me

---

325. *pledge:* test. 330. *die:* become susceptible of death. 337. *purpose:* speech.

I see not who partakes. In solitude
What happiness? who can enjoy alone,   365
Or, all enjoying, what contentment find?'
Thus I, presumptuous; and the Vision bright,
As with a smile more brightened, thus replied:
" 'What call'st thou solitude? Is not the Earth
With various living creatures, and the Air,   370
Replenished, and all these at thy command
To come and play before thee? Know'st thou not
Their language and their ways? They also know,
And reason not contemptibly; with these
Find pastime, and bear rule; thy realm is large.'   375
So spake the Universal Lord, and seemed
So ordering. I, with leave of speech implored,
And humble deprecation, thus replied:
" 'Let not my words offend thee, Heavenly Power;
My Maker, be propitious while I speak.   380
Hast thou not made me here thy substitute,
And these inferior far beneath me set?
Among unequals what society
Can sort, what harmony or true delight?
Which must be mutual, in proportion due   385
Given and received; but, in disparity,
The one intense, the other still remiss,
Cannot well suit with either, but soon prove
Tedious alike. Of fellowship I speak
Such as I seek, fit to participate   390
All rational delight, wherein the brute
Cannot be human consort. They rejoice
Each with their kind, lion with lioness;
So fitly them in pairs thou hast combined:
Much less can bird with beast, or fish with fowl,   395
So well converse, nor with the ox the ape;
Worse, then, can man with beast, and least of all.'
    "Whereto the Almighty answered, not displeased:
'A nice and subtle happiness, I see,
Thou to thyself proposest, in the choice   400
Of thy associates, Adam, and wilt taste
No pleasure, though in pleasure, solitary.

---

357 ff. Cf. Genesis 2 : 20 (See Appendix). 384. *sort:* be suitable. 387.
intense, remiss: aspiring, unaspiring. 402. *in pleasure:* in the midst of
pleasures.

What think'st thou, then, of me, and this my state?
Seem I to thee sufficiently possessed
Of happiness, or not, who am alone   405
From all eternity? for none I know
Second to me or like, equal much less.
How have I, then, with whom to hold converse,
Save with the creatures which I made, and those
To me inferior, infinite descents   410
Beneath what other creatures are to thee?'
    "He ceased. I lowly answered: 'To attain
The highth and depth of thy eternal ways
All human thoughts come short, Supreme of Things!
Thou in thyself art perfect, and in thee   415
Is no deficience found. Not so is Man,
But in degree—the cause of his desire
By conversation with his like to help
Or solace his defects. No need that thou
Should'st propagate, already infinite,   420
And through all numbers absolute, though One;
But Man by number is to manifest
His single imperfection, and beget
Like of his like, his image multiplied,
In unity defective; which requires   425
Collateral love, and dearest amity.
Thou, in thy secrecy although alone,
Best with thyself accompanied, seek'st not
Social communication—yet, so pleased,
Canst raise thy creature to what highth thou wilt   430
Of union or communion, deified;
I, by conversing, cannot these erect
From prone, nor in their ways complacence find.'
Thus I emboldened spake, and freedom used
Permissive, and acceptance found; which gained   435
This answer from the gracious Voice Divine:
    " 'Thus far to try thee, Adam, I was pleased,
And find thee knowing not of beasts alone,
Which thou hast rightly named, but of thyself—
Expressing well the spirit within thee free,   440
My image, not imparted to the brute;
Whose fellowship, therefore, unmeet for thee,
Good reason was thou freely shouldst dislike.

---

421. *numbers:* parts. 422. *by number:* in society.

And be so minded still. I, ere thou spak'st,
Knew it not good for Man to be alone,   445
And no such company as then thou saw'st
Intended thee—for trial only brought,
To see how thou couldst judge of fit and meet.
What next I bring shall please thee, be assured,
Thy likeness, thy fit help, thy other self,   450
Thy wish exactly to thy heart's desire.'
   " 'He ended, or I heard no more; for now
My earthly, by his heavenly overpowered,
Which it had long stood under, strained to the highth
In that celestial colloquy sublime,   455
As with an object that excels the sense,
Dazzled and spent, sunk down, and sought repair
Of sleep, which instantly fell on me, called
By Nature as in aid, and closed mine eyes.
Mine eyes he closed, but open left the cell   460
Of fancy, my internal sight; by which,
Abstract as in a trance, methought I saw,
Though sleeping, where I lay, and saw the Shape
Still glorious before whom awake I stood;
Who, stooping, opened my left side, and took   465
From thence a rib, with cordial spirits warm,
And life-blood streaming fresh; wide was the wound,
But suddenly with flesh filled up and healed.
The rib he formed and fashioned with his hands;
Under his forming hands a creature grew,   470
Man-like, but different sex, so lovely fair
That what seemed fair in all the world seemed now
Mean, or in her summed up, in her contained
And in her looks, which from that time infused
Sweetness into my heart unfelt before,   475
And into all things from her air inspired
The spirit of love and amorous delight.
She disappeared, and left me dark; I waked
To find her, or for ever to deplore
Her loss, and other pleasures all abjure: 480
When, out of hope, behold her not far off,
Such as I saw her in my dream, adorned
With what all Earth or Heaven could bestow

---

462. *Abstract:* abstracted out of myself. 466. *cordial spirits:* "vital spirits"
from the heart.

To make her amiable. On she came,
Led by her Heavenly Maker, though unseen   485
And guided by his voice, nor uninformed
Of nuptial sanctity and marriage rites.
Grace was in all her steps, heaven in her eye,
In every gesture dignity and love.
I, overjoyed, could not forbear aloud: 490
  " 'This turn hath made amends; thou hast fulfilled
Thy words, Creator bounteous and benign,
Giver of all things fair—but fairest this
Of all thy gifts!—nor enviest. I now see
Bone of my bone, flesh of my flesh, my Self   495
Before me. Woman is her name, of Man
Extracted; for this cause he shall forgo
Father and mother, and to his wife adhere,
And they shall be one flesh, one heart, one soul.'
  "She heard me thus; and, though divinely brought,   500
Yet innocence and virgin modesty,
Her virtue, and the conscience of her worth,
That would be wooed, and not unsought be won,
Not obvious, not obtrusive, but retired,
The more desirable—or, to say all,   505
Nature herself, though pure of sinful thought—
Wrought in her so, that, seeing me, she turned.
I followed her; she what was honour knew,
And with obsequious majesty approved
My pleaded reason. To the nuptial bower   510
I led her blushing like the Morn; all Heaven,
And happy constellations, on that hour
Shed their selectest influence; the Earth
Gave sign of gratulation, and each hill;
Joyous the birds; fresh gales and gentle airs   515
Whispered it to the woods, and from their wings
Flung rose, flung odours from the spicy shrub,
Disporting, till the amorous bird of night
Sung spousal, and bid haste the Evening-star
On his hill-top to light the bridal lamp.   520
  "Thus have I told thee all my state, and brought
My story to the sum of earthly bliss
Which I enjoy, and must confess to find

---

502. *conscience:* consciousness. 504. *obvious:* forward. 509. *obsequious:*
compliant.

In all things else delight indeed, but such
As, used or not, works in the mind no change,   525
Nor vehement desire—these delicacies
I mean of taste, sight, smell, herbs, fruits, and flowers,
Walks, and the melody of birds: but here,
Far otherwise, transported I behold,
Transported touch; here passion first I felt,   530
Commotion strange, in all enjoyments else
Superior and unmoved, here only weak
Against the charm of beauty's powerful glance.
Or Nature failed in me, and left some part
Not proof enough such object to sustain,   535
Or, from my side subducting, took perhaps
More than enough—at least on her bestowed
Too much of ornament, in outward show
Elaborate, of inward less exact.
For well I understand in the prime end   540
Of Nature her the inferior, in the mind
And inward faculties, which most excel;
In outward also her resembling less
His image who made both, and less expressing
The character of that dominion given   545
O'er other creatures. Yet when I approach
Her loveliness, so absolute she seems
And in herself complete, so well to know
Her own, that what she wills to do or say
Seems wisest, virtuousest, discreetest, best.   550
All higher Knowledge in her presence falls
Degraded; Wisdom in discourse with her
Loses, discountenanced, and like Folly shows;
Authority and Reason on her wait,
As one intended first, not after made   555
Occasionally; and, to consummate all,
Greatness of mind and nobleness their seat
Build in her loveliest, and create an awe
About her, as a guard angelic placed."
    To whom the Angel, with contracted brow: 560
"Accuse not Nature! she hath done her part;
Do thou but thine! and be not diffident
Of Wisdom; she deserts thee not, if thou
Dismiss not her, when most thou need'st her nigh,

556. *Occasionally:* for an occasion, accidentally.

By attribúting overmuch to things   565
Less excellent, as thou thyself perceiv'st.
For, what admir'st thou, what transports thee so?
An outside—fair, no doubt, and worthy well
Thy cherishing, thy honouring, and thy love;
Not thy subjection. Weigh with her thyself;   570
Then value. Oft-times nothing profits more
Than self-esteem, grounded on just and right
Well managed. Of that skill the more thou know'st,
The more she will acknowledge thee her head,
And to realities yield all her shows—   575
Made so adorn for thy delight the more,
So awful, that with honour thou may'st love
Thy mate, who sees when thou art seen least wise.
But, if the sense of touch, whereby mankind
Is propagated, seem such dear delight   580
Beyond all other, think the same voutsafed
To cattle and each beast; which would not be
To them made common and divulged, if aught
Therein enjoyed were worthy to subdue
The soul of Man, or passion in him move.   585
What higher in her society thou find'st
Attractive, human, rational, love still:
In loving thou dost well; in passion not,
Wherein true Love consists not. Love refines
The thoughts, and heart enlarges—hath his seat   590
In Reason, and is judicious, is the scale
By which to Heavenly Love thou may'st ascend,
Not sunk in carnal pleasure; for which cause
Among the beasts no mate for thee was found."
    To whom thus, half abashed, Adam replied: 595
"Neither her outside formed so fair, nor aught
In procreation, common to all kinds
(Though higher of the genial bed by far,
And with mysterious reverence, I deem),
So much delights me as those graceful acts,   600
Those thousand decencies, that daily flow
From all her words and actions, mixed with love
And sweet compliance, which declare unfeigned
Union of mind, or in us both one soul—
Harmony to behold in wedded pair   605

---

576. *adorn:* adorned. 598. *genial:* procreative. 601. *decencies:* graces.

More grateful than harmonious sound to the ear.
Yet these subject not; I to thee disclose
What inward thence I feel, not therefore foiled,
Who meet with various objects, from the sense
Variously representing, yet, still free,   610
Approve the best, and follow what I approve.

.   .   .   .

❧

BOOK IX

THE ARGUMENT

*Satan, having compassed the Earth, with meditated guile returns
as a mist by night into Paradise; enters into the Serpent sleeping.
Adam and Eve in the morning go forth to their labours, which Eve
proposes to divide in several places, each labouring apart: Adam con-
sents not, alleging the danger lest that enemy of whom they were
forewarned should attempt her found alone. Eve, loath to be thought
not circumspect or firm enough, urges her going apart, the rather
desirous to make trial of her strength; Adam at last yields. The Serpent finds her alone: his subtle approach, first gazing, then speaking,
with much flattery extolling Eve above all other creatures. Eve, wondering to hear the Serpent speak, asks how he attained to human
speech and such understanding not till now; the Serpent answers that
by tasting of a certain tree in the Garden he attained both to speech
and reason, till then void of both. Eve requires him to bring her to
that tree, and finds it to be the Tree of Knowledge forbidden: the
Serpent, now grown bolder, with many wiles and arguments induces
her at length to eat. She, pleased with the taste, deliberates a while
whether to impart thereof to Adam or not; at last brings him of the
fruit; relates what persuaded her to eat thereof. Adam, at first amazed,
but perceiving her lost, resolves, through vehemence of love, to perish
with her, and, extenuating the trespass, eats also of the fruit. The
effects thereof in them both; they seek to cover their nakedness; then
fall to variance and accusation of one another.*

No more of talk where God or Angel Guest
With Man, as with his friend, familiar used

---

608. *foiled:* overcome.

1. *God or Angel Guest:* In Book VIII Adam has recounted to his guest,
the angel Raphael, the friendly conversation he held with *God* after he
was created, and in Books V-VIII, as a whole, he has been on equally
friendly footing with the *Angel Guest*. All that intimacy between Heaven
and Earth is now to be lost.

To sit indulgent, and with him partake
Rural repast, permitting him the while
Venial discourse unblamed. I now must change 5
Those notes to tragic—foul distrust, and breach
Disloyal, on the part of man, revolt
And disobedience; on the part of Heaven,
Now alienated, distance and distaste,
Anger and just rebuke, and judgment given, 10
That brought into this World a world of woe,
Sin and her shadow Death, and Misery,
Death's harbinger. Sad task! yet argument
Not less but more heroic than the wrath
Of stern Achilles on his foe pursued 15
Thrice fugitive about Troy wall; or rage
Of Turnus for Lavinia disespoused;
Or Neptune's ire, or Juno's, that so long
Perplexed the Greek, and Cytherea's son:
If answerable style I can obtain 20
Of my celestial Patroness, who deigns
Her nightly visitation unimplored,
And dictates to me slumbering, or inspires
Easy my unpremeditated verse,
Since first this subject for heroic song 25
Pleased me, long choosing and beginning late,
Not sedulous by nature to indite
Wars, hitherto the only argument
Heroic deemed, chief mastery to dissect
With long and tedious havoc fabled knights 30
In battles feigned (the better fortitude
Of patience and heroic martyrdom
Unsung), or to describe races and games,
Or tilting furniture, emblazoned shields,
Impreses quaint, caparisons and steeds, 35

---

13 ff. Milton rejects the "old heroism" of the pagan epics which he associates with the passions, (*wrath, rage, ire*), in favor of a new heroism identified with self-control (31-3). 14-16. *wrath . . . wall:* theme of the Iliad, which begins with Achilles's wrath and closes soon after his pursuit and slaughter of Hector. 16. *rage . . . disespoused:* theme of the latter part of the Aeneid, where Turnus and Aeneas are rivals for Lavinia. 18-19. The sufferings of Odysseus, (*the Greek*) were caused by Neptune; those of Aeneas (*Cytherea's son*) by Juno. 21. *Patroness:* i.e., the Muse invoked at I 6. 27. *indite:* treat (in a literary composition). 34. *tilting furniture:* furnishings for tournaments. 35. *impreses:* symbolic designs on shields.

Bases and tinsel trappings, gorgeous knights
At joust and tournament; then marshalled feast
Served up in hall with sewers and seneschals:
The skill of artifice or office mean,
Not that which justly gives heroic name   40
To person or to poem! Me, of these
Nor skilled nor studious, higher argument
Remains, sufficient of itself to raise
That name, unless an age too late, or cold
Climate, or years, damp my intended wing   45
Depressed; and much they may if all be mine,
Not hers who brings it nightly to my ear.
    The Sun was sunk, and after him the Star
Of Hesperus, whose office is to bring
Twilight upon the Earth, short arbiter   50
'Twixt day and night, and now from end to end
Night's hemisphere had veiled the horizon round,
When Satan, who late fled before the threats
Of Gabriel out of Eden, now improved
In meditated fraud and malice, bent   55
On Man's destruction, maugre what might hap
Of heavier on himself, fearless returned.
By night he fled, and at midnight returned
From compassing the Earth—cautious of day
Since Uriel, Regent of the Sun, descried   60
His entrance, and forewarned the Cherubim
That kept their watch. Thence full of anguish driven,
The space of seven continued nights he rode
With darkness—thrice the equinoctial line
He circled, four times crossed the car of Night   65
From pole to pole, traversing each colure—

36. *Bases:* Both *bases* and *caparisons* (35) are ornamental coverings for horses. 37-8. *marshalled . . . seneschals:* i.e., a feast supervised by various Masters of Ceremony, such as marshalls, sewers (i.e., ushers), and sene-schals (stewards). 41. *Me:* i.e., to me. 43. *raise:* make memorable. 44. *an . . . late:* This may refer either to the common theory that the world and human talents were decaying, or to a feeling that the more secularized times into which Milton had survived would not value his poem. 44-5. *cold climate:* The sunny Mediterranean climates were held to be most pro-ductive of artistic genius. 54. *improved:* i.e., more proficient than ever (through his experience with Gabriel). 56. *maugre:* despite. 64-6. *thrice . . . colure:* Satan kept out of light's way for three days by circling the equator always at a point diametrically opposite to the sun, and for four days more by circling the earth longitudinally through the poles, twice via the equinoctial colure and twice via the solstitial colure.

On the eighth returned, and on the coast averse
From entrance or cherubic watch by stealth
Found unsuspected way. There was a place
(Now not, though Sin, not Time, first wrought the change)   70
Where Tigris, at the foot of Paradise,
Into the gulf shot underground, till part
Rose up a fountain by the Tree of Life.
In with the river sunk, and with it rose,
Satan, involved in rising mist; then sought   75
Where to lie hid. Sea he had searched and land
From Eden over Pontus, and the Pool
Mæotis, up beyond the river Ob;
Downward as far antarctic; and, in length,
West from Orontes to the ocean barred   80
At Darien, thence to the land where flows
Ganges and Indus. Thus the orb he roamed
With narrow search, and with inspection deep
Considered every creature, which of all
Most opportune might serve his wiles, and found   85
The Serpent subtlest beast of all the field.
Him, after long debate, irresolute
Of thoughts revolved, his final sentence chose
Fit vessel, fittest imp of fraud, in whom
To enter, and his dark suggestions hide   90
From sharpest sight; for in the wily snake
Whatever sleights none would suspicious mark,
As from his wit and native subtlety
Proceeding, which, in other beasts observed,
Doubt might beget of diabolic power   95
Active within beyond the sense of brute.
Thus he resolved, but first from inward grief
His bursting passion into plaints thus poured:
    "O Earth, how like to Heaven, if not preferred
More justly, seat worthier of Gods, as built   100
With second thoughts, reforming what was old!
For what God, after better, worse would build?
Terrestrial Heaven, danced round by other Heavens

77-8. *over . . . Ob:* i.e., over the Black Sea and the Sea of Azov beyond
the Obi River (in Siberia). 80. *Orontes:* the principal river of Syria. 81.
Darien: Isthmus of Panama. 88. *sentence:* verdict. 92. I.e., no matter what
acts of cunning he performed, no one would be suspicious. 95. *Doubt:*
suspicion.

That shine, yet bear their bright officious lamps,
Light above light, for thee alone, as seems,   105
In thee concentring all their precious beams
Of sacred influence! As God in Heaven
Is centre, yet extends to all, so thou
Centring receiv'st from all those orbs; in thee,
Not in themselves, all their known virtue appears,   110
Productive in herb, plant, and nobler birth
Of creatures animate with gradual life
Of growth, sense, reason, all summed up in Man.
With what delight could I have walked thee round,
If I could joy in aught—sweet interchange   115
Of hill and valley, rivers, woods, and plains,
Now land, now sea, and shores with forest crowned,
Rocks, dens, and caves! But I in none of these
Find place or refuge; and the more I see
Pleasures about me, so much more I feel   120
Torment within me, as from the hateful siege
Of contraries; all good to me becomes
Bane, and in Heaven much worse would be my state.
But neither here seek I, no, nor in Heaven,
To dwell, unless by mastering Heaven's Supreme;   125
Nor hope to be myself less miserable
By what I seek, but others to make such
As I, though thereby worse to me redound.
For only in destroying I find ease
To my relentless thoughts; and him destroyed,   130
Or won to what may work his utter loss,
For whom all this was made, all this will soon
Follow, as to him linked in weal or woe:
In woe then, that destruction wide may range!
To me shall be the glory sole among   135
The Infernal Powers, in one day to have marred
What he, Almighty styled, six nights and days
Continued making, and who knows how long
Before had been contriving? though perhaps
Not longer than since I in one night freed   140
From servitude inglorious well nigh half

---

104. *officious:* serviceable. 109. *receiv'st:* i.e., receivest benign influences.
112-13. I.e., ascending by ranks or "grades": as *growth* in vegetation, *growth*
and *sense* in animals, *growth, sense,* and *reason* in man.

The Angelic Name, the thinner left the throng
Of his adorers. He, to be avenged,
And to repair his numbers thus impaired—
Whether such virtue, spent of old, now failed   145
More Angels to create (if they at least
Are his created), or to spite us more—
Determined to advance into our room
A creature formed of earth, and him endow,
Exalted from so base original,   150
With heavenly spoils, our spoils. What he decreed
He effected; Man he made, and for him built
Magnificent this World, and Earth his seat,
Him Lord pronounced, and, O indignity!
Subjected to his service Angel-wings   155
And flaming ministers, to watch and tend
Their earthy charge. Of these the vigilance
I dread, and to elude, thus wrapt in mist
Of midnight vapour, glide obscure, and pry
In every bush and brake, where hap may find   160
The Serpent sleeping, in whose mazy folds
To hide me, and the dark intent I bring.
O foul descent! that I, who erst contended
With Gods to sit the highest, am now constrained
Into a beast, and, mixed with bestial slime,   165
This essence to incarnate and imbrute,
That to the highth of deity aspired!
But what will not ambition and revenge
Descend to? Who aspires must down as low
As high he soared, obnoxious, first or last,   170
To basest things. Revenge, at first though sweet,
Bitter ere long back on itself recoils.
Let it; I reck not, so it light well aimed,
Since higher I fall short, on him who next
Provokes my envy, this new favourite   175
Of Heaven, this Man of Clay, son of despite,
Whom, us the more to spite, his Maker raised
From dust: spite then with spite is best repaid."

---

142. *The . . . Name:* i.e., the ranks of angels. 145-9. I.e., either his creative
power was too much exhausted to create new angels to replace us, or else
he wishes to spite us by creating less worthy creatures (*of earth*) in our
place. 163-9. Milton repeatedly stresses Satan's increasing "de-gradation."
170. *obnoxious:* liable. 174. *Since . . . short:* since I cannot get at God
directly.

So saying, through each thicket, dank or dry,
Like a black mist low-creeping, he held on   180
His midnight search, where soonest he might find
The Serpent. Him sleeping soon he found,
In labyrinth of many a round self-rolled,
His head the midst, well stored with subtle wiles:
Not yet in horrid shade or dismal den,   185
Nor nocent yet, but on the grassy herb,
Fearless, unfeared, he slept. In at his mouth
The Devil entered, and his brutal sense,
In heart or head, possessing soon inspired
With act intelligential; but his sleep   190
Disturbed not, waiting close the approach of morn.
   Now whenas sacred light began to dawn
In Eden on the humid flowers, that breathed
Their morning incense, when all things that breathe
From the Earth's great altar send up silent praise   195
To the Creator, and his nostrils fill
With grateful smell, forth came the human pair,
And joined their vocal worship to the quire
Of creatures wanting voice; that done, partake
The season, prime for sweetest scents and airs;   200
Then commune how that day they best may ply
Their growing work—for much their work outgrew
The hands' dispatch of two gardening so wide:
And Eve first to her husband thus began:
   "Adam, well may we labour still to dress   205
This Garden, still to tend plant, herb, and flower,
Our pleasant task enjoined; but, till more hands
Aid us, the work under our labour grows,
Luxurious by restraint: what we by day
Lop overgrown, or prune, or prop, or bind,   210
One night or two with wanton growth derides,
Tending to wild. Thou, therefore, now advise,
Or hear what to my mind first thoughts present.
Let us divide our labours—thou where choice
Leads thee, or where most needs, whether to wind   215
The woodbine round this arbour, or direct
The clasping ivy where to climb; while I
In yonder spring of roses intermixed

---

186. *nocent:* harmful. 199. *wanting:* lacking. 211-12. *derides . . . wild:*
makes a mock of our labor, restoring all to wildness.

With myrtle find what to redress till noon.
For, while so near each other thus all day   220
Our task we choose, what wonder if so near
Looks intervene and smiles, or objects new
Casual discourse draw on, which intermits
Our day's work, brought to little, though begun
Early, and the hour of supper comes unearned!"   225
    To whom mild answer Adam thus returned:
"Sole Eve, associate sole, to me beyond
Compare above all living creatures dear!
Well hast thou motioned, well thy thoughts employed
How we might best fulfil the work which here   230
God hath assigned us, nor of me shalt pass
Unpraised; for nothing lovelier can be found
In woman than to study household good,
And good works in her husband to promote.
Yet not so strictly hath our Lord imposed   235
Labour as to debar us when we need
Refreshment, whether food, or talk between,
Food of the mind, or this sweet intercourse
Of looks and smiles; for smiles from reason flow
To brute denied, and are of love the food—   240
Love, not the lowest end of human life.
For not to irksome toil, but to delight,
He made us, and delight to reason joined.
These paths and bowers doubt not but our joint hands
Will keep from wilderness with ease, as wide   245
As we need walk, till younger hands ere long
Assist us. But, if much converse perhaps
Thee satiate, to short absence I could yield;
For solitude sometimes is best society,
And short retirement urges sweet return.   250
But other doubt possesses me, lest harm
Befall thee, severed from me; for thou know'st
What hath been warned us—what malicious foe,
Envying our happiness, and of his own
Despairing, seeks to work us woe and shame   255
By sly assault, and somewhere nigh at hand
Watches, no doubt, with greedy hope to find
His wish and best advantage, us asunder,
Hopeless to circumvent us joined, where each

---

253. *What . . . us:* in Books V-VIII. 258. *advantage:* i.e., Adam and Eve
separated (*us asunder*).

To other speedy aid might lend at need.   260
Whether his first design be to withdraw
Our fealty from God, or to disturb
Conjugal love—than which perhaps no bliss
Enjoyed by us excites his envy more—
Or this, or worse, leave not the faithful side   265
That gave thee being, still shades thee and protects.
The wife, where danger or dishonour lurks,
Safest and seemliest by her husband stays,
Who guards her, or with her the worst endures."
   To whom the virgin majesty of Eve,   270
As one who loves, and some unkindness meets,
With sweet austere composure thus replied:
   "Offspring of Heaven and Earth, and all Earth's lord!
That such an enemy we have, who seeks
Our ruin, both by thee informed I learn,   275
And from the parting Angel overheard,
As in a shady nook I stood behind,
Just then returned at shut of evening flowers.
But that thou shouldst my firmness therefore doubt
To God or thee, because we have a foe   280
May tempt it, I expected not to hear.
His violence thou fear'st not, being such
As we, not capable of death or pain,
Can either not receive, or can repel.
His fraud is, then, thy fear; which plain infers   285
Thy equal fear that my firm faith and love
Can by his fraud be shaken or seduced:
Thoughts, which how found they harbour in thy breast,
Adam! misthought of her to thee so dear?"
   To whom, with healing words, Adam replied: 290
"Daughter of God and Man, immortal Eve!—
For such thou art, from sin and blame entire—
Not diffident of thee do I dissuade
Thy absence from my sight, but to avoid
The attempt itself, intended by our foe.   295
For he who tempts, though in vain, at least asperses
The tempted with dishonour foul, supposed
Not incorruptible of faith, not proof

---

265. *Or . . . worse:* whether his aim is this or a worse one. 292. *entire:* i.e.,
whole, unharmed. 296-9. I.e., even Satan's attempt would dishonor Eve,
since it would imply a suspected weakness in her.

Against temptation. Thou thyself with scorn
And anger wouldst resent the offered wrong,   300
Though ineffectual found; misdeem not, then,
If such affront I labour to avert
From thee alone, which on us both at once
The enemy, though bold, will hardly dare;
Or, daring, first on me the assault shall light.   305
Nor thou his malice and false guile contemn—
Subtle he needs must be who could seduce
Angels—nor think superfluous others' aid.
I from the influence of thy looks receive
Access in every virtue—in thy sight   310
More wise, more watchful, stronger, if need were
Of outward strength; while shame, thou looking on,
Shame to be overcome or overreached,
Would utmost vigour raise, and raised unite.
Why shouldst not thou like sense within thee feel   315
When I am present, and thy trial choose
With me, best witness of thy virtue tried?"
    So spake domestic Adam in his care
And matrimonial love; but Eve, who thought
Less attribúted to her faith sincere,   320
Thus her reply with accent sweet renewed:
    "If this be our condition, thus to dwell
In narrow circuit straitened by a foe,
Subtle or violent, we not endued
Single with like defence wherever met,   325
How are we happy, still in fear of harm?
But harm precedes not sin: only our foe
Tempting affronts us with his foul esteem
Of our integrity: his foul esteem
Sticks no dishonour on our front, but turns   330
Foul on himself; then wherefore shunned or feared
By us? who rather double honour gain
From his surmise proved false, find peace within,
Favour from Heaven, our witness from the event.
And what is faith, love, virtue, unassayed   335
Alone, without exterior help sustained?
Let us not then suspect our happy state

---

310. *Access:* increase. 315. *sense:* i.e., sense of invigoration. 324-5. *we . . . met:* if each of us, singly, is not equipped with adequate means of defense against him wherever we meet him. 334. *event:* outcome.

Left so imperfect by the Maker wise
As not secure to single or combined.
Frail is our happiness, if this be so;   340
And Eden were no Eden, thus exposed."
    To whom thus Adam fervently replied:
"O Woman, best are all things as the will
Of God ordained them; his creating hand
Nothing imperfect or deficient left   345
Of all that he created—much less Man,
Or aught that might his happy state secure,
Secure from outward force. Within himself
The danger lies, yet lies within his power;
Against his will he can receive no harm.   350
But God left free the Will; for what obeys
Reason is free; and Reason he made right,
But bid her well be ware, and still erect,
Lest, by some fair appearing good surprised,
She dictate false, and misinform the Will   355
To do what God expressly hath forbid.
Not then mistrust, but tender love, enjoins
That I should mind thee oft; and mind thou me.
Firm we subsist, yet possible to swerve,
Since Reason not impossibly may meet   360
Some specious object by the foe suborned,
And fall into deception unaware,
Not keeping strictest watch, as she was warned.
Seek not temptation, then, which to avoid
Were better, and most likely if from me   365
Thou sever not: trial will come unsought.
Wouldst thou approve thy constancy, approve
First thy obedience; the other who can know,
Not seeing thee attempted, who attest?
But, if thou think trial unsought may find   370
Us both securer than thus warned thou seem'st,
Go; for thy stay, not free, absents thee more.
Go in thy native innocence; rely
On what thou hast of virtue; summon all;
For God towards thee hath done his part: do thine."   375
    So spake the Patriarch of Mankind; but Eve
Persisted; yet submiss, though last, replied:

---

339. I.e., as not safe whether we are alone or together. 358. *mind:* be vigilant
for. 367. *approve:* prove. 371. *securer:* more self-confident.

"With thy permission, then, and thus forewarned,
Chiefly by what thy own last reasoning words
Touched only, that our trial, when least sought,   380
May find us both perhaps far less prepared,
The willinger I go, nor much expect
A foe so proud will first the weaker seek;
So bent, the more shall shame him his repulse."
    Thus saying, from her husband's hand her hand   385
Soft she withdrew, and, like a wood-nymph light,
Oread or Dryad, or of Delia's train,
Betook her to the groves, but Delia's self
In gait surpassed and goddess-like deport,
Though not as she with bow and quiver armed,   390
But with such gardening tools as Art, yet rude,
Guiltless of fire had formed, or Angels brought.
To Pales, or Pomona, thus adorned,
Likest she seemed—Pomona when she fled
Vertumnus—or to Ceres in her prime,   395
Yet virgin of Proserpina from Jove.
Her long with ardent look his eye pursued
Delighted, but desiring more her stay.
Oft he to her his charge of quick return
Repeated; she to him as oft engaged   400
To be returned by noon amid the bower,
And all things in best order to invite
Noontide repast, or afternoon's repose.
O much deceived, much failing, hapless Eve,
Of thy presumed return! event perverse!   405
Thou never from that hour in Paradise
Found'st either sweet repast or sound repose;
Such ambush, hid among sweet flowers and shades,
Waited, with hellish rancour imminent,
To intercept thy way, or send thee back   410
Despoiled of innocence, of faith, of bliss.
    For now, and since first break of dawn, the Fiend,
Mere serpent in appearance, forth was come,
And on his quest where likeliest he might find
The only two of mankind, but in them   415

---

384. *so bent:* So intending (to attack first the weaker). 387. Mountain or
wood nymph, or one of Diana's huntress train. 393. *Pales, Pomona:* The
goddesses of flocks and fruits. 394. *Pomona . . . Jove:* i.e., Eve is young
and virginal, like Pomona or Ceres before they accepted lovers.

The whole included race, his purposed prey.
In bower and field he sought, where any tuft
Of grove or garden-plot more pleasant lay,
Their tendance or plantation for delight,
By fountain or by shady rivulet   420
He sought them both, but wished his hap might find
Eve separate; he wished, but not with hope
Of what so seldom chanced, when to his wish,
Beyond his hope, Eve separate he spies,
Veiled in a cloud of fragrance, where she stood,   425
Half-spied, so thick the roses bushing round
About her glowed, oft stooping to support
Each flower of tender stalk, whose head, though gay
Carnation, purple, azure, or specked with gold,
Hung drooping unsustained. Them she upstays   430
Gently with myrtle band, mindless the while
Herself, though fairest unsupported flower,
From her best prop so far, and storm so nigh.
Nearer he drew, and many a walk traversed
Of stateliest covert, cedar, pine, or palm;   435
Then voluble and bold, now hid, now seen
Among thick-woven arborets, and flowers
Imbordered on each bank, the hand of Eve:
Spot more delicious than those gardens feigned
Or of revived Adonis, or renowned   440
Alcinous, host of old Laertes' son,
Or that, not mystic, where the sapient king
Held dalliance with his fair Egyptian spouse.
Much he the place admired, the person more.
As one who, long in populous city pent,   445
Where houses thick and sewers annoy the air,
Forth issuing on a summer's morn, to breathe
Among the pleasant villages and farms
Adjoined, from each thing met conceives delight—
The smell of grain, or tedded grass, or kine,   450
Or dairy, each rural sight, each rural sound—
If chance with nymph-like step fair virgin pass,

---

419. *tendance:* i.e., object of cultivation. 431. *mindless:* heedless. 436.
voluble: turning. 438. *hand:* handiwork. 439 ff. The Garden of Adonis (cf.
Spenser's *Faerie Queene,* III vi, in vol. III); the Garden of Alcinous, the
Phaeacian king who entertained Odysseus (*Laertes' son*); and the garden
of King Solomon. 442. *not mystic:* i.e., real, historical, as opposed to
feigned in 439. 450. *tedded:* cut for haymaking. *kine:* cattle.

What pleasing seemed, for her now pleases more,
She most, and in her look sums all delight:
Such pleasure took the Serpent to behold   455
This flowery plat, the sweet recess of Eve
Thus early, thus alone. Her heavenly form
Angelic, but more soft and feminine,
Her graceful innocence, her every air
Of gesture or least action, overawed   460
His malice, and with rapine sweet bereaved
His fierceness of the fierce intent it brought.
That space the Evil One abstracted stood
From his own evil, and for the time remained
Stupidly good, of enmity disarmed,   465
Of guile, of hate, of envy, of revenge.
But the hot hell that always in him burns,
Though in mid Heaven, soon ended his delight,
And tortures him now more, the more he sees
Of pleasure not for him ordained. Then soon   470
Fierce hate he recollects, and all his thoughts
Of mischief, gratulating, thus excites:
    "Thoughts, whither have ye led me? with what sweet
Compulsion thus transported to forget
What hither brought us? hate, not love, nor hope   475
Of Paradise for Hell, hope here to taste
Of pleasure, but all pleasure to destroy,
Save what is in destroying; other joy
To me is lost. Then let me not let pass
Occasion which now smiles. Behold alone   480
The Woman, opportune to all attempts—
Her husband, for I view far round, not nigh,
Whose higher intellectual more I shun,
And strength, of courage haughty, and of limb
Heroic built, though of terrestrial mould;   485
Foe not informidable, exempt from wound—
I not; so much hath Hell debased, and pain
Enfeebled me, to what I was in Heaven.
She fair, divinely fair, fit love for Gods,
Not terrible, though terror be in love   490

---

453. *for her:* on her account. 456. *plat:* plot. 463. *abstracted:* i.e., remote,
outside of. 472. *gratulating:* gloating. 476. *hope:* nor hope. 486-7. *exempt
. . . not:* cf. 283, above. Adam and Eve, unfallen, are impervious in substance; Satan, because of his "de-gradation," is no longer so.

And beauty, not approached by stronger hate,
Hate stronger under show of love well feigned—
The way which to her ruin now I tend."
    So spake the Enemy of Mankind, enclosed
In serpent, inmate bad, and toward Eve   495
Addressed his way—not with indented wave,
Prone on the ground, as since, but on his rear,
Circular base of rising folds, that towered
Fold above fold, a surging maze; his head
Crested aloft, and carbuncle his eyes;   500
With burnished neck of verdant gold, erect
Amidst his circling spires, that on the grass
Floated redundant. Pleasing was his shape
And lovely; never since of serpent kind
Lovelier—not those that in Illyria changed   505
Hermione and Cadmus, or the god
In Epidaurus; nor to which transformed
Ammonian Jove, or Capitoline, was seen,
He with Olympias, this with her who bore
Scipio, the highth of Rome. With tract oblique   510
At first, as one who sought access but feared
To interrupt, sidelong he works his way.
As when a ship, by skilful steersman wrought
Nigh river's mouth or foreland, where the wind
Veers oft, as oft so steers, and shifts her sail,   515
So varied he, and of his tortuous train
Curled many a wanton wreath in sight of Eve,
To lure her eye. She, busied, heard the sound
Of rustling leaves, but minded not, as used
To such disport before her through the field   520
From every beast, more duteous at her call
Than at Circean call the herd disguised.
He, bolder now, uncalled before her stood,
But as in gaze admiring. Oft he bowed

---

491. *not:* i.e., unless. 500. *carbuncle:* red like carbuncles. 502. *spires:* coils.
503. *redundant:* wave-like. 505-6. *that . . . Cadmus:* i.e., that Harmonia
(Hermione) and her husband Cadmus were changed into. 506-7. *the . . .
Epidaurus:* i.e., Aesculapius, represented in serpent-form in his temple at
Epidaurus. 507-10. *nor . . . Rome:* nor the serpent's form in which
Jupiter Ammon loved Olympias, mother of Alexander the Great; and
Jupiter Capitoline loved Sempronia, mother of Scipio Africanus, the great
leader (*highth*) of Rome. 510. *tract:* track. 522. *herd disguised:* i.e., the
men turned into beasts by her arts.

His turret crest and sleek enamelled neck,   525
Fawning, and licked the ground whereon she trod.
His gentle dumb expression turned at length
The eye of Eve to mark his play; he, glad
Of her attention gained, with serpent-tongue
Organic, or impulse of vocal air,   530
His fraudulent temptation thus began:
    "Wonder not, sovran mistress (if perhaps
Thou canst who art sole wonder), much less arm
Thy looks, the heaven of mildness, with disdain,
Displeased that I approach thee thus, and gaze   535
Insatiate, I thus single, nor have feared
Thy awful brow, more awful thus retired.
Fairest resemblance of thy Maker fair,
Thee all things living gaze on, all things thine
By gift, and thy celestial beauty adore,   540
With ravishment beheld—there best beheld
Where universally admired. But here,
In this enclosure wild, these beasts among,
Beholders rude, and shallow to discern
Half what in thee is fair, one man except,   545
Who sees thee (and what is one?) who shouldst be seen
A Goddess among Gods, adored and served
By Angels numberless, thy daily train?"
    So glozed the Tempter, and his proem tuned.
Into the heart of Eve his words made way,   550
Though at the voice much marvelling; at length,
Not unamazed, she thus in answer spake:
    "What may this mean? Language of Man pronounced
By tongue of brute, and human sense expressed!
The first at least of these I thought denied   555
To beasts, whom God on their creation-day
Created mute to all articulate sound;
The latter I demur, for in their looks
Much reason, and in their actions, oft appears.
Thee, Serpent, subtlest beast of all the field   560
I knew, but not with human voice endued;

---

525. *turret:* towering. 529-30. *with . . . air:* i.e., using the serpent's actual
tongue, or in some way creating sound waves. 537. *awful:* awesome. 544-5.
I.e., except for Adam, Eve's beauty lacks a properly appreciative audience.
549. *glozed:* flattered. *proem:* formal introduction (as in an oration). 558.
demur: defer decision on.

Redouble, then, this miracle, and say,
How cam'st thou speakable of mute, and how
To me so friendly grown above the rest
Of brutal kind that daily are in sight: 565
Say, for such wonder claims attention due."
    To whom the guileful Tempter thus replied:
"Empress of this fair World, resplendent Eve!
Easy to me it is to tell thee all
What thou command'st, and right thou shouldst be obeyed.   570
I was at first as other beasts that graze
The trodden herb, of abject thoughts and low,
As was my food, nor aught but food discerned
Or sex, and apprehended nothing high:
Till on a day, roving the field, I chanced   575
A goodly tree far distant to behold,
Loaden with fruit of fairest colours mixed,
Ruddy and gold. I nearer drew to gaze;
When from the boughs a savoury odour blown,
Grateful to appetite, more pleased my sense   580
Than smell of sweetest fennel, or the teats
Of ewe or goat dropping with milk at even,
Unsucked of lamb or kid, that tend their play.
To satisfy the sharp desire I had
Of tasting those fair apples, I resolved   585
Not to defer; hunger and thirst at once,
Powerful persuaders, quickened at the scent
Of that alluring fruit, urged me so keen.
About the mossy trunk I wound me soon;
For, high from ground, the branches would require   590
Thy utmost reach, or Adam's: round the tree
All other beasts that saw, with like desire
Longing and envying stood, but could not reach.
Amid the tree now got, where plenty hung
Tempting so nigh, to pluck and eat my fill   595
I spared not; for such pleasure till that hour
At feed or fountain never had I found.
Sated at length, ere long I might perceive
Strange alteration in me, to degree
Of Reason in my inward powers, and Speech   600
Wanted not long, though to this shape retained.

---

581. Serpents were supposed to be fond of fennel (an aromatic vegetable)
and of stealing milk from sheep and goats. 599. *to:* even amounting to. 601.
though . . . retained: though I remained a serpent in shape.

---

605. *Middle:* the region *between* Heaven and Earth. 615. *overpraising:* i.e.,
of me. Eve's awakened vanity is evidenced in this show of false modesty.
622. *incorruptible:* undecayed. 624. *bearth:* i.e., "bear-th"—what Nature
bears. 634. *wandering fire:* will o' the wisp. 635. *unctuous:* oily. 635-7.
Cf. IV 557-8.

To bogs and mires, and oft through pond or pool,
There swallowed up and lost, from succour far:
So glistered the dire Snake, and into fraud
Led Eve, our credulous mother, to the Tree
Of Prohibition, root of all our woe;   645
Which when she saw, thus to her guide she spake:
   "Serpent, we might have spared our coming hither,
Fruitless to me, though fruit be here in excess,
The credit of whose virtue rest with thee—
Wondrous indeed, if cause of such effects!   650
But of this tree we may not taste nor touch;
God so commanded, and left that command
Sole daughter of his voice: the rest, we live
Law to ourselves; our Reason is our Law."
   To whom the Tempter guilefully replied: 655
"Indeed! Hath God then said that of the fruit
Of all these garden-trees ye shall not eat,
Yet lords declared of all in Earth or Air?"
   To whom thus Eve, yet sinless: "Of the fruit
Of each tree in the garden we may eat;   660
But of the fruit of this fair tree, amidst
The Garden, God hath said, 'Ye shall not eat
Thereof, nor shall ye touch it, lest ye die.'"
   She scarce had said, though brief, when now more bold
The Tempter, but, with show of zeal and love   665
To Man, and indignation at his wrong,
New part puts on, and, as to passion moved,
Fluctuates disturbed, yet comely, and in act
Raised, as of some great matter to begin.
As when of old some orator renowned   670
In Athens or free Rome, where eloquence
Flourished, since mute, to some great cause addressed,
Stood in himself collected, while each part,
Motion, each act, won audience ere the tongue
Sometimes in highth began, as no delay   675
Of preface brooking through his zeal of right:
So standing, moving, or to highth upgrown,
The Tempter, all impassioned, thus began:

---

649. *rest . . . thee:* i.e., will have to be judged by its effects on *you* (since
it is forbidden to *me*). 653. *the rest:* as for the rest. 667. *part:* rôle. 672.
since mute: i.e., no longer extant. 673. *part:* part of his body. 675. *in highth:*
in high feeling. 675-6. *as . . . brooking:* as if unable to endure the delay
of a formal introduction.

"O sacred, wise, and wisdom-giving Plant,
Mother of science! now I feel thy power   680
Within me clear, not only to discern
Things in their causes, but to trace the ways
Of highest agents, deemed however wise.
Queen of this Universe! do not believe
Those rigid threats of death. Ye shall not die.   685
How should ye? By the fruit? it gives you life
To knowledge. By the Threatener? look on me,
Me who have touched and tasted, yet both live,
And life more perfect have attained than Fate
Meant me, by venturing higher than my lot.   690
Shall that be shut to Man which to the Beast
Is open? or will God incense his ire
For such a petty trespass, and not praise
Rather your dauntless virtue, whom the pain
Of death denounced, whatever thing Death be,   695
Deterred not from achieving what might lead
To happier life, knowledge of Good and Evil?
Of good, how just! of evil—if what is evil
Be real, why not known, since easier shunned?
God therefore cannot hurt ye, and be just;   700
Not just, not God; not feared then, nor obeyed:
Your fear itself of death removes the fear.
Why then was this forbid! Why but to awe,
Why but to keep ye low and ignorant,
His worshipers? He knows that in the day   705
Ye eat thereof, your eyes that seem so clear,
Yet are but dim, shall perfectly be then
Opened and cleared, and ye shall be as Gods,
Knowing both good and evil, as they know.
That ye should be as Gods, since I as Man,   710
Internal Man, is but proportion meet—
I, of brute, human; ye, of human, Gods.
So ye shall die perhaps, by putting off
Human, to put on Gods—death to be wished,
Though threatened, which no worse than this can bring!   715
And what are Gods, that Man may not become

---

680. *science:* knowledge. 683. *highest agents:* e.g., God. 694. *pain:* penalty.
695. *denounced:* proclaimed. 701. *Not . . . God:* if he is not just, he is
not God. 710-12. I.e., if your advance is proportionate to mine (which was
from brute to human powers), it will be from human to godlike powers.
713-14. I.e., perhaps this change from human to godlike is what death is.

As they, participating godlike food?
The Gods are first, and that advantage use
On our belief, that all from them proceeds.
I question it; for this fair Earth I see,   720
Warmed by the Sun, producing every kind,
Them nothing; if they all things, who enclosed
Knowledge of good and evil in this tree,
That whoso eats thereof forthwith attains
Wisdom without their leave? and wherein lies   725
The offence, that Man should thus attain to know?
What can your knowledge hurt him, or this tree
Impart against his will, if all be his?
Or is it envy? and can envy dwell
In Heavenly breasts? These, these and many more   730
Causes import your need of this fair fruit.
Goddess humane, reach then, and freely taste!"
    He ended; and his words, replete with guile,
Into her heart too easy entrance won.
Fixed on the fruit she gazed, which to behold   735
Might tempt alone; and in her ears the sound
Yet rung of his persuasive words, impregned
With reason, to her seeming, and with truth.
Meanwhile the hour of noon drew on, and waked
An eager appetite, raised by the smell   740
So savoury of that fruit, which with desire,
Inclinable now grown to touch or taste,
Solicited her longing eye; yet first,
Pausing a while, thus to herself she mused:
    "Great are thy virtues, doubtless, best of fruits,   745
Though kept from Man, and worthy to be admired,
Whose taste, too long forborne, at first assay
Gave elocution to the mute, and taught
The tongue not made for speech to speak thy praise.
Thy praise he also who forbids thy use   750
Conceals not from us, naming thee the Tree
Of Knowledge, knowledge both of good and evil;
Forbids us then to taste. But his forbidding
Commends thee more, while it infers the good

718-19. I.e., because the gods come into being before we do, they delude us
with the belief that they created everything. 727. *him:* God. 737. *impregned:* pregnant. 738. *to . . . seeming:* as she thought. 754. *infers:*
suggests.

By thee communicated, and our want;   755
For good unknown sure is not had, or, had
And yet unknown, is as not had at all.
In plain, then, what forbids he but to know?
Forbids us good, forbids us to be wise!
Such prohibitions bind not. But, if Death   760
Bind us with after-bands, what profits then
Our inward freedom? In the day we eat
Of this fair fruit, our doom is we shall die!
How dies the Serpent? He hath eaten, and lives,
And knows, and speaks, and reasons, and discerns,   765
Irrational till then. For us alone
Was death invented? or to us denied
This intellectual food, for beasts reserved?
For beasts it seems; yet that one beast which first
Hath tasted envies not, but brings with joy   770
The good befallen him, author unsuspect,
Friendly to Man, far from deceit or guile.
What fear I then? rather, what know to fear
Under this ignorance of good and evil,
Of God or Death, of law or penalty?   775
Here grows the cure of all, this fruit divine,
Fair to the eye, inviting to the taste,
Of virtue to make wise. What hinders then
To reach, and feed at once both body and mind?"
So saying, her rash hand in evil hour   780
Forth-reaching to the fruit, she plucked, she eat.
Earth felt the wound, and Nature from her seat,
Sighing through all her works, gave signs of woe
That all was lost. Back to the thicket slunk
The guilty Serpent, and well might, for Eve,   785
Intent now only on her taste, naught else
Regarded; such delight till then, as seemed,
In fruit she never tasted, whether true,
Or fancied so through expectation high
Of knowledge; nor was Godhead from her thought.   790
Greedily she ingorged without restraint,
And knew not eating death. Satiate at length,
And hightened as with wine, jocund and boon,
Thus to herself she pleasingly began:

---

771. *author unsuspect:* i.e., a reliable authority. 792. *knew not:* knew not
she was. 793. *boon:* jovial.

"O sovran, virtuous, precious of all trees   795
In Paradise! of operation blest
To sapience, hitherto obscured, infamed,
And thy fair fruit let hang, as to no end
Created! but henceforth my early care,
Not without song, each morning, and due praise,   800
Shall tend thee, and the fertile burden ease
Of thy full branches, offered free to all;
Till, dieted by thee, I grow mature
In knowledge, as the Gods who all things know;
Though others envy what they cannot give—   805
For, had the gift been theirs, it had not here
Thus grown! Experience, next to thee I owe,
Best guide: not following thee, I had remained
In ignorance; thou open'st Wisdom's way,
And giv'st access, though secret she retire.   810
And I perhaps am secret: Heaven is high—
High, and remote to see from thence distinct
Each thing on Earth; and other care perhaps
May have diverted from continual watch
Our great Forbidder, safe with all his spies   815
About him. But to Adam in what sort
Shall I appear? Shall I to him make known
As yet my change, and give him to partake
Full happiness with me, or rather not,
But keep the odds of knowledge in my power   820
Without copartner? so to add what wants
In female sex, the more to draw his love,
And render me more equal, and perhaps—
A thing not undesirable—sometime
Superior; for, inferior, who is free?   825
This may be well; but what if God have seen,
And death ensue? Then I shall be no more;
And Adam, wedded to another Eve,
Shall live with her enjoying, I extinct!
A death to think! Confirmed, then, I resolve   830
Adam shall share with me in bliss or woe.
So dear I love him that with him all deaths
I could endure, without him live no life."

796-7. *of . . . sapience:* i.e., whose fruit produces wisdom. 807-8. *Experience
. . . guide:* i.e., next to the tree itself, I am most indebted to the experi-
mental method (which led me to try the fruit).

So saying, from the tree her step she turned,
But first low reverence done, as to the Power   835
That dwelt within, whose presence had infused
Into the plant sciential sap, derived
From nectar, drink of Gods. Adam the while,
Waiting desirous her return, had wove
Of choicest flowers a garland, to adorn   840
Her tresses, and her rural labours crown,
As reapers oft are wont their harvest-queen.
Great joy he promised to his thoughts, and new
Solace in her return, so long delayed;
Yet oft his heart, divine of something ill,   845
Misgave him. He the faltering measure felt,
And forth to meet her went, the way she took
That morn when first they parted. By the Tree
Of Knowledge he must pass; there he her met,
Scarce from the tree returning, in her hand   850
A bough of fairest fruit, that downy smiled,
New gathered, and ambrosial smell diffused.
To him she hasted; in her face excuse
Came Prologue, and Apology to prompt,
Which, with bland words at will, she thus addressed: 855
   "Hast thou not wondered, Adam, at my stay?
Thee I have missed, and thought it long, deprived
Thy presence—agony of love till now
Not felt, nor shall be twice; for never more
Mean I to try, what rash untried I sought,   860
The pain of absence from thy sight. But strange
Hath been the cause, and wonderful to hear.
This tree is not, as we are told, a tree
Of danger tasted, nor to evil unknown
Opening the way, but of divine effect   865
To open eyes, and make them Gods who taste;
And hath been tasted such. The Serpent wise,
Or not restrained as we, or not obeying,
Hath eaten of the fruit, and is become
Not dead, as we are threatened, but thenceforth   870
Endued with human voice and human sense,

---

837. *sciential sap:* sap that bestows knowledge. 842. *are wont:* are in the habit of doing for. 845. *divine of:* divining. 846. *measure:* heartbeat. 854. I.e., like the speaker of a prologue in a play, with Apology as prompter. 867. *tasted such:* proved such by tasting.

Reasoning to admiration, and with me
Persuasively hath so prevailed that I
Have also tasted, and have also found
The effects to correspond—opener mine eyes,   875
Dim erst, dilated spirits, ampler heart,
And growing up to Godhead; which for thee
Chiefly I sought, without thee can despise.
For bliss, as thou hast part, to me is bliss;
Tedious, unshared with thee, and odious soon.   880
Thou, therefore, also taste, that equal lot
May join us, equal joy, as equal love;
Lest, thou not tasting, different degree
Disjoin us, and I then too late renounce
Deity for thee, when fate will not permit."   885
    Thus Eve with countenance blithe her story told;
But in her cheek distemper flushing glowed.
On the other side, Adam, soon as he heard
The fatal trespass done by Eve, amazed,
Astonied stood and blank, while horror chill   890
Ran through his veins, and all his joints relaxed.
From his slack hand the garland wreathed for Eve
Down dropt, and all the faded roses shed.
Speechless he stood and pale, till thus at length
First to himself he inward silence broke: 895
    "O fairest of Creation, last and best
Of all God's works, creature in whom excelled
Whatever can to sight or thought be formed,
Holy, divine, good, amiable, or sweet!
How art thou lost! how on a sudden lost,   900
Defaced, deflowered, and now to death devote!
Rather, how hast thou yielded to transgress
The strict forbiddance, how to violate
The sacred fruit forbidden? Some cursèd fraud
Of enemy hath beguiled thee, yet unknown,   905
And me with thee hath ruined; for with thee
Certain my resolution is to die.
How can I live without thee? how forgo
Thy sweet converse, and love so dearly joined,
To live again in these wild woods forlorn?   910
Should God create another Eve, and I

872. *to admiration:* admirably.   876. *erst:* formerly.   883. *degree:* i.e.,
rank (in the hierarchy of beings).   901. *devote:* doomed.

Another rib afford, yet loss of thee
Would never from my heart. No, no! I feel
The link of nature draw me: flesh of flesh,
Bone of my bone thou art, and from thy state   915
Mine never shall be parted, bliss or woe."
    So having said, as one from sad dismay
Recomforted, and, after thoughts disturbed,
Submitting to what seemed remediless,
Thus in calm mood his words to Eve he turned: 920
    "Bold deed thou hast presumed, adventurous Eve,
And peril great provoked, who thus hast dared
Had it been only coveting to eye
That sacred food, sacred to abstinence;
Much more to taste it, under ban to touch.   925
But past who can recall, or done undo?
Not God Omnipotent, nor Fate! Yet so
Perhaps thou shalt not die; perhaps the fact
Is not so heinous now—foretasted fruit,
Profaned first by the Serpent, by him first   930
Made common and unhallowed ere our taste,
Nor yet on him found deadly. He yet lives—
Lives, as thou saidst, and gains to live, as Man,
Higher degree of life: inducement strong
To us, as likely, tasting, to attain   935
Proportional ascent; which cannot be
But to be Gods, or Angels, demi-gods.
Nor can I think that God, Creator wise,
Though threatening, will in earnest so destroy
Us, his prime creatures, dignified so high,   940
Set over all his works; which, in our fall,
For us created, needs with us must fail,
Dependent made. So God shall uncreate,
Be frustrate, do, undo, and labour lose—
Not well conceived of God; who, though his power   945
Creation could repeat, yet would be loath
Us to abolish, lest the Adversary
Triumph and say: 'Fickle their state whom God
Most favours; who can please him long? Me first

921-5. I.e., it was presumption even to eye that fruit, much less taste it.
933. *as Man:* i.e., in his new status, having human powers. 935. *as . . .
attain:* since it makes it likely that if *we* taste, we too shall attain.

He ruined, now Mankind; whom will he next?'—   950
Matter of scorn not to be given the Foe.
However, I with thee have fixed my lot,
Certain to undergo like doom. If death
Consort with thee, death is to me as life;
So forcible within my heart I feel   955
The bond of Nature draw me to my own—
My own in thee, for what thou art is mine:
Our state cannot be severed; we are one,
One flesh; to lose thee were to lose myself."
    So Adam; and thus Eve to him replied: 960
"O glorious trial of exceeding love,
Illustrious evidence, example high!
Engaging me to emulate; but short
Of thy perfection, how shall I attain,
Adam? from whose dear side I boast me sprung,   965
And gladly of our union hear thee speak,
One heart, one soul in both; whereof good proof
This day affords, declaring thee resolved,
Rather than death, or aught than death more dread,
Shall separate us, linked in love so dear,   970
To undergo with me one guilt, one crime,
If any be, of tasting this fair fruit;
Whose virtue (for of good still good proceeds,
Direct, or by occasion) hath presented
This happy trial of thy love, which else   975
So eminently never had been known.
Were it I thought death menaced would ensue
This my attempt, I would sustain alone
The worst, and not persuade thee—rather die
Deserted than oblige thee with a fact   980
Pernicious to thy peace, chiefly assured
Remarkably so late of thy so true,
So faithful, love unequaled. But I feel
Far otherwise the event—not death, but life
Augmented, opened eyes, new hopes, new joys,   985
Taste so divine that what of sweet before
Hath touched my sense, flat seems to this and harsh.

---

963. *Engaging . . . emulate:* requiring that I imitate it. 963-4. *short . . .
attain:* lacking thy perfection, how shall I equal thy *example high?* 980.
fact: deed. 984. *event:* consequence.

On my experience, Adam, freely taste,
And fear of death deliver to the winds."
   So saying, she embraced him, and for joy   990
Tenderly wept, much won that he his love
Had so ennobled as of choice to incur
Divine displeasure for her sake, or death.
In recompense (for such compliance bad
Such recompense best merits), from the bough   995
She gave him of that fair enticing fruit
With liberal hand. He scrupled not to eat,
Against his better knowledge, not deceived,
But fondly overcome with female charm.
Earth trembled from her entrails, as again   1000
In pangs, and Nature gave a second groan;
Sky loured, and, muttering thunder, some sad drops
Wept at completing of the mortal Sin
Original; while Adam took no thought,
Eating his fill, nor Eve to iterate   1005
Her former trespass feared, the more to soothe
Him with her loved society; that now,
As with new wine intoxicated both,
They swim in mirth, and fancy that they feel
Divinity within them breeding wings   1010
Wherewith to scorn the Earth. But that false fruit
Far other operation first displayed,
Carnal desire inflaming. He on Eve
Began to cast lascivious eyes; she him
As wantonly repaid; in lust they burn,   1015
Till Adam thus 'gan Eve to dalliance move:
   "Eve, now I see thou art exact of taste
And elegant—of sapience no small part;
Since to each meaning savour we apply,
And palate call judicious. I the praise   1020
Yield thee; so well this day thou hast purveyed.
Much pleasure we have lost, while we abstained
From this delightful fruit, nor known till now
True relish, tasting. If such pleasure be
In things to us forbidden, it might be wished   1025

1003-4. *Sin Original:* i.e., that which all men inherit. 1019-20. I.e., we use
the term *taste* to mean both the sense of taste and also judiciousness (as
in "a man of taste").

For this one tree had been forbidden ten.
But come; so well refreshed, now let us play,
As meet is, after such delicious fare;
For never did thy beauty, since the day
I saw thee first and wedded thee, adorned   1030
With all perfections, so inflame my sense
With ardour to enjoy thee, fairer now
Than ever—bounty of this virtuous tree!"
    So said he, and forbore not glance or toy
Of amorous intent, well understood   1035
Of Eve, whose eye darted contagious fire.
Her hand he seized, and to a shady bank,
Thick overhead with verdant roof embowered,
He led her, nothing loath; flowers were the couch,
Pansies, and violets, and asphodel,   1040
And hyacinth—Earth's freshest, softest lap.
There they their fill of love and love's disport
Took largely, of their mutual guilt the seal,
The solace of their sin, till dewy sleep
Oppressed them, wearied with their amorous play.   1045
    Soon as the force of that fallacious fruit,
That with exhilarating vapour bland
About their spirits had played, and inmost powers
Made err, was now exhaled, and grosser sleep,
Bred of unkindly fumes, with conscious dreams   1050
Encumbered, now had left them, up they rose
As from unrest, and, each the other viewing,
Soon found their eyes how opened, and their minds
How darkened. Innocence, that as a veil
Had shadowed them from knowing ill, was gone,   1055
Just confidence, and native righteousness,
And honour, from about them, naked left
To guilty Shame: he covered, but his robe
Uncovered more. So rose the Danite strong,
Herculean Samson, from the harlot-lap   1060
Of Philistean Dalilah, and waked
Shorn of his strength; they destitute and bare
Of all their virtue. Silent, and in face

1028. *meet:* fit. 1050. *unkindly:* unnatural. 1057. *naked left:* i.e., so that they were left naked. 1058. *he:* shame. 1062. *they:* i.e., just so, Adam and Eve waked.

Confounded, long they sat, as strucken mute;
Till Adam, though not less than Eve abashed,   1065
At length gave utterance to these words constrained:
  "O Eve, in evil hour thou didst give ear
To that false Worm, of whomsoever taught
To counterfeit Man's voice—true in our fall,
False in our promised rising; since our eyes   1070
Opened we find indeed, and find we know
Both good and evil, good lost and evil got:
Bad fruit of knowledge, if this be to know,
Which leaves us naked thus, of honour void,
Of innocence, of faith, of purity,   1075
Our wonted ornaments now soiled and stained,
And in our faces evident the signs
Of foul concupiscence; whence evil store;
Even shame, the last of evils; of the first
Be sure then. How shall I behold the face   1080
Henceforth of God or Angel, erst with joy
And rapture so oft beheld? Those Heavenly Shapes
Will dazzle now this earthly with their blaze
Insufferably bright. Oh, might I here
In solitude live savage, in some glade   1085
Obscured, where highest woods, impenetrable
To star or sunlight, spread their umbrage broad,
And brown as evening! Cover me, ye pines!
Ye cedars, with innumerable boughs
Hide me, where I may never see them more!   1090
But let us now, as in bad plight, devise
What best may, for the present, serve to hide
The parts of each from other that seem most
To shame obnoxious, and unseemliest seen—
Some tree, whose broad smooth leaves, together sewed,   1095
And girded on our loins, may cover round
Those middle parts, that this new comer, Shame,
There sit not, and reproach us as unclean."
    So counselled he, and both together went
Into the thickest wood. There soon they chose   1100

1070. *rising:* The godlike status the serpent had predicted for them. 1078.
whence . . . store: whence come abundant evils. 1079. *last:* worst. 1082-4.
Those . . . bright: Becoming an "earthly" substance through his sin, Adam
will no longer be able to stand the blinding light that surrounds "ethereal"
substance. 1094. *obnoxious:* liable.

The fig-tree—not that kind for fruit renowned,
But such as, at this day, to Indians known,
In Malabar or Decan spreads her arms
Branching so broad and long that in the ground
The bended twigs take root, and daughters grow   1105
About the mother tree, a pillared shade
High overarched, and echoing walks between:
There oft the Indian herdsman, shunning heat,
Shelters in cool, and tends his pasturing herds
At loop-holes cut through thickest shade. Those leaves   1110
They gathered, broad as Amazonian targe,
And with what skill they had, together sewed,
To gird their waist—vain covering, if to hide
Their guilt and dreaded shame! O how unlike
To that first naked glory! Such of late   1115
Columbus found th' American, so girt
With feathered cincture, naked else and wild,
Among the trees on isles and woody shores.
Thus fenced, and, as they thought, their shame in part
Covered, but not at rest or ease of mind,   1120
They sat them down to weep. Nor only tears
Rained at their eyes, but high winds worse within
Began to rise, high passions—anger, hate,
Mistrust, suspicion, discord—and shook sore
Their inward state of mind, calm region once   1125
And full of peace, now tost and turbulent:
For Understanding ruled not, and the Will
Heard not her lore, both in subjection now
To sensual Appetite, who, from beneath
Usurping over sovran Reason, claimed   1130
Superior sway. From thus distempered breast
Adam, estranged in look and altered style,
Speech intermitted thus to Eve renewed:
    "Would thou hadst harkened to my words, and stayed
With me, as I besought thee, when that strange   1135
Desire of wandering, this unhappy morn,
I know not whence possessed thee! We had then
Remained still happy—not, as now, despoiled

1101. *fig-tree:* i.e., the banyan tree. 1107. *and:* with. 1111. *targe:* shield.
1117. *cincture:* girdle. 1128. *her lore:* i.e., Understanding's teachings. 1132.
style: i.e., of speech. 1133. *intermitted:* i.e., which had been interrupted.

Of all our good, shamed, naked, miserable!
Let none henceforth seek needless cause to approve   1140
The faith they owe; when earnestly they seek
Such proof, conclude they then begin to fail."
    To whom, soon moved with touch of blame, thus Eve:
"What words have passed thy lips, Adam severe?
Imput'st thou that to my default, or will   1145
Of wandering, as thou call'st it, which who knows
But might as ill have happened thou being by,
Or to thyself perhaps? Hadst thou been there,
Or here the attempt, thou couldst not have discerned
Fraud in the Serpent, speaking as he spake;   1150
No ground of enmity between us known
Why he should mean me ill or seek to harm.
Was I to have never parted from thy side?
As good have grown there still, a lifeless rib.
Being as I am, why didst not thou, the head,   1155
Command me absolutely not to go,
Going into such danger as thou saidst?
Too facile then, thou didst not much gainsay,
Nay, didst permit, approve, and fair dismiss.
Hadst thou been firm and fixed in thy dissent,   1160
Neither had I transgressed, nor thou with me."
    To whom, then first incensed, Adam replied:
"Is this the love, is this the recompense
Of mine to thee, ingrateful Eve, expressed
Immutable when thou wert lost, not I—   1165
Who might have lived, and joyed immortal bliss,
Yet willingly chose rather death with thee?
And am I now upbraided as the cause
Of thy transgressing? not enough severe,
It seems, in thy restraint! What could I more?   1170
I warned thee, I admonished thee, foretold
The danger, and the lurking enemy
That lay in wait; beyond this had been force,
And force upon free will hath here no place.
But confidence then bore thee on, secure   1175
Either to meet no danger, or to find
Matter of glorious trial; and perhaps
I also erred in overmuch admiring

1140. *approve:* prove. 1159. *fair dismiss:* willingly let me go. 1164. *mine:*
i.e., my love. 1175. *secure:* confident.

What seemed in thee so perfect that I thought
No evil durst attempt thee. But I rue   1180
That error now, which is become my crime,
And thou the accuser. Thus it shall befall
Him who, to worth in women overtrusting,
Lets her will rule: restraint she will not brook;
And, left to herself, if evil thence ensue,   1185
She first his weak indulgence will accuse."
     Thus they in mutual accusation spent
The fruitless hours, but neither self-condemning;
And of their vain contést appeared no end.

THE END OF THE NINTH BOOK

∾

BOOK X

THE ARGUMENT

*Man's transgression known, the guardian Angels forsake Paradise.
and return up to Heaven to approve their vigilance, and are approved;
God declaring that the entrance of Satan could not be by them prevented. He sends his Son to judge the transgressors; who descends,
and gives sentence accordingly; then, in pity, clothes them both, and
reascends. Sin and Death, sitting till then at the gates of Hell, by
wondrous sympathy feeling the success of Satan in this new World,
and the sin by Man there committed, resolve to sit no longer confined
in Hell, but to follow Satan, their sire, up to the place of Man: to
make the way easier from Hell to this World to and fro, they pave
a broad highway or bridge over Chaos, according to the track that
Satan first made; then, preparing for Earth, they meet him, proud of
his success, returning to Hell; their mutual gratulation. Satan arrives
at Pandemonium; in full assembly relates, with boasting, his success
against Man; instead of applause is entertained with a general hiss by
all his audience, transformed, with himself also, suddenly into Serpents, according to his doom given in Paradise; then, deluded with
a show of the Forbidden Tree springing up before them, they, greedily
reaching to take of the fruit, chew dust and bitter ashes. The proceed-
ings of Sin and Death: God foretells the final victory of his Son over
them, and the renewing of all things; but, for the present, commands
his Angels to make several alterations in the Heavens and Elements.*

1184. *brook*: endure.

Adam, more and more perceiving his fallen condition, heavily bewails,
rejects the condolement of Eve; she persists, and at length appeases
him: then, to evade the curse likely to fall on their offspring, proposes
to Adam violent ways; which he approves not, but, conceiving better
hope, puts her in mind of the late promise made them, that her seed
should be revenged on the Serpent, and exhorts her, with him, to seek
peace of the offended Deity by repentance and supplication.

Meanwhile the heinous and despiteful act
Of Satan done in Paradise, and how
He, in the Serpent, had perverted Eve,
Her husband she, to taste the fatal fruit,
Was known in Heaven; for what can scape the eye   5
Of God all-seeing, or deceive his heart
Omniscient? who, in all things wise and just,
Hindered not Satan to attempt the mind
Of Man, with strength entire and free will armed
Complete to have discovered and repulsed   10
Whatever wiles of foe or seeming friend.
For still they knew, and ought to have still remembered,
The high injunction not to taste that fruit,
Whoever tempted; which they not obeying
Incurred (what could they less?) the penalty,   15
And, manifold in sin, deserved to fall.
Up into Heaven from Paradise in haste
The Angelic guards ascended, mute and sad
For Man; for of his state by this they knew,
Much wondering how the subtle Fiend had stolen   20
Entrance unseen. Soon as the unwelcome news
From Earth arrived at Heaven-gate, displeased
All were who heard; dim sadness did not spare
That time celestial visages, yet, mixed
With pity, violated not their bliss.   25
About the new-arrived, in multitudes,
The ethereal People ran, to hear and know
How all befell. They towards the throne supreme,
Accountable, made haste to make appear,
With righteous plea, their utmost vigilance,   30
And easily approved; when the Most High,

---

16. *manifold . . . sin:* i.e., having committed many sins—e.g., distrust of God, ingratitude, disobedience, pride, flattery, lust, etc. 19. *by this:* by this time. 31. *approved:* demonstrated.

Eternal Father, from his secret cloud
Amidst, in thunder uttered thus his voice:
  "Assembled Angels, and ye Powers returned
From unsuccessful charge, be not dismayed   35
Nor troubled at these tidings from the Earth,
Which your sincerest care could not prevent,
Foretold so lately what would come to pass,
When first this Tempter crossed the gulf from Hell.
I told ye then he should prevail, and speed   40
On his bad errand—Man should be seduced,
And flattered out of all, believing lies
Against his Maker; no decree of mine
Concurring to necessitate his fall,
Or touch with lightest moment of impulse   45
His free will, to her own inclining left
In even scale. But fallen he is; and now
What rests, but that the mortal sentence pass
On his transgression, Death denounced that day?
Which he presumes already vain and void,   50
Because not yet inflicted, as he feared,
By some immediate stroke, but soon shall find
Forbearance no acquittance ere day end.
Justice shall not return, as bounty, scorned.
But whom send I to judge them? whom but thee,   55
Vicegerent Son? To thee I have transferred
All judgment, whether in Heaven, or Earth, or Hell.
Easy it may be seen that I intend
Mercy colleague with justice, sending thee,
Man's friend, his Mediator, his designed   60
Both ransom and Redeemer voluntary,
And destined Man himself to judge Man fallen."
  So spake the Father; and, unfolding bright
Toward the right hand his glory, on the Son
Blazed forth unclouded deity. He full   65
Resplendent all his Father manifest
Expressed, and thus divinely answered mild:

---

35. *charge:* duty. 40. *then:* in III 92 ff. *speed:* succeed. 42. *all:* all he possessed. 48. *rests:* remains. *mortal sentence:* sentence punishing man with
mortality. 53. *Forbearance no acquittance:* that my withholding his penalty
does not mean he is acquitted. 54. *as . . . scorned:* scorned like my gen-
erosity (in bestowing Eden on them). 59. *sending thee:* since I send thee.
62. *destined Man:* i.e., one who is destined to become a man (Christ).

"Father Eternal, thine is to decree;
Mine both in Heaven and Earth to do thy will
Supreme, that thou in me, thy Son beloved,   70
May'st ever rest well pleased. I go to judge
On Earth these thy transgressors; but thou know'st,
Whoever judged, the worst on me must light,
When time shall be; for so I undertook
Before thee, and, not repenting, this obtain   75
Of right, that I may mitigate their doom
On me derived. Yet I shall temper so
Justice with mercy as may illustrate most
Them fully satisfied, and thee appease.
Attendance none shall need, nor train, where none   80
Are to behold the judgment but the judged,
Those two; the third best absent is condemned,
Convict by flight, and rebel to all law;
Conviction to the Serpent none belongs."
    Thus saying, from his radiant seat he rose   85
Of high collateral glory. Him Thrones and Powers,
Princedoms, and Dominations ministrant,
Accompanied to Heaven-gate, from whence
Eden and all the coast in prospect lay.
Down he descended straight; the speed of Gods   90
Time counts not, though with swiftest minutes winged.
    Now was the Sun in western cadence low
From noon, and gentle airs due at their hour
To fan the Earth now waked, and usher in
The evening cool, when he, from wrath more cool,   95
Came, the mild judge and intercessor both,
To sentence Man. The voice of God they heard
Now walking in the Garden, by soft winds
Brought to their ears, while day declined; they heard,
And from his presence hid themselves among   100
The thickest trees, both man and wife, till God,
Approaching, thus to Adam called aloud:
    "Where art thou, Adam, wont with joy to meet
My coming, seen far off? I miss thee here,
Not pleased, thus entertained with solitude,   105

70-1. Cf. III 168n. 77. *derived:* diverted. 78. *illustrate:* glorify. 80. I.e., ᵏ
need no attendants. 84. *Conviction:* legal process of trial. 92. *cadence:*
descent. 97 ff. Cf. Genesis 3:8 ff (in the Appendix).

Where obvious duty erewhile appeared unsought.
Or come I less conspicuous, or what change
Absents thee, or what chance detains? Come forth!"
    He came, and with him Eve, more loath, though first
To offend, discountenanced both, and discomposed.   110
Love was not in their looks, either to God
Or to each other, but apparent guilt,
And shame, and perturbation, and despair,
Anger, and obstinacy, and hate, and guile.
Whence Adam, faltering long, thus answered brief: 115
    "I heard thee in the Garden, and, of thy voice
Afraid, being naked, hid myself." To whom
The gracious Judge, without revile, replied:
    "My voice thou oft hast heard, and hast not feared,
But still rejoiced; how is it now become   120
So dreadful to thee? That thou art naked who
Hath told thee? Hast thou eaten of the tree
Whereof I gave thee charge thou shouldst not eat?"
To whom thus Adam, sore beset, replied:
    "O Heaven! in evil strait this day I stand   125
Before my Judge—either to undergo
Myself the total crime, or to accuse
My other self, the partner of my life,
Whose failing, while her faith to me remains,
I should conceal, and not expose to blame   130
By my complaint. But strict necessity
Subdues me, and calamitous constraint,
Lest on my head both sin and punishment,
However insupportable, be all
Devolved; though, should I hold my peace, yet thou   135
Wouldst easily detect what I conceal.
This Woman, whom thou mad'st to be my help,
And gav'st me as thy perfect gift, so good,
So fit, so acceptáble, so divine,
That from her hand I could suspect no ill,   140
And what she did, whatever in itself,
Her doing seemed to justify the deed—
She gave me of the tree, and I did eat."
To whom the Sovran Presence thus replied:

---

106. I.e., where you, who have an obvious duty to me, formerly appeared
without my calling for you. *Obvious* here means also "coming to meet,"
"welcoming." 141. *whatever in itself:* i.e., whatever character it has in itself.

"Was she thy God, that her thou didst obey   145
Before his voice? or was she made thy guide,
Superior, or but equal, that to her
Thou didst resign thy manhood, and the place
Wherein God set thee above her, made of thee
And for thee, whose perfection far excelled   150
Hers in all real dignity? Adorned
She was indeed, and lovely, to attract
Thy love, not thy subjection; and her gifts
Were such as under government well seemed—
Unseemly to bear rule; which was thy part   155
And person, hadst thou known thyself aright."
    So having said, he thus to Eve in few:
"Say, Woman, what is this which thou hast done?"
    To whom sad Eve, with shame nigh overwhelmed,
Confessing soon, yet not before her Judge   160
Bold or loquacious, thus abashed replied:
"The Serpent me beguiled, and I did eat."
    Which when the Lord God heard, without delay
To judgment he proceeded on the accused
Serpent, though brute, unable to transfer   165
The guilt on him who made him instrument
Of mischief, and polluted from the end
Of his creation—justly then accursed,
As vitiated in nature. More to know
Concerned not Man (since he no further knew),   170
Nor altered his offence; yet God at last
To Satan, first in sin, his doom applied,
Though in mysterious terms, judged as then best;
And on the Serpent thus his curse let fall:
    "Because thou hast done this, thou art accursed   175
Above all cattle, each beast of the field;
Upon thy belly grovelling thou shalt go,
And dust shalt eat all the days of thy life.
Between thee and the Woman I will put
Enmity, and between thine and her seed;   180
Her seed shall bruise thy head, thou bruise his heel."
    So spake this oracle—then verified
When Jesus, son of Mary, second Eve,

---

147. *but:* even. 154-5. *under . . . rule:* were well suited to be ruled, not to
rule. 165. *unable:* modifies *serpent:* Milton attributes some guilt to the serpent (perhaps because in Genesis the serpent alone is guilty), but suggests
that in some mysterious way the curse applies primarily to Satan.

Saw Satan fall like lightning down from Heaven,
Prince of the Air; then, rising from his grave,   185
Spoiled Principalities and Powers, triumphed
In open show, and, with ascension bright,
Captivity led captive through the Air,
The realm itself of Satan, long usurped,
Whom he shall tread at last under our feet,   190
Even he who now foretold his fatal bruise,
And to the Woman thus his sentence turned:
    "Thy sorrow I will greatly multiply
By thy conception; children thou shalt bring
In sorrow forth, and to thy husband's will   195
Thine shall submit; he over thee shall rule."
    On Adam last thus judgment he pronounced:
"Because thou hast hearkened to the voice of thy wife,
And eaten of the tree concerning which
I charged thee, saying, *Thou shalt not eat thereof,*   200
Cursed is the ground for thy sake; thou in sorrow
Shalt eat thereof all the days of thy life;
Thorns also and thistles it shall bring thee forth
Unbid; and thou shalt eat the herb of the field;
In the sweat of thy face thou shalt eat bread,   205
Till thou return unto the ground; for thou
Out of the ground was taken: know thy birth,
For dust thou art, and shalt to dust return."
    So judged he Man, both Judge and Saviour sent,
And the instant stroke of death, denounced that day,   210
Removed far off; then, pitying how they stood
Before him naked to the air, that now
Must suffer change, disdained not to begin
Thenceforth the form of servant to assume.
As when he washed his servants' feet, so now,   215
As father of his family, he clad
Their nakedness with skins of beasts, or slain,
Or, as the snake, with youthful coat repaid;

183-4. Cf. Luke 10:18, where Christ tells his disciples, "I beheld Satan as lightning fall from heaven." 185. *Prince . . . Air:* the title given to Satan by St. Paul (Ephesians 2:2). 186-7. *Spoiled . . . show:* St. Paul says of Christ (Colossians 2:15) that "having spoiled principalities and powers [of evil], he made a shew of them openly, triumphing over them." 187-8. *with . . . captive:* Psalms 68:18: "Thou hast ascended on high, thou hast led captivity captive." 189. *realm:* i.e., the air; cf. 185. 215. *servants':* the disciples—cf. John 13. 217-18. *or . . . repaid:* Milton refuses to decide whether the skins were those of beasts slain for the occasion, or "sloughs" for which they were repaid with a new pelt.

And thought not much to clothe his enemies.
Nor he their outward only with the skins   220
Of beasts, but inward nakedness, much more
Opprobrious, with his robe of righteousness
Arraying, covered from his Father's sight.
To him with swift ascent he up returned,
Into his blissful bosom reassumed   225
In glory as of old; to him, appeased,
All, though all-knowing, what had passed with Man
Recounted, mixing intercession sweet.
    Meanwhile, ere thus was sinned and judged on Earth,
Within the gates of Hell sat Sin and Death,   230
In counterview within the gates, that now
Stood open wide, belching outrageous flame
Far into Chaos, since the Fiend passed through,
Sin opening; who thus now to Death began:
    "O Son, why sit we here, each other viewing   235
Idly, while Satan, our great author, thrives
In other worlds, and happier seat provides
For us, his offspring dear? It cannot be
But that success attends him; if mishap,
Ere this he had returned, with fury driven   240
By his avengers, since no place like this
Can fit his punishment, or their revenge.
Methinks I feel new strength within me rise,
Wings growing, and dominion given me large
Beyond this Deep—whatever draws me on,   245
Or sympathy, or some connatural force,
Powerful at greatest distance to unite
With secret amity things of like kind
By secretest conveyance. Thou, my shade
Inseparable, must with me along;   250
For Death from Sin no power can separate.
But, lest the difficulty of passing back
Stay his return perhaps over this gulf
Impassable, impervious, let us try
(Adventurous work, yet to thy power and mine   255
Not unagreeable!) to found a path
Over this main from Hell to that new World

---

219. *thought . . . much:* did not begrudge. 228. *Recounted:* i.e., he
(Christ) recounted. 231. *counterview:* facing each other. 234. *opening:*
commencing (to speak). 241. *like this:* so wild as this. 257. *main:* **sea**
(of Chaos).

Where Satan now prevails—a monument
Of merit high to all the infernal host,
Easing their passage hence, for intercourse   260
Of transmigration, as their lot shall lead.
Nor can I miss the way, so strongly drawn
By this new-felt attraction and instinct."
　　Whom thus the meagre Shadow answered soon:
"Go whither fate and inclination strong   265
Leads thee; I shall not lag behind, nor err
The way, thou leading: such a scent I draw
Of carnage, prey innumerable, and taste
The savour of death from all things there that live.
Nor shall I to the work thou enterprisest   270
Be wanting, but afford thee equal aid."
　　So saying, with delight he snuffed the smell
Of mortal change on Earth. As when a flock
Of ravenous fowl, though many a league remote,
Against the day of battle, to a field   275
Where armies lie encamped come flying, lured
With scent of living carcases designed
For death the following day in bloody fight:
So scented the grim Feature, and upturned
His nostril wide into the murky air,   280
Sagacious of his quarry from so far.
Then both, from out Hell-gates, into the waste
Wide anarchy of Chaos, damp and dark,
Flew diverse, and, with power (their power was great)
Hovering upon the waters, what they met   285
Solid or slimy, as in raging sea
Tossed up and down, together crowded drove,
From each side shoaling, towards the mouth of Hell;
As when two polar winds, blowing adverse
Upon the Cronian sea, together drive   290
Mountains of ice, that stop the imagined way
Beyond Petsora eastward to the rich
Cathaian coast. The aggregated soil
Death with his mace petrific, cold and dry,
As with a trident smote, and fixed as firm   295

---

275. *Against:* anticipating. 281. *Sagacious:* keen-scented. 288. *shoaling:*
making a shoal. 290. *Cronian:* Arctic. 291. *imagined way:* the reputed
"northeast passage" to India and China (*Cathaian coast*). 292. *Petsora:*
river flowing from the Urals to the Arctic. 293-6. *The . . . once:* i.e.,

As Delos floating once; the rest his look
Bound with Gorgonian rigour not to move,
And with asphaltic slime; broad as the gate,
Deep to the roots of Hell the gathered beach
They fastened, and the mole immense wrought on   300
Over the foaming Deep high-arched, a bridge
Of length prodigious, joining to the wall
Immovable of this now fenceless World,
Forfeit to Death—from hence a passage broad,
Smooth, easy, inoffensive, down to Hell.   305
So, if great things to small may be compared,
Xerxes, the liberty of Greece to yoke,
From Susa, his Memnonian palace high,
Came to the sea, and over Hellespont
Bridging his way, Europe with Asia joined,   310
And scourged with many a stroke the indignant waves.
Now had they brought the work by wondrous art
Pontifical, a ridge of pendent rock
Over the vexed Abyss, following the track
Of Satan to the self-same place where he   315
First lighted from his wing, and landed safe
From out of Chaos to the outside bare
Of this round World. With pins of adamant
And chains they made all fast, too fast they made
And durable; and now in little space   320
The confines met of empyrean Heaven
And of this World, and on the left hand Hell,
With long reach interposed; three several ways
In sight to each of these three places led.
And now their way to Earth they had descried,   325
To Paradise first tending, when, behold
Satan, in likeness of an Angel bright,

Death isolates out of the four elements in Chaos—hot, cold, moist, dry (cf. II 898)—the cold and the dry and petrifies them into a solid with his mace, as Neptune once solidified out of sea-water the isle of Delos, which later Jove anchored in the Cyclades. 297. *Gorgonian:* like that of the Gorgons, whose sight turned all comers to stone. 300. *the . . . on:* i.e., extended the immense structure. 303. *fenceless:* defenseless. 305. *inoffensive:* unimpeded. 307-11. From his capital at Susa (supposedly established by Memnon), Xerxes of Persia came with an expedition to conquer Greece; when he sought to bridge the Hellespont, he had the waters whipped for daring to resist him. 312-13. *art Pontifical:* i.e., bridge-builder's art. 315-16. *where . . . wing:* as described in III 418-30. 323. *several:* distinct.

Betwixt the Centaur and the Scorpion steering
His zenith, while the Sun in Aries rose:
Disguised he came; but those his children dear   330
Their parent soon discerned, though in disguise.
He, after Eve seduced, unmindful slunk
Into the wood fast by, and, changing shape
To observe the sequel, saw his guileful act
By Eve, though all unweeting, seconded   335
Upon her husband—saw their shame that sought
Vain covertures; but, when he saw descend
The Son of God to judge them, terrified
He fled, not hoping to escape, but shun
The present—fearing, guilty, what his wrath   340
Might suddenly inflict; that past, returned
By night, and, listening where the hapless pair
Sat in their sad discourse and various plaint,
Thence gathered his own doom; which understood
Not instant, but of future time, with joy   345
And tidings fraught, to Hell he now returned,
And at the brink of Chaos, near the foot
Of this new wondrous pontifice, unhoped
Met who to meet him came, his offspring dear.
Great joy was at their meeting, and at sight   350
Of that stupendious bridge his joy increased.
Long he admiring stood, till Sin, his fair
Enchanting daughter, thus the silence broke:
  "O Parent, these are thy magnific deeds,
Thy trophies! which thou view'st as not thine own;   355
Thou art their author and prime architect.
For I no sooner in my heart divined
(My heart, which by a secret harmony
Still moves with thine, joined in connexion sweet)
That thou on Earth hadst prospered, which thy looks   360
Now also evidence, but straight I felt—
Though distant from thee worlds between, yet felt—
That I must after thee with this thy son;
Such fatal consequence unites us three.
Hell could no longer hold us in her bounds,   365

___

328-9. *Centaur, Scorpion, Aries:* signs of the Zodiac. Satan stays on the side of the sky opposite the sun, to avoid being seen by Uriel. 335. *unweeting:* unsuspecting. 345. *instant:* instantaneous. 346. *fraught:* freighted. 348. *pontifice:* bridge. 358-9. Cf. 246, 263.

Nor this unvoyageable gulf obscure
Detain from following thy illustrious track.
Thou hast achieved our liberty, confined
Within Hell-gates till now; thou us empowered
To fortify thus far, and overlay   370
With this portentous bridge the dark Abyss.
Thine now is all this World; thy virtue hath won
What thy hands builded not; thy wisdom gained,
With odds, what war hath lost, and fully avenged
Our foil in Heaven. Here thou shalt monarch reign,   375
There didst not; there let him still victor sway,
As battle hath adjudged, from this new World
Retiring, by his own doom alienated,
And henceforth monarchy with thee divide
Of all things, parted by the empyreal bounds,   380
His quadrature, from thy orbicular World,
Or try thee now more dangerous to his throne."
    Whom thus the Prince of Darkness answered glad:
"Fair daughter, and thou, son and grandchild both,
High proof ye now have given to be the race   385
Of Satan (for I glory in the name,
Antagonist of Heaven's Almighty King),
Amply have merited of me, of all
The Infernal Empire, that so near Heaven's door
Triumphal with triumphal act have met,   390
Mine with this glorious work, and made one realm
Hell and this World—one realm, one continent
Of easy thoroughfare. Therefore, while I
Descend through Darkness, on your road with ease,
To my associate Powers, them to acquaint   395
With these successes, and with them rejoice,
You two this way, among these numerous orbs,
All yours, right down to Paradise descend;
There dwell, and reign in bliss; thence on the Earth
Dominion exercise and in the air,   400
Chiefly on Man, sole lord of all declared;
Him first make sure your thrall, and lastly kill.
My substitutes I send ye, and create

---

375. *foil:* defeat. 378. *doom:* decision. 380-1. *parted . . . World:* i.e.,
separated by the boundaries of his Heaven (which Milton thinks of as
square, a *quadrature*) from thy round world. 382. *try:* test, find. 389.
Infernal Empire: i.e., all Hell's inhabitants. 390. I.e., have met my triumphal act (the Fall) with yours (the bridge).

Plenipotent on Earth, of matchless might
Issuing from me. On your joint vigour now   405
My hold of this new kingdom all depends,
Through Sin to Death exposed by my exploit.
If your joint power prevail, the affairs of Hell
No detriment need fear; go, and be strong."

   So saying, he dismissed them; they with speed   410
Their course through thickest constellations held,
Spreading their bane; the blasted stars looked wan,
And planets, planet-strook, real eclipse
Then suffered. The other way Satan went down
The causey to Hell-gate; on either side   415
Disparted Chaos overbuilt exclaimed,
And with rebounding surge the bars assailed,
That scorned his indignation. Through the gate,
Wide open and unguarded, Satan passed,
And all about found desolate; for those   420
Appointed to sit there had left their charge,
Flown to the upper World; the rest were all
Far to the inland retired, about the walls
Of Pandemonium, city and proud seat
Of Lucifer, so by allusion called   425
Of that bright star to Satan paragoned.
There kept their watch the legions, while the Grand
In council sat, solicitous what chance
Might intercept their Emperor sent; so he
Departing gave command, and they observed.   430
As when the Tartar from his Russian foe,
By Astracan, over the snowy plains,
Retires, or Bactrian Sophi, from the horns
Of Turkish crescent, leaves all waste beyond
The realm of Aladule, in his retreat   435
To Tauris or Casbeen; so these, the late
Heaven-banished host, left desert utmost Hell

413. *planet-strook:* a term applied to anyone under an evil influence from the stars—applied here to the effect of Sin and Death on the planets themselves. 415. *causey:* causeway. 416. *overbuilt:* built over (by the bridge). 426. *that bright star:* the planet Venus, called *Lucifer,* i.e., light-bringer, because it is the morning star. *paragoned:* compared. 427. *the Grand:* the grandees of Hell. 429. *so:* i.e., that they should remain in council. 432. *Astracan:* border city between the Tartars and the Russians. 433. *Bactrian Sophi:* Milton now turns to an alternative example—the retreat of a Persian *sophy* or shah before the Turk, leaving scorched earth behind him.

Many a dark league, reduced in careful watch
Round their metropolis, and now expecting
Each hour their great Adventurer from the search   440
Of foreign worlds. He through the midst unmarked,
In show plebian Angel militant
Of lowest order, passed, and, from the door
Of that Plutonian hall, invisible
Ascended his high throne, which, under state   445
Of richest texture spread, at the upper end
Was placed in regal lustre. Down a while
He sat, and round about him saw, unseen.
At last, as from a cloud, his fulgent head
And shape star-bright appeared, or brighter, clad   450
With what permissive glory since his fall
Was left him, or false glitter. All amazed
At that so sudden blaze, the Stygian throng
Bent their aspect, and whom they wished beheld,
Their mighty Chief returned: loud was the acclaim.   455
Forth rushed in haste the great consulting Peers,
Raised from their dark Divan, and with like joy
Congratulant approached him, who with hand
Silence, and with these words attention, won:
'Thrones, Dominations, Princedoms, Virtues, Powers!—   460
For in possession such, not only of right,
I call ye, and declare ye now, returned
Successful beyond hope, to lead ye forth
Triumphant out of this infernal pit
Abominable, accursed, the house of woe,   465
And dungeon of our tyrant! Now possess,
As lords, a spacious World, to our native Heaven
Little inferior, by my adventure hard
With peril great achieved. Long were to tell
What I have done, what suffered, with what pain   470
Voyaged the unreal, vast, unbounded Deep
Of horrible confusion—over which
By Sin and Death a broad way now is paved,
To expedite your glorious march; but I

---

438. *reduced:* led back (as in retreat). 442. *In show:* i.e., in the form of.
449. *fulgent:* shining. 451. *permissive:* i.e., permitted by God. 454. *aspect:*
look. 457. *Divan:* Council of State. 461-2. I.e., these titles are yours not only
on account of your rights to what you lost in Heaven, but also by virtue of
what you now actually possess (a universe as empire). 462. *returned:* having returned.

Toiled out my uncouth passage, forced to ride   47*
The untractable Abyss, plunged in the womb
Of unoriginal Night and Chaos wild,
That, jealous of their secrets, fiercely opposed
My journey strange, with clamorous uproar
Protesting Fate supreme; thence how I found   48(
The new-created World, which fame in Heaven
Long had foretold, a fabric wonderful,
Of absolute perfection; therein Man
Placed in a paradise, by our exile
Made happy. Him by fraud I have seduced   48:
From his Creator, and, the more to increase
Your wonder, with an apple! He, thereat
Offended—worth your laughter!—hath given up
Both his beloved Man and all his World
To Sin and Death a prey, and so to us,   490
Without our hazard, labour, or alarm,
To range in, and to dwell, and over Man
To rule, as over all he should have ruled.
True is, me also he hath judged; or rather
Me not, but the brute Serpent, in whose shape   495
Man I deceived. That which to me belongs
Is enmity, which he will put between
Me and Mankind: I am to bruise his heel;
His seed—when is not set—shall bruise my head!
A world who would not purchase with a bruise,   500
Or much more grievous pain? Ye have the account
Of my performance; what remains, ye Gods,
But up and enter now into full bliss?"
   So having said, a while he stood, expecting
Their universal shout and high applause   505
To fill his ear; when, contrary, he hears,
On all sides, from innumerable tongues
A dismal universal hiss, the sound
Of public scorn. He wondered, but not long
Had leisure, wondering at himself now more: 510
His visage drawn he felt to sharp and spare,
His arms clung to his ribs, his legs entwining

475. *uncouth:* unknown. 477. *unoriginal:* i.e., having no origin. 480. *how
I found:* grammatically, the object of *to tell* in 469. 499. *when . . . set:*
i.e., the date is not fixed. 511. *His . . . to:* I.e., he felt his visage narrowed
till it was.

Each other, till, supplanted, down he fell,
A monstrous serpent on his belly prone,
Reluctant, but in vain; a greater power   515
Now ruled him, punished in the shape he sinned,
According to his doom. He would have spoke,
But hiss for hiss returned with forkèd tongue
To forkèd tongue; for now were all transformed
Alike, to serpents all, as accessóries   520
To his bold riot. Dreadful was the din
Of hissing through the hall, thick-swarming now
With complicated monsters, head and tail—
Scorpion, and Asp, and Amphisbæna dire,
Cerastes horned, Hydrus, and Ellops drear,   525
And Dipsas (not so thick swarmed once the soil
Bedropt with blood of Gorgon, or the isle
Ophiusa); but still greatest he the midst,
Now Dragon grown, larger than whom the Sun
Engendered in the Pythian vale on slime,   530
Huge Python; and his power no less he seemed
Above the rest still to retain. They all
Him followed, issuing forth to the open field,
Where all yet left of that revolted rout,
Heaven-fallen, in station stood or just array,   535
Sublime with expectation when to see
In triumph issuing forth their glorious Chief.
They saw, but other sight instead—a crowd
Of ugly serpents! Horror on them fell,
And horrid sympathy; for what they saw   540
They felt themselves now changing. Down their arms,
Down fell both spear and shield; down they as fast,
And the dire hiss renewed, and the dire form
Catched by contagion, like in punishment
As in their crime. Thus was the applause they meant   545
Turned to exploding hiss, triumph to shame

---

513. *supplanted:* tripped. 515. *reluctant:* fighting against it. 523. *compli-cated:* tangled in folds. 524-6. *Amphisbaena . . . Dipsas:* Names of fabulous snakes. 526-7. *not . . . Gorgon:* Wherever blood dropped from the Gor-gon's head as Perseus carried it home, snakes sprang up. 528. *Ophiusa:* a name meaning *"snaky"* given to several islands by classical writers. *greatest he the midst:* i.e., greatest was he who stood in the midst (Satan). 531. *Py-thon:* the vast serpent that sprang from the mud after Deucation's flood. 534. *all:* all those who had been waiting outside the palace. 538. *Sublime:* uplifted. 541. *changing:* i.e., becoming.

Cast on themselves from their own mouths. There stood
A grove hard by, sprung up with this their change,
His will who reigns above, to aggravate
Their penance, laden with fair fruit, like that   550
Which grew in Paradise, the bait of Eve
Used by the Tempter. On that prospect strange
Their earnest eyes they fixed, imagining
For one forbidden tree a multitude
Now risen, to work them further woe or shame;   555
Yet, parched with scalding thirst and hunger fierce,
Though to delude them sent, could not abstain,
But on they rolled in heaps, and, up the trees
Climbing, sat thicker than the snaky locks
That curled Megæra. Greedily they plucked   560
The fruitage fair to sight, like that which grew
Near that bituminous lake where Sodom flamed;
This, more delusive, not the touch, but taste
Deceived; they, fondly, thinking to allay
Their appetite with gust, instead of fruit   565
Chewed bitter ashes, which the offended taste
With spattering noise rejected. Oft they assayed,
Hunger and thirst constraining; drugged as oft,
With hatefulest disrelish writhed their jaws
With soot and cinders filled; so oft they fell   570
Into the same illusion, not, as Man
Whom they triúmphed, once lapsed. Thus were they plagued,
And worn with famine long, and ceaseless hiss,
Till their lost shape, permitted, they resumed—
Yearly enjoined, some say, to undergo   575
This annual humbling certain numbered days,
To dash their pride, and joy for Man seduced.
However, some tradition they dispersed
Among the Heathen of their purchase got,
And fabled how the Serpent, whom they called   580

---

549. *His will:* in obedience to his will. 560. *Megaera:* As one of the Furies, Megaera had serpents in her hair. 561-4. *like . . . deceived:* Sodom (situated near the Dead Sea, *that bituminous lake*) was burnt to ashes for its wickedness (Genesis 19) and the fruits of that region were thereafter said to collapse like ashes on being picked. 565. *gust:* gusto. 568. *drugged:* nauseated. 570-3. *so . . . lapsed:* i.e., they fell *oft*—not, like man whom they *triumphed* over, once. 574. *permitted:* permitted by God. 578-84. Milton instances as a false pagan story—derived from the true Hebrew account—

Ophion, with Eurynome (the wide-
Encroaching Eve perhaps), had first the rule
Of high Olympus, thence by Saturn driven
And Ops, ere yet Dictæan Jove was born.
   Meanwhile in Paradise the Hellish pair   585
Too soon arrived—Sin there in power before,
Once actual, now in body, and to dwell
Habitual habitant; behind her Death,
Close following pace for pace, not mounted yet
On his pale horse; to whom Sin thus began: 590
   "Second of Satan sprung, all-conquering Death!
What think'st thou of our empire now? though earned
With travail difficult, not better far
Than still at Hell's dark threshold to have sat watch,
Unnamed, undreaded, and thyself half-starved?"   595
   Whom thus the Sin-born Monster answered soon:
"To me, who with eternal famine pine,
Alike is Hell, or Paradise, or Heaven—
There best where most with ravin I may meet:
Which here, though plenteous, all too little seems   600
To stuff this maw, this vast unhide-bound corpse."
   To whom the incestuous Mother thus replied:
"Thou, therefore, on these herbs, and fruits, and flowers,
Feed first; on each beast next, and fish, and fowl—
No homely morsels; and whatever thing   605
The scythe of Time mows down, devour unspared;
Till I, in Man residing through the race,
His thoughts, his looks, words, actions, all infect,
And season him thy last and sweetest prey."
   This said, they both betook them several ways,   610
Both to destroy, or unimmortal make
All kinds, and for destruction to mature
Sooner or later; which the Almighty seeing,
From his transcendent seat the Saints among,

---

the legend that a serpent-like Titan named Ophion and his wife Eurynome
were the first rulers of Olympus till expelled by Saturn and his wife Ops
—who were in turn to be expelled by their son Jove (called here Dictaean
from his temple at Dicte in Crete). 586. *in . . . before:* i.e., when Adam
and Eve fell. 590. *pale horse:* Revelation 6:8: ". . . and behold a pale
horse: and his name that sat on him was Death, and Hell followed with
him." 601. *unhide-bound:* i.e., not tight or distended (with food).

To those bright Orders uttered thus his voice: 615
"See with what heat these dogs of Hell advance
To waste and havoc yonder World, which I
So fair and good created, and had still
Kept in that state, had not the folly of Man
Let in these wasteful furies, who impute   620
Folly to me (so doth the Prince of Hell
And his adherents), that with so much ease
I suffer them to enter and possess
A place so heavenly, and, conniving, seem
To gratify my scornful enemies,   625
That laugh, as if transported with some fit
Of passion, I to them had quitted all,
At random yielded up to their misrule;
And know not that I called and drew them thither,
My Hell-hounds, to lick up the draff and filth   630
Which Man's polluting sin with taint hath shed
On what was pure; till, crammed and gorged, nigh burst
With sucked and glutted offal, at one sling
Of thy victorious arm, well-pleasing Son,
Both Sin and Death, and yawning Grave, at last   635
Through Chaos hurled, obstruct the mouth of Hell
For ever, and seal up his ravenous jaws.
Then Heaven and Earth, renewed, shall be made pure
To sanctity that shall receive no stain:
Till then the curse pronounced on both precedes."   640
   He ended, and the Heavenly audience loud
Sung Halleluiah, as the sound of seas,
Through multitude that sung: "Just are thy ways,
Righteous are thy decrees on all thy works;
Who can extenuate thee? Next, to the Son,   645
Destined restorer of Mankind, by whom
New Heaven and Earth shall to the ages rise,
Or down from Heaven descend." Such was their song,
While the Creator, calling forth by name
His mighty Angels, gave them several charge,   650
As sorted best with present things. The Sun
Had first his precept so to move, so shine,

---

615. *Orders:* ranks of angels. 617. *havoc:* plunder. 624. *conniving:* closing
my eyes. 638-9. As in Revelation 21. 641-3. *and . . . sung:* Revelation
19:6 refers to "The voice of a great multitude, . . . the voice of many
waters, . . . saying Alleluia!" 651. *sorted:* suited.

As might affect the Earth with cold and heat
Scarce tolerable, and from the north to call
Decrepit winter, from the south to bring   655
Solstitial summer's heat. To the blanc Moon
Her office they prescribed; to the other five
Their planetary motions and aspécts,
In *sextile, square,* and *trine,* and *opposite,*
Of noxious efficacy, and when to join   660
In synod unbenign; and taught the fixed
Their influence malignant when to shower—
Which of them, rising with the Sun or falling,
Should prove tempestuous. To the winds they set
Their corners, when with bluster to confound   665
Sea, air, and shore; the thunder when to roll
With terror through the dark aerial hall.
Some say he bid his Angels turn askance
The poles of Earth twice ten degrees and more
From the Sun's axle; they with labour pushed   670
Oblique the centric Globe: some say the Sun
Was bid turn reins from the equinoctial road
Like distant breadth—to Taurus with the seven
Atlantic Sisters, and the Spartan Twins,
Up to the Tropic Crab; thence down amain   675
By Leo, and the Virgin, and the Scales,
As deep as Capricorn, to bring in change
Of seasons to each clime. Else had the spring
Perpetual smiled on Earth with vernant flowers,
Equal in days and nights, except to those   680
Beyond the polar circles; to them day
Had unbenighted shone, while the low Sun,
To recompense his distance, in their sight
Had rounded still the horizon, and not known
Or east or west—which had forbid the snow   685
From cold Estotiland, and south as far

---

656. *blanc:* pale. 657. *five:* i.e., five planets (besides the moon). 659. Terms
used in describing the relative positions of the planets. 661. *synod:* i.e.,
"conjunction"—the meeting of planets in the same longitude. *fixed:* fixed
stars. 664. *they:* the angels. 665. *corners:* the four points of the compass.
668 ff. Milton gives two astronomical alternatives to account for the "fallen"
earth's loss of eternal spring. 673-7. *to . . . Capricorn:* This describes the
sun's annual course with relation to the zodiacal signs. The *seven . . .
Sisters* are the Pleiades. 678. *had:* would have (as in 682, 684, 685).
684-5. *not . . . west:* i.e., not risen or set.

Beneath Magellan. At that tasted fruit,
The Sun, as from Thyéstean banquet, turned
His course intended; else how had the world
Inhabited, though sinless, more than now   690
Avoided pinching cold and scorching heat?
These changes in the heavens, though slow, produced
Like change on sea and land—sideral blast,
Vapour, and mist, and exhalation hot,
Corrupt and pestilent. Now from the north   695
Of Norumbega, and the Samoed shore,
Bursting their brazen dungeon, armed with ice,
And snow, and hail, and stormy gust and flaw,
Boreas and Cæcias and Argestes loud
And Thrascias rend the woods, and seas upturn;   700
With adverse blast upturns them from the south
Notus and Afer, black with thundrous clouds
From Serraliona; thwart of these, as fierce
Forth rush the Levant and the Ponent winds,
Eurus and Zephyr, with their lateral noise,   705
Sirocco and Libecchio. Thus began
Outrage from lifeless things; but Discord first,
Daughter of Sin, among the irrational
Death introduced through fierce antipathy.
Beast now with beast 'gan war, and fowl with fowl,   710
And fish with fish. To graze the herb all leaving
Devoured each other; nor stood much in awe
Of Man, but fled him, or with countenance grim
Glared on him passing. These were from without
The growing miseries; which Adam saw   715
Already in part, though hid in gloomiest shade,
To sorrow abandoned, but worse felt within,
And, in a troubled sea of passion tost,

---

687. *Magellan:* the straits of Magellan. 688. *Thyestean banquet:* the horrible feast at which Thyestes ate his sons. 693. *sideral blast:* a malign influence from the stars. 696. *Norumbega, Samoed:* Names referring vaguely to the arctic shores of Canada and Russia. 699-700. The names are those of north winds. 702. *Notus, Afer:* south winds. 703. *Serraliona:* Sierra Leone (in Africa). *thwart of:* across. 704-5. *the . . . Zephyr:* the east (Eurus) and west (Zephyr) winds, blowing from the sun's rising (Levant) and its setting (Ponent). 705. *lateral:* at right angles to the north and south winds. 706. *Sirocco and Libecchio:* the southeast and southwest winds. 711. *leaving:* ceasing.

Thus to disburden sought with sad complaint:
  "O miserable of happy! Is this the end   720
Of this new glorious World, and me so late
The glory of that glory? who now, become
Accursed of blessèd, hide me from the face
Of God, whom to behold was then my highth
Of happiness! Yet well, if here would end   725
The misery! I deserved it, and would bear
My own deservings. But this will not serve:
All that I eat or drink, or shall beget,
Is propagated curse. O voice, once heard
Delightfully, *Increase and multiply*,   730
Now death to hear! for what can I increase
Or multiply but curses on my head?
Who, of all ages to succeed, but, feeling
The evil on him brought by me, will curse
My head? 'Ill fare our Ancestor impure!   735
For this we may thank Adam!' but his thanks
Shall be the execration: so, besides
Mine own that bide upon me, all from me
Shall with a fierce reflux on me redound—
On me, as on their natural centre, light;   740
Heavy, though in their place. O fleeting joys
Of Paradise, dear bought with lasting woes!
Did I request thee, Maker, from my clay
To mould me Man? Did I solicit thee
From darkness to promote me, or here place   745
In this delicious Garden? As my will
Concurred not to my being, it were but right
And equal to reduce me to my dust,
Desirous to resign and render back
All I received, unable to perform   750
Thy terms too hard, by which I was to hold
The good I sought not. To the loss of that,
Sufficient penalty, why hast thou added
The sense of endless woes? Inexplicable
Thy justice seems. Yet, to say truth, too late   755
I thus contest; then should have been refused
Those terms, whatever, when they were proposed.

729-30. *O . . . multiply*: Cf. Genesis 1:28. 737-8. *besides . . . from me*: i.e., besides my own evils, which remain with me, the evils that are inherited from me. 748. *equal*: just.

Thou didst accept them: wilt thou enjoy the good,
Then cavil the conditions? And, though God
Made thee without thy leave, what if thy son   760
Prove disobedient, and, reproved, retort,
'Wherefore didst thou beget me? I sought it not!'
Wouldst thou admit for his contempt of thee
That proud excuse? yet him not thy election,
But natural necessity, begot.   765
God made thee of choice his own, and of his own
To serve him; thy reward was of his grace;
Thy punishment, then, justly is at his will.
Be it so, for I submit, his doom is fair,
That dust I am, and shall to dust return: 770
O welcome hour whenever! Why delays
His hand to execute what his decree
Fixed on this day? Why do I overlive?
Why am I mocked with death, and lengthened out
To deathless pain? How gladly would I meet   775
Mortality, my sentence, and be earth
Insensible! how glad would lay me down
As in my mother's lap! There I should rest,
And sleep secure; his dreadful voice no more
Would thunder in my ears; no fear of worse   780
To me and to my offspring would torment me
With cruel expectation. Yet one doubt
Pursues me still—lest all I cannot die;
Lest that pure breath of life, the Spirit of Man
Which God inspired, cannot together perish   785
With this corporeal clod. Then, in the grave,
Or in some other dismal place, who knows
But I shall die a living death? O thought
Horrid, if true! Yet why? It was but breath
Of life that sinned: what dies but what had life   790
And sin? The body properly hath neither.
All of me, then, shall die: let this appease
The doubt, since human reach no further knows.
For, though the Lord of all be infinite,
Is his wrath also? Be it, Man is not so,   795
But mortal doomed. How can he exercise
Wrath without end on Man, whom death must end?

---

758. *thou:* Adam addresses himself. 764. *election:* free will. 783. *all:* wholly.
795. *Be it:* even supposing his wrath *is* infinite.

Can he make deathless death? That were to make
Strange contradiction; which to God himself
Impossible is held, as argument   800
Of weakness, not of power. Will he draw out,
For anger's sake, finite to infinite
In punished Man, to satisfy his rigour
Satisfied never? That were to extend
His sentence beyond dust and Nature's law;   805
By which all causes else according still
To the reception of their matter act,
Not to the extent of their own sphere. But say
That death be not one stroke, as I supposed,
Bereaving sense, but endless misery   810
From this day onward, which I feel begun
Both in me and without me, and so last
To perpetuity——Ay me! that fear
Comes thundering back with dreadful revolution
On my defenceless head! Both Death and I   815
Am found eternal, and incorporate both:
Nor I on my part single; in me all
Posterity stands cursed. Fair patrimony
That I must leave ye, sons! Oh, were I able
To waste it all myself, and leave ye none!   820
So disinherited, how would ye bless
Me, now your curse! Ah, why should all Mankind,
For one man's fault, thus guiltless be condemned?
If guiltless! But from me what can proceed
But all corrupt—both mind and will depraved   825
Not to do only, but to will the same
With me? How can they, then, acquitted stand
In sight of God? Him, after all disputes,
Forced I absolve. All my evasions vain
And reasonings, though through mazes, lead me still   830
But to my own conviction: first and last
On me, me only, as the source and spring
Of all corruption, all the blame lights due.
So might the wrath! Fond wish! couldst thou support

806-7. I.e., according to nature's law, all agents other than God act with an effect determined by the qualities of what they act on (the *reception of their matter*), not by their own qualities (*the extent of their own sphere*). 816. *incorporate:* united in body. 817. *nor . . . single:* nor am I singly cursed. 831. *conviction:* i.e., of guilt.

That burden, heavier than the earth to bear—   835
Than all the world much heavier, though divided
With that bad Woman? Thus, what thou desir'st,
And what thou fear'st, alike destroys all hope
Of refuge, and concludes thee miserable
Beyond all past example and future—   840
To Satan only like, both crime and doom.
O Conscience! into what abyss of fears
And horrors hast thou driven me; out of which
I find no way, from deep to deeper plunged!"
      Thus Adam to himself lamented loud   845
Through the still night—not now, as ere Man fell,
Wholesome and cool and mild, but with black air
Accompanied, with damps and dreadful gloom;
Which to his evil conscience represented
All things with double terror. On the ground   850
Outstretched he lay, on the cold ground, and oft
Cursed his creation; Death as oft accused
Of tardy execution, since denounced
The day of his offence. "Why comes not Death,"
Said he, "with one thrice-ácceptable stroke   855
To end me? Shall Truth fail to keep her word,
Justice divine not hasten to be just?
But Death comes not at call; Justice divine
Mends not her slowest pace for prayers or cries.
O woods, O fountains, hillocks, dales, and bowers!   860
With other echo late I taught your shades
To answer, and resound far other song."
Whom thus afflicted when sad Eve beheld,
Desolate where she sat, approaching nigh,
Soft words to his fierce passion she assayed;   865
But her, with stern regard, he thus repelled:
      "Out of my sight, thou serpent! That name best
Befits thee, with him leagued, thyself as false
And hateful: nothing wants, but that thy shape
Like his, and colour serpentine, may show   870
Thy inward fraud, to warn all creatures from thee
Henceforth, lest that too heavenly form, pretended
To hellish falsehood, snare them. But for thee
I had persisted happy, had not thy pride
And wandering vanity, when least was safe,   875

853-4. *since . . . offence:* i.e., since it (death) was the penalty to be ex-
acted the day he disobeyed. 872. *pretended:* serving as a cloak.

Rejected my forewarning, and disdained
Not to be trusted—longing to be seen,
Though by the Devil himself; him overweening
To overreach; but with the Serpent meeting
Fooled and beguiled, by him thou, I by thee,   880
To trust thee from my side, imagined wise,
Constant, mature, proof against all assaults,
And understood not all was but a show,
Rather than solid virtue, all but a rib
Crookèd by nature—bent, as now appears,   885
More to the part siníster—from me drawn;
Well if thrown out, as supernumerary
To my just number found! Oh, why did God,
Creator wise, that peopled highest Heaven
With Spirits masculine, create at last   890
This novelty on Earth, this fair defect
Of Nature, and not fill the World at once
With men as Angels, without feminine;
Or find some other way to generate
Mankind? This mischief had not then befallen,   895
And more that shall befall—innumerable
Disturbances on Earth through female snares,
And strait conjunction with this sex. For either
He never shall find out fit mate, but such
As some misfortune brings him, or mistake;   900
Or whom he wishes most shall seldom gain,
Through her perverseness, but shall see her gained
By a far worse or, if she love, withheld
By parents; or his happiest choice too late
Shall meet, already linked and wedlock-bound   905
To a fell adversary, his hate or shame:
Which infinite calamity shall cause
To human life, and household peace confound."
    He added not, and from her turned; but Eve,
Not so repulsed, with tears that ceased not flowing,   910
And tresses all disordered, at his feet
Fell humble, and, embracing them, besought
His peace, and thus proceeded in her plaint:

878-9. *him . . . overreach:* over-confident that you could outwit him. 886.
sinister: (1) left (not right) (2) ill-omened. 887. *supernumerary:* superfluous. 891. I.e., woman. 898. *strait:* close. 899. *He:* a man. 906. *fell:*
brutal.

"Forsake me not thus, Adam! witness Heaven
What love sincere and reverence in my heart   915
I bear thee, and unweeting have offended,
Unhappily deceived! Thy suppliant
I beg, and clasp thy knees; bereave me not
Whereon I live, thy gentle looks, thy aid,
Thy counsel in this uttermost distress,   920
My only strength and stay. Forlorn of thee,
Whither shall I betake me, where subsist?
While yet we live, scarce one short hour perhaps,
Between us two let there be peace; both joining,
As joined in injuries, one enmity   925
Against a foe by doom express assigned us,
That cruel Serpent. On me exercise not
Thy hatred for this misery befallen—
On me already lost, me than thyself
More miserable. Both have sinned; but thou   930
Against God only; I against God and thee,
And to the place of judgment will return,
There with my cries importune Heaven, that all
The sentence, from thy head removed, may light
On me, sole cause to thee of all this woe,   935
Me, me only, just object of His ire."
     She ended, weeping; and her lowly plight,
Immovable till peace obtained from fault
Acknowledged and deplored, in Adam wrought
Commiseration. Soon his heart relented   940
Towards her, his life so late, and sole delight,
Now at his feet submissive in distress—
Creature so fair his reconcilement seeking,
His counsel whom she had displeased, his aid.
As one disarmed, his anger all he lost,   945
And thus with peaceful words upraised her soon:
     "Unwary, and too desirous, as before
So now, of what thou know'st not, who desir'st
The punishment all on thyself! Alas!
Bear thine own first, ill able to sustain   950
His full wrath whose thou feel'st as yet least part,
And my displeasure bear'st so ill. If prayers
Could alter high decrees, I to that place

919. *Whereon I live:* of that which I live on. 926. *by . . . express:* by God's specific sentence. 951. *whose:* i.e., whose wrath.

Would speed before thee, and be louder heard,
That on my head all might be visited,   955
Thy frailty and infirmer sex forgiven,
To me committed, and by me exposed.
But rise; let us no more contend, nor blame
Each other, blamed enough elsewhere, but strive
In offices of love how we may lighten   960
Each other's burden in our share of woe;
Since this day's death denounced, if aught I see,
Will prove no sudden, but a slow-paced evil,
A long day's dying, to augment our pain,
And to our seed (O hapless seed!) derived."   965
    To whom thus Eve, recovering heart, replied:
"Adam, by sad experiment I know
How little weight my words with thee can find,
Found so erroneous, thence by just event
Found so unfortunate. Nevertheless,   970
Restored by thee, vile as I am, to place
Of new acceptance, hopeful to regain
Thy love, the sole contentment of my heart,
Living or dying, from thee I will not hide
What thoughts in my unquiet breast are risen,   975
Tending to some relief of our extremes,
Or end, though sharp and sad, yet tolerable,
As in our evils, and of easier choice.
If care of our descent perplex us most,
Which must be born to certain woe, devoured   980
By Death at last (and miserable it is
To be to others cause of misery,
Our own begotten, and of our loins to bring
Into this cursèd world a woeful race,
That, after wretched life, must be at last   985
Food for so foul a monster), in thy power
It lies, yet ere conception, to prevent
The race unblest, to being yet unbegot.
Childless thou art; childless remain. So Death
Shall be deceived his glut, and with us two   990
Be forced to satisfy his ravenous maw.
But, if thou judge it hard and difficult,

959. *elsewhere:* i.e., at that place (953) where Christ judged them. 969. *event:* consequence. 978. *As . . . evils:* in such evils as ours. 979. *descent:* descendants. 990. *deceived . . . glut:* disappointed of his glutting.

Conversing, looking, loving, to abstain
From love's due rites, nuptial embraces sweet,
And with desire to languish without hope   995
Before the present object languishing
With like desire—which would be misery
And torment less than none of what we dread—
Then, both ourselves and seed at once to free
From what we fear for both, let us make short;   1000
Let us seek Death, or, he not found, supply
With our own hands his office on ourselves.
Why stand we longer shivering under fears
That show no end but death, and have the power,
Of many ways to die the shortest choosing,   1005
Destruction with destruction to destroy?"
    She ended here, or vehement despair
Broke off the rest; so much of death her thoughts
Had entertained as dyed her cheeks with pale.
But Adam, with such counsel nothing swayed,   1010
To better hopes his more attentive mind
Labouring had raised, and thus to Eve replied:
    "Eve, thy contempt of life and pleasure seems
To argue in thee something more sublime
And excellent than what thy mind contemns: 1015
But self-destruction therefore sought refutes
That excellence thought in thee, and implies
Not thy contempt, but anguish and regret
For loss of life and pleasure overloved.
Or, if thou covet death, as utmost end   1020
Of misery, so thinking to evade
The penalty pronounced, doubt not but God
Hath wiselier armed his vengeful ire than so
To be forestalled. Much more I fear lest death
So snatched will not exempt us from the pain   1025
We are by doom to pay; rather such acts
Of contumacy will provoke the Highest
To make death in us live. Then let us seek
Some safer resolution—which methinks
I have in view, calling to mind with heed   1030
Part of our sentence, that thy seed shall bruise
The Serpent's head. Piteous amends! unless
Be meant whom I conjecture, our grand foe,
Satan, who in the Serpent hath contrived

996. *the . . . object:* i.e., Eve.

Against us this deceit. To crush his head   1035
Would be revenge indeed—which will be lost
By death brought on ourselves, or childless days
Resolved as thou proposest; so our foe
Shall scape his punishment ordained, and we
Instead shall double ours upon our heads.   1040
No more be mentioned, then, of violence
Against ourselves, and wilful barrenness
That cuts us off from hope, and savours only
Rancour and pride, impatience and despite,
Reluctance against God and his just yoke   1045
Laid on our necks. Remember with what mild
And gracious temper he both heard and judged,
Without wrath or reviling. We expected
Immediate dissolution, which we thought
Was meant by death that day; when, lo! to thee   1050
Pains only in child-bearing were foretold,
And bringing forth, soon recompensed with joy,
Fruit of thy womb. On me the curse aslope
Glanced on the ground. With labour I must earn
My bread; what harm? Idleness had been worse;   1055
My labour will sustain me; and, lest cold
Or heat should injure us, his timely care
Hath, unbesought, provided, and his hands
Clothed us unworthy, pitying while he judged.
How much more, if we pray him, will his ear   1060
Be open, and his heart to pity incline,
And teach us further by what means to shun
The inclement seasons, rain, ice, hail, and snow!
Which now the sky, with various face, begins
To show us in this mountain, while the winds   1065
Blow moist and keen, shattering the graceful locks
Of these fair spreading trees; which bids us seek
Some better shroud, some better warmth to cherish
Our limbs benumbed, ere this diurnal star
Leave cold the night, how we his gathered beams   1070
Reflected may with matter sere foment,

1045. *reluctance:* struggle against. 1053-4. *aslope Glanced:* glanced off me
(instead of wounding me seriously). 1058. *provided:* i.e., provided with
clothes. 1068. *shroud:* covering. 1069. *this . . . star:* the sun. 1070-3.
how . . . fire: i.e., how we may make a fire by a burning-glass or else by
friction. The clause is object of *which* in 1067. 1071. *sere:* dry. *foment:*
warm.

Or by collision of two bodies grind
The air attrite to fire; as late the clouds,
Justling, or pushed with winds, rude in their shock,
Tine the slant lightning, whose thwart flame, driven down,   1075
Kindles the gummy bark of fir or pine,
And sends a comfortable heat from far,
Which might supply the Sun. Such fire to use,
And what may else be remedy or cure
To evils which our own misdeeds have wrought,   1080
He will instruct us praying, and of grace
Beseeching him; so as we need not fear
To pass commodiously this life, sustained
By him with many comforts, till we end
In dust, our final rest and native home.   1085
What better can we do than, to the place
Repairing where he judged us, prostrate fall
Before him reverent, and there confess
Humbly our faults, and pardon beg, with tears
Watering the ground, and with our sighs the air   1090
Frequenting, sent from hearts contrite, in sign
Of sorrow unfeigned and humiliation meek?
Undoubtedly he will relent, and turn
From his displeasure, in whose look serene,
When angry most he seemed and most severe,   1095
What else but favour, grace, and mercy shone?"
    So spake our Father penitent; nor Eve
Felt less remorse. They, forthwith to the place
Repairing where he judged them, prostrate fell
Before him reverent, and both confessed   1100
Humbly their faults, and pardon begged, with tears
Watering the ground, and with their sighs the air
Frequenting, sent from hearts contrite, in sign
Of sorrow unfeigned and humiliation meek.

THE END OF THE TENTH BOOK

❧

1073. *attrite:* rubbed, heated by friction. 1075. *Tine:* kindle. 1078. *supply:*
replace. 1081. *praying:* if we pray. 1091. *frequenting:* filling.

BOOK XI

THE ARGUMENT

The Son of God presents to his Father the prayers of our first parents now repenting, and intercedes for them. God accepts them, but declares that they must no longer abide in Paradise; sends Michael with a band of Cherubim to dispossess them, but first to reveal to Adam future things: Michael's coming down. Adam shows to Eve certain ominous signs: he discerns Michael's approach; goes out to meet him: the angel denounces their departure. Eve's lamentation. Adam pleads, but submits: the Angel leads him up to a high hill; sets before him in vision what shall happen till the Flood.

❧

BOOK XII

THE ARGUMENT

The Angel Michael continues, from the Flood, to relate what shall succeed; then, in the mention of Abraham, comes by degrees to explain who that Seed of the Woman shall be which was promised Adam and Eve in the Fall: his incarnation, death, resurrection, and ascension; the state of the Church till his second coming. Adam, greatly satisfied and recomforted by these relations and promises, descends the hill with Michael; wakens Eve, who all this while had slept, but with gentle dreams composed to quietness of mind and submission. Michael in either hand leads them out of Paradise, the fiery sword waving behind them, and the Cherubim taking their stations to guard the place.

. . . .

*T*HEN to the Heaven of Heavens he shall ascend
With victory, triumphing through the air
Over his foes and thine; there shall surprise
The Serpent, Prince of Air, and drag in chains
Through all his realm, and there confounded leave;   455
Then enter into glory, and resume
His seat at God's right hand, exalted high

---

451. *he:* Christ (after the Crucifixion).   452. *air:* Cf. Satan's title, 454.

Above all names in Heaven; and thence shall come,
When this World's dissolution shall be ripe,
With glory and power, to judge both quick and dead—   460
To judge the unfaithful dead, but to reward
His faithful, and receive them into bliss,
Whether in Heaven or Earth; for then the Earth
Shall all be Paradise, far happier place
Than this of Eden, and far happier days."   465
    So spake the Archangel Michael; then paused,
As at the World's great period; and our Sire,
Replete with joy and wonder, thus replied:
    "O Goodness infinite, Goodness immense,
That all this good of evil shall produce,   470
And evil turn to good—more wonderful
Than that which by creation first brought forth
Light out of darkness! Full of doubt I stand,
Whether I should repent me now of sin
By me done and occasioned, or rejoice   475
Much more that much more good thereof shall spring—
To God more glory, more good-will to men
From God—and over wrath grace shall abound.
But say, if our Deliverer up to Heaven
Must reascend, what will betide the few,   480
His faithful, left among the unfaithful herd,
The enemies of truth. Who then shall guide
His people, who defend? Will they not deal
Worse with his followers than with him they dealt?"
    "Be sure they will," said the Angel; "but from Heaven   485
He to his own a Comforter will send,
The promise of the Father, who shall dwell,
His Spirit, within them, and the law of faith
Working through love upon their hearts shall write,
To guide them in all truth, and also arm   490
With spiritual armour, able to resist
Satan's assaults, and quench his fiery darts—
What man can do against them—not afraid,
Though to the death; against such cruelties
With inward consolations recompensed,   495

---

460. *quick:* living. 467. *period:* end. 478. *over . . . abound:* Romans 5:20:
"Where sin abounded, grace did much more abound." 486. *Comforter:*
the Holy Spirit. 493. *What . . . them:* i.e., to the extent that man can.

And oft supported so as shall amaze
Their proudest persecutors. For the Spirit,
Poured first on his Apostles, whom he sends
To evangelize the nations, then on all
Baptized, shall them with wondrous gifts endue   500
To speak all tongues, and do all miracles,
As did their Lord before them. Thus they win
Great numbers of each nation to receive
With joy the tidings brought from Heaven: at length,
Their ministry performed, and race well run,   505
Their doctrine and their story written left,
They die; but in their room, as they forewarn,
Wolves shall succeed for teachers, grievous wolves,
Who all the sacred mysteries of Heaven
To their own vile advantages shall turn   510
Of lucre and ambition, and the truth
With superstitions and traditions taint,
Left only in those written records pure,
Though not but by the Spirit understood.
Then shall they seek to avail themselves of names,   515
Places, and titles, and with these to join
Secular power, though feigning still to act
By spiritual; to themselves appropriating
The Spirit of God, promised alike and given
To all believers; and, from that pretence,   520
Spiritual laws by carnal power shall force
On every conscience—laws which none shall find
Left them enrolled, or what the Spirit within
Shall on the heart engrave. What will they then
But force the Spirit of Grace itself, and bind   525
His consort, Liberty? what but unbuild
His living temples, built by faith to stand—
Their own faith, not another's? for, on Earth,
Who against faith and conscience can be heard
Infallible? Yet many will presume: 530
Whence heavy persecution shall arise
On all who in the worship persevere
Of Spirit and Truth; the rest, far greater part,

---

508. So St. Paul says to the church at Ephesus (Acts 20:29): "After my departing shall grievous wolves enter in among you." Cf. *Lycidas*, 128. 513. *written records:* the Scriptures. 514. I.e., though the Scriptures can be properly interpreted only by the aid of the Holy Spirit.

Will deem in outward rites and specious forms
Religion satisfied; Truth shall retire   535
Bestuck with slanderous darts, and works of Faith
Rarely be found. So shall the World go on,
To good malignant, to bad men benign,
Under her own weight groaning, till the day
Appear of respiration to the just   540
And vengeance to the wicked, at return
Of Him so lately promised to thy aid,
The Woman's Seed—obscurely then foretold,
Now amplier known thy Saviour and thy Lord;
Last in the clouds from Heaven to be revealed   545
In glory of the Father, to dissolve
Satan with his perverted World; then raise
From the conflagrant mass, purged and refined,
New Heavens, new Earth, Ages of endless date
Founded in righteousness and peace and love,   550
To bring forth fruits, joy and eternal bliss."
     He ended; and thus Adam last replied:
"How soon hath thy prediction, Seer blest,
Measured this transient World, the race of Time,
Till Time stand fixed! Beyond is all abyss—   555
Eternity, whose end no eye can reach.
Greatly instructed I shall hence depart,
Greatly in peace of thought, and have my fill
Of knowledge, what this vessel can contain;
Beyond which was my folly to aspire.   560
Henceforth I learn that to obey is best,
And love with fear the only God, to walk
As in his presence, ever to observe
His providence, and on him sole depend,
Merciful over all his works, with good   565
Still overcoming evil, and by small
Accomplishing great things, by things deemed weak
Subverting worldly-strong, and worldly-wise
By simply meek; that suffering for Truth's sake
Is fortitude to highest victory,   570
And to the faithful death the gate of life;
Taught this by his example whom I now

540. *respiration:* breathing-space, respite. 549. *New . . . earth:* Revelation
21:1—"And I saw a new heaven and a new earth: for the first heaven and
the first earth were passed away." 554. *race:* product. 559. *vessel:* body.
569-71. *that . . . life:* grammatically the object of *learn* in 561.

Acknowledge my Redeemer ever blest."
   To whom thus also the Angel last replied:
"This having learned, thou hast attained the sum   575
Of wisdom; hope no higher, though all the stars
Thou knew'st by name, and all the ethereal powers,
All secrets of the Deep, all Nature's works,
Or works of God in heaven, air, earth, or sea,
And all the riches of this world enjoy'dst,   580
And all the rule, one empire. Only add
Deeds to thy knowledge answerable; add faith;
Add virtue, patience, temperance; add love,
By name to come called Charity, the soul
Of all the rest: then wilt thou not be loath   585
To leave this Paradise, but shalt possess
A Paradise within thee, happier far.
Let us descend now, therefore, from this top
Of speculation; for the hour precise
Exacts our parting hence; and, see! the guards,   590
By me encamped on yonder hill, expect
Their motion, at whose front a flaming sword,
In signal of remove, waves fiercely round.
We may no longer stay. Go, waken Eve;
Her also I with gentle dreams have calmed,   595
Portending good, and all her spirits composed
To meek submission: thou, at season fit,
Let her with thee partake what thou hast heard—
Chiefly what may concern her faith to know,
The great deliverance by her seed to come   600
(For by the Woman's Seed) on all mankind—
That ye may live, which will be many days,
Both in one faith unanimous; though sad
With cause for evils past, yet much more cheered
With meditation on the happy end."   605
   He ended, and they both descend the hill.
Descended, Adam to the bower where Eve
Lay sleeping ran before, but found her waked;
And thus with words not sad she him received:
   "Where thou return'st and whither went'st I know; 610
For God is also in sleep, and dreams advise,

---

587. I.e., as Satan contains a hell. 589. *speculation:* outlook. 601. *For . . .
Seed:* with reference to the Immaculate Conception. 602. *many days:* i.e.,
a long time. (In Genesis, Adam lives 930 years.)

Which he hath sent propitious, some great good
Presaging, since, with sorrow and heart's distress
Wearied, I fell asleep: but now lead on,
In me is no delay; with thee to go   615
Is to stay here; without thee here to stay
Is to go hence unwilling; thou to me
Art all things under Heaven, all places thou,
Who for my wilful crime art banished hence.
This further consolation yet secure   620
I carry hence: though all by me is lost,
Such favour I unworthy am voutsafed,
By me the Promised Seed shall all restore."
   So spake our mother Eve; and Adam heard
Well pleased, but answered not; for now too nigh   625
The Archangel stood, and from the other hill
To their fixed station, all in bright array,
The Cherubim descended, on the ground
Gliding meteorous, as evening mist
Risen from a river o'er the marish glides,   630
And gathers ground fast at the labourer's heel
Homeward returning. High in front advanced,
The brandished sword of God before them blazed,
Fierce as a comet; which with torrid heat,
And vapour as the Libyan air adust,   635
Began to parch that temperate clime; whereat
In either hand the hastening Angel caught
Our lingering parents, and to the eastern gate
Led them direct, and down the cliff as fast
To the subjected plain—then disappeared.   640
They, looking back, all the eastern side beheld
Of Paradise, so late their happy seat,
Waved over by that flaming brand; the gate
With dreadful faces thronged and fiery arms.
Some natural tears they dropped, but wiped them soon;   645
The world was all before them, where to choose
Their place of rest, and Providence their guide.
They, hand in hand, with wandering steps and slow,
Through Eden took their solitary way.

THE END

---

630. *marish:* marsh. 635. *as . . . adust:* i.e., scorching like a wind from the
Libyan desert. 640. *subjected:* spread out below.

Samson Agonistes

A DRAMATIC POEM
(1671)

THE ARGUMENT

*Samson, made captive, blind, and now in the prison at Gaza, there
to labour as in a common workhouse, on a festival day, in the general cessation from labour, comes forth into the open air, to a place
nigh, somewhat retired, there to sit a while and bemoan his condition. Where he happens at length to be visited by certain friends, and
equals of his tribe, which make the Chorus, who seek to comfort him
what they can; then by his old father, Manoa, who endeavours the
like, and withal tells him his purpose to procure his liberty by ransom;
lastly, that this feast was proclaimed by the Philistines as a day of
thanksgiving for their deliverance from the hands of Samson—which
yet more troubles him. Manoa then departs to prosecute his endeavour
with the Philistian lords for Samson's redemption: who, in the meanwhile, is visited by other persons, and, lastly, by a public officer to
require his coming to the feast before the lords and people, to play or
show his strength in their presence. He at first refuses, dismissing the
public officer with absolute denial to come; at length, persuaded inwardly that this was from God, he yields to go along with him, who
came now the second time with great threatenings to fetch him. The
Chorus yet remaining on the place, Manoa returns full of joyful hope
to procure ere long his son's deliverance; in the midst of which discourse an Ebrew comes in haste, confusedly at first, and afterwards
more distinctly, relating the catastrophe—what Samson had done to
the Philistines, and by accident to himself; wherewith the Tragedy
ends.*

THE PERSONS

SAMSON	HARAPHA *of Gath*
MANOA, *the father of Samson*	PUBLIC OFFICER
DALILA, *his wife*	MESSENGER

CHORUS OF DANITES

The Scene: Before the Prison in Gaza

Title: For the Biblical story, see the Appendix.

SAMS. A little onward lend thy guiding hand
To these dark steps, a little further on;
For yonder bank hath choice of sun or shade.
There I am wont to sit, when any chance
Relieves me from my task of servile toil,   5
Daily in the common prison else enjoined me,
Where I, a prisoner chained, scarce freely draw
The air, imprisoned also, close and damp,
Unwholesome draught. But here I feel amends—
The breath of heaven fresh blowing, pure and sweet,   10
With day-spring born; here leave me to respire.
This day a solemn feast the people hold
To Dagon, their sea-idol, and forbid
Laborious works. Unwillingly this rest
Their superstition yields me; hence, with leave   15
Retiring from the popular noise, I seek
This unfrequented place to find some ease—
Ease to the body some, none to the mind
From restless thoughts, that, like a deadly swarm
Of hornets armed, no sooner found alone   20
But rush upon me thronging, and present
Times past, what once I was, and what am now.
O, wherefore was my birth from Heaven foretold
Twice by an Angel, who at last, in sight
Of both my parents, all in flames ascended   25
From off the altar where an offering burned,
As in a fiery column charioting
His godlike presence, and from some great act
Or benefit revealed to Abraham's race?
Why was my breeding ordered and prescribed   30
As of a person separate to God,
Designed for great exploits, if I must die
Betrayed, captived, and both my eyes put out,
Made of my enemies the scorn and gaze,
To grind in brazen fetters under task   35
With this heaven-gifted strength? O glorious strength,
Put to the labour of a beast, debased
Lower than bond-slave! Promise was that I

---

11. *day-spring:* daybreak.   13. *Dagon:* Cf. Par. Lost, I 462-3.   20. *no . . . alone:* as soon as they find me alone.   24. *Twice:* Judges 13:3-5, 9-20. 31. *separate . . . God:* Samson was reared as a Nazarite—i.e., one dedicated (to God). (Judges 13:5).

Should Israel from Philistian yoke deliver!
Ask for this great deliverer now, and find him   40
Eyeless in Gaza, at the mill with slaves,
Himself in bonds under Philistian yoke.
Yet stay; let me not rashly call in doubt
Divine prediction. What if all foretold
Had been fulfilled but through mine own default?   45
Whom have I to complain of but myself?
Who this high gift of strength committed to me,
In what part lodged, how easily bereft me,
Under the seal of silence could not keep,
But weakly to a woman must reveal it,   50
O'ercome with importunity and tears.
O impotence of mind in body strong!
But what is strength without a double share
Of wisdom? Vast, unwieldy, burdensome,
Proudly secure, yet liable to fall   55
By weakest subtleties; not made to rule,
But to subserve where wisdom bears command.
God, when he gave me strength, to show withal
How slight the gift was, hung it in my hair.
But peace! I must not quarrel with the will   60
Of highest dispensation, which herein
Haply had ends above my reach to know.
Suffices that to me strength is my bane,
And proves the source of all my miseries—
So many, and so huge, that each apart   65
Would ask a life to wail. But, chief of all,
O loss of sight, of thee I most complain!
Blind among enemies! O worse than chains,
Dungeon, or beggary, or decrepit age!
Light, the prime work of God, to me is extinct,   70
And all her various objects of delight
Annulled, which might in part my grief have eased.
Inferior to the vilest now become
Of man or worm, the vilest here excel me:
They creep, yet see; I, dark in light, exposed   75
To daily fraud, contempt, abuse, and wrong,
Within doors, or without, still as a fool,

47-9. The verb of this clause is *keep:* the object is *gift.* 51. *importunity:* persistent solicitation. 55. *secure:* self-confident. 70. *prime:* i.e., first as well as greatest. 77. *still:* always.

In power of others, never in my own—
Scarce half I seem to live, dead more than half.
O dark, dark, dark, amid the blaze of noon,   80
Irrecoverably dark, total eclipse
Without all hope of day!
O first-created beam, and thou great Word,
"Let there be light, and light was over all,"
Why am I thus bereaved thy prime decree?   85
The Sun to me is dark
And silent as the Moon,
When she deserts the night,
Hid in her vacant interlunar cave.
Since light so necessary is to life,   90
And almost life itself, if it be true
That light is in the soul,
She all in every part, why was the sight
To such a tender ball as the eye confined,
So obvious and so easy to be quenched,   95
And not, as feeling, through all parts diffused,
That she might look at will through every pore?
Then had I not been thus exiled from light,
As in the land of darkness, yet in light,
To live a life half dead, a living death,   100
And buried; but, O yet more miserable!
Myself my sepulchre, a moving grave;
Buried, yet not exempt,
By privilege of death and burial,
From worst of other evils, pains, and wrongs;   105
But made hereby obnoxious more
To all the miseries of life,
Life in captivity
Among inhuman foes.
But who are these? for with joint pace I hear   110
The tread of many feet steering this way;
Perhaps my enemies, who come to stare
At my affliction, and perhaps to insult—
Their daily practice to afflict me more.

---

84. God's first decree at Creation, used here (in apposition with Word) to define the creative nature. 85. *bereaved . . . decree:* i.e., deprived of light (which was God's first decree). 88-9. I.e., the dark of the moon. 93. *She:* the soul. 106. *obnoxious:* liable.

CHOR. This, this is he; softly a while;   115
Let us not break in upon him.
O change beyond report, thought, or belief!
See how he lies at random, carelessly diffused,
With languished head unpropt,
As one past hope, abandoned,   120
And by himself given over,
In slavish habit, ill-fitted weeds
O'er-worn and soiled.
Or do my eyes misrepresent? Can this be he,
That heroic, that renowned,   125
Irresistible Samson? whom, unarmed,
No strength of man, or fiercest wild beast, could withstand;
Who tore the lion as the lion tears the kid;
Ran on embattled armies clad in iron,
And, weaponless himself,   130
Made arms ridiculous, useless the forgery
Of brazen shield and spear, the hammered cuirass,
Chalybean-tempered steel, and frock of mail
Adamantean proof:
But safest he who stood aloof,   135
When insupportably his foot advanced,
In scorn of their proud arms and warlike tools,
Spurned them to death by troops. The bold Ascalonite
Fled from his lion ramp; old warriors turned
Their plated backs under his heel,   140
Or grovelling soiled their crested helmets in the dust.
Then with what trivial weapon came to hand,
The jaw of a dead ass, his sword of bone,
A thousand foreskins fell, the flower of Palestine,
In Ramath-lechi, famous to this day: 145
Then by main force pulled up, and on his shoulders bore,
The gates of Azza, post and massy bar,
Up to the hill by Hebron, seat of giants old—
No journey of a sabbath-day, and loaded so—
Like whom the Gentiles feign to bear up Heaven.   150

---

118. *diffused:* sprawled. 122. *habit:* dress. *weeds:* clothes. 131. *forgery:* forging. 133. *Chalybean:* from the Chalybees, a people of Asia Minor famous for their ironsmiths. 134. As hard as adamant. 136. *insupportably:* irresistibly. 138. *Ascalonite:* citizen of Askalon, one of the chief Philistine cities, like Gaza. 147. *Azza:* Gaza. 148. *giants:* Near Hebron had once dwelt "the giants, the sons of Anak" (Numbers 13:33). 149. Mosaic law limited the length of Sabbath journeys. 150. I.e., Atlas.

Which shall I first bewail—
Thy bondage or lost sight,
Prison within prison
Inseparably dark?
Thou art become (O worst imprisonment!)   155
The dungeon of thyself; thy soul
(Which men enjoying sight oft without cause complain)
Imprisoned now indeed,
In real darkness of the body dwells,
Shut up from outward light   160
To incorporate with gloomy night;
For inward light, alas!
Puts forth no visual beam.
O mirror of our fickle state,
Since man on earth, unparalleled,   165
The rarer thy example stands,
By how much from the top of wondrous glory,
Strongest of mortal men,
To lowest pitch of abject fortune thou art fallen.
For him I reckon not in high estate   170
Whom long descent of birth,
Or the sphere of fortune, raises;
But thee, whose strength, while virtue was her mate,
Might have subdued the Earth,
Universally crowned with highest praises.   175
    SAMS. I hear the sound of words; their sense the air
Dissolves unjointed ere it reach my ear.
    CHOR. He speaks: let us draw nigh. Matchless in might,
The glory late of Israel, now the grief!
We come, thy friends and neighbours not unknown,   180
From Eshtaol and Zora's fruitful vale,
To visit or bewail thee; or, if better,
Counsel or consolation we may bring,
Salve to thy sores: apt words have power to swage
The tumours of a troubled mind,   185
And are as balm to festered wounds.

---

163. *visual beam:* sight (conceived as a beam radiating *from* the eye). 164-
169. Samson is an unparalleled *mirror* of the fickleness of human fortune
in having fallen so low from so high a *top of . . . glory.* 181. *Zora* was
Samson's father's native city, and *Eshtaol* lay nearby. 182. *if better:* i.e., if
we can do something better for you. 184. *swage:* assuage. 185. *tumours:*
swellings.

SAMS. Your coming, friends, revives me; for I learn
Now of my own experience, not by talk,
How counterfeit a coin they are who 'friends'
Bear in their superscription (of the most   190
I would be understood). In prosperous days
They swarm, but in adverse withdraw their head,
Not to be found, though sought. Ye see, O friends,
How many evils have enclosed me round;
Yet that which was the worst now least afflicts me,   195
Blindness; for, had I sight, confused with shame,
How could I once look up, or heave the head,
Who, like a foolish pilot, have shipwracked
My vessel trusted to me from above,
Gloriously rigged, and for a word, a tear,   200
Fool! have divulged the secret gift of God
To a deceitful woman? Tell me, friends,
Am I not sung and proverbed for a fool
In every street? Do they not say, 'How well
Are come upon him his deserts'? Yet why?   205
Immeasurable strength they might behold
In me; of wisdom nothing more than mean.
This with the other should at least have paired;
These two, proportioned ill, drove me transverse.
   CHOR. Tax not divine disposal. Wisest men   210
Have erred, and by bad women been deceived;
And shall again, pretend they ne'er so wise.
Deject not, then, so overmuch thyself,
Who hast of sorrow thy full load besides.
Yet, truth to say, I oft have heard men wonder   215
Why thou should'st wed Philistian women rather
Than of thine own tribe fairer, or as fair,
At least of thy own nation, and as noble.
   SAMS. The first I saw at Timna, and she pleased
Me, not my parents, that I sought to wed   220
The daughter of an infidel. They knew not
That what I motioned was of God; I knew
From intimate impulse, and therefore urged
The marriage on, that, by occasion hence,
I might begin Israel's deliverance—   225
The work to which I was divinely called.

---

197. *heave:* lift up. 208. *paired:* matched. 209. *transverse:* astray. 210.
disposal: ordering of events. 219. *Timna:* Philistine city.

She proving false, the next I took to wife
(O that I never had! fond wish too late!)
Was in the vale of Sorec, Dalila,
That specious monster, my accomplished snare.   230
I thought it lawful from my former act,
And the same end, still watching to oppress
Israel's oppressors. Of what now I suffer
She was not the prime cause, but I myself,
Who, vanquished with a peal of words, (O weakness!)   235
Gave up my fort of silence to a woman.
   CHOR. In seeking just occasion to provoke
The Philistine, thy country's enemy,
Thou never wast remiss, I bear thee witness;
Yet Israel still serves with all his sons.   240
   SAMS. That fault I take not on me, but transfer
On Israel's governors and heads of tribes,
Who, seeing those great acts which God had done
Singly by me against their conquerors,
Acknowledged not, or not at all considered,   245
Deliverance offered. I, on the other side,
Used no ambition to commend my deeds;
The deeds themselves, though mute, spoke loud the doer.
But they persisted deaf, and would not seem
To count them things worth notice, till at length   250
Their lords, the Philistines, with gathered powers,
Entered Judea, seeking me, who then
Safe to the rock of Etham was retired—
Not flying, but forecasting in what place
To set upon them, what advantaged best.   255
Meanwhile the men of Judah, to prevent
The harass of their land, beset me round;
I willingly on some conditions came
Into their hands, and they as gladly yield me
To the Uncircumcised a welcome prey,   260
Bound with two cords. But cords to me were threads
Touched with the flame: on their whole host I flew
Unarmed, and with a trivial weapon felled
Their choicest youth; they only lived who fled.

---

230. *accomplished:* (1) resourceful, (2) successful. 231-2. *I . . . end:* I
justified this marriage by precedent of the former one, and because it had
the same objective. 245. *considered:* valued. 248. *doer:* i.e., God. 262-4. *on
. . . youth:* a slaughter already described by the Chorus at 142-5.

Had Judah that day joined, or one whole tribe,   265
They had by this possessed the towers of Gath,
And lorded over them whom now they serve.
But what more oft, in nations grown corrupt,
And by their vices brought to servitude,
Than to love bondage more than liberty—   270
Bondage with ease than strenuous liberty—
And to despise, or envy, or suspect,
Whom God hath of his special favour raised
As their deliverer? If he aught begin,
How frequent to desert him, and at last   275
To heap ingratitude on worthiest deeds!
   CHOR. Thy words to my remembrance bring
How Succoth and the fort of Penuel
Their great deliverer contemned,
The matchless Gideon, in pursuit   280
Of Madian, and her vanquished kings;
And how ingrateful Ephraim
Had dealt with Jephtha, who by argument,
Not worse than by his shield and spear,
Defended Israel from the Ammonite,   285
Had not his prowess quelled their pride
In that sore battle when so many died
Without reprieve, adjudged to death
For want of well pronouncing *Shibboleth*.
   SAMS. Of such examples add me to the roll.   290
Me easily indeed mine may neglect,
But God's proposed deliverance not so.
   CHOR. Just are the ways of God,
And justifiable to men,
Unless there be who think not God at all.   295
If any be, they walk obscure;
For of such doctrine never was there school,
But the heart of the fool,
And no man therein doctor but himself.

---

266. *Gath:* name of a Palestine city, here used for the whole country. 278-81.
The men of Succoth and Penuel refused to assist Gideon in freeing them
from the kings of Midian (*Madian*). Cf. Judges 8:4-9. 282-9. The Ephra-
imite Hebrews refused to assist Jephthah and his Gileadite Hebrews against
the Ammonites. Afterwards, in retaliation, the Gileadites slew many of the
Ephraimites, distinguishing them as they sought to escape by their inability
to pronounce *Shibboleth*. (Judges 12: 1 ff.) 298. Psalms 14:1 "The fool
hath said in his heart, There is no God." 299. *doctor:* teacher.

Yet more there be who doubt his ways not just,   300
As to his own edícts found contradicting,
Then give the reins to wandering thought,
Regardless of his glory's diminution,
Till, by their own perplexities involved,
They ravel more, still less resolved,   305
But never find self-satisfying solution.
    As if they would confine the Interminable,
And tie him to his own prescript,
Who made our laws to bind us, not himself,
And hath full right to exempt   310
Whomso it pleases him by choice
From national obstriction, without taint
Of sin, or legal debt;
For with his own laws he can best dispense.
    He would not else, who never wanted means,   315
Nor in respect of the enemy just cause,
To set his people free,
Have prompted this heroic Nazarite,
Against his vow of strictest purity,
To seek in marriage that fallacious bride,   320
Unclean, unchaste.
    Down, Reason, then; at least, vain reasonings down;
Though Reason here aver
That moral verdit quits her of unclean:
Unchaste was subsequent; her stain, not his.   325
    But see! here comes thy reverend sire,
With careful step, locks white as down,
Old Manoa: advise
Forthwith how thou ought'st to receive him.
    sams. Ay me! another inward grief, awaked   330
With mention of that name, renews the assault.
    man. Brethren and Men of Dan (for such ye seem
Though in this uncouth place), if old respect,
As I suppose, towards your once gloried friend,
My son, now captive, hither hath informed   335
Your younger feet, while mine, cast back with age,
Came lagging after, say if he be here.

---

305. *ravel:* confuse themselves. 307. *the Interminable:* the infinite (i.e.,
God). 312. *national obstriction:* Mosaic prohibition of marriage with Gentiles. 323-4. Though reason affirms that a *moral* verdict acquits Dalila of
being unclean (all Gentiles being *legally* unclean by Mosaic law). 324.
verdit: verdict. 332. *Dan:* Samson's and Manoa's tribe.

CHOR. As signal now in low dejected state
As erst in highest, behold him where he lies.
    MAN. O miserable change! Is this the man,   340
That invincible Samson, far renowned,
The dread of Israel's foes, who with a strength
Equivalent to Angels' walked their streets,
None offering fight; who, single combatant,
Duelled their armies ranked in proud array,   345
Himself an army—now unequal match
To save himself against a coward armed
At one spear's length? O ever-failing trust
In mortal strength! and, oh, what not in man
Deceivable and vain? Nay, what thing good   350
Prayed for, but often proves our woe, our bane?
I prayed for children, and thought barrenness
In wedlock a reproach; I gained a son,
And such a son as all men hailed me happy:
Who would be now a father in my stead?   355
Oh, wherefore did God grant me my request,
And as a blessing with such pomp adorned?
Why are his gifts desirable, to tempt
Our earnest prayers, then, given with solemn hand
As graces, draw a scorpion's tail behind?   360
For this did the Angel twice descend? for this
Ordained thy nurture holy, as of a plant
Select and sacred? glorious for a while,
The miracle of men; then in an hour
Ensnared, assaulted, overcome, led bound,   365
Thy foes' derision, captive, poor, and blind,
Into a dungeon thrust, to work with slaves!
Alas! methinks whom God hath chosen once
To worthiest deeds, if he through frailty err,
He should not so o'erwhelm, and as a thrall   370
Subject him to so foul indignities,
Be it but for honour's sake of former deeds.
    SAMS. Appoint not heavenly disposition, father.
Nothing of all these evils hath befallen me
But justly; I myself have brought them on;   375

---

338. *signal:* striking. 339. *erst:* formerly. 354. *as:* that. 356-7. (1) Why did
God grant me a son, and (2), why one of such eminence (since he was only
to be brought low). 369. *he:* i.e., the man chosen. 370. *He:* God. *thrall:*
slave. 373. *Appoint:* fix to a point, or specific path of action.

Sole author I, sole cause. If aught seem vile,
As vile hath been my folly, who have profaned
The mystery of God, given me under pledge
Of vow, and have betrayed it to a woman,
A Canaanite, my faithless enemy.   380
This well I knew, nor was at all surprised,
But warned by oft experience. Did not she
Of Timna first betray me, and reveal
The secret wrested from me in her highth
Of nuptial love professed, carrying it straight   385
To them who had corrupted her, my spies
And rivals? In this other was there found
More faith, who, also in her prime of love,
Spousal embraces, vitiated with gold,
Though offered only, by the scent conceived   390
Her spurious first-born, Treason against me?
Thrice she assayed, with flattering prayers and sighs,
And amorous reproaches, to win from me
My capital secret, in what part my strength
Lay stored, in what part summed, that she might know;   395
Thrice I deluded her, and turned to sport
Her importunity, each time perceiving
How openly and with what impudence
She purposed to betray me, and (which was worse
Than undissembled hate) with what contempt   400
She sought to make me traitor to myself.
Yet, the fourth time, when mustering all her wiles,
With blandished parleys, feminine assaults,
Tongue-batteries, she surceased not day nor night
To storm me, over-watched and wearied out,   405
At times when men seek most repose and rest,
I yielded, and unlocked her all my heart,
Who, with a grain of manhood well resolved,
Might easily have shook off all her snares;
But foul effeminacy held me yoked   410
Her bond-slave. O indignity, O blot
To honour and religion! servile mind

---

380. *Canaanite:* i.e., a Philistine living in Canaan. 390-1. The very smell of
gold (even when only proposed, not actually given) was enough to make
her conceive a bastard first-born child—namely, *treason against me.* 394.
capital: (1) important; (2) having to do with my head. 402. *mustering:*
Cf. the many following metaphors which compare Dalila's solicitations to a
siege. 405. *over-watched:* tired from being kept awake.

Rewarded well with servile punishment!
The base degree to which I now am fallen,
These rags, this grinding, is not yet so base   415
As was my former servitude, ignoble,
Unmanly, ignominious, infamous,
True slavery; and that blindness worse than this,
That saw not how degenerately I served.
    MAN. I cannot praise thy marriage-choices, son—   420
Rather approved them not; but thou didst plead
Divine impulsion prompting how thou might'st
Find some occasion to infest our foes.
I state not that; this I am sure—our foes
Found soon occasion thereby to make thee   425
Their captive, and their triumph; thou the sooner
Temptation found'st, or over-potent charms,
To violate the sacred trust of silence
Deposited within thee—which to have kept
Tacit was in thy power. True; and thou bear'st   430
Enough, and more, the burden of that fault;
Bitterly hast thou paid, and still art paying,
That rigid score. A worse thing yet remains:
This day the Philistines a popular feast
Here celebrate in Gaza, and proclaim   435
Great pomp, and sacrifice, and praises loud,
To Dagon, as their god who hath delivered
Thee, Samson, bound and blind, into their hands—
Them out of thine, who slew'st them many a slain.
So Dagon shall be magnified, and God,   440
Besides whom is no god, compared with idols,
Disglorified, blasphemed, and had in scorn
By the idolatrous rout amidst their wine;
Which to have come to pass by means of thee,
Samson, of all thy sufferings think the heaviest,   445
Of all reproach the most with shame that ever
Could have befallen thee and thy father's house.
    SAMS. Father, I do acknowledge and confess
That I this honour, I this pomp, have brought
To Dagon, and advanced his praises high   450
Among the Heathen round—to God have brought
Dishonour, obloquy, and oped the mouths
Of idolists and atheists; have brought scandal

---

423. *infest*: annoy.

To Israel, diffidence of God, and doubt
In feeble hearts, propense enough before   455
To waver, or fall off and join with idols:
Which is my chief affliction, shame and sorrow,
The anguish of my soul, that suffers not
Mine eye to harbour sleep, or thoughts to rest.
This only hope relieves me, that the strife   460
With me hath end. All the contest is now
'Twixt God and Dagon. Dagon hath presumed,
Me overthrown, to enter lists with God,
His deity comparing and preferring
Before the God of Abraham. He, be sure,   465
Will not connive, or linger, thus provoked,
But will arise, and his great name assert.
Dagon must stoop, and shall ere long receive
Such a discomfit as shall quite despoil him
Of all these boasted trophies won on me,   470
And with confusion blank his worshipers.
    MAN. With cause this hope relieves thee; and these words
I as a prophecy receive; for God
(Nothing more certain) will not long defer
To vindicate the glory of his name   475
Against all competition, nor will long
Endure it doubtful whether God be Lord
Or Dagon. But for thee what shall be done?
Thou must not in the meanwhile, here forgot,
Lie in this miserable loathsome plight   480
Neglected. I already have made way
To some Philistian lords, with whom to treat
About thy ransom. Well they may by this
Have satisfied their utmost of revenge,
By pains and slaveries, worse than death, inflicted   485
On thee, who now no more canst do them harm.
    SAMS. Spare that proposal, father; spare the trouble
Of that solicitation. Let me here,
As I deserve, pay on my punishment,
And expiate, if possible, my crime,   490
Shameful garrulity. To have revealed
Secrets of *men,* the secrets of a friend,

---

454. *diffidence:* distrust. 455. *propense:* inclined. 463. *Me overthrown:* now
that I am overthrown. 466. *connive:* ignore. 469. *discomfit:* defeat. 471.
blank: confound.

How heinous had the fact been, how deserving
Contempt and scorn of all—to be excluded
All friendship, and avoided as a blab,   495
The mark of fool set on his front!
But I *God's* counsel have not kept, his holy secret
Presumptuously have published, impiously,
Weakly at least and shamefully—a sin
That Gentiles in their parables condemn   500
To their Abyss and horrid pains confined.
   MAN. Be penitent, and for thy fault contrite;
But act not in thy own affliction, son.
Repent the sin; but, if the punishment
Thou canst avoid, self-preservation bids;   505
Or the execution leave to high disposal,
And let another hand, not thine, exact
Thy penal forfeit from thyself. Perhaps
God will relent, and quit thee all his debt;
Who ever more approves and more accepts   510
(Best pleased with humble and filial submission)
Him who, imploring mercy, sues for life,
Than who, self-rigorous, chooses death as due;
Which argues over-just, and self-displeased
For self-offence more than for God offended.   515
Reject not, then, what offered means who knows
But God hath set before us to return thee
Home to thy country and his sacred house,
Where thou may'st bring thy offerings, to avert
His further ire, with prayers and vows renewed.   520
   SAMS. His pardon I implore; but, as for life,
To what end should I seek it? When in strength
All mortals I excelled, and great in hopes,
With youthful courage, and magnanimous thoughts
Of birth from Heaven foretold and high exploits,   525
Full of divine instinct, after some proof
Of acts indeed heroic, far beyond
The sons of Anak, famous now and blazed,
Fearless of danger, like a petty god

---

493. *fact:* deed. 499-501. *a . . . confined:* e.g., Tantalus, who suffered in
Hades for his failure to keep the gods' secrets. 509. *quit . . . debt:* cancel
your debt to him. 514-15. I.e., choosing to die argues that one is too rigorous, displeased more for having offended one's self-esteem than for having
offended God. 516-17. *what . . . us:* the means available, which, for all
we know, God may have provided.

I walked about, admired of all, and dreaded   530
On hostile ground, none daring my affront—
Then, swollen with pride, into the snare I fell
Of fair fallacious looks, venereal trains,
Softened with pleasure and voluptuous life,
At length to lay my head and hallowed pledge   535
Of all my strength in the lascivious lap
Of a deceitful concubine, who shore me,
Like a tame wether, all my precious fleece,
Then turned me out ridiculous, despoiled,
Shaven, and disarmed among my enemies.   540
   CHOR. Desire of wine and all delicious drinks,
Which many a famous warrior overturns,
Thou could'st repress; nor did the dancing ruby,
Sparkling out-poured, the flavour, or the smell,
Or taste that cheers the heart of gods and men,   545
Allure thee from the cool crystálline stream.
   SAMS. Wherever fountain or fresh current flowed
Against the eastern ray, translucent, pure
With touch ethereal of Heaven's fiery rod,
I drank, from the clear milky juice allaying   550
Thirst, and refreshed; nor envied them the grape
Whose heads that turbulent liquor fills with fumes.
   CHOR. O madness! to think use of strongest wines
And strongest drinks our chief support of health,
When God with these forbidden made choice to rear   555
His mighty champion, strong above compare,
Whose drink was only from the liquid brook!
   SAMS. But what availed this temperance, not complete
Against another object more enticing?
What boots it at one gate to make defence,   560
And at another to let in the foe,
Effeminately vanquished? by which means,
Now blind, disheartened, shamed, dishonoured, quelled,
To what can I be useful? wherein serve
My nation, and the work from Heaven imposed,   565
But to sit idle on the household hearth,
A burdenous drone; to visitants a gaze,

---

531. *my affront:* to confront me. 533. *venereal trains:* lures of passion. 537.
me: from me. 548-9. *pure . . . rod:* purified by sunlight. 560. *What . . .
it:* What good is it.

Or pitied object; these redundant locks,
Robustious to no purpose, clustering down,
Vain monument of strength; till length of years   570
And sedentary numbness craze my limbs
To a contemptible old age obscure.
Here rather let me drudge, and earn my bread,
Till vermin, or the draff of servile food,
Consume me, and oft-invocated death   575
Hasten the welcome end of all my pains.
    MAN. Wilt thou then serve the Philistines with that gift
Which was expressly given thee to annoy them?
Better at home lie bed-rid, not only idle,
Inglorious, unemployed, with age outworn.   580
But God, who caused a fountain at thy prayer
From the dry ground to spring, thy thirst to allay
After the brunt of battle, can as easy
Cause light again within thy eyes to spring,
Wherewith to serve him better than thou hast.   585
And I persuade me so: Why else this strength
Miraculous yet remaining in those locks?
His might continues in thee not for naught,
Nor shall his wondrous gifts be frustrate thus.
    SAMS. All otherwise to me my thoughts portend—   590
That these dark orbs no more shall treat with light,
Nor the other light of life continue long,
But yield to double darkness nigh at hand;
So much I feel my genial spirits droop,
My hopes all flat: Nature within me seems   595
In all her functions weary of herself;
My race of glory run, and race of shame,
And I shall shortly be with them that rest.
    MAN. Believe not these suggestions, which proceed
From anguish of the mind, and humours black   600
That mingle with thy fancy. I, however,
Must not omit a father's timely care
To prosecute the means of thy deliverance
By ransom or how else: meanwhile be calm,
And healing words from these thy friends admit.   605

---

568. *redundant:* (1) superabundant; (2) flowing (from Latin *unda,* wave).
574. *draff:* refuse. 590. *portend:* fortell. 593. *double darkness:* blindness plus death.

SAMS. Oh, that torment should not be confined
To the body's wounds and sores,
With maladies innumerable
In heart, head, breast, and reins,
But must secret passage find   610
To the inmost mind,
There exercise all his fierce accidents,
And on her purest spirits prey,
As on entrails, joints, and limbs,
With answerable pains, but more intense,   615
Though void of corporal sense!
    My griefs not only pain me
As a lingering disease,
But, finding no redress, ferment and rage;
Nor less than wounds immedicable   620
Rankle, and fester, and gangrene,
To black mortification.
Thoughts, my tormentors, armed with deadly stings,
Mangle my apprehensive tenderest parts,
Exasperate, exulcerate, and raise   625
Dire inflammation, which no cooling herb
Or med'cinal liquor can assuage,
Nor breath of vernal air from snowy Alp.
Sleep hath forsook and given me o'er
To death's benumbing opium as my only cure;   630
Thence faintings, swoonings of despair,
And sense of Heaven's desertion.
    I was His nursling once and choice delight,
His destined from the womb,
Promised by heavenly message twice descending.   635
Under his special eye
Abstemious I grew up and thrived amain;
He led me on to mightiest deeds,
Above the nerve of mortal arm,
Against the Uncircumcised, our enemies: 640
But now hath cast me off as never known,
And to those cruel enemies,
Whom I by his appointment had provoked,

---

609. *reins:* kidneys. 612. *accidents:* symptoms. 615. *answerable:* correspond-
ing. 620. *immedicable:* not responsive to medication. 622. *mortification:*
the "deadness" which requires amputation. 624. *apprehensive:* sensitive. 637.
amain: mightily.

Left me all helpless, with the irreparable loss
Of sight, reserved alive to be repeated   645
The subject of their cruelty or scorn.
Nor am I in the list of them that hope;
Hopeless are all my evils, all remediless.
This one prayer yet remains, might I be heard,
No long petition—speedy death,   650
The close of all my miseries and the balm.
  CHOR. Many are the sayings of the wise,
In ancient and in modern books enrolled,
Extolling patience as the truest fortitude,
And to the bearing well of all calamities,   655
All chances incident to man's frail life,
Consolatories writ
With studied argument, and much persuasion sought,
Lenient of grief and anxious thought.
But with the afflicted in his pangs their sound   660
Little prevails, or rather seems a tune
Harsh, and of dissonant mood from his complaint,
Unless he feel within
Some source of consolation from above,
Secret refreshings that repair his strength   665
And fainting spirits uphold.
  God of our fathers! what is Man,
That thou towards him with hand so various—
Or might I say contrarious?—
Temper'st thy providence through his short course: 670
Not evenly, as thou rul'st
The angelic orders, and inferior creatures mute,
Irrational and brute?
Nor do I name of men the common rout,
That, wandering loose about,   675
Grow up and perish as the summer fly;
Heads without name, no more remembered;
But such as thou hast solemnly elected,
With gifts and graces eminently adorned,
To some great work, thy glory,   680
And people's safety, which in part they effect.

---

645. *repeated:* made repeatedly. 657. *consolatories:* works of consolation.
659. *lenient:* softening. 667 ff. Cf. Psalm 8:4—"What is man that thou art
mindful of him?" 672. *angelic orders:* the nine ranks of angels.

Yet toward these, thus dignified, thou oft,
Amidst their highth of noon,
Changest thy countenance and thy hand, with no regard
Of highest favours past   685
From thee on them, or them to thee of service.
    Nor only dost degrade them, or remit
To life obscured, which were a fair dismission,
But throw'st them lower than thou didst exalt them high—
Unseemly falls in human eye,   690
Too grievous for the trespass or omission;
Oft leav'st them to the hostile sword
Of heathen and profane, their carcasses
To dogs and fowls a prey, or else captived,
Or to the unjust tribunals, under change of times,   695
And condemnation of the ungrateful multitude.
If these they scape, perhaps in poverty
With sickness and disease thou bow'st them down,
Painful diseases and deformed,
In crude old age;   700
Though not disordinate, yet causeless suffering
The punishment of dissolute days. In fine,
Just or unjust alike seem miserable,
For oft alike both come to evil end.
    So deal not with this once thy glorious champion,   705
The image of thy strength, and mighty minister.
What do I beg? how hast thou dealt already!
Behold him in this state calamitous, and turn
His labours, for thou canst, to peaceful end.
    But who is this? what thing of sea or land—   710
Female of sex it seems—
That, so bedecked, ornate, and gay,
Comes this way sailing,
Like a stately ship

---

682. *dignified:* in a position of dignity. 691. More generous than the sin
(whether of omission or commission) deserved. 692 ff. These lines may be
contemporary in reference as well as general. The bodies of Cromwell and
some of his followers were exhumed in 1661 and hung on the gallows *to
dogs and fowls a prey;* the regicide judges were executed or imprisoned, and
were subject to *condemnation of the ungrateful multitude;* Milton himself
was reduced to poverty through loss of his government income, and in addition suffered from the gout. 700. *crude:* early. 701-2. *Though . . . days:*
Though they have not been dissolute, they suffer as if they had been.

Of Tarsus, bound for the isles   715
Of Javan or Gadire,
With all her bravery on, and tackle trim,
Sails filled, and streamers waving,
Courted by all the winds that hold them play;
An amber scent of odorous perfume   720
Her harbinger, a damsel train behind?
Some rich Philistian matron she may seem;
And now, at nearer view, no other certain
Than Dalila thy wife.
    SAMS. My wife! my traitress! let her not come near me. 725
    CHOR. Yet on she moves; now stands and eyes thee fixed,
About to have spoke; but now, with head declined,
Like a fair flower surcharged with dew, she weeps,
And words addressed seem into tears dissolved,
Wetting the borders of her silken veil.   730
But now again she makes address to speak.
    DAL. With doubtful feet and wavering resolution
I came, still dreading thy displeasure, Samson;
Which to have merited, without excuse,
I cannot but acknowledge. Yet, if tears   735
May expiate (though the fact more evil drew
In the perverse event than I foresaw),
My penance hath not slackened, though my pardon
No way assured. But conjugal affection,
Prevailing over fear and timorous doubt,   740
Hath led me on, desirous to behold
Once more thy face, and know of thy estate,
If aught in my ability may serve
To lighten what thou suffer'st, and appease
Thy mind with what amends is in my power—   745
Though late, yet in some part to recompense
My rash but more unfortunate misdeed.
    SAMS. Out, out, hyæna! These are thy wonted arts,
And arts of every woman false like thee—
To break all faith, all vows, deceive, betray;   750
Then, as repentant, to submit, beseech,
And reconcilement move with feigned remorse,

715-16. *the . . . Gadire:* i.e., the Greek isles, or Cadiz. 717. *bravery:* finery.
719. *hold them play:* play with them. 720. *amber:* ambergris, used in perfumes. 729. *addressed:* prepared. 731. *address:* preparation. 738. *pardon:*
pardon is. 742. *estate:* state. 752. *move:* urge.

Confess, and promise wonders in her change—
Not truly penitent, but chief to try
Her husband, how far urged his patience bears,   755
His virtue or weakness which way to assail:
Then, with more cautious and instructed skill,
Again transgresses, and again submits;
That wisest and best men, full oft beguiled,
With goodness principled not to reject   760
The penitent, but ever to forgive,
Are drawn to wear out miserable days,
Entangled with a poisonous bosom-snake,
If not by quick destruction soon cut off,
As I by thee, to ages an example.   765
    DAL. Yet hear me, Samson; not that I endeavour
To lessen or extenuate my offence,
But that, on the other side, if it be weighed
By itself, with aggravations not surcharged,
Or else with just allowance counterpoised,   770
I may, if possible, thy pardon find
The easier towards me, or thy hatred less.
First granting, as I do, it was a weakness
In me, but incident to all our sex,
Curiosity, inquisitive, importúne   775
Of secrets, then with like infirmity
To publish them—both common female faults—
Was it not weakness also to make known
For importunity, that is for naught,
Wherein consisted all thy strength and safety?   780
To what I did thou show'dst me first the way.
But I to enemies revealed, and should not!
Nor should'st thou have trusted that to woman's frailty:
Ere I to thee, thou to thyself wast cruel.
Let weakness, then, with weakness come to parle,   785
So near related, or the same of kind;
Thine forgive mine, that men may censure thine
The gentler, if severely thou exact not
More strength from me than in thyself was found.

---

759. *that:* so that. 760. *principled:* acting on the principle. 773-80. Granting
my weakness, curiosity, a weakness common to all my sex, which is first
eager to know secrets, and then eager to publish them (two common female faults); was it not also weakness in you to divulge your secret merely
on account of my entreaties—that is to say, for no good reason. 785. *parle:*
parley, discussion of terms of truce.

And what if love, which thou interpret'st hate,   790
The jealousy of love, powerful of sway
In human hearts, nor less in mine towards thee,
Caused what I did? I saw thee mutable
Of fancy; feared lest one day thou would'st leave me
As her at Timna; sought by all means, therefore,   795
How to endear, and hold thee to me firmest:
No better way I saw than by importuning
To learn thy secrets, get into my power
Thy key of strength and safety. Thou wilt say,
"Why, then, revealed?" I was assured by those   800
Who tempted me that nothing was designed
Against thee but safe custody and hold.
That made for me; I knew that liberty
Would draw thee forth to perilous enterprises,
While I at home sat full of cares and fears,   805
Wailing thy absence in my widowed bed;
Here I should still enjoy thee, day and night,
Mine and love's prisoner, not the Philistines',
Whole to myself, unhazarded abroad,
Fearless at home of partners in my love.   810
These reasons in Love's law have passed for good,
Though fond and reasonless to some perhaps;
And love hath oft, well meaning, wrought much woe,
Yet always pity or pardon hath obtained.
Be not unlike all others, not austere   815
As thou art strong, inflexible as steel.
If thou in strength all mortals dost exceed,
In uncompassionate anger do not so.
    SAMS. How cunningly the sorceress displays
Her own transgressions, to upbraid me mine!   820
That malice, not repentance, brought thee hither
By this appears. I gave, thou say'st, the example,
I led the way—bitter reproach, but true;
I to myself was false ere thou to me.
Such pardon, therefore, as I give my folly   825
Take to thy wicked deed; which when thou seest
Impartial, self-severe, inexorable,
Thou wilt renounce thy seeking, and much rather

---

796. *endear:* endear myself. 803. *That . . . me:* i.e., your being kept in
custody, and hence from straying, was in my interest. 826-8. *which . . .
seeking:* i.e., when you see I do not pardon myself, you will not expect me
to pardon you.

Confess it feigned. Weakness is thy excuse,
And I believe it—weakness to resist   830
Philistian gold. If weakness may excuse,
What murtherer, what traitor, parricide,
Incestuous, sacrilegious, but may plead it?
All wickedness is weakness; that plea, therefore,
With God or man will gain thee no remission.   835
But love constrained thee! Call it furious rage
To satisfy thy lust. Love seeks to have love;
My love how could'st thou hope, who took'st the way
To raise in me inexpiable hate,
Knowing, as needs I must, by thee betrayed?   840
In vain thou striv'st to cover shame with shame,
Or by evasions thy crime uncover'st more.
    DAL. Since thou determin'st weakness for no plea
In man or woman, though to thy own condemning,
Hear what assaults I had, what snares besides,   845
What sieges girt me round, ere I consented;
Which might have awed the best-resolved of men,
The constantest, to have yielded without blame.
It was not gold, as to my charge thou lay'st,
That wrought with me. Thou know'st the magistrates   850
And princes of my country came in person,
Solicited, commanded, threatened, urged,
Adjured by all the bonds of civil duty
And of religion—pressed how just it was,
How honourable, how glorious, to entrap   855
A common enemy, who had destroyed
Such numbers of our nation: and the priest
Was not behind, but ever at my ear,
Preaching how meritorious with the gods
It would be to ensnare an irreligious   860
Dishonourer of Dagon. What had I
To oppose against such powerful arguments?
Only my love of thee held long debate,
And combated in silence all these reasons
With hard contest. At length, that grounded maxim,   865
So rife and celebrated in the mouths

---

836 ff. Samson now rebuts her second argument (cf. 790 ff.). 840. *Knowing:* knowing myself. 850. *wrought with:* influenced. 853. *Adjured:* adjured me. 854. *pressed:* urged. 866. *rife:* common.

Of wisest men, that to the public good
Private respects must yield, with grave authority
Took full possession of me, and prevailed;
Virtue, as I thought, truth, duty, so enjoining.   870
   SAMS. I thought where all thy circling wiles would end—
In feigned religion, smooth hypocrisy!
But had thy love, still odiously pretended,
Been, as it ought, sincere, it would have taught thee
Far other reasonings, brought forth other deeds.   875
I, before all the daughters of my tribe
And of my nation, chose thee from among
My enemies, loved thee, as too well thou knew'st,
Too well; unbosomed all my secrets to thee,
Not out of levity, but overpowered   880
By thy request, who could deny thee nothing;
Yet now am judged an enemy. Why, then,
Didst thou at first receive me for thy husband—
Then, as since then, thy country's foe professed?
Being once a wife, for me thou wast to leave   885
Parents and country; nor was I their subject,
Nor under their protection, but my own;
Thou mine, not theirs. If aught against my life
Thy country sought of thee, it sought unjustly,
Against the law of nature, law of nations;   890
No more thy country, but an impious crew
Of men conspiring to uphold their state
By worse than hostile deeds, violating the ends
For which our country is a name so dear;
Not therefore to be obeyed. But zeal moved thee;   895
To please thy gods thou didst it! gods unable
To acquit themselves and prosecute their foes
But by ungodly deeds—the contradiction
Of their own deity—Gods cannot be:
Less therefore to be pleased, obeyed, or feared.   900
These false pretexts and varnished colours failing,
Bare in thy guilt, how foul must thou appear!

---

879. *Too well:* The phrase goes with *loved* in 878. 884. I.e., since I was just
as much your country's enemy then as later. 886 ff. The Philistine state
had no claims on me (not being a citizen), nor any right by international
law to use you (as my wife) against me; and if these men were ready to
violate law, then they must not be called *thy country,* but only a group of
criminals whom there was no need to obey.

DAL. In argument with men a woman ever
Goes by the worse, whatever be her cause.
 SAMS. For want of words, no doubt, or lack of breath!   905
Witness when I was worried with thy peals.
 DAL. I was a fool, too rash, and quite mistaken
In what I thought would have succeeded best.
Let me obtain forgiveness of thee, Samson;
Afford me place to show what recompense   910
Towards thee I intend for what I have misdone,
Misguided. Only what remains past cure
Bear not too sensibly, nor still insist
To afflict thyself in vain. Though sight be lost,
Life yet hath many solaces, enjoyed   915
Where other senses want not their delights—
At home, in leisure and domestic ease,
Exempt from many a care and chance to which
Eye-sight exposes, daily, men abroad.
I to the lords will intercede, not doubting   920
Their favourable ear, that I may fetch thee
From forth this loathsome prison-house, to abide
With me, where my redoubled love and care,
With nursing diligence, to me glad office,
May ever tend about thee to old age,   925
With all things grateful cheered, and so supplied
That what by me thou hast lost thou least shalt miss.
 SAMS. No, no; of my condition take no care;
It fits not; thou and I long since are twain;
Nor think me so unwary or accursed   930
To bring my feet again into the snare
Where once I have been caught. I know thy trains,
Though dearly to my cost, thy gins, and toils.
Thy fair enchanted cup, and warbling charms,
No more on me have power; their force is nulled;   935
So much of adder's wisdom I have learned,
To fence my ear against thy sorceries.
If in my flower of youth and strength, when all men
Loved, honoured, feared me, thou alone could hate me,

---

904. *Goes by:* gets. 906. *peals:* Cf. 235. 913. *sensibly:* sensitively. 916. *want:*
lack. 924. *to . . . office:* a task I shall enjoy. 927. *what . , . lost:* i.e., sight.
933. *gins, and toils:* snares and nets. 934. A comparison of Dalila's wiles to
those of Circe (and Comus). 936. *adder's wisdom:* deafness (adders were
believed to be deaf).

Thy husband, slight me, sell me, and forgo me,   940
How would'st thou use me now, blind, and thereby
Deceivable, in most things as a child
Helpless, thence easily contemned and scorned,
And last neglected! How would'st thou insult,
When I must live uxorious to thy will   945
In perfect thraldom! how again betray me,
Bearing my words and doings to the lords
To gloss upon, and, censuring, frown or smile!
This jail I count the house of liberty
To thine, whose doors my feet shall never enter.   950
   DAL. Let me approach at least, and touch thy hand.
   SAMS. Not for thy life, lest fierce remembrance wake
My sudden rage to tear thee joint by joint.
At distance I forgive thee; go with that;
Bewail thy falsehood, and the pious works   955
It hath brought forth to make thee memorable
Among illustrious women, faithful wives;
Cherish thy hastened widowhood with the gold
Of matrimonial treason: so farewell.
   DAL. I see thou art implacable, more deaf   960
To prayers than winds and seas. Yet winds to seas
Are reconciled at length, and sea to shore:
Thy anger, unappeasable, still rages,
Eternal tempest never to be calmed.
Why do I humble thus myself, and, suing   965
For peace, reap nothing but repulse and hate,
Bid go with evil omen, and the brand
Of infamy upon my name denounced?
To mix with thy concernments I desist
Henceforth, nor too much disapprove my own.   970
Fame, if not double-faced, is double-mouthed,
And with contrary blast proclaims most deeds;
On both his wings, one black, the other white,
Bears greatest names in his wild aery flight.
My name, perhaps, among the Circumcised   975
In Dan, in Judah, and the bordering tribes,
To all posterity may stand defamed,
With malediction mentioned, and the blot
Of falsehood most unconjugal traduced.
But in my country, where I most desire,   980

---

948. *gloss:* comment, enlarge. 950. *To:* compared to. 967. *Bid go:* being
bidden (by you) to go. 978. *and:* and with.

In Ecron, Gaza, Asdod, and in Gath,
I shall be named among the famousest
Of women, sung at solemn festivals,
Living and dead recorded, who, to save
Her country from a fierce destroyer, chose   985
Above the faith of wedlock bands, my tomb
With odours visited and annual flowers;
Not less renowned than in Mount Ephraim
Jael, who, with inhospitable guile,
Smote Sisera sleeping, through the temples nailed.   990
Nor shall I count it heinous to enjoy
The public marks of honour and reward
Conferred upon me for the piety
Which to my country I was judged to have shown.
At this whoever envies or repines,   995
I leave him to his lot, and like my own.
   CHOR. She's gone—a manifest serpent by her sting
Discovered in the end, till now concealed.
   SAMS. So let her go. God sent her to debase me,
And aggravate my folly, who committed   1000
To such a viper his most sacred trust
Of secrecy, my safety, and my life.
   CHOR. Yet beauty, though injurious, hath strange power,
After offence returning, to regain
Love once possessed, nor can be easily   1005
Repulsed, without much inward passion felt,
And secret sting of amorous remorse.
   SAMS. Love-quarrels oft in pleasing concord end;
Not wedlock-treachery endangering life.
   CHOR. It is not virtue, wisdom, valour, wit,   1010
Strength, comeliness of shape, or amplest merit,
That woman's love can win, or long inherit;
But what it is, hard is to say,
Harder to hit,
Which way soever men refer it,   1015
(Much like thy riddle, Samson) in one day
Or seven though one should musing sit.
   If any of these, or all, the Timnian bride
Had not so soon preferred

---

981. I.e., in the chief Palestine cities. 989. *Jael:* an example from Jewish history (cf. Judges 4-5) of the patriotic heroism Dalila now claims for herself. 1012. *inherit:* keep. 1018. *these:* the qualities mentioned in 1010-11.

Thy paranymph, worthless to thee compared,   1020
Successor in thy bed,
Nor both so loosely disallied
Their nuptials, nor this last so treacherously
Had shorn the fatal harvest of thy head.
Is it for that such outward ornament   1025
Was lavished on their sex, that inward gifts
Were left for haste unfinished, judgment scant,
Capacity not raised to apprehend
Or value what is best
In choice, but oftest to affect the wrong?   1030
Or was too much of self-love mixed,
Of constancy no root infixed,
That either they love nothing, or not long?
   Whate'er it be, to wisest men and best,
Seeming at first all heavenly under virgin veil,   1035
Soft, modest, meek, demure,
Once joined, the contrary she proves—a thorn
Intestine, far within defensive arms
A cleaving mischief, in his way to virtue
Adverse and turbulent; or by her charms   1040
Draws him awry, enslaved
With dotage, and his sense depraved
To folly and shameful deeds, which ruin ends.
What pilot so expert but needs must wreck,
Embarked with such a steers-mate at the helm?   1045
   Favored of Heaven who finds
One virtuous, rarely found,
That in domestic good combines!
Happy that house! his way to peace is smooth:
But virtue which breaks through all opposition,   1050
And all temptation can remove,
Most shines and most is acceptable above.
   Therefore God's universal law
Gave to the man despotic power
Over his female in due awe,   1055
Nor from that right to part an hour,

1020. *paranymph:* groomsman—i.e., the "companion" to whom the father of
the woman of Timnath gave her instead of to Samson. 1022. *both:* the
woman of Timnath and Dalila. 1025. *for that:* because. 1038. *Intestine:* domestic. 1039. *cleaving:* clinging. 1046. *Favoured:* The man is favoured.
1053. *God's . . . law:* Cf. 1 Timothy 2:12—"I suffer not a woman . . . to
usurp authority over the man."

Smile she or lour:
So shall he least confusion draw
On his whole life, not swayed
By female usurpation, nor dismayed.   1060
  But had we best retire? I see a storm.
  SAMS. Fair days have oft contracted wind and rain.
  CHOR. But this another kind of tempest brings.
  SAMS. Be less abstruse; my riddling days are past.
  CHOR. Look now for no enchanting voice, nor fear   1065
The bait of honeyed words; a rougher tongue
Draws hitherward; I know him by his stride,
The giant Harapha of Gath, his look
Haughty, as is his pile high-built and proud.
Comes he in peace? What wind hath blown him hither   1070
I less conjecture than when first I saw
The sumptuous Dalila floating this way:
His habit carries peace, his brow defiance.
  SAMS. Or peace or not, alike to me he comes.
  CHOR. His fraught we soon shall know; he now arrives.   1075
  HAR. I come not, Samson, to condole thy chance,
As these perhaps, yet wish it had not been,
Though for no friendly intent. I am of Gath;
Men call me Harapha, of stock renowned
As Og, or Anak, and the Emins old   1080
That Kiriathaim held. Thou know'st me now,
If thou at all art known. Much I have heard
Of thy prodigious might and feats performed,
Incredible to me, in this displeased,
That I was never present on the place   1085
Of those encounters, where we might have tried
Each other's force in camp or listed field;
And now am come to see of whom such noise
Hath walked about, and each limb to survey,
If thy appearance answer loud report.   1090
  SAMS. The way to know were not to see, but taste.
  HAR. Dost thou already single me? I thought
Gyves and the mill had tamed thee. O that fortune
Had brought me to the field where thou art famed

1062. *contracted:* brought together. 1064. *riddling:* for the allusion, cf.
above 382-5. 1068. *Harapha:* the name is Hebrew for "great." 1069. *pile:*
frame. 1075. *fraught:* freight, i.e., business. 1076. *condole:* condole with.
1080. *Og . . . Emins:* Giants mentioned in the Old Testament. The Emins
were defeated at *Kiriathaim* (1081). 1087. *in . . . field:* in battle or tournament. 1092. *single:* challenge.

To have wrought such wonders with an ass's jaw!   1095
I should have forced thee soon wish other arms,
Or left thy carcass where the ass lay thrown;
So had the glory of prowess been recovered
To Palestine, won by a Philistine
From the unforeskinned race, of whom thou bear'st   1100
The highest name for valiant acts. That honour,
Certain to have won by mortal duel from thee,
I lose, prevented by thy eyes put out.
 SAMS. Boast not of what thou would'st have done, but do
What then thou would'st; thou seest it in thy hand.   1105
 HAR. To combat with a blind man I disdain,
And thou hast need much washing to be touched.
 SAMS. Such usage as your honourable lords
Afford me, assassinated and betrayed;
Who durst not with their whole united powers   1110
In fight withstand me single and unarmed,
Nor in the house with chamber-ambushes
Close-banded durst attack me, no, not sleeping,
Till they had hired a woman with their gold,
Breaking her marriage-faith, to circumvent me.   1115
Therefore, without feigned shifts, let be assigned
Some narrow place enclosed, where sight may give thee,
Or rather flight, no great advantage on me;
Then put on all thy gorgeous arms, thy helmet
And brigandine of brass, thy broad habergeon,   1120
Vant-brace and greaves and gauntlet; add thy spear,
A weaver's beam, and seven-times-folded shield:
I only with an oaken staff will meet thee,
And raise such outcries on thy clattered iron,
Which long shall not withhold me from thy head,   1125
That in a little time, while breath remains thee,
Thou oft shalt wish thyself at Gath, to boast
Again in safety what thou would'st have done
To Samson, but shalt never see Gath more.
 HAR. Thou durst not thus disparage glorious arms   1130
Which greatest heroes have in battle worn,

1102. *mortal duel:* duel to the death. 1105. *in . . . hand:* in thy power.
1109. *assassinated:* attacked (not killed) by assassins. 1116. *feigned shifts:*
treacheries. 1120. *brigandine:* armour of overlapping metal plates sewn to
a flexible material. *habergeon:* tunic of mail. 1121. *Vant-brace:* vambrace
(cf. *avant-bras*), armor for the forearm. 1122. *A . . . beam:* thick as the
cylinder which feeds the warp to the loom. *seven . . . folded:* having seven
layers.

Their ornament and safety, had not spells
And black enchantments, some magician's art,
Armed thee or charmed thee strong, which thou from Heaven
Feign'dst at thy birth was given thee in thy hair, 1135
Where strength can least abide, though all thy hairs
Were bristles ranged like those that ridge the back
Of chafed wild boars or ruffled porcupines.

   SAMS. I know no spells, use no forbidden arts;
My trust is in the Living God, who gave me, 1140
At my nativity, this strength, diffused
No less through all my sinews, joints, and bones,
Than thine, while I preserved these locks unshorn,
The pledge of my unviolated vow.
For proof hereof, if Dagon be thy god, 1145
Go to his temple, invocate his aid
With solemnest devotion, spread before him
How highly it concerns his glory now
To frustrate and dissolve these magic spells,
Which I to be the power of Israel's God 1150
Avow, and challenge Dagon to the test,
Offering to combat thee, his champion bold,
With the utmost of his godhead seconded:
Then thou shalt see, or rather to thy sorrow
Soon feel, whose God is strongest, thine or mine. 1155

   HAR. Presume not on thy God. Whate'er he be,
Thee he regards not, owns not, hath cut off
Quite from his people, and delivered up
Into thy enemies' hand; permitted them
To put out both thine eyes, and fettered send thee 1160
Into the common prison, there to grind
Among the slaves and asses, thy comrades,
As good for nothing else, no better service
With those thy boisterous locks; no worthy match
For valour to assail, nor by the sword 1165
Of noble warrior, so to stain his honour,
But by the barber's razor best subdued.

   SAMS. All these indignities, for such they are
From thine, these evils I deserve and more,
Acknowledge them from God inflicted on me 1170
Justly, yet despair not of his final pardon,

1138. *chafed, ruffled:* angry, and hence bristling. 1164. *boisterous:* thick.
1168. *indignities:* taunts. 1169. *from thine:* coming from your nation.

Whose ear is ever open, and his eye
Gracious to re-admit the suppliant;
In confidence whereof I once again
Defy thee to the trial of mortal fight,   1175
By combat to decide whose god is God,
Thine, or whom I with Israel's sons adore.
    HAR. Fair honour that thou dost thy God, in trusting
He will accept thee to defend his cause,
A murtherer, a revolter, and a robber!   1180
    SAMS. Tongue-doughty giant, how dost thou prove me these?
    HAR. Is not thy nation subject to our lords?
Their magistrates confessed it when they took thee
As a league-breaker, and delivered bound
Into our hands; for hadst thou not committed   1185
Notorious murder on those thirty men
At Ascalon, who never did thee harm,
Then, like a robber, stripp'dst them of their robes?
The Philistines, when thou hadst broke the league,
Went up with armèd powers thee only seeking,   1190
To others did no violence nor spoil.
    SAMS. Among the daughters of the Philistines
I chose a wife, which argued me no foe,
And in your city held my nuptial feast;
But your ill-meaning politician lords,   1195
Under pretence of bridal friends and guests,
Appointed to await me thirty spies,
Who, threatening cruel death, constrained the bride
To wring from me, and tell to them, my secret,
That solved the riddle which I had proposed.   1200
When I perceived all set on enmity,
As on my enemies, wherever chanced,
I used hostility, and took their spoil,
To pay my underminers in their coin.
My nation was subjected to your lords!   1205
It was the force of conquest; force with force
Is well ejected when the conquered can.
But I, a private person, whom my country
As a league-breaker gave up bound, presumed
Single rebellion, and did hostile acts!   1210

1178. *Fair:* i.e., it is a fair. 1181. *Tongue-doughty:* brave mainly in tongue.
1195-7. This is the interpretation given by Josephus (*Antiquities,* V viii 6).

I was no private, but a person raised
With strength sufficient and command from Heaven
To free my country. If their servile minds
Me, their deliverer sent, would not receive,
But to their masters gave me up for nought,   1215
The unworthier they; whence to this day they serve.
I was to do my part from Heaven assigned,
And had performed it if my known offence
Had not disabled me, not all your force.
These shifts refuted, answer thy appellant,   1220
Though by his blindness maimed for high attempts,
Who now defies thee thrice to single fight,
As a petty enterprise of small enforce.
    HAR. With thee, a man condemned, a slave enrolled,
Due by the law to capital punishment?   1225
To fight with thee no man of arms will deign.
    SAMS. Cam'st thou for this, vain boaster, to survey me,
To descant on my strength, and give thy verdict?
Come nearer; part not hence so slight informed;
But take good heed my hand survey not thee.   1230
    HAR. O Baal-zebub! can my ears unused
Hear these dishonours, and not render death?
    SAMS. No man with-holds thee; nothing from thy hand
Fear I incurable; bring up thy van;
My heels are fettered, but my fist is free.   1235
    HAR. This insolence other kind of answer fits.
    SAMS. Go, baffled coward, lest I run upon thee,
Though in these chains, bulk without spirit vast,
And with one buffet lay thy structure low,
Or swing thee in the air, then dash thee down,   1240
To the hazard of thy brains and shattered sides.
    HAR. By Astaroth, ere long thou shalt lament
These braveries, in irons loaden on thee.
    CHOR. His giantship is gone somewhat crest-fallen,
Stalking with less unconscionable strides,   1245
And lower looks, but in a sultry chafe.
    SAMS. I dread him not, nor all his giant brood,

1220. *shifts:* excuses (for not fighting Samson). *appellant:* challenger.
1221. *high attempts:* deeds really great. 1228. *descant:* comment (unfavorably). 1231. *Baal-zebub:* the Philistines' sun-god, and the Beelzebub of
Par. Lost. unused: unaccustomed. 1234. *van:* front troops (i.e., "start something"). 1243. *braveries:* boasts. 1245. *unconscionable:* absurdly arrogant.

Though fame divulge him father of five sons,
All of gigantic size, Goliah chief.

  CHOR. He will directly to the lords, I fear,   1250
And with malicious counsel stir them up
Some way or other yet further to afflict thee.

  SAMS. He must allege some cause, and offered fight
Will not dare mention, lest a question rise
Whether he durst accept the offer or not;   1255
And that he durst not plain enough appeared.
Much more affliction than already felt
They cannot well impose, nor I sustain,
If they intend advantage of my labours,
The work of many hands, which earns my keeping,   1260
With no small profit daily to my owners.
But come what will; my deadliest foe will prove
My speediest friend, by death to rid me hence;
The worst that he can give to me the best.
Yet so it may fall out, because their end   1265
Is hate, not help to me, it may with mine
Draw their own ruin who attempt the deed.

  CHOR. O, how comely it is, and how reviving
To the spirits of just men long oppressed,
When God into the hands of their deliverer   1270
Puts invincible might,
To quell the mighty of the earth, the oppressor,
The brute and boisterous force of violent men,
Hardy and industrious to support
Tyrannic power, but raging to pursue   1275
The righteous, and all such as honour truth!
He all their ammunition
And feats of war defeats,
With plain heroic magnitude of mind
And celestial vigour armed;   1280
Their armories and magazines contemns,
Renders them useless, while
With wingèd expedition
Swift as the lightning glance he executes
His errand on the wicked, who, surprised,   1285
Lose their defence, distracted and amazed.

1248-9. Milton identifies his Harapha with the unnamed giant of 2 Samuel
21, who has five sons—the fifth, Goliath. 1277. *He:* the deliverer. 1286.
defence: defensive power.

But patience is more oft the exercise
Of saints, the trial of their fortitude,
Making them each his own deliverer,
And victor over all   1290
That tyranny or fortune can inflict.
Either of these is in thy lot,
Samson, with might endued
Above the sons of men; but sight bereaved
May chance to number thee with those   1295
Whom patience finally must crown.
  This Idol's day hath been to thee no day of rest,
Labouring thy mind
More than the working day thy hands.
And yet, perhaps, more trouble is behind;   1300
For I descry this way
Some other tending; in his hand
A sceptre or quaint staff he bears,
Comes on amain, speed in his look.
By his habit I discern him now   1305
A public officer, and now at hand.
His message will be short and voluble.
    OFF. Ebrews, the prisoner Samson here I seek.
    CHOR. His manacles remark him; there he sits.
    OFF. Samson, to thee our lords thus bid me say: 1310
This day to Dagon is a solemn feast,
With sacrifices, triumph, pomp, and games;
Thy strength they know surpassing human rate,
And now some public proof thereof require
To honour this great feast, and great assembly.   1315
Rise, therefore, with all speed, and come along,
Where I will see thee heartened and fresh clad,
To appear as fits before the illustrious lords.
    SAMS. Thou know'st I am an Ebrew; therefore tell them
Our law forbids at their religious rites   1320
My presence; for that cause I cannot come.
    OFF. This answer, be assured, will not content them.
    SAMS. Have they not sword-players, and every sort
Of gymnic artists, wrestlers, riders, runners,
Jugglers and dancers, antics, mummers, mimics,   1325
But they must pick me out, with shackles tired,
And over-laboured at their public mill,

1303. *quaint:* cunningly made. 1307. *voluble:* expressive. 1309. *remark:* designate. 1325. *mummers:* pantomimists.

To make them sport with blind activity?
Do they not seek occasion of new quarrels,
On my refusal, to distress me more,   1330
Or make a game of my calamities?
Return the way thou cam'st; I will not come.
   OFF. Regard thyself; this will offend them highly.
   SAMS. Myself! my conscience, and internal peace.
Can they think me so broken, so debased   1335
With corporal servitude, that my mind ever
Will condescend to such absurd commands?
Although their drudge, to be their fool or jester,
And, in my midst of sorrow and heart-grief,
To show them feats, and play before their god—   1340
The worst of all indignities, yet on me
Joined with extreme contempt! I will not come.
   OFF. My message was imposed on me with speed,
Brooks no delay: is this thy resolution?
   SAMS. So take it with what speed thy message needs.   1345
   OFF. I am sorry what this stoutness will produce.
   SAMS. Perhaps thou shalt have cause to sorrow indeed.
   CHOR. Consider, Samson; matters now are strained
Up to the highth, whether to hold or break.
He's gone, and who knows how he may report   1350
Thy words by adding fuel to the flame?
Expect another message, more imperious,
More lordly thundering than thou well wilt bear.
   SAMS. Shall I abuse this consecrated gift
Of strength, again returning with my hair   1355
After my great transgression—so requite
Favour renewed, and add a greater sin
By prostituting holy things to idols,
A Nazarite, in place abominable,
Vaunting my strength in honour to their Dagon?   1360
Besides how vile, contemptible, ridiculous,
What act more execrably unclean, profane?
   CHOR. Yet with this strength thou serv'st the Philistines,
Idolatrous, uncircumcised, unclean.
   SAMS. Not in their idol-worship, but by labour   1365
Honest and lawful to deserve my food
Of those who have me in their civil power.

1333. *Regard:* look out for. 1342. *Joined:* enjoined. 1344. *Brooks:* allows of.
1346. *stoutness:* pride. 1357. *Favour:* God's favour. 1360. *Vaunting:* exhibiting.

CHOR. Where the heart joins not, outward acts defile not.
SAMS. Where outward force constrains, the sentence holds:
But who constrains me to the temple of Dagon,   1370
Not dragging? The Philistian lords command:
Commands are no constraints. If I obey them,
I do it freely, venturing to displease
God for the fear of man, and man prefer,
Set God behind; which, in his jealousy,   1375
Shall never, unrepented, find forgiveness.
Yet that he may dispense with me, or thee,
Present in temples at idolatrous rites
For some important cause, thou need'st not doubt.
    CHOR. How thou wilt here come off surmounts my reach.   1380
    SAMS. Be of good courage; I begin to feel
Some rousing motions in me, which dispose
To something extraordinary my thoughts.
I with this messenger will go along—
Nothing to do, be sure, that may dishonour   1385
Our Law, or stain my vow of Nazarite.
If there be aught of presage in the mind,
This day will be remarkable in my life
By some great act, or of my days the last.
    CHOR. In time thou hast resolved: the man returns.   1390
    OFF. Samson, this second message from our lords
To thee I am bid say: Art thou our slave,
Our captive, at the public mill our drudge,
And dar'st thou, at our sending and command,
Dispute thy coming? Come without delay;   1395
Or we shall find such engines to assail
And hamper thee, as thou shalt come of force,
Though thou wert firmlier fastened than a rock.
    SAMS. I could be well content to try their art,
Which to no few of them would prove pernicious;   1400
Yet, knowing their advantages too many,
Because they shall not trail me through their streets
Like a wild beast, I am content to go.
Masters' commands come with a power resistless
To such as owe them absolute subjection;   1405

1369. *the sentence:* the thought that the Chorus has just uttered. 1377-8.
dispense . . . present: allow one by his special dispensation to be present.
1387. i.e., I have a presentiment that. 1402. *Because:* in order that.

And for a life who will not change his purpose?
(So mutable are all the ways of men!)
Yet this be sure, in nothing to comply
Scandalous or forbidden in our Law.
   OFF. I praise thy resolution. Doff these links: 1410
By this compliance thou wilt win the lords
To favour, and perhaps to set thee free.
   SAMS. Brethren, farewell. Your company along
I will not wish, lest it perhaps offend them
To see me girt with friends; and how the sight   1415
Of me, as of a common enemy,
So dreaded once, may now exasperate them
I know not. Lords are lordliest in their wine;
And the well-feasted priest then soonest fired
With zeal, if aught religion seem concerned;   1420
No less the people, on their holy-days,
Impetuous, insolent, unquenchable.
Happen what may, of me expect to hear
Nothing dishonourable, impure, unworthy
Our God, our Law, my nation, or myself;   1425
The last of me or no I cannot warrant.
   CHOR. Go, and the Holy One
Of Israel be thy guide
To what may serve his glory best, and spread his name
Great among the Heathen round;   1430
Send thee the Angel of thy birth, to stand
Fast by thy side, who from thy father's field
Rode up in flames after his message told
Of thy conception, and be now a shield
Of fire; that Spirit that first rushed on thee   1435
In the camp of Dan,
Be efficacious in thee now at need!
For never was from Heaven imparted
Measure of strength so great to mortal seed,
As in thy wondrous actions hath been seen.   1440
But wherefore comes old Manoa in such haste
With youthful steps? Much livelier than erewhile
He seems: supposing here to find his son,
Or of him bringing to us some glad news?
   MAN. Peace with you, brethren! My inducement hither   1445
Was not at present here to find my son,

1420. *aught:* in any way. 1426. Whether this is the last time you will ever
see me, I cannot be sure. 1431. *Send:* may He send.

By order of the lords new parted hence
To come and play before them at their feast.
I heard all as I came; the city rings,
And numbers thither flock: I had no will,   1450
Lest I should see him forced to things unseemly.
But that which moved my coming now was chiefly
To give ye part with me what hope I have
With good success to work his liberty.

   CHOR. That hope would much rejoice us to partake   1455
With thee. Say, reverend sire; we thirst to hear.

   MAN. I have attempted, one by one, the lords,
Either at home, or through the high street passing,
With supplication prone and father's tears,
To accept of ransom for my son, their prisoner.   1460
Some much averse I found, and wondrous harsh,
Contemptuous, proud, set on revenge and spite;
That part most reverenced Dagon and his priests:
Others more moderate seeming, but their aim
Private reward, for which both God and State   1465
They easily would set to sale: a third
More generous far and civil, who confessed
They had enough revenged, having reduced
Their foe to misery beneath their fears;
The rest was magnanimity to remit,   1470
If some convenient ransom were proposed.
What noise or shout was that? It tore the sky.

   CHOR. Doubtless the people shouting to behold
Their once great dread, captive and blind before them,
Or at some proof of strength before them shown.   1475

   MAN. His ransom, if my whole inheritance
May compass it, shall willingly be paid
And numbered down. Much rather I shall choose
To live the poorest in my tribe, than richest,
And he in that calamitous prison left.   1480
No, I am fixed not to part hence without him.
For his redemption all my patrimony,
If need be, I am ready to forgo
And quit. Not wanting him, I shall want nothing.

   CHOR. Fathers are wont to lay up for their sons;   1485
Thou for thy son art bent to lay out all:
Sons wont to nurse their parents in old age;

1450. *will:* alternative. 1453. *give . . . me:* share with you. 1457. *attempted:* tried, appealed to. 1487. *wont:* are wont.

Thou in old age car'st how to nurse thy son,
Made older than thy age through eye-sight lost.
   MAN. It shall be my delight to tend his eyes.   1490
And view him sitting in his house, ennobled
With all those high exploits by him achieved,
And on his shoulders waving down those locks
That of a nation armed the strength contained.
And I persuade me God had not permitted   1495
His strength again to grow up with his hair
Garrisoned round about him like a camp
Of faithful soldiery, were not his purpose
To use him further yet in some great service—
Not to sit idle with so great a gift   1500
Useless, and thence ridiculous, about him.
And, since his strength with eye-sight was not lost,
God will restore him eye-sight to his strength.
   CHOR. Thy hopes are not ill founded, nor seem vain,
Of his delivery, and thy joy thereon   1505
Conceived, agreeable to a father's love;
In both which we, as next, participate.
   MAN. I know your friendly minds, and . . . O, what noise!
Mercy of Heaven! what hideous noise was that?
Horribly loud, unlike the former shout.   1510
   CHOR. Noise call you it, or universal groan,
As if the whole inhabitation perished?
Blood, death, and deathful deeds, are in that noise,
Ruin, destruction at the utmost point.
   MAN. Of ruin indeed methought I heard the noise.   1515
Oh! it continues; they have slain my son.
   CHOR. Thy son is rather slaying them: that outcry
From slaughter of one foe could not ascend.
   MAN. Some dismal accident it needs must be.
What shall we do—stay here, or run and see?   1520
   CHOR. Best keep together here, lest, running thither,
We unawares run into danger's mouth.
This evil on the Philistines is fallen:
From whom could else a general cry be heard?
The sufferers, then, will scarce molest us here;   1525
From other hands we need not much to fear.
What if, his eye-sight (for to Israel's God
Nothing is hard) by miracle restored,

1495-8. *had not . . . were not:* would not have . . . if it were not. 1507.
next: next of kin.

He now be dealing dole among his foes,
And over heaps of slaughtered walk his way?   1530
   MAN. That were a joy presumptuous to be thought.
   CHOR. Yet God hath wrought things as incredible
For his people of old; what hinders now?
   MAN. He can, I know, but doubt to think he will;
Yet hope would fain subscribe, and tempts belief.   1535
A little stay will bring some notice hither.
   CHOR. Of good or bad so great, of bad the sooner;
For evil news rides post, while good news baits.
And to our wish I see one hither speeding—
An Ebrew, as I guess, and of our tribe.   1540
   MESS. O, whither shall I run, or which way fly
The sight of this so horrid spectacle,
Which erst my eyes beheld, and yet behold?
For dire imagination still pursues me.
But providence or instinct of nature seems,   1545
Or reason, though disturbed and scarce consulted,
To have guided me aright, I know not how,
To thee first, reverend Manoa, and to these
My countrymen, whom here I knew remaining,
As at some distance from the place of horror,   1550
So in the sad event too much concerned.
   MAN. The accident was loud, and here before thee
With rueful cry; yet what it was we hear not.
No preface needs; thou seest we long to know.
   MESS. It would burst forth; but I recover breath   1555
And sense distract, to know well what I utter.
   MAN. Tell us the sum; the circumstance defer.
   MESS. Gaza yet stands; but all her sons are fallen,
All in a moment overwhelmed and fallen.
   MAN. Sad! but thou know'st to Israelites not saddest   1560
The desolation of a hostile city.
   MESS. Feed on that first; there may in grief be surfeit.
   MAN. Relate by whom.
   MESS.   By Samson.
   MAN.   That still lessens
The sorrow, and converts it nigh to joy.

1529. *dole:* pain. 1537. I.e., news of so great a good or evil will soon arrive,
and if it is of evil, sooner than if it is of good. 1538. *baits:* travels slowly.
1543. *erst:* just now. 1552. *here:* arrived here. 1555. *recover:* must recover.
1556. *distract:* distracted.

MESS. Ah! Manoa, I refrain too suddenly   1565
To utter what will come at last too soon,
Lest evil tidings, with too rude irruption
Hitting thy agèd ear, should pierce too deep.
  MAN. Suspense in news is torture; speak them out.
  MESS. Then take the worst in brief: Samson is dead.   1570
  MAN. The worst indeed! O, all my hope's defeated
To free him hence! but Death, who sets all free,
Hath paid his ransom now and full discharge.
What windy joy this day had I conceived,
Hopeful of his delivery, which now proves   1575
Abortive as the first-born bloom of spring
Nipt with the lagging rear of winter's frost!
Yet, ere I give the reins to grief, say first
How died he; death to life is crown or shame.
All by him fell, thou say'st; by whom fell he?   1580
What glorious hand gave Samson his death's wound?
  MESS. Unwounded of his enemies he fell.
  MAN. Wearied with slaughter, then, or how? explain.
  MESS. By his own hands.
  MAN.   Self-violence! What cause
Brought him so soon at variance with himself   1585
Among his foes?
  MESS.   Inevitable cause—
At once both to destroy and be destroyed.
The edifice, where all were met to see him,
Upon their heads and on his own he pulled.
  MAN. O lastly over-strong against thyself!   1590
A dreadful way took'st to thy revenge.
More than enough we know; but, while things yet
Are in confusion, give us, if thou canst,
Eye-witness of what first or last was done,
Relation more particular and distinct.   1595
  MESS. Occasions drew me early to this city;
And, as the gates I entered with sun-rise,
The morning trumpets festival proclaimed
Through each high street. Little I had dispatched,
When all abroad was rumoured that this day   1600
Samson should be brought forth, to show the people
Proof of his mighty strength in feats and games.
I sorrowed at his captive state, but minded

1574. *windy:* vain.   1596. *Occasions:* my affairs.   1599. *dispatched:* accomplished.

Not to be absent at that spectacle.
The building was a spacious theatre,   1605
Half round on two main pillars vaulted high,
With seats where all the lords, and each degree
Of sort, might sit in order to behold;
The other side was open, where the throng
On banks and scaffolds under sky might stand: 1610
I among these aloof obscurely stood.
The feast and noon grew high, and sacrifice
Had filled their hearts with mirth, high cheer, and wine,
When to their sports they turned. Immediately
Was Samson as a public servant brought,   1615
In their state livery clad: before him pipes
And timbrels; on each side went armèd guards;
Both horse and foot before him and behind,
Archers and slingers, cataphracts, and spears.
At sight of him the people with a shout   1620
Rifted the air, clamouring their god with praise,
Who had made their dreadful enemy their thrall.
He patient, but undaunted, where they led him,
Came to the place; and what was set before him,
Which without help of eye might be assayed,   1625
To heave, pull, draw, or break, he still performed
All with incredible, stupendious force,
None daring to appear antagonist.
At length, for intermission sake, they led him
Between the pillars; he his guide requested   1630
(For so from such as nearer stood we heard),
As over-tired, to let him lean a while
With both his arms on those two massy pillars,
That to the archèd roof gave main support.
He unsuspicious led him; which when Samson   1635
Felt in his arms, with head a while inclined,
And eyes fast fixed, he stood, as one who prayed,
Or some great matter in his mind revolved:
At last, with head erect, thus cried aloud.
"Hitherto, Lords, what your commands imposed   1640
I have performed, as reason was, obeying,
Not without wonder or delight beheld;

1607-8. *each . . . sort:* each rank of the better class (as opposed to *throng,*
1609). 1610. *banks:* benches. 1619. *cataphracts:* heavily armed soldiers on
heavily armoured horses. *spears:* spearmen. 1641-2. *obeying, beheld:* obeying you and beheld by you.

Now, of my own accord, such other trial
I mean to show you of my strength yet greater
As with amaze shall strike all who behold."   1645
This uttered, straining all his nerves, he bowed;
As with the force of winds and waters pent
When mountains tremble, those two massy pillars
With horrible convulsion to and fro
He tugged, he shook, till down they came, and drew   1650
The whole roof after them with burst of thunder
Upon the heads of all who sat beneath,
Lords, ladies, captains, counsellors, or priests,
Their choice nobility and flower, not only
Of this, but each Philistian city round,   1655
Met from all parts to solemnize this feast.
Samson, with these immixed, inevitably
Pulled down the same destruction on himself;
The vulgar only scaped, who stood without.
   CHOR. O dearly bought revenge, yet glorious!   1660
Living or dying thou hast fulfilled
The work for which thou wast foretold
To Israel, and now liest victorious
Among thy slain self-killed
Not willingly, but tangled in the fold   1665
Of dire Necessity, whose law in death conjoined
Thee with thy slaughtered foes, in number more
Than all thy life had slain before.
   SEMICHOR. While their hearts were jocund and sublime,
Drunk with idolatry, drunk with wine   1670
And fat regorged of bulls and goats,
Chaunting their idol, and preferring
Before our living Dread, who dwells
In Silo, his bright sanctuary,
Among them he a spirit of phrenzy sent,   1675
Who hurt their minds,
And urged them on with mad desire
To call in haste for their destroyer.

1659. *vulgar:* the "throng," cf. 1609. 1665-7. *Not . . . foes:* Milton's effort
to clear Samson of the charge of suicide: the argument seems to be that
Samson died self-killed but not because he chose suicide; rather because he
chose to take the offered opportunity to kill his enemies, and that opportunity necessarily involved death for himself. 1669. *sublime:* uplifted. 1671.
regorged: belched up. 1672. *Chaunting . . . preferring:* chanting to . . .
preferring him. 1675. *he:* God. 1675 ff. The reference is to the idea, central
in Greek tragedy, that whom the gods would destroy, they first make mad.

They, only set on sport and play,
Unweetingly importuned   1680
Their own destruction to come speedy upon them.
So fond are mortal men,
Fallen into wrath divine,
As their own ruin on themselves to invite,
Insensate left, or to sense reprobate,   1685
And with blindness internal struck.
   SEMICHOR. But he, though blind of sight,
Despised, and thought extinguished quite,
With inward eyes illuminated,
His fiery virtue roused   1690
From under ashes into sudden flame,
And as an evening dragon came,
Assailant on the perchèd roosts
And nests in order ranged
Of tame villatic fowl, but as an eagle   1695
His cloudless thunder bolted on their heads.
So Virtue, given for lost,
Depressed and overthrown, as seemed,
Like that self-begotten bird
In the Arabian woods embost,   1700
That no second knows nor third,
And lay erewhile a holocaust,
From out her ashy womb now teemed,
Revives, reflourishes, then vigorous most
When most unactive deemed;   1705
And, though her body die, her fame survives,
A secular bird, ages of lives.
   MAN. Come, come; no time for lamentation now,
Nor much more cause. Samson hath quit himself
Like Samson, and heroicly hath finished   1710

1679. *set on:* intending. 1680. *Unweetingly:* unwittingly. 1682. *fond:* foolish. 1685. The line puns on two meanings of "sense": (1) left foolish (sense-
less); (2) abandoned to sensuality (sense). 1689. *inward eyes:* i.e., a contrast of Samson's case with that of the Philistines (*blindness internal,* 1686).
1692. *dragon:* a monster usually represented as breathing fire and having
wings; hence its relevance to 1689-91 and 1693-5. 1697. *given:* given up.
1699-1707. The Arabian phoenix, of which there is only one specimen alive
at a time (1701), and which reproduces itself in a new specimen by being
consumed with flame (1702-4). Ll. 1704-7, though they continue the phoenix
image, refer especially to virtue: the immortal fame of a great man's virtue
even though his body (as in Samson's case) dies.

A life heroic, on his enemies
Fully revenged—hath left them years of mourning,
And lamentation to the sons of Caphtor
Through all Philistian bounds; to Israel
Honour hath left and freedom, let but them   1715
Find courage to lay hold on this occasion;
To himself and father's house eternal fame;
And, which is best and happiest yet, all this
With God not parted from him, as was feared,
But favouring and assisting to the end.   1720
Nothing is here for tears, nothing to wail
Or knock the breast; no weakness, no contempt,
Dispraise, or blame; nothing but well and fair,
And what may quiet us in a death so noble.
Let us go find the body where it lies   1725
Soaked in his enemies' blood, and from the stream
With lavers pure, and cleansing herbs, wash off
The clotted gore. I, with what speed the while
(Gaza is not in plight to say us nay),
Will send for all my kindred, all my friends,   1730
To fetch him hence, and solemnly attend,
With silent obsequy and funeral train,
Home to his father's house. There will I build him
A monument, and plant it round with shade
Of laurel ever green and branching palm,   1735
With all his trophies hung, and acts enrolled
In copious legend, or sweet lyric song.
Thither shall all the valiant youth resort,
And from his memory inflame their breasts
To matchless valour and adventures high;   1740
The virgins also shall, on feastful days,
Visit his tomb with flowers, only bewailing
His lot unfortunate in nuptial choice,
From whence captivity and loss of eyes.
    CHOR. All is best, though we oft doubt   1745
What the unsearchable dispose
Of Highest Wisdom brings about,
And ever best found in the close.
Oft He seems to hide his face,

1713. *sons of Caphtor:* Philistines. 1728. *what speed:* what speed I can. 1735.
laurel, palm: symbols of victory. 1746. *dispose:* disposal. 1748. *in . . .
close:* in the conclusion.

But unexpectedly returns,   1750
And to his faithful champion hath in place
Bore witness gloriously; whence Gaza mourns,
And all that band them to resist
His uncontrollable intent.
His servants He, with new acquist   1755
Of true experience from this great event,
With peace and consolation hath dismissed,
And calm of mind, all passion spent.

THE END

❦

1751. *in place:* on this spot. 1755. *acquist:* acquisition.

Appendix

Genesis

In the beginning God created the heaven and the earth. And the earth was without form, and void; and darkness was upon the face of the deep. And the Spirit of God moved upon the face of the waters. And God said, Let there be light: and there was light. And God saw the light, that it was good: and God divided the light from the darkness. And God called the light Day, and the darkness he called Night. And the evening and the morning were the first day.

And God said, Let there be a firmament in the midst of the waters, and let it divide the waters from the waters. And God made the firmament, and divided the waters which were under the firmament from the waters which were above the firmament: and it was so. And God called the firmament Heaven. And the evening and the morning were the second day.

And God said, Let the waters under the heaven be gathered together unto one place, and let the dry land appear: and it was so. And God called the dry land Earth; and the gathering together of the waters called he Seas: and God saw that it was good. And God said, Let the earth bring forth grass, the herb yielding seed, and the fruit tree yielding fruit after his kind, whose seed is in itself, upon the earth: and it was so. And the earth brought forth grass, and herb yielding seed after his kind, and the tree yielding fruit, whose seed was in itself, after his kind: and God saw that it was good. And the evening and the morning were the third day.

And God said, Let there be lights in the firmament of the heaven to divide the day from the night; and let them be for signs, and for seasons, and for days, and years: and let them be for lights in the firmament of the heaven to give light upon the earth: and it was so. And God made two great lights; the greater light to rule the day, and the lesser light to rule the night: he made the stars also. And God set them in the firmament of the heaven to give light upon the earth, and to rule over the day and over the night, and to divide the light from the darkness: and God saw that it was good. And the evening and the morning were the fourth day. And God said, Let the waters bring forth abundantly the moving creature that hath life, and fowl that may fly above the earth in the open firmament of heaven. And God created great whales, and every living creature that moveth, which the waters brought forth abundantly, after their kind, and every winged fowl after his kind: and God saw that it was good. And God blessed them, saying, Be fruitful, and multiply, and fill the waters in the seas, and let fowl multiply in the earth. And the evening and the morning were the fifth day.

And God said, Let the earth bring forth the living creature after his kind, cattle, and creeping thing, and beast of the earth after his kind: and it was so. And God made the beast of the earth after his kind, and cattle after their kind, and everything that creepeth upon the earth after his kind: and God saw that it was good.

And God said, Let us make man in our image, after our likeness: and let them have dominion over the fish of the sea, and over the fowl of the air, and over the cattle, and over all the earth, and over every creeping thing that creepeth upon the earth. So God created man in his own image, in the image of God created he him; male and female created he them. And God blessed them, and God said unto them, Be fruitful, and multiply, and replenish the earth, and subdue it: and have dominion over the fish of the sea, and over the fowl of the air, and over every living thing that moveth upon the earth.

And God said, Behold, I have given you every herb bearing seed, which is upon the face of all the earth, and every tree, in the which is the fruit of a tree yielding seed; to you it shall be for meat. And to every beast of the earth, and to every fowl of the air, and to every thing that creepeth upon the earth, wherein there is life, I have given every green herb for meat: and it was so. And God saw every thing that he had made, and, behold, it was very good. And the evening and the morning were the sixth day.

II

Thus the heavens and the earth were finished, and all the host of them. And on the seventh day God ended his work which he had made; and he rested on the seventh day from all his work which he had made. And God blessed the seventh day, and sanctified it: because that in it he had rested from all his work which God created and made.

These are the generations of the heavens and of the earth when they were created, in the day that the Lord God made the earth and the heavens, and every plant of the field before it was in the earth, and every herb of the field before it grew: for the Lord God had not caused it to rain upon the earth, and there was not a man to till the ground. But there went up a mist from the earth, and watered the whole face of the ground. And the Lord God formed man of the dust of the ground, and breathed into his nostrils the breath of life; and man became a living soul.

And the Lord God planted a garden eastward in Eden; and there he put the man whom he had formed. And out of the ground made the Lord God to grow every tree that is pleasant to the sight, and good for food; the tree of life also in the midst of the garden, and the tree of knowledge of good and evil. And a river went out of Eden to water the garden; and from thence it was parted, and became into four heads. The name of the first is Pison: that is it which compasseth the whole land of Havilah, where there is gold; and the gold of that land is good: there is bdellium and the onyx stone. And the name of the second river is Gihon: the same is it that compasseth the whole land of Ethiopia. And the name of the third river is Hiddekel: that is it which goeth toward the east of Assyria. And the fourth river is Euphrates. And the Lord God took the man, and put him into the garden of Eden to dress it and to keep it. And the Lord God commanded the man, saying, Of every tree of the garden thou mayest freely eat: but of the tree of the knowledge of good and evil, thou shalt not eat of it: for in the day that thou eatest thereof thou shalt surely die.

And the Lord God said, It is not good that the man should be alone; I will make him an help meet for him. And out of the ground the Lord God formed every beast of the field, and every fowl of the air; and brought them unto Adam to see what he would call them: and whatsoever Adam called every living creature, that was the name thereof. And Adam gave names to all cattle, and to the fowl of the air, and to every beast of the field; but for Adam there was not found an help meet for him. And the Lord God caused a deep sleep to fall upon Adam, and he slept: and he took one of his ribs, and closed up the flesh instead thereof; and the rib, which the Lord God had taken from man, made he a woman, and brought her unto the man. And Adam said, This is now bone of my bones, and flesh of my flesh: she shall be called Woman, because she was taken out of

Man. Therefore shall a man leave his father and his mother, and shall cleave unto his wife: and they shall be one flesh. And they were both naked, the man and his wife, and were not ashamed.

III

Now the serpent was more subtil than any beast of the field which the Lord God had made. And he said unto the woman, Yea, hath God said, Ye shall not eat of every tree of the garden? And the woman said unto the serpent, We may eat of the fruit of the trees of the garden: but of the fruit of the tree which is in the midst of the garden, God hath said, Ye shall not eat of it, neither shall ye touch it, lest ye die. And the serpent said unto the woman, Ye shall not surely die: for God doth know that in the day ye eat thereof, then your eyes shall be opened, and ye shall be as gods, knowing good and evil. And when the woman saw that the tree was good for food, and that it was pleasant to the eyes, and a tree to be desired to make one wise, she took of the fruit thereof, and did eat, and gave also unto her husband with her; and he did eat. And the eyes of them both were opened, and they knew that they were naked; and they sewed fig leaves together, and made themselves aprons. And they heard the voice of the Lord God walking in the garden in the cool of the day: and Adam and his wife hid themselves from the presence of the Lord God amongst the trees of the garden. And the Lord God called unto Adam, and said unto him, Where art thou? And he said, I heard thy voice in the garden, and I was afraid, because I was naked; and I hid myself. And he said, Who told thee that thou wast naked? Hast thou eaten of the tree, whereof I commanded thee that thou shouldest not eat? And the man said, The woman whom thou gavest to be with me, she gave me of the tree, and I did eat. And the Lord God said unto the woman. What is this that thou hast done? And the woman said, The serpent beguiled me, and I did eat. And the Lord God said unto the serpent, Because thou hast done this, thou art cursed above all cattle, and above every beast of the field; upon thy belly shalt thou go, and dust shalt thou eat all the days of thy life: and I will put enmity between thee and the woman, and between thy seed and her seed; it shall bruise thy head, and thou shalt bruise his heel. Unto the woman he said, I will greatly multiply thy sorrow and thy conception; in sorrow thou shalt bring forth children; and thy desire shall be to thy husband, and he shall rule over thee. And unto Adam he said, Because thou hast hearkened unto the voice of thy wife, and hast eaten of the tree, of which I commanded thee, saying, Thou shalt not eat of it: cursed is the ground for thy sake; in sorrow shalt thou eat of it all the days of thy life; thorns also and thistles shall it bring forth to thee; and thou shalt eat the herb of the field; in the sweat of thy face shalt thou eat bread, till thou return unto the ground; for out of it wast thou taken: for dust thou art, and unto dust shalt thou return. And Adam called his wife's name Eve; because she was the mother of all living. Unto Adam also and to his wife did the Lord God make coats of skins, and clothed them.

And the Lord God said, Behold, the man is become as one of us, to know good and evil: and now, lest he put forth his hand, and take also of the tree of life, and eat, and live forever: therefore the Lord God sent him forth from the garden of Eden, to till the ground from whence he was taken. So he drove out the man; and he placed at the east of the garden of Eden Cherubims, and a flaming sword which turned every way, to keep the way of the tree of life.

∾

Judges

XIII

And the children of Israel did evil again in the sight of the Lord; and the Lord delivered them into the hand of the Philistines forty years. And there was a certain man of Zorah, of the family of the Danites, whose name was Manoah; and his wife was barren, and bare not. And the angel of the Lord appeared unto the woman, and said unto her, Behold now, thou art barren, and bearest not: but thou shalt conceive, and bear a son. Now therefore beware, I pray thee, and drink not wine nor strong drink, and eat not any unclean thing: for, lo, thou shalt conceive, and bear a son; and no razor shall come on his head: for the child shall be a Nazarite unto God from the womb: and he shall begin to deliver Israel out of the hand of the Philistines. Then the woman came and told her husband, saying, A man of God came unto me, and his countenance was like the countenance of an angel of God, very terrible: but I asked him not whence he was, neither told he me his name: but he said unto me, Behold, thou shalt conceive, and bear a son; and now drink no wine nor strong drink, neither eat any unclean thing: for the child shall be a Nazarite to God from the womb to the day of his death.

Then Manoah intreated the Lord, and said, O my Lord, let the man of God which thou didst send come again unto us, and teach us what we shall do unto the child that shall be born. And God hearkened to the voice of Manoah; and the angel of God came again unto the woman as she sat in the field: but Manoah her husband was not with her. And the woman made haste, and ran, and shewed her husband, and said unto him, Behold, the man hath appeared unto me, that came unto me the other day. And Manoah arose, and went after his wife, and came to the man, and said unto him, Art thou the man that spakest unto the woman? And he said, I am. And Manoah said, Now let thy words come to pass. How shall we order the child, and how shall we do unto him? And the angel of the Lord said unto Manoah, Of all that I said unto the woman let her beware. She may not eat of anything that cometh of the vine, neither let her drink wine or strong drink, nor eat any unclean thing: all that I commanded her let her observe.

And Manoah said unto the angel of the Lord, I pray thee, let us detain thee, until we shall have made ready a kid for thee. And the angel of the Lord said unto Manoah, Though thou detain me, I will not eat of thy bread: and if thou wilt offer a burnt offering, thou must offer it unto the Lord. For Manoah knew not that he was an angel of the Lord, And Manoah said unto the angel of the Lord, What is thy name, that when thy sayings come to pass we may do thee honour? And the angel of the Lord said unto him, Why askest thou thus after my name, seeing it is secret? So Manoah took a kid with a meat offering, and offered it upon a rock unto the Lord: and the angel did wonderously; and Manoah and his wife looked on. For it came to pass, when the flame went up toward heaven from off the altar, that the angel of the Lord ascended in the flame of the altar. And Manoah and his wife looked on it, and fell on their faces to the ground. But the angel of the Lord did no more appear to Manoah and to his wife. Then Manoah knew that he was an angel of the Lord. And Manoah said unto his wife, We shall surely die, because we have seen God. But his wife said unto him, If the Lord were pleased to kill us, he would not have received a burnt offering and a meat offering at our hands, neither would he have shewed us all these things, nor would as at this time have told us such things as these.

And the woman bare a son, and called his name Samson: and the child grew, and the Lord blessed him. And the Spirit of the Lord began to move him at times in the camp of Dan between Zorah and Eshtaol.

XIV

And Samson went down to Timnath, and saw a woman in Timnath of the daughters of the Philistines. And he came up, and told his father and his mother, and said, I have seen a woman in

Timnath of the daughters of the Philistines: now therefore get her for me to wife. Then his father and his mother said unto him, Is there never a woman among the daughters of thy brethren, or among all my people, that thou goest to take a wife of the uncircumcised Philistines? And Samson said unto his father, Get her for me; for she pleaseth me well. But his father and his mother knew not that it was of the Lord, that he sought an occasion against the Philistines: for at that time the Philistines had dominion over Israel.

Then went Samson down, and his father and his mother, to Timnath, and came to the vineyards of Timnath: and, behold, a young lion roared against him. And the Spirit of the Lord came mightily upon him, and he rent him as he would have rent a kid, and he had nothing in his hand: but he told not his father or his mother what he had done. And he went down, and talked with the woman; and she pleased Samson well.

And after a time he returned to take her, and he turned aside to see the carcass of the lion: and, behold, there was a swarm of bees and honey in the carcass of the lion. And he took thereof in his hands, and went on eating, and came to his father and mother, and he gave them, and they did eat: but he told not them that he had taken the honey out of the carcass of the lion.

So his father went down unto the woman: and Samson made there a feast; for so used the young men to do. And it came to pass, when they saw him, that they brought thirty companions to be with him.

And Samson said unto them, I will now put forth a riddle unto you: if ye can certainly declare it me within the seven days of the feast, and find it out, then I will give you thirty sheets and thirty change of garments: but if ye cannot declare it me, then shall ye give me thirty sheets and thirty change of garments. And they said unto him, Put forth thy riddle, that we may hear it. And he said unto them, Out of the eater came forth meat, and out of the strong came forth sweetness. And they could not in three days expound the riddle. And it came to pass on the seventh day, that they said unto Samson's wife, Entice thy husband, that he may declare unto us the riddle, lest we burn thee and thy father's house with fire: have ye called us to take that we have? is it not so? And Samson's wife wept before him, and said, Thou dost but hate me, and lovest me not: thou hast put forth a riddle unto the children of my people, and hast not told it me. And he said unto her, Behold, I have not told it my father nor my mother, and shall I tell it thee? And she wept before him the seven days, while their feast lasted: and it came to pass on the seventh day, that he told her, because she lay sore upon him: and she told the riddle to the children of her people. And the men of the city said unto him on the seventh day before the sun went down, What is sweeter than honey? and what is stronger than a lion? And he said unto them, If ye had not plowed with my heifer, ye had not found out my riddle.

And the Spirit of the Lord came upon him, and he went down to Ashkelon, and slew thirty men of them, and took their spoil, and gave change of garments unto them which expounded the riddle. And his anger was kindled, and he went up to his father's house. But Samson's wife was given to his companion, whom he had used as his friend.

XV

But it came to pass within a while after, in the time of wheat harvest, that Samson visited his wife with a kid; and he said, I will go in to my wife into the chamber. But her father would not suffer him to go in. And her father said, I verily thought that thou hadst utterly hated her; therefore I gave her to thy companion: is not her younger sister fairer than she? take her, I pray thee, instead of her.

And Samson said concerning them, Now shall I be more blameless than the Philistines, though I do them a displeasure. And Samson went and caught three hundred foxes, and took firebrands, and turned tail to tail, and put a firebrand in the midst between two tails. And when he had set the brands on fire, he let them go into the standing corn of the Philistines, and burnt up both the shocks, and also the standing corn, with the vineyards and olives.

Then the Philistines said, Who hath done this? And they answered, Samson, the son in law of the Timnite, because he had taken his wife, and given her to his companion. And the Philistines came up, and burnt her and her father with fire.

And Samson said unto them, Though ye have done this, yet will I be avenged of you, and after that I will cease. And he smote them hip and thigh with a great slaughter: and he went down and dwelt in the top of the rock Etam.

Then the Philistines went up, and pitched in Judah, and spread themselves in Lehi. And the men of Judah said, Why are ye come up against us? And they answered, To bind Samson are we come up, to do to him as he hath done to us. Then three thousand men of Judah went to the top of the rock Etam, and said to Samson, Knowest thou not that the Philistines are rulers over us? what is this that thou hast done unto us? And he said unto them, As they did unto me, so have I done unto them. And they said unto him, We are come down to bind thee, that we may deliver thee into the hand of the Philistines. And Samson said unto them, Swear unto me, that ye will not fall upon me yourselves. And they spake unto him, saying, No; but we will bind thee fast, and deliver thee into their hand: but surely we will not kill thee. And they bound him with two new cords, and brought him up from the rock.

And when he came unto Lehi, the Philistines shouted against him: and the Spirit of the Lord came mightily upon him, and the cords that were upon his arms became as flax that was burnt with fire, and his bands loosed from off his hands. And he found a new jawbone of an ass, and put forth his hand, and took it, and slew a thousand men therewith. And Samson said, With the jawbone of an ass, heaps upon heaps, with the jaw of an ass have I slain a thousand men. And it came to pass, when he had made an end of speaking, that he cast away the jawbone out of his hand, and called that place Ramath-lehi.

And he was sore athirst, and called on the Lord, and said, Thou hast given this great deliverance into the hand of thy servant: and now shall I die for thirst, and fall into the hand of the uncircumcised? But God clave an hollow place that was in the jaw, and there came water thereout; and when he had drunk, his spirit came again, and he revived: wherefore he called the name thereof En-hakkore, which is in Lehi unto this day. And he judged Israel in the days of the Philistines twenty years.

XVI

Then went Samson to Gaza, and saw there an harlot, and went in unto her. And it was told the Gazites, saying, Samson is come hither. And they compassed him in, and laid wait for him all night in the gate of the city, and were quiet all the night, saying, In the morning, when it is day, we shall kill him. And Samson lay till midnight, and arose at midnight, and took the doors of the gate of the city, and the two posts, and went away with them, bar and all, and put them upon his shoulders, and carried them up to the top of an hill that is before Hebron.

And it came to pass afterward, that he loved a woman in the valley of Sorek, whose name was Delilah. And the lords of the Philistines came up unto her, and said unto her, Entice him, and see wherein his great strength lieth, and by what means we may prevail against him, that we may bind him to afflict him: and we will give thee every one of us eleven hundred pieces of silver.

And Delilah said to Samson, Tell me, I pray thee, wherein thy great strength lieth, and wherewith thou mightest be bound to afflict thee. And Samson said unto her, If they bind me with seven green withes that were never dried, then shall I be weak, and be as another man. Then the lords of the Philistines brought up to her seven green withes which had not been dried, and she bound him with them. Now there were men lying in wait, abiding with her in the chamber. And she said unto him, The Philistines be upon thee, Samson. And he brake the withes, as a thread of tow is broken when it toucheth the fire. So his strength was not known. And Delilah said unto Samson, Behold, thou hast mocked me, and told me lies: now tell me, I pray thee, wherewith thou mightest be bound. And he said unto her, If they bind me fast with new ropes that never were occupied, then shall I be weak, and as another man. Delilah therefore took new ropes, and bound him therewith, and said unto him, The Philistines be upon thee, Samson. And there were liers in wait abiding in the chamber. And he brake them from off his arms like a thread. And Delilah said unto Samson, Hitherto thou hast mocked me, and told me lies: tell me wherewith thou mightest be bound. And he said unto her, If thou weavest the seven locks of my head with the web. And she fastened it with a pin, and said unto him, The Philistines be upon thee, Samson. And he awaked out of his sleep, and went away with the pin of the beam, and with the web.

And she said unto him, How canst thou say, I love thee, when thine heart is not with me? thou hast mocked me these three times, and hast not told me wherein thy great strength lieth. And it came to pass, when she pressed him daily with her words, and urged him, so that his soul was vexed unto death; that he told her all his heart, and said unto her, There hath not come a razor upon mine head; for I have been a Nazarite unto God from my mother's womb; if I be shaven, then my strength will go from me, and I shall become weak, and be like any other man. And when Delilah saw that he had told her all his heart, she sent and called for the lords of the Philistines, saying, Come up this once, for he hath shewed me all his heart. Then the lords of the Philistines came up unto her, and brought money in their hand. And she made him sleep upon her knees; and she called for a man, and she caused him to shave off the seven locks of his head; and she began to afflict him, and his strength went from him. And she said, The Philistines be upon thee, Samson. And he awoke out of his sleep, and said, I will go out as at other times before, and shake myself. And he wist not that the Lord was departed from him.

But the Philistines took him, and put out his eyes, and brought him down to Gaza, and bound him with fetters of brass; and he did grind in the prison house. Howbeit the hair of his head began to grow again after he was shaven. Then the lords of the Philistines gathered them together for to offer a great sacrifice unto Dagon their god, and to rejoice: for they said, Our god hath delivered Samson our enemy into our hand. And when the people saw him, they praised their god: for they said, Our god hath delivered into our hands our enemy, and the destroyer of our country, which slew many of us. And it came to pass, when their hearts were merry, that they said, Call for Samson, that he may make us sport. And they called for Samson out of the prison house; and he made them sport: And they set him between the pillars. And Samson said unto the lad that held him by the hand, Suffer me that I may feel the pillars whereupon the house standeth, that I may lean upon them. Now the house was full of men and women; and all the lords of the Philistines were there; and there were upon the roof about three thousand men and women, that beheld while Samson made sport. And Samson called unto the Lord, and said, O Lord God, remember me, I pray thee, and strengthen me, I pray thee, only this once, O God, that I may be at once avenged of the Philistines for my two eyes. And Samson took hold of the two middle pillars upon which the house stood, and on which it was borne up, of the one with his right hand, and of the other with his left. And Samson said, Let me die with the Philistines. And he bowed himself with all his might; and the house fell upon the lords, and upon all the people that were therein. So the dead which he slew at his death were more than they which he slew in his life. Then his brethren and all the house of his father came down, and took him, and brought him up, and buried him between Zorah and Eshtaol in the buryingplace of Manoah his father. And he judged Israel twenty years.

Bibliographical References

The indispensable life of Milton is still that by David Masson (7 vols., 1859-94). For contemporary biographies, see H. Darbishire (ed.), *Early Lives of Milton* (1932); for autobiography, J. S. Diekhoff, *Milton on Himself* (1939); and for a modern biographical study, J. H. Hanford, *John Milton, Englishman* (1949), whose *A Milton Handbook* (4th ed., 1946) is also valuable. Background studies of the age and its climate of opinion are D. Saurat, *Milton: Man and Thinker* (1925, revised 1944); H. J. C. Grierson, *Cross Currents in English Literature of the XVIIth Century* (1929); B. Willey, *The Seventeenth Century Background* (1934); G. W. Whiting, *Milton's Literary Milieu* (1939); and D. Bush, *English Literature in the Earlier Seventeenth Century, 1600-1660* (Oxford History of English Literature, V, 1945).

In the recent literature of criticism of Milton's poetry, the following warrant special notice: Sir Walter A. Raleigh, *Milton* (1900); E. E. Stoll, "Milton," in *Poets and Playwrights* (1930); E. M. W. Tillyard, *Milton* (1930), and *The Miltonic Setting* (1938); T. S. Eliot, "A Note on the Verse of John Milton," in *Essays and Studies of the English Association* (1935), and *Milton* (1948). In the study of individual poems, the following books and essays will be found helpful:

ODE: Cf. A. S. P. Woodhouse, "Notes on Milton's Early Development," *University of Toronto Quarterly*, XIII (1943); A. Barker, "The Pattern of Milton's Nativity Ode," *Ibid.*, X (1940).

COMUS: Cf. E. Welsford, *The Court Masque* (1927); A. S. P. Woodhouse, "The Argument of Milton's Comus," *University of Toronto Quarterly*, XI (1941); E. M. W. Tillyard, "The Action of Comus," in *Essays and Studies of the English Association*, XXVIII (1942).

LYCIDAS: Cf. J. H. Hanford, "The Pastoral Elegy and Milton's 'Lycidas,'" *Publications of the Modern Language Association*, XXV (1910); P. E. More, "How to Read Lycidas," in *The American Review* (1936); J. C. Ransom, "A Poem Nearly Anonymous," in *The World's Body* (1938); J. E. Hardy, "Lycidas," in *The Kenyon Review*, VII (1945); D. Daiches, "The Nature of Poetry," in his *A Study of Literature* (1948). R. P. Adams, "The Archetypal Pattern of Death and Rebirth in Milton's 'Lycidas,'" *Publications of the Modern Language Association*, LXIV (1949): C. W. Mayerson, "The Orpheus Image in 'Lycidas,'" *Ibid.*

AREOPAGITICA: Cf. W. E. Gilman, *Milton's Rhetoric: Studies in His Defense of Liberty* (1939); Sir H. J. C. Grierson, *Milton and Wordsworth* (1937); D. M. Wolfe, *Milton in the Puritan Revolution* (1941); A. Barker, *Milton and the Puritan Dilemma* (1942); D. Bush, *The Renaissance and English Humanism* (1940); W. Haller, "For the Liberty of Unlicensed

Printing," in *The American Scholar,* XIV (1945); H. Read, "On Milton's Areopagitica," in *Adelphi* XXI (1944); A. S. P. Woodhouse, "Milton, Puritanism and Liberty," *University of Toronto Quarterly,* IV (1935).

PARADISE LOST: Cf. C. S. Lewis, *A Preface to Paradise Lost* (1942); C. M. Bowra, *From Virgil to Milton* (1945); D. Bush, *Paradise Lost in Our Time* (1945); J. S. Diekhoff, *Milton's Paradise Lost* (1946); B. Rajan, *Paradise Lost and the Seventeenth-Century Reader* (1947); A. J. A. Waldock, *Paradise Lost and Its Critics* (1947).

SAMSON AGONISTES: Cf. W. R. Parker, *Milton's Debt to Greek Tragedy in Samson Agonistes* (1937); F. M. Krouse, *Milton's Samson and the Christian Tradition* (1949); and the works listed in Krouse's bibliography.